Steck-Vaughn

GED

LANGUAGE ARTS, WRITING

PROGRAM CONSULTANTS

Liz Anderson, Director of Adult Education/Skills Training
Northwest Shoals Community College
Muscle Shoals, Alabama

Mary Ann Corley, Ph.D., Director
Lindy Boggs National Center for Community Literacy
Loyola University New Orleans
New Orleans, Louisiana

Nancy Dunlap, Adult Education Coordinator
Northside Independent School District
San Antonio, Texas

Roger M. Hansard, Director of Adult Education
CCARE Learning Center
Tazewell, Tennessee

Nancy Lawrence, M.A.
Education and Curriculum Consultant
Butler, Pennsylvania

Pat L. Taylor, STARS Consultant for GEDTS
Adult Education/GED Programs
Mesa, Arizona

STECK-VAUGHN
ELEMENTARY · SECONDARY · ADULT · LIBRARY

A Harcourt Company

www.steck-vaughn.com

Acknowledgments

Executive Editor: Ellen Northcutt

Supervising Editor: Julie Higgins

Associate Editor: Sarah Combs

Associate Director of Design: Cynthia Ellis

Designers: Rusty Kaim
Katie Nott

Media Researcher: Sarah Fraser

Editorial Development: Learning Unlimited, Oak Park, Illinois

Production Development: LaurelTech

Photography: Cover (in/out box) ©Imagebank; (mail, journal) ©Digital Studios; p.i ©Digital Studios; p.32 ©Bob Daemmrich Photo, Inc.; p.92 ©Superstock; p.134 ©Rob Lewine/The Stock Market; p.186 ©Jim Erickson/The Stock Market.

ISBN 0-7398-2831-2

10 11 073 07 06

Contents

What Are the GED Tests?

You have taken a big step in your life by deciding to take the GED Tests. By the time that you have opened this book, you have made a second important decision: to put in the time and effort to prepare for the tests. You may feel nervous about what is ahead, which is only natural. Relax and read the following pages to find out more about the GED Tests in general and the Language Arts, Writing Test in particular.

The GED Tests are the five tests of General Educational Development. The GED Testing Service of the American Council on Education makes them available to adults who did not graduate from high school. When you pass the GED Tests, you will receive a certificate that is regarded as equivalent to a high school diploma. Employers in private industry and government, as well as admissions officers in colleges and universities, accept the GED certificate as they would a high school diploma.

The GED Tests cover the same subjects that people study in high school. The five subject areas include: Language Arts, Writing and Language Arts, Reading (which, together, are equivalent to high school English), Social Studies, Science, and Mathematics. You will not be required to know all the information that is usually taught in high school. However, across the five tests you will be tested on your ability to read and process information, solve problems, and communicate effectively. Some of the states in the U.S. also require a test on the U.S. Constitution or on state government. Check with your local adult education center to see if your state requires such a test.

Each year more than 800,000 people take the GED Tests. Of those completing the test battery, 70 percent earn their GED certificates. The *Steck-Vaughn GED Series* will help you pass the GED Tests by providing instruction and practice in the skill areas needed to pass, practice with test items like those found on the GED Test, test-taking tips, timed-test practice, and evaluation charts to help track your progress.

There are five separate GED Tests. The chart on page 2 gives you information on the content, number of items, and time limit for each test. Because states have different requirements for how many tests you take in a day or testing period, you need to check with your local adult education center for the requirements in your state, province, or territory.

The Tests of General Educational Development

Test	Content Areas	Items	Time Limit
Language Arts, Writing, Part I	Organization 15% Sentence Structure 30% Usage 30% Mechanics 25%	50 questions	75 minutes
Language Arts, Writing, Part II	Essay		45 minutes
Social Studies	U.S. History 25% World History 15% Civics and Government 25% Geography 15% Economics 20%	50 questions	70 minutes
Science	Life Science 45% Earth and Space Science 20% Physical Science 35%	50 questions	80 minutes
Language Arts, Reading	Nonfiction Texts 25% Literary Texts 75% • Prose Fiction • Poetry • Drama	40 questions	65 minutes

Mathematics	Number Operations
	  and Number Sense 25%
	Measurement and
	  Geometry 25%
	Data Analysis, Statistics,
	  and Probability 25%
	Algebra 25%
		Part I: 25 questions with optional use of a calculator
		Part II: 25 questions without a calculator
			90 minutes

In addition to these content areas, you will be asked to answer items based on work- and consumer-related texts across all five tests. These do not require any specialized knowledge, but will ask you to draw upon your own observations and life experiences.

The Language Arts, Reading, Social Studies, and Science Tests will ask you to answer questions by interpreting reading passages, diagrams, charts and graphs, maps, cartoons, and practical and historical documents.

The Language Arts, Writing Test will ask you to detect and correct common errors in edited American English as well as decide on the most effective organization of text. The Essay portion of the Writing Test will ask you to write an essay offering your opinion or an explanation on a single topic of general knowledge.

The Mathematics Test will ask you to solve a variety of word problems, many with graphics, using basic computation, analytical, and reasoning skills.

GED Scores

After you complete each GED Test, you will receive a score for that test. Once you have completed all five GED Tests, you will receive a total score. The total score is an average of all the other scores. The highest score possible on a single test is 800. The scores needed to pass the GED vary depending on where you live. Contact your local adult education center for the minimum passing scores for your state, province, or territory.

Where Can You Go to Take the GED Tests?

The GED Tests are offered year-round throughout the United States and its possessions, on U.S. military bases worldwide, and in Canada. To find out when and where tests are held near you, contact the GED Hot Line at 1-800-62-MY-GED (1-800-626-9433) or one of these institutions in your area:

- An adult education center
- A continuing education center
- A local community college
- A public library
- A private business school or technical school
- The public board of education

In addition, the GED Hot Line and the institutions can give you information regarding necessary identification, testing fees, writing implements, and on the scientific calculator to be used on the GED Mathematics Test. Also, check on the testing schedule at each institution; some testing centers are open several days a week, and others are open only on weekends.

Other GED Resources

- www.acenet.edu This is the official site for the GED Testing Service. Just follow the GED links throughout the site for information on the test.

- www.steckvaughn.com Follow the Adult Learners link to learn more about available GED preparation materials and www.gedpractice.com. This site also provides other resources for adult learners.

- www.nifl.gov/nifl/ The National Institute for Literacy's site provides information on instruction, federal policies, and national initiatives that affect adult education.

- www.doleta.gov U.S. Department of Labor's Employment and Training Administration site offers information on adult training programs.

Why Should You Take the GED Tests?

A GED certificate is widely recognized as the equivalent of a high school diploma and can help you in the following ways:

Employment

People with GED certificates have proven their determination to succeed by following through with their education. They generally have less difficulty changing jobs or moving up in their present companies. In many cases, employers will not hire someone who does not have a high school diploma or the equivalent.

Education

Many technical schools, vocational schools, or other training programs may require a high school diploma or the equivalent in order to enroll in their programs. However, to enter a college or university, you must have a high school diploma or the equivalent.

Personal Development

The most important thing is how you feel about yourself. You now have the unique opportunity to accomplish an important goal. With some effort, you can attain a GED certificate that will help you in the future and make you feel proud of yourself now.

How to Prepare for the GED Tests

Classes for GED preparation are available to anyone who wants to prepare to take the GED Tests. Most GED preparation programs offer individualized instruction and tutors who can help you identify areas in which you may need help. Many adult education centers offer free day or night classes. The classes are usually informal and allow you to work at your own pace and with other adults who also are studying for the GED Tests.

If you prefer to study by yourself, the *Steck-Vaughn GED Series* has been developed to guide your study through skill instruction and practice exercises. *Steck-Vaughn GED Exercise* books and www.gedpractice.com are also available to provide you with additional practice for each test. In addition to working on specific skills, you will be able to take practice GED Tests (like those in this book) in order to check your progress. For information about classes available near you, contact one of the resources in the list on page 3.

What You Need to Know to Pass the Language Arts, Writing, Part I Test

The GED Language Arts, Writing Test is divided into two parts. Part I is a proofreading and editing test in multiple-choice format, and Part II is an essay based on a single given topic.

On Part I, you will read several documents, 12–22 sentences long, that, when corrected, will be examples of good writing. The texts include instructional or "how-to" documents (dressing for success, leasing a car, etc.), workplace communications (letters, memos, applications, etc.), and informational documents.

Always read the passage before you start answering the questions. First, you should be anticipating the questions as you read through the text and see errors. Second, some questions (for instance, verb tense items) require you to have a sense of the text as a whole. Finally, an understanding of the whole text is essential for answering questions that focus on improving the organization of the piece.

Content Areas

Organization

Fifteen percent of the test items are based on improving the organization of written materials. These items include topics such as making text divisions within paragraphs, creating effective paragraph divisions within documents, selecting and placing an effective topic sentence, unifying a document, and removing irrelevant ideas.

Sentence Structure

Thirty percent of the test items reflect effective and correct sentence structure. This includes correcting errors in the construction of sentences—sentence fragments, run-on sentences, and comma splices. This content area also includes correcting mistakes in sentence structure such as improper subordination of ideas, dangling or misplaced modifiers, and lack of parallel structure.

Usage

Thirty percent of the test items ask you to correct errors in usage. Usage includes using a verb or pronoun that agrees with the subject of the sentence. Correct usage also includes determining the right verb tense or form for the situation. Pronoun forms and references are also tested in usage questions.

Mechanics

Twenty-five percent of the test items examine punctuation, spelling, and capitalization. Punctuation items include correct comma use in sentences as well as overuse of commas. Spelling items focus on possessives, contractions, and homonyms and other commonly confused words.

Item Types

The items on the Language Arts, Writing, Part I Test fall into three basic types. About half of the items ask you to make a correction, about a third ask you to make a revision to an underlined portion of a sentence, and the rest ask you to determine an alternate way of presenting an idea.

Correction

A correction item can involve one sentence or more from the document. It asks you to choose the correction to an error or to choose the alternative "(5) no correction is necessary."

Revision

These items provide you with a stem with a part underlined that may or may not include an error. It asks you to choose from four possible corrections or to choose option (1), which is the same as the underlined section. If you choose (1) you are saying that the selection from the document is correct as presented.

Construction Shift

Rather than testing errors, these items test your ability to form a sentence in a new way or to combine ideas from two sentences to form a new sentence. You have to decide which choice will result in a sentence that is free of errors and keeps the meaning of the original sentence(s).

The *Steck-Vaughn GED Language Arts, Writing* book teaches the skills needed to pass Language Arts, Writing, Part I. It also introduces basic writing skills through *Writing Link* activities within each unit. Writing skills along with editing skills are essential for writing an effective essay on Part II of the test. For more information on Part II of the Writing Test, see the *Steck-Vaughn GED Essay* book.

Sample Passage and Items

The following is a sample paragraph and test items. Although the paragraph is much shorter than those on the GED Test, the items that follow are similar to those on the test. Following each item is an explanation of the skill area that the item tests as well as an explanation of the correct answer.

Questions 1 through 5 refer to the following paragraph.

(1) Some parents look forward to there children leaving home at last. (2) This group of parents want peace and quiet. (3) A number of adult children, however, move back home. (4) Parents continue to support them. (5) Sometimes the parents charge rent to their children. (6) People often pay rent on apartments unless they buy condominiums or homes.

1. Sentence 1: **Some parents look forward to there children leaving home at last.**

   What correction should be made to sentence 1?

   (1) change parents to parent's
   (2) change look to looks
   (3) replace to with too
   (4) replace there with their
   (5) no correction is necessary

Answer: (4) replace there with their

Explanation: This is an example of a correction item. The item tests spelling, which is a topic in the area of Mechanics. Option (4) is correct because it replaces *there* with *their,* which is the possessive form: *parents look forward to their children leaving home.* Option (1) is incorrect because the possessive form for parents is not needed. Option (2) is incorrect because it gives the plural subject *parents* a singular verb. Option (3) incorrectly replaces *to* with its homonym *too,* which means "also."

2. Sentence 2: **This group of parents want peace and quiet.**

   Which is the best way to write the underlined portion of this sentence? If the original is the best way, choose option (1).

   (1) group of parents want
   (2) group of parents, want
   (3) group of parents wanting
   (4) group of parents wants
   (5) group of parents to want

Answer: (4) group of parents wants

Explanation: This is an example of an item that requires a revision of a sentence. This is a Usage item that focuses on a problem with subject/verb agreement. Option (4) is correct because it gives the singular subject, *group*, a singular verb, *wants*. Items that are constructed like the one above indicate that if the sentence is correct as written, you should choose option (1). However, option (1) does not solve the subject agreement problem. In option (2), a comma incorrectly separates the subject from the verb. Option (3) changes the verb to a form that makes a sentence fragment. Option (5) also changes the verb to an incorrect verb form.

3. Sentences 3 and 4: **A number of adult children, however, move back home. Parents continue to support them.**

The most effective combination of sentences 3 and 4 would include which of the following groups of words?

(1) home where parents
(2) home even if parents
(3) home, but parents
(4) home; instead, parents
(5) home, parents

Answer: (1) home where parents

Explanation: This is an example of a construction shift item. This item requires you to combine two sentences to form a new one, which is in the area of Sentence Structure. You must choose the words that best connect the two sentences while keeping the meaning the same. The new sentence could read something like: *A number of adult children move back home where their parents continue to support them.* Option (1) is correct because it uses the word *where* to put the ideas in the two sentences together. Option (2) implies that the children would have moved home regardless, an idea not present in the two sentences. Options (3) and (4) show an unintended contrast between the two ideas. Option (5) incorrectly connects the sentences using only a comma.

4. Sentence 6: **People often pay rent on apartments unless they buy condominiums or homes.**

What revision should be made to sentence 6?

(1) move sentence 6 to follow sentence 1
(2) move sentence 6 to follow sentence 2
(3) move sentence 6 to follow sentence 3
(4) remove sentence 6
(5) no revision is necessary

Answer: (4) remove sentence 6

Explanation: This is an example of a question that tests the organization of the text. The correct answer removes the sentence because while it is related to the general subject of "paying rent" it is unrelated to the topic of the paragraph—children moving back home with their parents. Options (1), (2), and (3) do not solve the problem with the unrelated sentence, and option (5) is incorrect because the text does need to be revised.

The *Steck-Vaughn GED Language Arts, Writing* book helps you develop the necessary proofreading and editing skills by giving detailed explanations for each answer. The answer key for each item has an explanation of why the correct answer is right and the incorrect answers are wrong. By studying these explanations, you will learn strategies for understanding and thinking about these topics. To prepare for the essay portion of the test, consider reviewing the *Steck-Vaughn GED Essay* book.

Test-Taking Skills

The GED Language Arts, Writing Test will test your ability to apply reading and critical thinking skills to text. This book will help you prepare for this test. In addition, there are some specific ways that you can improve your performance on the test.

Answering the Test Items

- Never skim the directions. Read them carefully so that you know exactly what to do. If you are unsure, ask the test-giver if the directions can be explained.

- Read each question carefully to make sure that you know what it is asking.

- Read all of the answer options carefully, even if you think you know the right answer. Some of the answers may not seem wrong at first glance, but one answer will be the correct one.

- Before you answer a question, be sure that there is evidence in the passage to support your choice. Don't rely on what you know outside the context of the passage.

- Answer all the items. If you cannot find the correct answer, reduce the number of possible answers by eliminating all the answers you know are wrong. Then go back to the passage to figure out the correct answer. If you still cannot decide, make your best guess.

- Fill in your answer sheet carefully. To record your answers, mark one numbered space on the answer sheet beside the number that corresponds to the item. Mark only one answer space for each item; multiple answers will be scored as incorrect.

- Remember that the GED is a timed test. When the test begins, write down the time you have to finish. Then keep an eye on the time. Do not take a long time on any one item. Answer each item as best you can and go on. If you are spending a lot of time on one item, skip it, making a very light mark next to the item number on the sheet. If you finish before time is up, go back to the items you skipped or were unsure of and give them more thought. (Be sure to erase any extraneous marks you have made.)

- Don't change an answer unless you are certain your answer was wrong. Usually the first answer you choose is the correct one.

- If you feel that you are getting nervous, stop working for a moment. Take a few deep breaths and relax. Then begin working again.

Study Skills

Study Regularly

- If you can, set aside an hour to study every day. If you do not have time every day, set up a schedule of the days you can study. Be sure to pick times when you will be the most relaxed and least likely to be bothered by outside distractions.

- Let others know your study time. Ask them to leave you alone for that period. It helps if you explain to others why this is important.

- You should be relaxed when you study, so find an area that is comfortable for you. If you cannot study at home, go to the library. Most public libraries have areas for reading and studying. If there is a college or university near you, find out if you can use its library. All libraries have dictionaries, encyclopedias, and other resources you can use if you need more information while you're studying.

Organize Your Study Materials

- Be sure to have pens, sharp pencils, and paper for any notes you might want to take.

- Keep all of your books together. If you are taking an adult education class, you probably will be able to borrow some books or other study material.

- Make a notebook or folder for each subject you are studying. Folders with pockets are useful for storing loose papers.

- Keep all of your materials in one place so you do not waste time looking for them each time you study.

Read Regularly

- Read the newspaper, read magazines, read books. Read whatever appeals to you—but read! Regular, daily reading is the best way to improve your reading skills.

- Use the library to find material you like to read. Check the magazine section for publications of interest to you. Most libraries subscribe to hundreds of magazines ranging in interest from news to cars to music to sewing to sports. If you are not familiar with the library, ask a librarian for help. Get a library card so that you can check out material to use at home.

Take Notes

- Take notes on things that interest you or things that you think might be useful.

- When you take notes, do not copy the words directly from the book. Restate the information in your own words.

- Take notes any way you want. You do not have to write in full sentences as long as you can understand your notes later.

- Use outlines, charts, or diagrams to help you organize information and make it easier to learn.

- You may want to take notes in a question-and-answer form, such as: *What is the main idea? The main idea is . . .*

Improve Your Vocabulary

- As you read, do not skip a word you do not know. Instead, try to figure out what the word means. First, omit it from the sentence. Read the sentence without the word and try to put another word in its place. Is the meaning of the sentence the same?

- Make a list of unfamiliar words, look them up in the dictionary, and write down the meanings.

- Since a word may have several meanings, it is best to look up the word while you have the passage with you. Then you can try out the different meanings in the context.

- When you read the definition of a word, restate it in your own words. Use the word in a sentence or two.

- Use the Glossary at the end of this book to review the meanings of the key terms. All of the words you see in **boldface** type are defined in the Glossary. In addition, definitions of other important words are included. Use this list to review important vocabulary for the content areas you are studying.

Make a List of Subject Areas that Give You Trouble

As you go through this book, make a note whenever you do not understand something. Then ask your teacher or another person for help. Later go back and review the topic.

Taking the Test

Before the Test

- If you have never been to the test center, go there the day before you take the test. If you drive, find out where to park.

- Prepare the things you need for the test: your admission ticket (if necessary), acceptable identification, some sharpened No. 2 pencils with erasers, a watch, glasses, a jacket or sweater (in case the room is cold), and a snack to eat during breaks.

- Eat a meal and get a good night's sleep. If the test is early in the morning, set the alarm.

The Day of the Test

- Eat a good breakfast. Wear comfortable clothing. Make sure that you have all of the materials you need.

- Try to arrive at the test center about twenty minutes early. This allows time if, for example, there is a last-minute change of room.

- If you are going to be at the test center all day, you might pack a lunch. If you have to find a restaurant or if you wait a long time to be served, you may be late for the rest of the test.

Using this Book

- Start with the Pretest. It is identical to the real test in format and length. It will give you an idea of what the GED Language Arts, Writing Test is like. Then use the Pretest Performance Analysis Chart at the end of the test to figure out your areas of strength and the areas you need to review. The chart will refer you to units and page numbers to study. You also can use the Study Planner on page 31 to plan your work after you take the Pretest and again, after the Posttest.

- As you study, use the Cumulative Review and the Performance Analysis Chart at the end of each unit to find out if you need to review any lessons before continuing. Use the GED Writing Link activities throughout the book to develop your basic writing skills and to practice writing regularly. Use the Writer's Checklist (pages 314–325) to edit your own writing. This will help you to prepare for the essay portion of the test.

- After you complete your review, use the Posttest to decide if you are ready for the real GED Test. The Performance Analysis Chart will tell you if you need additional review. Then use the Simulated Test and its Performance Analysis Chart as a final check of your test-readiness.

LANGUAGE ARTS, WRITING, PART I

Directions

The Language Arts, Writing Pretest is intended to measure your ability to use clear and effective English. It is a test of English as it should be written, not as it might be spoken.

This test consists of paragraphs with numbered sentences. Some of the sentences contain errors in sentence structure, organization, usage, or mechanics (spelling, punctuation, and capitalization). After reading the numbered sentences, answer the multiple-choice questions that follow. Some questions refer to sentences that are correct as written. The best answer for these questions is the one that leaves the sentence as originally written. The best answer for some questions is the one that produces a sentence that is consistent with the verb tense and point of view used throughout the paragraph.

You should spend no more than 75 minutes answering the 50 questions on this test. Work carefully, but do not spend too much time on any one question. Do not skip any items. Make a reasonable guess when you are not sure of an answer. You will not be penalized for incorrect answers.

When time is up, mark the last item you finished. This will tell you whether you can finish the real GED Test in the time allowed. Then complete the test.

Record your answers to the questions on a copy of the answer sheet on page 331. Be sure that all required information is properly recorded on the answer sheet.

To record your answers, mark the numbered space on the answer sheet that corresponds to the answer you choose for each question on the test.

Example:

Sentence 1: **We were all honored to meet governor Phillips.**

What correction should be made to sentence 1?

(1) change honored to honoring
(2) insert a comma after honored
(3) change meet to met
(4) change governor to Governor
(5) no correction is necessary   ① ② ③ ● ⑤

In this example, the word governor should be capitalized; therefore, answer space 4 would be marked on the answer sheet.

Do not rest the point of your pencil on the answer sheet while you are considering your answer. Make no stray or unnecessary marks. If you change an answer, erase your first mark completely. Mark only one answer space for each question; multiple answers will be scored as incorrect. Do not fold or crease your answer sheet.

When you finish the test, use the Performance Analysis Chart on page 30 to determine whether you are ready to take the real GED Test and, if not, which skill areas need additional review.

Directions: Choose the one best answer to each question.

Questions 1 through 6 refer to the following paragraphs.

Daydreaming

(A)

(1) Daydreaming is a common pastime for most people. (2) Songs, legends, and movies often contains stories about daydreaming. (3) Daydreaming is fine as long as you are being the one in control and don't let it control you.

(B)

(4) Daydreaming has several positive psychological aspects. (5) For example, it can help you relax unwind, and improve your mood when you're having a bad day. (6) Sometimes you may daydream while doing a boring, repetitive job. (7) An example of such a job is pushing a lawn mower around the yard. (8) Daydreaming is a good way to occupy your mind while your body is otherwise engaged.

(C)

(9) For one thing, it can be dangerous to daydream while supervising children, using machinery, or operating electrical controls. (10) You might find yourself daydreaming while driving a car. (11) Especially while driving alone along a straight road for a long time. (12) Most of all, you need to be careful that you don't get to the point where you will begin to confuse dreams with reality. (13) Daydreaming, like many other things, is usually all right if not done to excess.

1. Sentence 2: **Songs, legends, and movies often contains stories about daydreaming.**

   What correction should be made to sentence 2?

   (1) remove the comma after Songs
   (2) insert a comma after movies
   (3) change contains to contain
   (4) change contains to will contain
   (5) no correction is necessary

2. Sentence 3: **Daydreaming is fine as long as you are being the one in control and don't let it control you.**

   Which is the best way to write the underlined portion of the text? If the original is the best way, choose option (1).

   (1) are being the one in control
   (2) have been in control
   (3) will be in control
   (4) are the controlling one
   (5) control it

3. Sentence 5: **For example, it can help you relax unwind, and improve your mood when you're having a bad day.**

   What correction should be made to sentence 5?

   (1) remove the comma after example
   (2) insert a comma after relax
   (3) change your to you're
   (4) insert a comma after mood
   (5) change you're to your

4. Sentences 6 and 7: **Sometimes you may daydream while doing a boring, repetitive job. An example of such a job is pushing a lawn mower around the yard.**

   The most effective combination of sentences 6 and 7 would include which group of words?

   (1) job, as to push
   (2) job for instance push
   (3) job, such as pushing
   (4) job or you could be pushing
   (5) job and you can push

5. Which sentence below would be most effective at the beginning of paragraph C?

   (1) Like most things, however, daydreaming can have a negative side as well.
   (2) Sometimes people daydream at other times too.
   (3) It's common to daydream during boring classes or sermons.
   (4) You might daydream on a long car trip.
   (5) Intense daydreaming can make you miss important conversations or phone calls.

6. Sentences 10 and 11: **You might find yourself daydreaming while driving a car. Especially while driving alone along a straight road for a long time.**

   Which is the best way to write the underlined portion of the text? If the original is the best way, choose option (1).

   (1) car. Especially
   (2) car, especially
   (3) car especially
   (4) car, even especially
   (5) car. And especially

WARNING: NOTICE TO DIGGERS

from the City of Smithville Utility Service

(A)

(1) Every Spring, landlords and homeowners throughout the state begin construction, renovation, and landscaping projects. (2) Please be warned, however, that anyone who uses large machinery to dig holes must follow these digging guidelines. (3) A person digging with hand tools are the only exception.

(B)

(4) State law requires that a digger must provide plans to the local building department at least five days before work begins. (5) They will issue a permit and notify the utility companies. (6) The utility companies, in turn, will locate and mark all their underground systems. (7) Once marked, a digger can safely proceed with plans.

(C)

(8) This process helps avoid damaging homes or other structures. (9) State law also mandates that a contractor or other digger "pre-mark" the boundary of any proposed hole. (10) White paint, taped stakes, or other clearly visible signs, are acceptable. (11) Such markings will further ensure that no underground cables or pipes will be damaged by digging.

7. Sentence 1: **Every Spring, landlords and homeowners throughout the state begin construction, renovation, and landscaping projects.**

What correction should be made to sentence 1?

(1) change Spring to spring
(2) remove the comma after Spring
(3) change state to State
(4) change begin to will begin
(5) remove the comma after construction

8. Sentence 3: **A person digging with hand tools are the only exception.**

What correction should be made to sentence 3?

(1) insert is after person
(2) insert a comma after digging
(3) change tools to tool's
(4) insert a comma after tools
(5) change are to is

9. Sentence 5: **They will issue a permit and notify the utility companies.**

Which is the best way to write the underlined portion of the text? If the original is the best way, choose option (1).

(1) They
(2) It
(3) One
(4) The building department
(5) The diggers

10. Sentence 7: **Once marked, a digger can safely proceed with plans.**

Which is the best way to write the underlined portion of the text? If the original is the best way, choose option (1).

(1) Once marked,
(2) Upon marking,
(3) Marking the systems,
(4) Once the systems are marked,
(5) Once, having marked the systems,

11. Which revision should be made to paragraph C?

(1) move sentence 8 to the end of paragraph B
(2) remove sentence 8
(3) move sentence 8 to follow sentence 9
(4) remove sentence 9
(5) no revision is necessary

12. Sentence 10: **White paint, taped stakes, or other clearly visible signs, are acceptable.**

What correction should be made to sentence 10?

(1) remove the comma after paint
(2) remove the comma after signs
(3) change are to being
(4) change are to is
(5) no correction is necessary

Handy Around the House

(A)

(1) Anyone can learn to be a handy person around the house. (2) Start with simple things like changing a light bulb, oiling a lock, and the screws in the door can be tightened. (3) Many reference guides are full of helpful hints even for such simple jobs. (4) Nowadays, you can probably even order these books over the Internet.

(B)

(5) As you try more difficult jobs, you first need to analyze the steps. (6) It often helps to consider what preparations are necessary and to make a list before you start. (7) For example, if you decide to paint the walls in your bedroom, figure out the tasks to be done and there order. (8) You need to decide on the color and the type of paint to use. (9) There is oil-based paint and latex paint on the market. (10) An adequate paintbrush to do the trim and a good roller to do the large, flat areas. (11) Painting can be messy, too, and you will need to cover the floor.

(C)

(12) If you want to try more technical jobs, you should first consult someone who has experience. (13) No one is born with handy skills, the best way to learn is by doing.

13. Sentence 2: **Start with simple things like changing a light bulb, oiling a lock, and the screws in the door can be tightened.**

The most effective revision of sentence 2 would include which group of words?

(1) you can tighten the screws
(2) the door screws can be tightened
(3) tightening door screws
(4) to tighten the screws
(5) make the screws tighter

14. Which revision should be made to paragraph A?

(1) remove sentence 1
(2) move sentence 2 to the end of the paragraph
(3) remove sentence 2
(4) remove sentence 4
(5) no revision is necessary

15. Sentence 7: **For example, if you decide to paint the walls in your bedroom, figure out the tasks to be done and there order.**

What correction should be made to sentence 7?

(1) change your to you're
(2) remove the comma after bedroom
(3) change be done to have been done
(4) insert a comma after done
(5) change there to their

16. Sentence 9: **There is oil-based paint and latex paint on the market.**

Which is the best way to write the underlined portion of the text? If the original is the best way, choose option (1).

(1) is
(2) are
(3) being
(4) have been
(5) will be

17. Sentence 10: **An adequate paintbrush to do the trim and a good roller to do the large, flat areas.**

The most effective revision of sentence 10 would begin with which group of words?

(1) An adequate paintbrush and a good roller
(2) Being sure to have an adequate
(3) You will also need an adequate
(4) With an adequate paintbrush
(5) An adequate paintbrush being needed

18. Sentence 13: **No one is born with handy skills, the best way to learn is by doing.**

Which is the best way to write the underlined portion of the text? If the original is the best way, choose option (1).

(1) skills, the
(2) skills the
(3) skills. The
(4) skills and the
(5) skills whereas the

Transforming Inventions

(A)

(1) We have come a long way from the 15th century, when johannes gutenberg invented the printing press. (2) Today's Internet sends bookloads of text around the world in seconds. (3) Yet the printing press had its own dramatic effect on human culture and the flow of ideas.

(B)

(4) All written material was done by hand. (5) There were few books and very little written information. (6) It took an hour or more to hand print a page. (7) Months or even years to do an entire book such as the Bible. (8) With the printing press, many copies could quickly and easily be made of a page once type for that page had been set. (9) It meant information could spread more widely and rapidly, allowing people to become more educated and knowledge to advance. (10) The printing press may be the single most important invention ever made and yet exception may be taken to that if you consider the personal computer.

(C)

(11) Today, computers give us the Internet and instant access to millions of books and massive amounts of information. (12) In fact, some people say we get too much information. (13) Perhaps people would have felt overwhelmed by the printing press. (14) Everyone just needs time to get used to inventions that change their lives.

19. Sentence 1: **We have come a long way from the 15th century, when johannes gutenberg invented the printing press.**

    What correction should be made to sentence 1?

    (1) insert a comma after <u>way</u>
    (2) change <u>century</u> to <u>Century</u>
    (3) change <u>johannes gutenberg</u> to <u>Johannes Gutenberg</u>
    (4) change <u>invented</u> to <u>was inventing</u>
    (5) no correction is necessary

20. Sentence 4: **All written material was done by hand.**

    Which revision should be made to sentence 4?

    (1) move sentence 4 to the end of paragraph A
    (2) replace <u>All</u> with <u>For instance, all</u>
    (3) replace <u>All</u> with <u>Prior to the invention of the printing press, all</u>
    (4) remove sentence 4
    (5) no revision is necessary

21. Sentences 6 and 7: **It took an hour or more to hand print a <u>page. Months</u> or even years to do an entire book such as the Bible.**

Which is the best way to write the underlined portion of the text? If the original is the best way, choose option (1).

(1) page. Months
(2) page months
(3) page. Therefore, months
(4) page such as months
(5) page and months

22. Sentence 8: **With the printing press, <u>many copies could quickly and easily be made of a page</u> once type for that page had been set.**

Which is the best way to write the underlined portion of the text? If the original is the best way, choose option (1).

(1) many copies could quickly and easily be made of a page
(2) many copies of a page could be made quickly and easily
(3) many copies could be made quickly and easily of a page
(4) quickly and easily, many copies could be made of a page
(5) many copies could be made of a page quickly and easily

23. Sentence 9: **<u>It meant</u> information could spread more widely and rapidly, allowing people to become more educated and knowledge to advance.**

Which is the best way to write the underlined portion of the text? If the original is the best way, choose option (1).

(1) It meant
(2) Meaning
(3) This process meant
(4) With this,
(5) Then

24. Sentence 10: **The printing press may be the single most important invention ever made and yet exception may be taken to that if you consider the personal computer.**

The most effective revision of sentence 10 would include which group of words?

(1) made, yet taking exception to that
(2) Either the printing press or the personal computer is the single most important
(3) Taking exception to the printing press being
(4) made except, perhaps, for the personal computer
(5) made, yet considering the personal computer

25. Sentence 13: **Perhaps people <u>would have felt</u> overwhelmed by the printing press.**

Which is the best way to write the underlined portion of the text? If the original is the best way, choose option (1).

(1) would have felt
(2) have felt
(3) felt
(4) had felt
(5) feel

Customer Service Department
Fuller Stores
67 Second Avenue
Bayside, CT 06226

To Whom It May Concern:

(A)

(1) Yesterday morning, I had gone to the Fuller Store in Lakeville to purchase the Media Radio that was advertised in the Sunday paper. (2) According to the advertisement, the model X12 radio would be available at all stores for $47.95.

(B)

(3) Unfortunately, I had several problems in the home entertainment department in Lakeville. (4) First, I had to wait ten minutes before even seeing any sales clerk. (5) When I finally spoke to a clerk, they said that the store didn't carry the model at all. (6) Then a second clerk said the model was out of stock. (7) At that point, I found Joe Forest, who was the supervisor. (8) Joe Forest said that the store did carry the radio, but it wasn't on sale. (9) Since I hadn't brought the ad with me I could not show it to him. (10) Before I could ask him to check, he disappeared. (11) I was about to leave when I spotted the radio, on sale at the right price. (12) I purchased it immediately and left. (13) My experience at the store was so frustrating, however, that I wont shop there again. (14) If you want to keep customers, I suggest you improve your staff training right away.

Sincerely,

Arvis Black

26. Sentence 1: **Yesterday morning, I had gone to the Fuller Store in Lakeville to purchase the Media Radio that was advertised in the Sunday paper.**

Which is the best way to write the underlined portion of the text? If the original is the best way, choose option (1).

(1) have gone
(2) have went
(3) has gone
(4) was going
(5) went

27. Sentence 5: **When I finally spoke to a clerk, they said that the store didn't carry the model at all.**

What correction should be made to sentence 5?

(1) change spoke to speaked
(2) remove the comma after clerk
(3) replace they with she
(4) insert a comma after model
(5) no correction is necessary

28. Sentences 7 and 8: **At that point, I found Joe Forest, who was the supervisor. Joe Forest said that the store did carry the radio, but it wasn't on sale.**

The most effective combination of sentences 7 and 8 would include which group of words?

(1) Joe Forest, the supervisor, who said
(2) Joe Forest, who was the supervisor and who said
(3) Joe Forest, being the supervisor, who said
(4) supervisor, and Joe Forest said
(5) supervisor, so he said

29. Which revision would make the letter more effective?

Begin a new paragraph

(1) with sentence 9
(2) with sentence 10
(3) with sentence 11
(4) with sentence 12
(5) with sentence 13

30. Sentence 9: **Since I hadn't brought the ad with me I could not show it to him.**

What correction should be made to sentence 9?

(1) remove Since
(2) change hadn't to had'nt
(3) insert a comma after me
(4) change show to shown
(5) replace it with the ad

31. Sentence 11: **I was about to leave when I spotted the radio, on sale at the right price.**

What correction should be made to sentence 11?

(1) change to leave to leaving
(2) insert a comma after leave
(3) change spotted to had spotted
(4) remove the comma after radio
(5) replace right with write

32. Sentence 13: **My experience at the store was so frustrating, however, that I wont shop there again.**

What correction should be made to sentence 13?

(1) insert a comma after store
(2) change was to been
(3) remove the comma after frustrating
(4) remove the comma after however
(5) change wont to won't

CONSUMER ALERT!

Brought to you by your local Better Business Bureau

How to Shop Online Safely

(A)

(1) Shopping online become popular now that more and more people are connected to the Internet. (2) Everything is available online with a credit card. (3) This includes everything from discount clothing to bus or train tickets. (4) Many people find Internet shopping fast and convenient.

(B)

(5) There are, however, some risks involved. (6) Delivery of orders is not always reliable shipping and handling fees can add a whopping 15 percent to the cost.

(C)

(7) Laws about returning unwanted purchases don't always apply to on-line businesses. (8) Giving out credit card numbers on an unsecured site might allow someone to steal your personal information.

(D)

(9) Consumer advocates say there are several things you can do to protect yourself. (10) For example, one should stick to well-known businesses when shopping on-line. (11) On-line retailers who don't list a telephone number are sometimes fakes. (12) Make sure you check the return policy and shipping fees before making a purchase. (13) As long as you are careful online buying can be a helpful new way of shopping.

33. Sentence 1: **Shopping online become popular now that more and more people are connected to the Internet.**

   Which is the best way to write the underlined portion of the text? If the original is the best way, choose option (1).

   (1) become
   (2) becoming
   (3) became
   (4) has become
   (5) had become

34. Sentences 2 and 3: **Everything is available online with a credit card. This includes everything from discount clothing to bus or train tickets.**

   The most effective combination of sentences 2 and 3 would include which group of words?

   (1) credit card, and this includes
   (2) Including discount clothing and bus or train tickets,
   (3) One can buy with a credit card everything
   (4) Everything from discount clothing to bus or train tickets is
   (5) Everything you can charge on a credit card

35. Sentence 6: **Delivery of orders is not always reliable shipping and handling fees can add a whopping 15 percent to the cost.**

   What correction should be made to sentence 6?

   (1) insert a comma after orders
   (2) change is to are
   (3) insert , and after reliable
   (4) insert a comma after shipping
   (5) no correction is necessary

36. Which revision would improve the text?

   (1) move sentence 6 to the beginning of paragraph B
   (2) combine paragraphs B and C
   (3) move sentence 7 to the end of paragraph C
   (4) move sentence 8 to the beginning of paragraph D
   (5) remove sentence 8

37. Sentence 10: **For example, one should stick to well-known businesses when shopping online.**

   What correction should be made to sentence 10?

   (1) remove the comma after example
   (2) change one to you
   (3) replace should stick with is sticking
   (4) change businesses to business's
   (5) insert a comma after businesses

38. Sentence 13: **As long as you are careful online buying can be a helpful new way of shopping.**

   What correction should be made to sentence 13?

   (1) replace you are with one is
   (2) insert a comma after careful
   (3) change can be to will have been
   (4) replace way with weigh
   (5) no correction is necessary

How to Deal with a Feverish Child

(A)

(1) Unless describing a child, it is accurate to say that a person's normal temperature is 98.6°F. (2) According to pediatricians, a normal child's temperature falls within the range of 97° to 100°F. (3) What should parents do when their child is feverish? (4) Here are some helpful guidelines.

(B)

(5) For infants under three months, all temperatures above 100°F need medical attention. (6) Be aware that an illness is not always symptomatized by fever. (7) Your baby's temperature may fall within normal range. (8) He or she may still be vomiting or gasping for air. (9) In such cases, call your doctor immediately.

(C)

(10) For an older child with a fever a sponge bath with cool water is a good idea. (11) Non-aspirin pain relievers may also help. (12) Make sure you don't give a child more than the recommended dose. (13) If you're not sure of how much medicine to give your child, call your doctor for advice. (14) A child's dosage is usually determined by one's weight.

39. Sentence 1: **Unless describing a child, it is accurate to say that a person's normal temperature is 98.6°F.**

Which is the best way to write the underlined portion of the text? If the original is the best way, choose option (1).

(1) Unless describing a child
(2) Unless you are describing a child
(3) Unless a child is described
(4) Unless one describes a child
(5) Unless a child is being described

40. Sentence 3: **What should parents do when their child is feverish?**

What correction should be made to sentence 3?

(1) change do to be doing
(2) insert a comma after do
(3) replace their with there
(4) change is to is being
(5) no correction is necessary

41. Sentences 7 and 8: **Your baby's temperature may fall within normal range. He or she may still be vomiting or gasping for air.**

Which is the best way to write the underlined portion of the text? If the original is the best way, choose option (1).

(1) range. He
(2) range. So he
(3) range, yet he
(4) range, he
(5) range he

42. Sentence 10: **For an older child with a fever a sponge bath with cool water is a good idea.**

Which is the best way to write the underlined portion of the text? If the original is the best way, choose option (1).

(1) fever a
(2) fever. A
(3) fever, so a
(4) fever, a
(5) fever, then a

43. Which revision should be made to paragraph C?

(1) move sentence 10 to the end of paragraph B
(2) remove sentence 12
(3) move sentence 13 to follow sentence 11
(4) move sentence 13 to the end of paragraph C
(5) remove sentence 13

44. Sentence 14: **A child's dosage is usually determined by one's weight.**

What correction should be made to sentence 14?

(1) change child's to childs
(2) change is to being
(3) change one's to ones
(4) replace one's with his or her
(5) no correction is necessary

MEMORANDUM

TO: All Employees
FROM: A. Weston, Human Resources Specialist
RE: Job Opening

(A)

(1) The Human Resources Department is pleased to announce a new job opening. (2) The department looks for a full-time assistant to the supervisor of personnel records.

(B)

(3) Candidates for the position must have proven skills and be able to perform certain duties. (4) The assistant needs to have strong typing skills, be well organized, and attention to details. (5) The assistant will be responsible for distributing, collecting, and recording time sheets, sick-time authorization forms, and vacation vouchers for all branches. (6) He or she will verify the accuracy of employee time records each week. (7) The assistant will also be involved in distributing information to the branches, finally, the selected candidate will report to the supervisor.

(C)

(8) Minimum qualifications for the position include a high school diploma or it's equivalent and a familiarity with computers. (9) The hiree will be expected to learn database software and to get along with a variety of staff. (10) The salary level for this position, as for all office assistants, start at Level 3.

(D)

(11) In keeping with our policy to hire from within the company if possible, all current employees who apply will be interviewed. (12) If you have any questions or wish to apply for this position, see my assistant, Ray Forbes.

45. Sentence 2: **The department <u>looks</u> for a full-time assistant to the supervisor of personnel records.**

Which is the best way to write the underlined portion of the text? If the original is the best way, choose option (1).

(1) looks
(2) looked
(3) looking
(4) is looking
(5) was looking

46. Sentence 3: **Candidates for the position must have proven skills and be able to perform certain duties.**

Which revision should be made to sentence 3?

(1) move sentence 3 to the end of paragraph A
(2) remove sentence 3
(3) move sentence 3 to follow sentence 4
(4) move sentence 3 to the end of paragraph B
(5) no revision is necessary

47. Sentence 4: **The assistant needs to have strong typing skills, be well organized, and attention to details.**

The most effective revision of sentence 4 would include which group of words?

(1) Needing strong typing skills,
(2) having strong typing skills
(3) type well
(4) have good organization
(5) pay attention to details

48. Sentence 7: **The assistant will also be involved in distributing information to the <u>branches, finally, the</u> selected candidate will report to the supervisor.**

Which is the best way to write the underlined portion of the text? If the original is the best way, choose option (1).

(1) branches, finally, the
(2) branches, finally the
(3) branches. Finally, the
(4) branches finally, the
(5) branches, so finally, the

49. Sentence 8: **Minimum qualifications for the position include a high school diploma or it's equivalent and a familiarity with computers.**

What correction should be made to sentence 8?

(1) insert a comma after <u>position</u>
(2) replace <u>high school</u> with <u>High School</u>
(3) insert a comma after <u>diploma</u>
(4) change <u>it's</u> to <u>its</u>
(5) no correction is necessary

50. Sentence 10: **The salary level for this position, as for all office assistants, <u>start</u> at Level 3.**

Which is the best way to write the underlined portion of the text? If the original is the best way, choose option (1).

(1) start
(2) started
(3) starts
(4) are starting
(5) will have started

Answers start on page 263.

Pretest Performance Analysis Chart
Language Arts, Writing

This chart can help you determine your strengths and weaknesses on the content and skill areas of the Language Arts, Writing Test. Use the Answers and Explanations on pages 263–266 to check your answers to the test. Then circle on the chart the numbers of the test items you answered correctly. Put the total number correct for each content area and skill area in each row and column. If you answered fewer than 50 questions correctly, look at the total items correct in each column and row and decide which areas are difficult for you. Use the page references to study those areas. Use a copy of the Language Arts, Writing Study Planner on page 31 to guide your studying.

Item Type / Content Area	Correction	Revision	Construction Shift	Number Correct	Page References
Sentence Structure (Pages 32–91)					
Sentences/Sentence Fragments		6, 21	17	____/3	34–41
Compound Sentences/ Combining Ideas		41		____/1	42–49
Subordinating Ideas			28, 34	____/2	54–61
Run-ons/Comma Splices	35	18, 48	24	____/4	62–69
Modifiers		10, 22, 39		____/3	72–77
Parallel Structure			13, 47	____/2	78–83
Organization (Pages 92–133)					
Paragraph Structure/ Unity and Coherence	11, 14, 43, 46			____/4	94–101
Topic Sentences			5	____/1	104–109
Paragraph Division			29, 36	____/2	112–117
Transitions	20			____/1	120–125
Usage (Pages 134–185)					
Subject-Verb Agreement	1, 8	16, 50		____/4	136–145
Verb Forms	40	33		____/2	148–155
Verb Tenses		2, 25, 26, 45		____/4	158–165
Pronouns	27, 37, 44	9, 23		____/5	168–177
Mechanics (Pages 186–226)					
Capitalization	7, 19			____/2	188–195
Commas	3, 12, 30, 31, 38	42	4	____/7	196–203
Spelling	15, 32, 49			____/3	208–217

1–40 → Use the Study Planner on page 31 to organize your work in this book.
41–50 → Use the tests in this book to practice for the GED.

For additional help, see the _Steck-Vaughn GED Language Arts, Writing Exercise Book._

Language Arts, Writing Study Planner

These charts will help you to organize your study after you take the Language Arts, Writing Pretest and Posttest. After each test, use your results from the Number Correct column on the corresponding Performance Analysis Chart to complete the study planner. Place a check mark next to the areas in which you need more practice. Copy the page numbers from the Performance Analysis Chart. Review your study habits by keeping track of the start and finish dates for each practice. These charts will help you to see your progress as you practice to improve your skills and prepare for the GED Test.

Pretest (pages 13–29): Use results from your **Performance Analysis Chart** (page 30).

Content	Correct/Total	✓	Page Numbers	Date Started	Date Finished
Sentence Structure	_____/15				
Organization	_____/8				
Usage	_____/15				
Mechanics	_____/12				

Posttest (pages 227–243): Use results from your **Performance Analysis Chart** (page 244).

Content	Correct/Total	✓	Page Numbers	Date Started	Date Finished
Sentence Structure	_____/15				
Organization	_____/8				
Usage	_____/15				
Mechanics	_____/12				

Sentence Structure

Whenever you write a note, a report at work, a postcard, or a letter to a friend, you write in sentences. In order to express your thoughts effectively, you need to write complete, correct sentences. A complete sentence is the basic building block of written material.

Part I of the GED Language Arts, Writing Test will test your ability to recognize and revise problems in sentences and paragraphs. Thirty percent of the questions on the test are about sentence structure, or the way sentences are put together. This unit focuses on key topics in sentence structure. It will show you ways to express your ideas in clear, correct, and logical sentences.

Clear, correct sentences help you express your ideas effectively.

The lessons in this unit include:

Lesson 1: **Sentences and Sentence Fragments**
A complete sentence is the basic building block of writing. A fragment is only a part of a sentence. You can correct a fragment by adding a subject or a verb or by joining it to another sentence.

Lesson 2: **Compound Sentences**
To make their writing more varied and interesting, good writers often combine sentences that are short, choppy, or repetitive. You can learn to vary your writing by creating compound sentences that contain the right punctuation and connecting words.

Lesson 3: **Subordinating Ideas**
In addition to a main idea, some sentences contain supporting ideas. You can clarify the relationship between the main idea and its subordinate parts with special conjunctions and correct punctuation.

Lesson 4: **Run-ons and Comma Splices**
A run-on sentence consists of two or more sentences that are strung together without correct connecting words or punctuation. You can correct run-ons by using appropriate punctuation and connecting words.

Lesson 5: **Misplaced and Dangling Modifiers**
Modifiers are words or phrases that describe other words or phrases. When you misplace modifiers, they may appear to describe the wrong word or phrase. You can usually correct this problem by moving the modifier.

Lesson 6: **Parallel Structure**
Problems in parallel structure result from writing a series of words, phrases, or clauses in different forms. You can improve your writing by putting items in a series in the same form.

To use the skills in this unit in your own writing, see the Writer's Checklist on page 314.

> ## WRITING LINKS
>
> In this unit, you will practice these types of writing skills:
>
> ⊙ Writing Your Thoughts in Complete Sentences
>
> ⊙ Detailed Writing
>
> ⊙ Using Modifiers

Lesson 1

GED SKILL Sentences and Sentence Fragments

Complete Sentences

To write clearly, you should use complete sentences. A sentence is complete when it meets the following requirements.

subject
tells who or what a sentence is about

verb
tells what the subject is or does

RULE 1 A complete sentence has a subject and a verb. The **subject** names who or what the sentence is about. The **verb** tells what the subject is or does.

No Subject: Teaches her son to drive a car with a stick shift.
Complete: <u>Gloria</u> teaches her son to drive a car with a stick shift.

No Verb: A car with an automatic transmission.
Complete: A car with an automatic transmission <u>is</u> easy to drive.

Sometimes the subject of a sentence is not stated, but it is understood to be the word *you.*

Complete: Learn to drive safely.

Identify a complete sentence by asking: *Does the sentence have a subject? Does it have a complete verb? Does it express a complete thought?* If the answer to all those questions is yes, the sentence is complete.

RULE 2 A complete sentence expresses a complete thought.

Incomplete: Because it gets better mileage.
Complete: Ramon plans to buy a car with a standard transmission because it gets better mileage.

RULE 3 A complete sentence ends with punctuation. Most statements end with a period. A question ends with a question mark. A strong statement or command ends with an exclamation point.

Statement: Gloria prefers to drive a car with a stick shift.
Question: Is Ramon a good driver?
Exclamation: Get out of his way!

Put a check mark next to the complete sentence.

_____ a. The equipment to Dallas via Relay Shipping.

_____ b. Hoping the package arrived in time for the meeting!

_____ c. Because it was delivered without any delay.

_____ d. Relay Shipping tracks packages via the Internet.

You were correct if you decided that *option d* is the complete sentence. *Option a* is missing a verb, *option b* is missing a subject, and *option c* has a subject and a verb but is an incomplete thought.

GED SKILL FOCUS

A. Write *C* if a sentence is complete. Write *I* if it is incomplete and explain your answer.

I 1. The airline searching for David's luggage.

    This incomplete sentence is missing a verb.

_____ 2. When his luggage was not unloaded from his flight.

_____

_____ 3. The airline recorded David's name and phone number.

_____

_____ 4. Delivered his suitcase to his house three hours later.

_____

_____ 5. David was relieved.

_____

B. Correct this article by inserting punctuation after the complete sentences. Underline any incomplete sentences. There are six statements, three questions, and one exclamation.

Q: I live in Los Angeles How can I renew my passport

A: You have several options Can you wait seven to ten days for your passport If so, getting a renewal form at the post office Fill it out and send it via overnight mail With the necessary documentation You can also apply in person at the passport office However, you'll probably have to wait in line

Do you need the passport immediately Then the same-day renewal service While you're at the passport office Finally, let me be the first to wish you a safe trip Have a fabulous time

C. Write about the following topic.

The article you corrected in Exercise B is about getting a passport. Think of a time that you had to get an official document such as a passport or a driver's license. Write a paragraph about what you did. Use complete sentences and correct end punctuation.

Answers start on page 266.

Sentence Fragments

You have been working with complete sentences. If you mistakenly write an incomplete sentence, you have written a **sentence fragment.** When you edit a piece of writing and you see a sentence fragment, you can use one of these methods to correct it. The method that you choose will depend on the situation and on what you think will most improve the piece of writing.

METHOD 1 If a fragment is missing a subject, add a subject.

Fragment: Went to the interview with her resume.
Correct: <u>Lia</u> went to the interview with her resume.

METHOD 2 If a fragment is missing a complete verb, make the verb complete.

Fragment: Dr. Parks <u>asking</u> about her last job.
Correct: Dr. Parks <u>is asking</u> about her last job.

METHOD 3 Add or change words to make an incomplete thought complete.

Fragment: Not a bad job, only boring.
Correct: Her last job was not bad, only boring.

METHOD 4 Attach the fragment to a complete sentence. This is a good method to use when a fragment has a subject and verb but still does not express a complete thought.

Fragment: Lia took the job. <u>Because she wanted a challenge.</u>
Correct: Lia took the job because she wanted a challenge.
Correct: Because she wanted a challenge, Lia took the job.

The second correction shows that when you attach a fragment to a sentence, you may also need to add or rearrange words.

The underlined statement that follows is a fragment. Put a check mark next to the best way to correct it.

Jay lost weight. <u>Once he started exercising.</u>

_____ a. add a subject

_____ b. add a verb

_____ c. add words to complete the thought

_____ d. attach it to the sentence before it

You were correct if you chose *option d*. The fragment already has the subject *he* (*option a*) and the verb *started* (*option b*), but it is not a complete thought. You could add words to the fragment to make it a complete thought (*option c*). However, the best way to correct it is to attach it to the preceding sentence because that sentence is short and choppy, and the meaning of the fragment is related closely to it.

---

sentence fragment
an incomplete
sentence

TIP

You can fix a fragment in various ways. However, on the GED Test, there will always be **only one** correct answer.

A. Correct the fragments by adding words or attaching the fragments to complete sentences.

1. Used to cook for the family.

   Mothers used to cook for the family.

2. Today, many teens prepare dinner for the family. Because their working parents come home late.

   _____

   _____

3. Microwave cooking, take-out food, or packaged macaroni and cheese easy favorites.

   _____

   _____

4. Teens feel they are accomplishing an important task. Making them feel grown-up and valuable.

   _____

   _____

5. Important to their self-esteem.

   _____

B. Edit the paragraph below by correcting the sentence fragments. There are eight fragments.

    Dry cleaning ~~costing~~ *costs* a lot of money. I know some good ways to remove stains from ~~clothing. Without~~ *clothing without* going to the dry cleaners. For example, I wasn't upset. When my child came home with ink on her new sweater. First, I sprayed the ink with some hair spray. That I keep around just for stains. When the stain was completely saturated, wiped it off with a sponge. Fruit stains, too, will disappear. If you first soak them in cool water. Then hot water with a few drops of ammonia. The stain must be gone before washing. Because soap sets fruit stains. If you know of any other practical methods to remove stains, please let me know.

C. Write about the following topic.

    The paragraph that you edited in Exercise B gave advice about removing stains from clothes. What is something that you know how to clean or fix? Write a short paragraph explaining how to clean or fix that item. Then edit your writing for fragments and correct end punctuation.

Answers start on page 267.

Directions: Choose the one best answer to each question.

Questions 1 through 5 refer to the following business letter.

Dear Sir:

(1) On June 15, I ordered a pair of blue pants in boys' size 8 from your outlet catalog. (2) I was sent a pair of green pants instead. (3) That I promptly returned. (4) Then I received the right color, but in size 4, not 8. (5) I was transferred to voice mail when I called the customer service line to complain. (6) 15 days since I left that message. (7) This unacceptable treatment of a customer. (8) I will cancel my store charge account. (9) An apology and full reimbursement within one week.

1. Sentences 2 and 3: **I was sent a pair of green pants instead. That I promptly returned.**

   Which is the best way to write the underlined portion of the text? If the original is the best way, choose option (1).

   (1) instead. That
   (2) instead! That
   (3) instead that
   (4) instead and
   (5) instead. And that

2. Sentence 5: **I was transferred to voice mail when I called the customer service line to complain.**

   What correction should be made to sentence 5?

   (1) insert Even though before I was
   (2) change mail when to mail! When
   (3) change mail when to mail. When
   (4) remove when
   (5) no correction is necessary

3. Sentence 6: **15 days since I left that message.**

   What correction should be made to sentence 6?

   (1) insert It has been before 15
   (2) change 15 to Fifteen
   (3) insert ago after days
   (4) insert with your voice mail after message
   (5) no correction is necessary

4. Sentence 7: **This unacceptable treatment of a customer.**

   What correction should be made to sentence 7?

   (1) replace This with Making this
   (2) insert is after This
   (3) replace treatment of with treatment. Of
   (4) replace of with given to
   (5) insert by your store after customer

5. Sentences 8 and 9: **I will cancel my store charge account. An apology and full reimbursement within one week.**

   The most effective combination of sentences 8 and 9 would include which group of words?

   (1) account give me an
   (2) account demanding an
   (3) account unless I receive an
   (4) account and an
   (5) account with an

TIP Read a GED selection carefully. Think about how you would correct or improve it. Then when you read the questions, you may already have an idea about the correct answers.

Questions 6 through 9 refer to the following paragraph.

Microwave Ovens

(1) Microwave ovens have transformed cooking because of their convenience in today's fast-paced society. (2) In the past, most people cooked with gas or electricity. (3) Today, many people prefer microwave ovens for their speed of cooking. (4) Which is one of their best qualities. (5) Less expensive than gas or electric ranges, too. (6) Where space is a consideration, microwave ovens are also conveniently small. (7) In fact, most people use the microwave as an addition to, not a replacement for, a full-size gas or electric oven. (8) Stove manufacturers not being worried.

6. Sentence 1: **Microwave ovens have transformed cooking because of their convenience in today's fast-paced society.**

   What correction should be made to sentence 1?

   (1) insert they after ovens
   (2) change have to having
   (3) change cooking because to cooking. Because
   (4) change convenience in to convenience. In
   (5) no correction is necessary

7. Sentences 3 and 4: **Today, many people prefer microwave ovens for their speed of cooking. Which is one of their best qualities.**

   Which is the best way to write the underlined portion of the text? If the original is the best way, choose option (1).

   (1) cooking. Which is one
   (2) cooking, which is one
   (3) cooking. One
   (4) cooking and one
   (5) cooking. Being one

8. Sentence 5: **Less expensive than gas or electric ranges, too.**

   What correction should be made to sentence 5?

   (1) replace Less with Microwaves are less
   (2) insert to use after expensive
   (3) insert either after than
   (4) change gas or to gas. Or
   (5) insert are after ranges

9. Sentences 7 and 8: **In fact, most people use the microwave as an addition to, not a replacement for, a full-size gas or electric oven. Stove manufacturers not being worried.**

   If you rewrote sentences 7 and 8 beginning with

   Stove manufacturers, however,

   the next words should be

   (1) not being worried because most
   (2) not worrying because, in fact
   (3) they aren't worried because most
   (4) are not worried because most
   (5) not worried because in fact,

   TIP Some GED questions give the option "no correction is necessary." If you think that is the correct answer, reread the sentence carefully to see whether there really are no errors.

Answers start on page 267.

Directions: This is a ten-minute practice test. After ten minutes, mark the last question you finished. Then complete the test and check your answers. If most of your answers were correct, but you didn't finish, try to work faster next time. Choose the one best answer to each question.

Questions 1 through 4 refer to the following paragraphs.

What We Eat

(A)

(1) Parents complain that their children's eyes are bigger than their stomachs. (2) When the children estimate how much candy or treats they can eat. (3) As it turns out, adults also depend too much on their perception when estimating amounts of food.

(B)

(4) People definitely make a connection between what they see and how much they eat. (5) Unfortunately, underestimating their daily food intake by almost 25 percent. (6) A nutritionist recently demonstrated a helpful way to avoid guessing the quantity of a serving. (7) First measured the food into the serving size listed on the label. (8) Then he placed the measured portion in the middle of a large, empty plate. (9) What a serving really looks like.

1. Sentences 1 and 2: **Parents complain that their children's eyes are bigger than their stomachs. When the children estimate how much candy or treats they can eat.**

   Which is the best way to write the underlined portion of the text? If the original is the best way, choose option (1).

   (1) stomachs. When
   (2) stomachs when
   (3) stomachs! When
   (4) stomachs. Especially when
   (5) stomachs. This when

2. Sentence 5: **Unfortunately, underestimating their daily food intake by almost 25 percent.**

   What correction should be made to sentence 5?

   (1) insert are after Unfortunately,
   (2) replace underestimating with they underestimate
   (3) replace their with they're
   (4) insert this after intake
   (5) change intake by to intake. By

3. Sentence 7: **First measured the food into the serving size listed on the label.**

   Which is the best way to write the underlined portion of the text? If the original is the best way, choose option (1).

   (1) First measured
   (2) First, measured
   (3) He first measured
   (4) First. He measured
   (5) First measuring

4. Sentences 8 and 9: **Then he placed the measured portion in the middle of a large, empty plate. What a serving really looks like.**

   The most effective combination of sentences 8 and 9 would include which group of words?

   (1) plate to show what
   (2) measured and served portion
   (3) portion, what a serving really looks like, in
   (4) looks like, then he
   (5) plate and what

Questions 5 through 8 refer to the following paragraphs.

Finesse Computer Systems

To Our Valued Customers:

(A)

(1) Finesse Computer wants to make it easier for you to visit our Web sites. (2) We've set up our systems to help you store the information you wish to share with us. (3) Your name, street and e-mail addresses, and telephone number. (4) Then you select your unique Finesse password, which you will be asked to enter at the beginning of your Web search. (5) You won't have to reenter all your personal information. (6) For downloading an article from our archives or to purchase a new product. (7) Simply type in your password, and the system will access the information automatically.

(B)

(8) The information we store for you will not be shared with anyone else, and your personal information cannot be accessed by others. (9) Your information updated at any time by typing in your password and editing the information on file.

5. Sentences 2 and 3: **We've set up our systems to help you store the information you wish to share with us. Your name, street and e-mail addresses, and telephone number.**

Which is the best way to write the underlined portion of the text? If the original is the best way, choose option (1).

(1) us. Your
(2) us your
(3) us; such as your
(4) us being your
(5) us because your

6. Sentence 4: **Then you select your unique Finesse password, which you will be asked to enter at the beginning of your Web search.**

What correction should be made to sentence 4?

(1) insert as after Then
(2) replace you select with selecting
(3) change password, which to password. Which
(4) replace your with you're
(5) no correction is necessary

7. Sentences 5 and 6: **You won't have to reenter all your personal information. For downloading an article from our archives or to purchase a new product.**

The most effective combination of sentences 5 and 6 would include which group of words?

(1) for the reason of downloading
(2) when you want to download
(3) reenter and download
(4) information and for
(5) information because

8. Sentence 9: **Your information updated at any time by typing in your password and editing the information on file.**

What correction should be made to sentence 9?

(1) insert can be before updated
(2) change updated to updating
(3) change time by to time. By
(4) change editing to having edited
(5) insert you have after the information

Answers start on page 267.

GED SKILL Compound Sentences

Coordinating Conjunctions

You have been writing complete sentences, which are also called **independent clauses.** An independent clause can stand by itself as a simple sentence. Two or more independent clauses can be combined into one **compound sentence.** Writing a compound sentence is an effective way for you to show how the ideas in the clauses are related.

coordinating conjunction
a word that connects the independent clauses in a compound sentence

METHOD To write a compound sentence, combine independent clauses with a **coordinating conjunction.** The coordinating conjunction shows the relationship between the clauses.

Coordinating conjunction	Relationship
and	connects two related ideas
but, yet	contrasts two ideas
for	shows a cause
so	shows an effect
or	gives choices
nor	gives negative choices

TIP

To combine two sentences effectively, read both sentences and look for the relationship between their ideas. Then use a comma and a coordinating conjunction that correctly expresses that relationship.

RULE When you write a compound sentence with a coordinating conjunction, use a comma before the conjunction.

Separate: Jack joined a group of actors. They are quite talented.
Combined: Jack joined a group of actors, and they are quite talented. (The word *and* connects the two related ideas.)

Separate: Their first play is a hilarious comedy. It's sure to be a hit.
Combined: Their first play is a hilarious comedy, so it's sure to be a hit. (The word *so* shows an effect.)

Put a check mark next to the compound sentence that correctly combines independent clauses.

_____ a. My mother works at High Mills, she's worked there ten years.

_____ b. She started as a sewer, but she wanted to be a designer.

_____ c. After six years she finished college so she was promoted to the design department.

You were correct if you decided that *option b* is a correct compound sentence. Its two independent clauses are joined by both a comma and the coordinating conjunction *but. Option a* contains only a comma with no conjunction. *Option c* does not include a comma.

A. Combine each pair of clauses to write a compound sentence. Choose the correct coordinating conjunction and add the necessary comma.

1. (so, yet) People want their lawns to be insect-free. Many of them use chemical pesticides.

   People want their lawns to be insect-free, so many of them use chemical pesticides.

2. (for, or) Chemical pesticides in grass can pose a hazard. Children often play on the grass.

   _____

3. (and, but) Some thoughtful parents still use pesticides. They follow instructions for use and disposal carefully.

   _____

4. (or, so) Others prefer to use biodegradable sprays. They choose natural bug repellents, like marigolds.

   _____

5. (and, nor) Professional exterminators must be certified. They should apply pesticides properly.

   _____

B. Read the paragraph below. The places where sentences can be combined are underlined. Make compound sentences by changing punctuation and adding coordinating conjunctions.

The moon's gravitational pull affects the tides on <u>Earth. Some</u> *Earth, but some* people believe it affects humans more. People have been accused of behaving strangely under a full moon. The number of violent crimes seems to <u>rise. Accidents</u> are more frequent. Some people feel more <u>creative. Others</u> feel depressed. Do you postpone a <u>haircut? Do</u> you fail to clip your nails during the full moon? Some people believe in these <u>superstitions. They're</u> unlikely to admit to it in public.

C. Write about the following topic.

The paragraph you edited in Exercise B described superstitions about a full moon. Write a paragraph that explains why you do or do not believe a particular superstition. Then edit your paragraph for the correct use of compound sentences.

Answers start on page 268.

Other Connectors

There are two other ways to combine independent clauses in compound sentences.

METHOD 1 Combine sentences using a semicolon when the ideas are closely related.

Separate: Nuclear weapons threaten all our lives. Failure to solve this problem could have serious consequences.

Combined: Nuclear weapons threaten all our lives; failure to solve this problem could have serious consequences.

METHOD 2 Combine sentences using a semicolon and a **conjunctive adverb.** The conjunctive adverb you choose should show the relationship between the two ideas being combined.

Conjunctive adverbs	Relationship
also, furthermore, moreover, besides	connect two ideas
however, still, nevertheless, instead, nonetheless	contrast two ideas
similarly, likewise	compare two ideas
therefore, thus, consequently	show a result
next, then, meanwhile, finally, subsequently	show time order
for example, for instance	give examples

RULE When you use a conjunctive adverb to connect two clauses, put a semicolon before it and a comma after it.

Separate: People are interested in avoiding nuclear war. They do not always agree on the best way to do so.

Combined: People are interested in avoiding nuclear war; however, they do not always agree on the best way to do so. (*However* contrasts the two ideas.)

Put a check mark next to the sentences that correctly combine ideas in compound sentences.

_____ a. Social Security provides many forms of financial help; it currently pays retirement, disability, and other benefits.

_____ b. Most people retire at age 65; next, a new law is increasing that age to 67.

_____ c. Some people retire at age 62; consequently, they receive lower benefits.

_____ d. Retirees also receive Medicare; which pays for medical services.

You were correct if you chose *options a* and *c*. *Option b* incorrectly uses *next*, a time-order connecting word, when the relationship is a contrast. *Option d* is incorrect because *which pays for medical services* is not an independent clause.

A. Choose the correct conjunctive adverb. Add punctuation as needed.

1. (nevertheless, moreover) El Niño is a fascinating cyclical weather system

    ; moreover, _____ scientists are finding some useful data from studying it.

2. (likewise, however) Old forecasting methods relied on weather data from the past

    _____ El Niño has changed that.

3. (for instance, finally) Now meteorologists also look at current conditions

    _____ recent changes in ocean temperatures, soil wetness, and snowfall are examined.

4. (consequently, besides) Climates near the equator change little season to season

    _____ weather predictions there are the most accurate.

5. (nevertheless, next) Weather patterns to the north and south are more unpredictable

    _____ data on El Niño can be helpful in predicting seasonal temperatures and precipitation.

B. Read this paragraph about painting a room. The places where sentences can be combined are underlined. Make compound sentences with either (1) a semicolon or (2) a semicolon, conjunctive adverb, and comma.

First, you should pick your color scheme. *; then, determine* Determine the kind and amount of paint you'll need. Most people use latex paint. It is easier to apply. Oil-based paint lasts longer. It is hard to apply and messy to clean up. Lightweight furniture can be moved to another room. Heavy or bulky furniture can be dragged to the center of the room. Cover everything in the room with drop cloths. Remove hardware from doors, windows, and curtain rods. Unscrew switch plates and electric outlet plates. Patch any cracks in the plaster or ceiling. Fill small holes with plastic wood. Sand the walls with coarse sandpaper and the woodwork with fine sandpaper. Your room is now ready to paint.

C. Write about the following topic.

The paragraph that you edited in Exercise B explained how to prepare a room for painting. What is something that you know how to do? Write a paragraph explaining the steps that are involved. Then edit your paragraph to make sure compound sentences are written correctly.

Answers start on page 268.

Directions: Choose the <u>one best answer</u> to each question.

<u>Questions 1 through 4</u> refer to the following paragraph.

Internet Tax Filing

(1) The Internal Revenue Service has simplified tax time with electronic filing. (2) You can prepare and file your tax forms very quickly over the Internet, so your tax refund may arrive in three weeks instead of six. (3) To file electronically, you'll need a personal computer with a modem and commercial tax preparation software. (4) The software records all your personal and financial information and the modem transmits it to the IRS. (5) The IRS then checks your forms for errors. (6) Some forms may be rejected. (7) The IRS has a customer service department to help in such cases. (8) A service representative can tell you what's missing or incomplete, so you can correct it and file again. (9) Once your return is accepted, you have to send in additional forms, such as the special signature document and your W-2 forms. (10) You can also pay electronically, you can have the IRS deposit your refund directly into your checking account.

1. Sentence 2: **You can prepare and file your tax forms very quickly over the <u>Internet, so your</u> tax refund may arrive in three weeks instead of six.**

   Which is the best way to write the underlined portion of the text? If the original is the best way, choose option (1).

   (1) Internet, so your
   (2) Internet, your
   (3) Internet so, your
   (4) Internet so your
   (5) Internet. So your

2. Sentence 4: **The software records all your personal and financial information and the modem transmits it to the IRS.**

   What correction should be made to sentence 4?

   (1) remove <u>and</u> after <u>information</u>
   (2) insert a comma after <u>and</u>
   (3) insert a comma after <u>information</u>
   (4) remove <u>the modem</u>
   (5) no correction is necessary

3. Sentences 6 and 7: **Some forms may be rejected. The IRS has a customer service department to help in such cases.**

   The most effective combination of sentences 6 and 7 would include which group of words?

   (1) rejected, the
   (2) rejected the,
   (3) rejected therefore the
   (4) rejected but the
   (5) rejected, but the

4. Sentence 10: **You can also pay electronically, you can have the IRS deposit your refund directly into your checking account.**

   What correction should be made to sentence 10?

   (1) remove the comma
   (2) insert <u>or</u> after the comma
   (3) insert <u>however</u> after the comma
   (4) insert a comma after <u>deposit</u>
   (5) no correction is necessary

TIP

Some questions on the GED Test ask, "Which way is the best way to write the underlined portion of the text?" In those question types, option (1) is always the same as the original.

Questions 5 through 9 refer to the following business letter.

Dear New Cellular Phone Customer:

(1) Your monthly access charges will be billed on the twenty-fifth of every month. (2) Your first bill includes prorated charges from April 8, the date you began service, and the regular access charge for May. (3) Two months are combined on the first bill, it may be larger than subsequent bills. (4) In addition, you get one free hour of cellular airtime each month. (5) That airtime must be used within the month. (6) Additional taxes, tolls, and special charges will be recorded separately. (7) Charges for calls begin at the time of pick-up and, they end at the time of disconnection. (8) You are billed for all answered calls but there is no charge for busy signals or unanswered rings. (9) Calls are billed in full minutes; for example, a call of 5 minutes and 15 seconds will be billed as a 6-minute call.

5. Sentence 3: **Two months are combined on the first bill, it may be larger than subsequent bills.**

   What correction should be made to sentence 3?

   (1) insert , and after combined
   (2) insert similarly after the comma
   (3) insert so after the comma
   (4) remove the comma
   (5) no correction is necessary

6. Sentences 4 and 5: **In addition, you get one free hour of cellular airtime each month. That airtime must be used within the month.**

   The most effective combination of sentences 4 and 5 would include which group of words?

   (1) month for example that
   (2) month and airtime
   (3) month however airtime
   (4) month so, the airtime
   (5) month, but it

7. Sentence 7: **Charges for calls begin at the time of pick-up and, they end at the time of disconnection.**

   What correction should be made to sentence 7?

   (1) change pick-up and, to pick-up, and
   (2) replace and with nonetheless
   (3) remove and
   (4) remove the comma
   (5) no correction is necessary

8. Sentence 8: **You are billed for all answered calls but there is no charge for busy signals or unanswered rings.**

   Which is the best way to write the underlined portion of the text? If the original is the best way, choose option (1).

   (1) calls but
   (2) calls, but
   (3) calls, however,
   (4) calls and
   (5) calls. But

9. Sentence 9: **Calls are billed in full minutes; for example, a call of 5 minutes and 15 seconds will be billed as a 6-minute call.**

   What correction should be made to sentence 9?

   (1) replace for example with nevertheless
   (2) replace for example with but
   (3) remove the comma
   (4) insert a comma after 5 minutes
   (5) no correction is necessary

TIP

On the GED Test, you may see an option that uses a conjunctive adverb without a semicolon to connect two clauses. Remember, that type of sentence construction is never correct.

Answers start on page 268.

GED Mini-Test • Lesson 2

Directions: This is a ten-minute practice test. After ten minutes, mark the last question you finished. Then complete the test and check your answers. If most of your answers were correct, but you didn't finish, try to work faster next time. Choose the one best answer to each question.

Questions 1 through 4 refer to the following paragraphs.

Tour Jackets

(A)

(1) During the Vietnam War, many of the sailors and soldiers wore personally decorated jackets known as "Pleiku" or tour jackets. (2) The jackets were hand-sewn with colorful designs. (3) Maps, dragons, flags, and the like. (4) Later, the owners added elaborate patches, or they embroidered messages that indicated where they were stationed. (5) The jackets became completely personalized; each individual's was different.

(B)

(6) The first to wear the tour jackets were sailors. (7) The Navy issued each sailor a complete working uniform yet the jacket was the only Navy clothing that could be embellished. (8) Decorating jackets, then, began with sailors. (9) Became more common among soldiers in the war later.

1. Sentences 2 and 3: **The jackets were hand-sewn with colorful designs. Maps, dragons, flags, and the like.**

   The most effective combination of sentences 2 and 3 would include which groups of words?

   (1) designs, and maps
   (2) designs such as maps
   (3) hand-sewn maps with
   (4) The maps were hand-sewn
   (5) Their jackets with maps

2. Sentence 4: **Later, the owners added elaborate patches, or they embroidered messages that indicated where they were stationed.**

   Which is the best way to write the underlined portion of the text? If the original is the best way, choose option (1).

   (1) patches, or they
   (2) patches or they
   (3) patches. Or they
   (4) patches or, they
   (5) patches, or, they

3. Sentence 7: **The Navy issued each sailor a complete working uniform yet the jacket was the only Navy clothing that could be embellished.**

   Which is the best way to write the underlined portion of the text? If the original is the best way, choose option (1).

   (1) uniform yet
   (2) uniform, thus
   (3) uniform. And
   (4) uniform yet,
   (5) uniform, yet

4. Sentence 9: **Became more common among soldiers in the war later.**

   What correction should be made to sentence 9?

   (1) change Became to Becoming
   (2) change Became to It became
   (3) insert a comma after war
   (4) change war to War
   (5) no correction is necessary

Questions 5 through 9 refer to the following paragraphs.

Using the Library

(A)

(1) A popular misconception about libraries is that it's hard to find information in them. (2) Libraries hold an enormous number of reference books. (3) These books are kept together in a special section. (4) Is filled with books used to find facts. (5) Reference librarians are trained to find any kind of information you might want. (6) Suppose you want to find the address of an organization, perhaps you want information on buying a home. (7) A reference librarian can help but you have to ask.

(B)

(8) Libraries have more to offer than just books. (9) Some libraries provide typewriters and computers for the use of their patrons. (10) Who don't have other access to these devices. (11) Libraries must be viewed as one of our greatest public resources, they provide so many services.

5. Sentences 3 and 4: **These books are kept together in a special section. Is filled with books used to find facts.**

   The most effective combination of sentences 3 and 4 would include which group of words?

   (1) section, so it is
   (2) section and filled
   (3) section, yet filled
   (4) section being filled
   (5) section that is filled

6. Sentence 6: **Suppose you want to find the address of an organization, perhaps you want information on buying a home.**

   What correction should be made to sentence 6?

   (1) remove the comma
   (2) insert or after the comma
   (3) insert a comma after perhaps
   (4) replace perhaps with likewise
   (5) insert a comma after information

7. Sentence 7: **A reference librarian can help but you have to ask.**

   Which is the best way to write the underlined portion of the text? If the original is the best way, choose option (1).

   (1) help but
   (2) help, but
   (3) help. But
   (4) help but,
   (5) help

8. Sentences 9 and 10: **Some libraries provide typewriters and computers for the use of their patrons. Who don't have other access to these devices.**

   Which is the best way to write the underlined portion of the text? If the original is the best way, choose option (1).

   (1) patrons. Who
   (2) patrons, yet they
   (3) patrons. They
   (4) patrons, but
   (5) patrons who

9. Sentence 11: **Libraries must be viewed as one of our greatest public resources, they provide so many services.**

   What correction should be made to sentence 11?

   (1) remove must be
   (2) insert a comma after viewed
   (3) remove the comma
   (4) insert for after the comma
   (5) no correction is necessary

Answers start on page 269.

Writing Your Thoughts in Complete Sentences

You have learned how to tell if a sentence expresses a complete thought. You have also learned how to relate ideas in compound sentences. These skills can help you when you write the essay on the GED Test. In fact, complete, clearly written sentences are the building blocks in almost every kind of writing you do in your life.

Look at the paragraph below. Can you easily understand what the writer is trying to say?

> Family life. Ups and downs. Older sister. Did really care for each other, though. Father who was never home. Needed structure. Had my grandmother living with us. Got on my nerves. Stress. But helped, too.

Now read the improved paragraph. Look at how the use of complete sentences makes the writer's point easier to understand. Each sentence has a subject and a verb and expresses a complete idea. Some sentences are compound, with two complete, related ideas.

> When I was growing up, my family life certainly had its ups and downs. My moody older sister could be difficult to live with, yet we really cared for each other. Having a father who worked a lot and was never home was challenging. However, we all appreciated the structure of our family, which included our grandmother who lived with us. I admit that family members sometimes got on my nerves and there was stress at home. At those times, I think about the help my family gave me, too.

Rewrite these phrases from the first paragraph as complete sentences using ideas of your own. Notice how writing a complete sentence gives clear meaning to the ideas.

older sister: *An older sister can offer advice and support.*

needed structure: _____

got on my nerves: _____

stress: _____

Be sure that each of your sentences includes a subject and a verb and expresses a complete thought. Compare your sentences to these: *People who need structure do well in a family. My brothers got on my nerves all the time. Stress is a part of life, but it should not overwhelm you.*

The Personal Link

TIP

The only way to become a better writer is to practice. All the writing you do will help you prepare for the GED Writing Test—both the editing section and the essay.

Personal writing can take many different forms; it is the writing people do in their everyday lives. It includes personal details and thoughts. Even though personal writing is sometimes informal, it is most often written in complete sentences. Here are some examples of personal writing.

A note to a delivery person:

Please do not leave my package here. Instead, give it to my neighbor across the hall, Enid Jones, in apartment 17. She will sign for it.

A letter to a friend:

Dear Carmen,

I haven't heard from you in a while, so I decided to drop you a line. What's new? Did you get the job you were applying for? Has your mom gotten out of the hospital? Please tell her I said "hi" and hope she feels better soon. My life is going pretty well these days. My job is challenging, but the people in the store are really nice. Renee says "hi." Write soon!

Love,
Maria

A letter to a housing supervisor:

Dear Supervisor Davidson:

As you requested, here is the list of people who live at 234 East Drive. I live here with my mother, Mary Howard, my aunt, Gwen Holt, my brother and his wife, Mr. and Mrs. John Howard, and their son, John, Jr. As you can see, there are six of us, which is under the limit of eight, as stated in my lease. Please let me know if you need any further information.

Sincerely,
Jean Howard

On a separate sheet of paper, write a note of at least four sentences to a friend. Tell your friend what is happening with your family.

The Personal Link

One very personal form of writing is journal writing. A **journal** is a notebook in which you can write anything you want. What you write is for your eyes only.

A journal is a good way for you to express and explore your thoughts and feelings. It is also a great source of ideas to include in other forms of writing, such as the GED essay. If you decide to keep a journal, get a special notebook for that use.

In your journal or on a separate sheet of paper, write down three things that you like about your family and three things that you do not like. Remember, your journal is for only you to read. Be honest about how you feel.

The GED Link

The essay that you will write on the GED Writing Test, Part II is different from the personal writing you have done so far. For one thing, the reader of a GED essay is a scorer—someone you do not know who will read your essay and decide how well it is written.

You will use your own thoughts and experiences in your GED essay. However, instead of limiting your writing to personal details, you will also write more generally about the topic. You will want to include experiences and ideas other than your own—things you have read about, heard about on the news, or discussed with a friend.

Read the paragraph about the family on page 50 again. Then compare it with the paragraph below.

Family life is sometimes more difficult than single life; sometimes a family makes life easier. We have all heard stories about the little brother or sister who would never leave us alone. My younger brother was like that, and he sometimes made me feel more like a parent than a kid growing up. There is no question that having a brother or a sister can infringe on our personal freedom. However, many times a sibling can be an ally—someone who sticks up for us in the neighborhood or when a parent accuses us of some misdeed.

Can you see a difference between the original paragraph on page 50 and the one above? The one on page 50 describes the writer's family in personal detail. The paragraph above includes a personal detail but also talks about families in general—not just one person's own family life, but the family life of people he has heard about or read about.

1. **Read the paragraphs below. Label each one *personal* or *general essay* writing.**

   a. The life of the American family is a complex one. There is no such thing as the "perfect family life."

   general essay

   b. My stepmother is a real pain. Yesterday, she asked me to do the laundry, then didn't give me any money for the machines! I get so tired of her problems.

   _____

   c. The relationship between a stepparent and a son or daughter can be a challenging one. Although my stepmother is a pain, there are some stepmothers who add a lot of joy to their stepchildren's lives.

   _____

2. **Write at least a few sentences on the following topic. You can use some of the ideas you wrote about in The Personal Link, but try to include some ideas about the topic in general.**

   Being part of a family is easier for some people than others. Do the benefits of being a family member outweigh the challenges? Give examples to support your opinion.

Edit

Look at the sentences you wrote in the GED Link. Edit them to make sure they are complete and correctly punctuated. Use a caret (^) to show something you want to add. Use a single line to cross out words and ideas you do not want to keep.

A family made up of people ^can be ~~which~~ who are not blood relatives.

Portfolio Reminder

Throughout this book, you will see reminders to put your writing in your **portfolio.** Try to save as much of your work as you can.

Answers start on page 270.

GED SKILL Subordinating Ideas

Complex Sentences

You know that an independent clause has a subject and verb and expresses a complete thought. A dependent clause, or subordinate clause, has a subject and verb but does not express a complete thought.

Subordinate clause: Until the sun set.

You also know that a compound sentence consists of two independent clauses joined by a coordinating conjunction. You can create a **complex sentence** when you join an independent clause and a subordinate clause. The subordinate clause adds information or details to the main independent clause.

Complex sentence: The fireworks did not start until the sun set.

A subordinate clause is introduced by a **subordinating conjunction.** Here are some subordinating conjuctions and relationships they show.

> **Time:** after, before, once, since, until, when, whenever, while
> **Result/effect:** in order that, so, so that
> **Location:** where, wherever
> **Condition:** if, even if, unless
> **Choice:** whether
> **Concession:** although, even though, though
> **Reason/cause:** as, because, since

METHOD A subordinate clause is a sentence fragment if it is not connected to an independent clause. You can correct the fragment by attaching it to an independent clause to create a complex sentence.

Independent clause
and fragment: The game was canceled. Because it rained.
Complex sentence: The game was canceled because it rained.

RULE Use a comma after a subordinate clause at the beginning of a sentence. You usually do not need a comma before a subordinate clause at the end of a sentence.

Complex sentence: Because it rained, the game was canceled.
Complex sentence: The game was canceled because it rained.

Put a check mark next to the correct complex sentence.

_____ a. Once the tow truck removed the broken-down truck.

_____ b. Once the truck was removed, the traffic jam was cleared.

You were correct if you chose *option b*. It is a correctly punctuated complex sentence. *Option a* is a subordinate clause (fragment).

Sidebar

complex sentence contains an independent clause and a subordinate clause, connected by a subordinating conjunction

A. Combine the clauses into complex sentences using the subordinating conjunctions in parentheses. Add or change words and punctuation as needed.

1. (when) Bob quit smoking. He gained weight.

   When Bob quit smoking, he gained weight.

2. (even though) People may put on pounds. They still should quit smoking.

   _____

3. (after) People tend to gain weight for several years. They kick the habit.

   _____

4. (because) Smoking represses hunger. The heaviest smokers put on the most weight.

   _____

5. (so that) People need to exercise. Weight gain can be limited.

   _____

B. Edit this paragraph. Insert a comma in each sentence that begins with a subordinate clause. Attach each subordinate-clause fragment to an independent clause.

Although many would deny it. Judges and juries are swayed by a witness's appearance. Even though justice is supposed to be impartial juries tend to believe attractive people more often. That is why lawyers hire jury consultants to advise witnesses. When a witness is more believable he or she is more valuable to a client. Witnesses are told to dress as they would for a job interview or business meeting. While fashionable clothing isn't forbidden. A plain suit with a white blouse or shirt is the best choice. Whether they're male or female people who wear sandals can expect to be ignored. In a suit, you're seen as a trustworthy person. It also satisfies a jury. Because you give the appearance of understanding and following society's rules.

C. Write about the following topic.

What kind of advice would you give about appearance to someone who was preparing for a job interview or an important presentation? Write a paragraph giving your advice. Then edit your paragraph for correct complex sentences.

Answers start on page 270.

Combining Details

Very simple ideas or single details often don't need their own sentences. Try combining them with sentences nearby to reduce choppy writing.

A simple sentence has a subject, a verb, and one idea. Simple sentences are often short. Too many short, simple sentences—or too many short, simple clauses in a compound sentence—will make your writing seem choppy and repetitious.

There are several methods for combining details to make your writing flow more smoothly. Notice that while all three methods solve the problem slightly differently, each contains the same details, eliminates repetition, and shows the relationship of ideas.

METHOD 1 Combine details into one longer simple sentence.

Choppy: Many different needles are required for hand sewing. The needles vary according to eye shape. They vary according to length. They vary according to point.

Choppy: The needles vary according to eye shape, and they vary according to length, and they vary according to point.

Smooth: Needles for hand sewing vary according to eye shape, length, and point.

METHOD 2 Combine details into one compound sentence.

Smooth: Hand sewing requires different needles, so they vary according to eye shape, length, and point.

METHOD 3 Combine details into one complex sentence.

Smooth: Because hand sewing requires different needles, they vary according to eye shape, length, and point.

Put a check mark next to the smoothest, most effective writing.

_____ a. On average, women in the United States live longer than men. They live about seven years longer than men who are generally stronger than women.

_____ b. On average, women in the United States live seven years longer than men, even though men are physically stronger.

_____ c. On average, women in the United States live seven years longer than men. That means men, on average, have shorter lives than women. Men are typically stronger than women.

You were correct if you chose *option b*. It combines all the ideas smoothly and shows how they are related in one clear complex sentence. *Option a* combines some ideas, but repeats information unnecessarily. *Option c* does not combine any of the ideas and repeats the same information in different ways.

A. Here are directions for making hot cocoa. Combine the details in each group into a sentence. There is more than one way to rewrite the directions.

1. You will need milk. You will need cocoa. You will also need sugar.

   You will need milk, cocoa, and sugar.

2. Pour 8 ounces of milk in a saucepan. Place $2\frac{1}{2}$ tablespoons of cocoa in the saucepan. Put 2 tablespoons of sugar in the saucepan.

   _____

   _____

3. Heat the mixture. Stir the mixture constantly.

   _____

   _____

4. The mixture should be piping hot. The mixture shouldn't boil.

   _____

   _____

5. Serve the cocoa plain. Top it with marshmallows.

   _____

   _____

B. Read the notice. On another sheet of paper, try to combine all the information into only six or seven sentences. There is more than one way to rewrite the information.

The Zoning Board announces a public hearing. The hearing is on Tuesday, November 30, at 8:10 P.M. It will be held in the East Lake City Hall. A petition by Allied Hardware will be discussed.

Allied Hardware wants a building variance. The company wants to construct a parking lot. The parking lot will be in a residential neighborhood. Parking lots are not usually permitted in residential neighborhoods. Allied Hardware's petition is on file with the Zoning Board. Its plans are on file there, too. They are available for public inspection in the Office of City Zoning.

Residents may comment on the variance request. Residents can register their names on the Comments Roster. It is posted in the Office of City Zoning.

C. Write about the following topic.

In Exercise B, you rewrote an announcement about a public hearing. Write an announcement for an event you read about or would like to attend. Then edit your announcement for short, choppy sentences and other errors.

Answers start on page 271.

Directions: Choose the <u>one best answer</u> to each question.

Questions 1 through 4 refer to the following paragraph.

Impulse Shopping

(1) Supermarkets are designed to encourage us to buy on impulse. (2) When we enter we generally move in the direction the store has chosen, down the "power" aisle. (3) It is a rare shopper who can reach the dairy products in the rear of the store without picking up unplanned items. (4) Then we stand in the checkout line and see more impulse buys. (5) We see magazines. (6) We see candy and other small items. (7) Even though we may have wanted only a quart of milk. (8) We'll probably walk out with several items. (9) We can avoid impulse buying. (10) We have to understand why we do it.

1. Sentence 2: **When we enter we generally move in the direction the store has chosen, down the "power" aisle.**

   What correction should be made to sentence 2?

   (1) replace <u>When</u> with <u>Because</u>
   (2) insert a comma after <u>enter</u>
   (3) change <u>enter we</u> to <u>enter. We</u>
   (4) insert a comma after <u>generally</u>
   (5) insert a comma after <u>direction</u>

> **TIP**
> A subordinating conjunction and a subject and verb at the beginning of the sentence will help you determine if you need to use a comma.

2. Sentences 4, 5, and 6: **Then we stand in the checkout line and see more impulse buys. We see magazines. We see candy and other small items.**

   The most effective combination of sentences 4, 5, and 6 would include which group of words?

   (1) Standing in the checkout line and seeing
   (2) Then we stand and see
   (3) buys such as magazines, candy, and
   (4) buys, we see magazines
   (5) buys, seeing magazines

3. Sentences 7 and 8: **Even though we may have wanted only a quart of <u>milk. We'll</u> probably walk out with several items.**

   Which is the best way to write the underlined portion of the text? If the original is the best way, choose option (1).

   (1) milk. We'll
   (2) milk, and we'll
   (3) milk, so we'll
   (4) milk we'll
   (5) milk, we'll

4. Sentences 9 and 10: **We can avoid impulse buying. We have to understand why we do it.**

   The most effective combination of sentences 9 and 10 would include which group of words?

   (1) buying, and we
   (2) buying, so we
   (3) Because we can
   (4) if we understand
   (5) although we do not

Questions 5 through 8 refer to the following paragraph.

Fit and Healthy

(1) Being fit is practically a national obsession. (2) Fitness books are numerous. (3) So are commercial exercise programs. (4) Unfortunately, there is no magic formula for getting into shape. (5) How do you become fit and stay fit? (6) If you really want to get into shape you need to make serious, permanent lifestyle changes. (7) Exercise must be one of those changes. (8) You don't need to pay for membership in an expensive health club. (9) You can simply buy a good pair of shoes and take a brisk walk in them several times a week, and the shoes should be made especially for walking. (10) Finally, keep a positive attitude. (11) Frequently remind yourself how much better you look and feel. (12) Since you've changed your behavior.

5. Sentences 2 and 3: **Fitness books are numerous. So are commercial exercise programs.**

The most effective combination of sentences 2 and 3 would include which group of words?

(1) numerous, so are
(2) books and commercial exercise programs are
(3) in addition, commercial exercise programs
(4) but so are commercial exercise programs
(5) Numerous fitness books and commercial

TIP One way to combine details is to combine subjects. For example, *Stan worked at the warehouse. Ivan did too.* becomes *Stan and Ivan worked at the warehouse.* You can also combine verbs: *Stan unloaded shipments. He also checked inventory.* becomes *Stan unloaded shipments and checked inventory.*

6. Sentence 6: **If you really want to get into shape you need to make serious, permanent lifestyle changes.**

What correction should be made to sentence 6?

(1) change If you to You
(2) insert a comma after want
(3) insert a comma after shape
(4) change shape you to shape. You
(5) no correction is necessary

7. Sentence 9: **You can simply buy a good pair of shoes and take a brisk walk in them several times a week, and the shoes should be made especially for walking.**

The most effective revision of sentence 9 would include which group of words?

(1) make sure that the shoes
(2) Buying a good pair of shoes and walking
(3) You can simply buy and walk
(4) the shoes should be good for walking
(5) a good pair of walking shoes

8. Sentences 11 and 12: **Frequently remind yourself how much better you look and feel. Since you've changed your behavior.**

Which is the best way to write the underlined portion of the text? If the original is the best way, choose option (1).

(1) feel. Since you've
(2) feel, and since you've
(3) feel since you've
(4) feel although you've
(5) feel. You've

Answers start on page 271.

Directions: This is a ten-minute practice test. After ten minutes, mark the last question you finished. Then complete the test and check your answers. If most of your answers were correct, but you didn't finish, try to work faster next time. Choose the one best answer to each question.

Questions 1 through 4 refer to the following memo.

Memorandum

To: All Departments
From: Marie, Photocopy Manager
Re: New Copier

(A)

(1) If your department has a major copying project due you should plan on having the copying completed before Friday night. (2) Beginning this weekend, the photocopy machines will be removed. (3) The old photocopiers will be replaced with 26 Task copiers. (4) The new copiers work at twice the speed and perform additional functions, including making double-sided copies and collating.

(B)

(5) Removing machines is a slow process, and installing machines is a slow process, and so copy machine service will probably be interrupted next week. (6) The interruption should not last too long and we apologize for any inconvenience. (7) Once the installation is complete, everyone will be happier with the improved equipment. (8) In the meantime, please let office management know if there is anything we can do to help you.

1. Sentence 1: **If your department has a major copying project due you should plan on having the copying completed before Friday night.**

   What correction should be made to sentence 1?

   (1) replace If with When
   (2) replace your with you're
   (3) insert a comma after due
   (4) insert then after due
   (5) no correction is necessary

2. Sentences 2 and 3: **Beginning this weekend, the photocopy machines will be removed. The old photocopiers will be replaced with 26 Task copiers.**

   Which is the best way to write the underlined portion of the text? If the original is the best way, choose option (1).

   (1) removed. The old photocopiers will be replaced
   (2) removed, the old photocopiers will be replaced
   (3) removed the old photocopiers will be replaced
   (4) removed so they will be replaced
   (5) removed and replaced

3. Sentence 5: **Removing machines is a slow process, and installing machines is a slow process, and so copy machine service will probably be interrupted next week.**

   The most effective revision of sentence 5 would begin with which group of words?

   (1) Because removing and installing machines
   (2) Both removing machines and installing
   (3) Whenever you remove or install machines
   (4) Due to interrupted copy machine service
   (5) The slow process will interrupt

4. Sentence 6: **The interruption should not last too long and we apologize for any inconvenience.**

   What correction should be made to sentence 6?

   (1) replace The with While the
   (2) insert a comma after long
   (3) replace and with but
   (4) remove we
   (5) insert a comma after apologize

Questions 5 through 9 refer to the following paragraphs.

Moving Tips

(A)

(1) Whether you're going across town or across the country. (2) Moving is one of life's stressful experiences. (3) So that you have an easier time experienced movers suggest making a "home change-over" list.

(B)

(4) For example, let the utility companies know the date that you're moving. (5) Fill out a Change of Address form at the post office. (6) Be sure to know your new address. (7) Know the date you want your mail switched, too. (8) Some movers recommend packing a survival kit. (9) This kit contains items such as basic tools, snacks and drinks, and tissue. (10) You will probably need these things at some point on moving day, so make sure you keep your kit with you.

5. Sentences 1 and 2: **Whether you're going across town or across the country. Moving is one of life's stressful experiences.**

Which is the best way to write the underlined portion of the text? If the original is the best way, choose option (1).

(1) country. Moving
(2) country moving
(3) country, moving
(4) country, and moving
(5) country because moving

6. Sentence 3: **So that you have an easier time experienced movers suggest making a "home change-over" list.**

What correction should be made to sentence 3?

(1) replace So that with Because
(2) insert a comma after time
(3) change suggest to suggested
(4) insert a comma after suggest
(5) no correction is necessary

7. Sentences 6 and 7: **Be sure to know your new address. Know the date you want your mail switched, too.**

Which is the best way to write the underlined portion of the text? If the original is the best way, choose option (1).

(1) address. Know
(2) address, know
(3) address, while knowing
(4) address. And know
(5) address and

8. Sentences 8 and 9: **Some movers recommend packing a survival kit. This kit contains items such as basic tools, snacks and drinks, and tissue.**

The most effective combination of sentences 8 and 9 would include which group of words?

(1) survival kit, and this
(2) survival kit such as
(3) survival kit containing
(4) packing basic tools
(5) movers recommending a kit with

9. Sentence 10: **You will probably need these things at some point on moving day, so make sure you keep your kit with you.**

What correction should be made to sentence 10?

(1) insert a comma after things
(2) remove the comma after day
(3) replace so with and
(4) replace your with you're
(5) no correction is necessary

Answers start on page 272.

GED SKILL **Run-ons and Comma Splices**

Run-on Sentences

A **run-on sentence** consists of two or more independent clauses joined incorrectly. There are several ways to correct run-ons.

run-on sentence
two or more independent clauses that are run together without proper punctuation and/or connecting words

METHOD 1 Separate the clauses in a run-on sentence by making two sentences.

Run-on: It's easy to get caught up in the excitement of an auction it's so fast and noisy.

Correct: It's easy to get caught up in the excitement of an auction. It's so fast and noisy.

METHOD 2 Separate the clauses with a semicolon alone or with a semicolon, conjunctive adverb, and comma.

Run-on: A man at an auction sneezed he wound up owning a moth-eaten moose head.

Correct: A man at an auction sneezed; he wound up owning a moth-eaten moose head.

Correct: A man at an auction sneezed; consequently, he wound up owning a moth-eaten moose head.

TIP

To decide if a long sentence is a run-on, check to see if there are too many ideas that are not connected with the correct punctuation and connecting words.

METHOD 3 Separate the clauses with both a comma and a coordinating conjunction. Remember that the seven coordinating conjunctions are *and, but, or, nor, for, so,* and *yet.*

Run-on: Decide ahead of time how much to spend you won't be tempted to overbid.

Correct: Decide ahead of time how much to spend, and you won't be tempted to overbid.

METHOD 4 Make one independent clause a dependent clause with a subordinate conjunction. Use a comma if necessary.

Correct: If you decide ahead of time how much to spend, you won't be tempted to overbid.

Put a check mark next to the correct sentence.

_____ a. Agnes is not efficient, but she's learning quickly.

_____ b. Agnes is not efficient she's learning quickly.

You were correct if you chose *option a.* It correctly creates a compound sentence with a comma and the coordinating conjunction *but. Option b* is a run-on sentence.

A. Write _R_ for run-on sentences and _C_ for correct sentences. Rewrite the run-ons correctly.

_R_ 1. Consumers need help buying used cars they want to avoid overpriced ones.

   Consumers need help buying used cars if they want to avoid overpriced ones.

____ 2. Some dishonest dealers sell salvaged cars, and they don't inform buyers about a car's defects.

_____

____ 3. The cars look fine they have cosmetic repairs.

_____

____ 4. Consumers must be careful, and they should follow a few sensible guidelines.

_____

____ 5. Moveable parts of the car should line up with each other the seams should be straight and even.

_____

____ 6. The car should have an in-state license plate badly damaged cars are often moved between states.

_____

B. Edit this paragraph for four more run-on sentences.

   It's not often a child rescues his ~~mother it~~ mother; however, it did happen recently. A mother-son team of Southern Right whales was trapped in shallow water off the coast of Argentina an out-going tide had confused them. Human volunteers doused them with water to keep the whales' skin safely wet. At the first high tide, the calf swam into deeper water he wouldn't leave his mother, who seemed half-asleep. The calf and the volunteers slowly moved the mother toward deeper water. The volunteers pushed the calf bumped the mother's head with its tail. Eventually the mother woke up from her drowsy state then she and her calf were able to swim back to the ocean. Apparently, their ordeal left them with only minor bruises.

C. Write about the following topic.

   Think of a time you helped another person or an animal out of a difficult or dangerous situation. Describe the situation and what you did. Then edit your paragraph for run-on sentences and other errors.

Answers start on page 272.

Comma Splices and Run-ons Connected with *and*

comma splice
a run-on sentence in which independent clauses are connected only by a comma

A **comma splice** occurs when independent clauses are joined only with a comma; the coordinating conjunction is missing.

METHOD 1 The easiest way to correct a comma splice is to add a coordinating conjunction after the comma.

Comma splice: A learning disability is a handicap, you can't see any obvious signs like other disabilities.

Correct: A learning disability is a handicap, yet you can't see any obvious signs like other disabilities.

You can also fix a comma splice by using any of the methods for fixing a run-on explained on page 62.

Another kind of run-on is created when too many independent clauses are strung together, connected only by the word *and*. Often, these lengthy sentences connect ideas that are not closely enough related to be combined in one sentence.

METHOD 2 Correct a run-on with too many independent clauses by dividing it into more than one sentence. One or more sentences may become compound sentences.

Run-on: There are many types of learning disorders and they can interfere with a person's speaking or writing and these disorders sometimes produce problems with reading or math and they may affect attention or self-control.

Correct: There are many types of learning disorders. They can interfere with a person's speaking or writing. These disorders sometimes produce problems with reading and math, and they may affect attention or self-control.

Put a check mark next to the correct sentences.

_____ a. Babies like toys that make noise, but be sure no small pieces can break off for baby to swallow.

_____ b. Big, lightweight toys are fun, and they are easy to grab and hold.

_____ c. They shouldn't have sharp edges, avoid points as well.

_____ d. You can buy a tube and you place toys or toy parts in it and if the parts can fit in it then they are too small for a baby and you should get rid of the toy.

You were correct if you chose *options a* and *b*. They are correctly combined compound sentences. *Option c* is a comma splice because it combines two independent clauses with only a comma. *Option d* has too many clauses connected with just the word *and*.

A. Edit these comma splices and run-on sentences.

1. Muscles are tough elastic tissue they enable other body parts to move.

   . They (handwritten correction above "they")

2. Americans lose only about 15 percent of muscle strength before the age of 50 and after that, they lose almost twice as much muscle strength and after 70, the rate of loss falls even faster.

3. This can lead to many health problems, people may fall frequently, become obese, or have brittle bones.

4. Strength training seems to help, lifting light weights or doing push-ups rebuilds muscles fast.

5. If you are over 45, visit your doctor before you start strength training and people of any age who haven't exercised in many years should also get a checkup and anyone who has high blood pressure or is taking medications should go to their doctor first.

B. Edit this paragraph for three more comma splices and one run-on with *and*.

It may come as a surprise, snug pajamas are the safest kind of sleepwear for small children. *but* (handwritten correction above) Snug-fitting cotton pajamas seem to be the safest, loose-fitting T-shirts or nightgowns have air pockets that may speed up a fire less oxygen fits under snug clothing. Synthetic or polyester material must be treated with chemicals. Snug-fitting cotton pajamas don't have to be treated and that's why they cost less and many people feel that cotton is more comfortable than polyester anyway. Children shouldn't sleep in bathrobes either, robes catch on fire more easily than pajamas. Bathrobe belts can also be a problem, they can get caught around a sleeping child's neck. Finally, be sure to wash flame-resistant pajamas according to the instructions; otherwise, the chemicals that make them safe could be washed away.

C. Write about the following topic.

Write a paragraph explaining a safety issue you feel strongly about. Tell why it's important and what people can do to protect themselves. Then edit your paragraph for run-ons, comma splices, and other errors.

Answers start on page 273.

Directions: Choose the one best answer to each question.

Questions 1 through 4 refer to the following letter.

Dear Dr. Winger:

(A)

(1) Thank you for responding to our evaluation of your program at City Hospital you are correct in observing the difference in the evaluation this year. (2) The reason is that our agency is shifting its emphasis from hospital-based programs to community-based settings. (3) We also had more time for our evaluations this year, so the report is more detailed.

(B)

(4) Your program is in non-compliance in several areas, there is no reason to be too concerned. (5) We evaluate many hospital programs and almost all fail to comply in one or more areas and total compliance is not an absolute requirement for funding. (6) We will provide an objective view of your operation and an explanation of our new evaluation process in our annual report.

1. Sentence 1: **Thank you for responding to our evaluation of your program at City Hospital you are correct in observing the difference in the evaluation this year.**

   Which is the best way to write the underlined portion of the text? If the original is the best way, choose option (1).

   (1) City Hospital you are correct
   (2) City Hospital, You are correct
   (3) City Hospital, you are correct
   (4) City Hospital. You are correct
   (5) City Hospital and you are correct

2. Sentence 3: **We also had more time for our evaluations this year, so the report is more detailed.**

   What correction should be made to sentence 3?

   (1) insert a comma after time
   (2) remove the comma
   (3) insert and after the comma
   (4) remove so
   (5) no correction is necessary

3. Sentence 4: **Your program is in non-compliance in several areas, there is no reason to be too concerned.**

   What correction should be made to sentence 4?

   (1) replace Your with Because your
   (2) remove the comma
   (3) replace the comma with and
   (4) insert however after the comma
   (5) insert but after the comma

4. Sentence 5: **We evaluate many hospital programs and almost all fail to comply in one or more areas and total compliance is not an absolute requirement for funding.**

   The most effective revision of sentence 5 would include which group of words?

   (1) programs, and almost all fail to comply in one or more areas. Total
   (2) While evaluating many hospital programs,
   (3) Many hospital programs fail evaluation
   (4) total compliance not being an absolute requirement
   (5) hospital programs that fail to comply

Questions 5 through 9 refer to the following paragraph.

On-the-Job Injuries

(1) Not all on-the-job injuries involve heavy equipment, some office occupations can also involve injuries. (2) Workers who type constantly, such as data entry operators, may suffer from carpal tunnel syndrome their fingers may literally seize up from the repetitive finger movements. (3) Both changing position frequently and keeping one's keyboard lower than the elbows help avoid injury. (4) Studies have uncovered other injuries at seemingly "safe" jobs, staring for long periods at computer screens can cause severe eyestrain. (5) To reduce eyestrain, stay at least 20 inches from the screen, and use diffuse overhead lighting. (6) In some offices back injuries are common workers can lower their risk by squatting when they lift objects off the floor.

5. Sentence 1: **Not all on-the-job injuries involve heavy equipment, some office occupations can also involve injuries.**

   Which is the best way to write the underlined portion of the text? If the original is the best way, choose option (1).

   (1) equipment, some
   (2) equipment some
   (3) equipment, however some
   (4) equipment so that some
   (5) equipment. Some

6. Sentence 2: **Workers who type constantly, such as data entry operators, may suffer from carpal tunnel syndrome their fingers may literally seize up from the repetitive finger movements.**

   Which is the best way to write the underlined portion of the text? If the original is the best way, choose option (1).

   (1) syndrome their
   (2) syndrome, their
   (3) syndrome. Their
   (4) syndrome for their
   (5) syndrome and their

7. Sentence 3: **Both changing position frequently and keeping one's keyboard lower than the elbows help avoid injury.**

   What correction should be made to sentence 3?

   (1) replace Both with By both
   (2) insert a comma after frequently
   (3) remove and
   (4) insert to after elbows
   (5) no correction is necessary

8. Sentence 4: **Studies have uncovered other injuries at seemingly "safe" jobs, staring for long periods at computer screens can cause severe eyestrain.**

   The most effective revision of sentence 4 would include which group of words?

   (1) jobs and staring
   (2) Whereas studies have uncovered
   (3) because staring for long periods
   (4) jobs; for example,
   (5) have uncovered that staring

9. Sentence 6: **In some offices back injuries are common workers can lower their risk by squatting when they lift objects off the floor.**

   What correction should be made to sentence 6?

   (1) replace In with Because in
   (2) insert a comma after common
   (3) insert and after common
   (4) replace common workers with common. Workers
   (5) no correction is necessary

> **TIP**
> Be careful to distinguish between two compound clauses separated by *and* (which require a comma) and two subjects separated by *and*. Do not use a comma between two subjects.

Answers start on page 273.

Directions: This is a ten-minute practice test. After ten minutes, mark the last question you finished. Then complete the test and check your answers. If most of your answers were correct, but you didn't finish, try to work faster next time. Choose the one best answer to each question.

Questions 1 through 4 refer to the following application.

Conditions of Credit

(1) I have read this application everything I have stated in it is true. (2) I authorize Ocean Pacific Bank to check my credit, employment history, and any other relevant information. (3) I agree to be responsible for all bills charged to the account, I am at least 18 years of age. (4) I also understand that information about me or my account may be shared by the Bank with its related companies. (5) However, refuse to allow such sharing of personal or credit information with outside companies. (6) If I refuse, I agree to inform Ocean Pacific in a letter and I need to include my name, address, and home telephone number, as well as any applicable Ocean Pacific Bank account numbers. (7) The information in this application is accurate as of the date signed below.

1. Sentence 1: **I have read this application everything I have stated in it is true.**

   Which is the best way to write the underlined portion of the text? If the original is the best way, choose option (1).

   (1) application everything
   (2) application, everything
   (3) application, therefore everything
   (4) application and everything
   (5) application, and everything

2. Sentence 3: **I agree to be responsible for all bills charged to the account, I am at least 18 years of age.**

   What correction should be made to sentence 3?

   (1) change bills charged to bills. Charged
   (2) remove the comma
   (3) change the comma to a period
   (4) insert yet after the comma
   (5) replace I am with being

3. Sentence 5: **However, refuse to allow such sharing of personal or credit information with outside companies.**

   What correction should be made to sentence 5?

   (1) insert I can after the comma
   (2) replace refuse with refusing
   (3) replace refuse with my refusal
   (4) insert a comma after personal
   (5) no correction is necessary

4. Sentence 6: **If I refuse, I agree to inform Ocean Pacific in a letter and I need to include my name, address, and home telephone number, as well as any applicable Ocean Pacific Bank account numbers.**

   The most effective revision of sentence 6 would include which group of words?

   (1) If I refuse yet agree
   (2) including a letter to Ocean Pacific
   (3) letter, needing to include
   (4) letter and include my name,
   (5) I agree to include, if I refuse,

Questions 5 through 9 refer to the following paragraphs.

Car Repairs

(A)

(1) If you want to receive good service on your car. (2) Do your homework before you bring it in for repairs. (3) First, follow the servicing schedule the automaker recommends, keep a record of all service and repairs. (4) Second, as you drive, note any unusual sounds you hear and drips, leaks, or smoke you see. (5) Write this information down so that you can remember and describe the symptoms.

(B)

(6) Let's say you bring your car in and you want to insist on a diagnosis on the spot but you shouldn't. (7) Ask questions about fees, labor rates, and guarantees first. (8) Finally, leave a telephone number the mechanic can call you back with an estimate.

5. Sentences 1 and 2: **If you want to receive good service on your car. Do your homework before you bring it in for repairs.**

Which is the best way to write the underlined portion of the text? If the original is the best way, choose option (1).

(1) car. Do
(2) car, doing
(3) car, do
(4) car, and do
(5) car do

6. Sentence 3: **First, follow the servicing schedule the automaker recommends, keep a record of all service and repairs.**

Which is the best way to write the underlined portion of the text? If the original is the best way, choose option (1).

(1) recommends, keep
(2) recommends keep
(3) recommends to keep
(4) recommends, and keep
(5) recommends moreover keep

7. Sentence 5: **Write this information down so that you can remember and describe the symptoms.**

What correction should be made to sentence 5?

(1) replace Write with If you write
(2) change Write to Writing
(3) insert a comma after down
(4) insert a comma after remember
(5) no correction is necessary

8. Sentence 6: **Let's say you bring your car in and you want to insist on a diagnosis on the spot but you shouldn't.**

The most effective revision of sentence 6 would begin with which group of words?

(1) When you bring your car in, don't insist
(2) Bringing your car in, insisting
(3) Let's say you bring your car in and insist
(4) If you insist on a diagnosis,
(5) Bring your car in, not to insist

9. Sentence 8: **Finally, leave a telephone number the mechanic can call you back with an estimate.**

What correction should be made to sentence 8?

(1) insert you after Finally,
(2) change leave to leaving
(3) insert a comma after number
(4) insert so that after number
(5) change can call to will be calling

Answers start on page 274.

GED WRITING LINK **Detailed Writing**

You have been combining details to make smooth, interesting, varied sentences. This skill will prepare you for correcting short choppy sentences on the editing section of the GED Writing Test. In addition, when you write your essay on the GED Test, you will improve your score if you write sentences with interesting details and examples. Of course, this is a good skill for any writing that you do.

These sentences were written in a note to a friend. Most of the sentences are choppy, and there are few details.

> Saturday we were looking for something to do. It couldn't cost much money. That's because Jake doesn't get paid until next week. So we went downtown. Hundreds of cow statues had been erected. Some were painted. Some had jewels all over them. Others were dressed up. The kids had a blast. They climbed on the cows. They swung from their horns. Even the adults liked the cows. What fun! It didn't even cost us a dime!

Now read another version of that note. Notice the details that help you see and understand what the writer is writing about. Notice also that the details are combined in sentences that are smooth and pleasing to read.

> Saturday we were looking for something to do that didn't cost much because Jake doesn't get paid until next week. So we decided to go downtown, where hundreds of cow statues had been erected along the sidewalks. Some cows were painted bright colors or even jeweled. Others were dressed in patchwork material or covered in glittering glass. The kids had a blast climbing on the cows and swinging from their horns. Even the adults were laughing and posing for pictures with their favorite cows. What fun, and it didn't even cost us a dime!

Here are three details from the note above. Explain how each added detail helps you understand or picture what the writer is writing about.

Along the sidewalks: _makes it clear where the cows were_

Covered in glittering glass: _____

Adults were laughing and posing for pictures: _____

_____

Adding *covered in glittering glass* helps you picture the cows. Saying *adults were laughing and posing* explains how the people reacted. These types of details make the writing more interesting.

The Personal Link

1. Write a note of at least a few sentences to a friend. Tell about a good time that you had when you didn't have to spend much money.

_____

_____

_____

_____

_____

_____

2. In your journal or on a separate piece of paper, list three things you feel you need or want to spend money on. Include details that would help explain each item and why you included it on your list.

The GED Link

Write at least a few sentences on the following topic. You can use some of the ideas you wrote about in The Personal Link if you wish. You may also write down other thoughts in your journal to get details for your sentences.

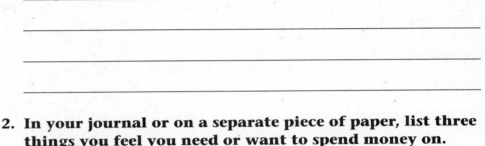

Some people claim that money cannot buy happiness. Do you agree or disagree with that statement? Give examples to support your opinion.

Edit

Look at the detailed sentences you just wrote in The Personal Link and The GED Link exercises. Edit them to make sure they are complete and correctly punctuated. Use the editing marks you have learned if you need to delete or insert words or punctuation marks.

Portfolio Reminder

If you started a portfolio in the first Writing Link, put your edited sentences in it.

Answers start on page 275.

GED SKILL Misplaced and Dangling Modifiers

misplaced modifier
a word or phrase placed too far from the word or phrase it describes

When you write, you can use a modifier to describe another word or phrase. A modifier can be a single word, such as the adjective *soft* in *soft pillow* or the adverb *soundly* in *sleep soundly*. A modifier can also be a phrase, such as *on the bed* in *My husband is sleeping on the bed.*

When a modifier is put in the wrong place in a sentence, it can confuse the reader or change the meaning of the sentence. Then it is called a **misplaced modifier.** A misplaced modifier appears to describe the wrong word or phrase, or it is unclear which word or phrase the modifier is describing.

RULE 1 Place a modifier near the word or phrase it describes.

Misplaced: Our hands blistered when we paddled painfully.
(Does *painfully* modify *paddled*?)
Correct: Our hands blistered painfully when we paddled.
Unclear: Our canoe was wooden, which was the only choice.
(Does the phrase *which was the only choice* modify *canoe* or *wooden*?)
Correct: Our canoe, which was the only choice, was wooden.

dangling modifier
a phrase placed at the beginning of a sentence that lacks the subject the modifier is describing

A **dangling modifier** is another problem modifier. A modifier is dangling when the sentence lacks the subject that the modifier is describing.

RULE 2 Avoid dangling modifiers.

METHOD 1 Fix a dangling modifier by making it into a subordinate clause.

METHOD 2 Fix a dangling modifier by changing the subject of the sentence to the word that the modifier is describing.

Dangling: Paddling down the river, the canoe overturned.
(Who is the subject of *Paddling down the river*? As written, it seems that the canoe is!)
Correct: As we paddled down the river, the canoe overturned.
Correct: Paddling down the river, we overturned the canoe.

Put a check mark next to the sentence that has a misplaced or dangling modifier.

_____ a. I made dinner for a friend at his house.

_____ b. Looking in the refrigerator, the vegetables were rotten.

You were correct if you chose *option b.* There is no subject for the opening phrase (*who* is looking in the refrigerator—the vegetables?), so it has a dangling modifier.

TIP

Misplaced modifiers can be hard to spot because a reader automatically tries to interpret a sentence even if it's confusing. Be sure to read exactly what a sentence is saying, rather than what you think it means to say.

A. Write *C* for correct sentences. Write *M* for sentences with misplaced modifiers. Underline the misplaced modifiers you find. Then rewrite the sentence correctly.

M 1. When buying clothes, one size does not fit all.

  When customers buy clothes, one size does not fit all.

____ 2. Today's clothing sizes are based on two-dimensional body measurements of young Caucasians taken over 60 years ago.

_____

____ 3. A new three-dimensional sizing database of 8,000 volunteers is being developed of all shapes, sizes, ages, and ethnicities.

_____

____ 4. The project managers promise when the database is finished that a customer will be able to trust the size on a label.

_____

____ 5. Soon customers will be able to trust sizes, and then shopping for clothes will be easier.

_____

____ 6. Of course, high-end fashion designers will still want women to believe that their clothes are smaller who buy expensive designer dresses.

_____

B. Edit this paragraph to correct three more misplaced or dangling modifiers.

      Vitamins and iron can reach starving people in scientifically enriched "golden rice" *around the world*. ~~around the world~~. Almost 400 million people in poor countries who are deficient in vitamin A risk suffering from infections and blindness. Additionally, millions of people suffer from iron deficiency. Causing anemia and retarded development in children, pregnant women with iron-poor blood have a special problem. Hoping for a major improvement in the health of millions around the world, this golden rice might be the answer.

C. Write about the following topic.

      What are your views on food? What kind of diet do you have? What kind do you think you should have? Write a paragraph explaining your views. Then edit your paragraph for misplaced modifiers and other errors.

Answers start on page 275.

Directions: Choose the <u>one best answer</u> to each question.

<u>Questions 1 through 4</u> refer to the following paragraph.

Lower Your Insurance

(1) Is your car insurance too high? (2) By installing anti-theft devices, your insurance cost will decrease. (3) The best way to save money is by etching your vehicle identification number into the windows, costing about $20. (4) Etched windows make it hard to break a car down into sellable pieces for car thieves. (5) Etched windows can save you up to $50 on your comprehensive rate, depending on where you live. (6) Other popular devices cost between $300 and $800 but can save you as much as 35% on insurance rates. (7) Whichever you choose, installing anti-theft devices gives you both lower rates and peace of mind.

1. Sentence 2: **By installing anti-theft devices, your insurance cost will decrease.**

   What correction should be made to sentence 2?

   (1) replace <u>By installing</u> with <u>If you install</u>
   (2) remove the comma
   (3) insert <u>and</u> after the comma
   (4) change <u>will decrease</u> to <u>decreasing</u>
   (5) no correction is necessary

TIP

When a GED Test question asks you how best to revise or rewrite a sentence, change the words around in your head first. Then match how you would change the sentence with one of the options given.

2. Sentence 3: **The best way to save money is by etching your vehicle identification number into the windows, costing about $20.**

   The most effective revision of sentence 3 would begin with which group of words?

   (1) Costing about $20,
   (2) Being the cheapest way to save,
   (3) To save money,
   (4) Etching your vehicle identification number,
   (5) Your vehicle identification number

3. Sentence 4: **Etched windows make it hard to break a car down into sellable pieces for car thieves.**

   The most effective revision of sentence 4 would include which group of words?

   (1) By etching windows, it
   (2) If you etch windows, you make
   (3) making it hard to break
   (4) hard for car thieves to break
   (5) break into sellable pieces

4. Sentence 7: **Whichever you choose, installing anti-theft devices gives you both lower rates and peace of mind.**

   What correction should be made to sentence 7?

   (1) replace <u>Whichever you choose</u> with <u>Selecting either one,</u>
   (2) remove the comma
   (3) replace <u>installing</u> with <u>you can install</u>
   (4) insert a comma after <u>rates</u>
   (5) no correction is necessary

Questions 5 through 9 refer to the following letter of recommendation.

Dear Ms. Lang:

(1) As senior crew supervisor, Erica Ortiz supervises 24 gardeners in six landscaping crews for Strong Landscapers, Inc. (2) She makes sure when leaving each morning that the crews have their job assignments and tools. (3) Erica started as the only female supervisor at Strong Landscapers, quickly gaining the respect of crew members in 1998. (4) Hardworking, well-organized, and dedicated, she has done a commendable job of supervising the gardening crews. (5) Erica also has a great reputation among our customers, representing Strong Landscapers proudly in the community. (6) With pleasure, Erica Ortiz is recommended for a managerial position in the landscaping field.

5. Sentence 1: **As senior crew supervisor, Erica Ortiz supervises 24 gardeners in six landscaping crews for Strong Landscapers, Inc.**

Which is the best way to write the underlined portion of the text? If the original is the best way, choose option (1).

(1) As senior crew supervisor, Erica Ortiz
(2) As Erica Ortiz, senior crew supervisor,
(3) Erica Ortiz is senior crew supervisor
(4) Erica Ortiz being senior crew supervisor
(5) Erica Ortiz, she is senior crew supervisor

6. Sentence 2: **She makes sure when leaving each morning that the crews have their job assignments and tools.**

The most effective revision of sentence 2 would include which group of words?

(1) Making sure that the crews have
(2) When leaving each morning, she
(3) makes sure that the morning job assignments
(4) sure that the crews have their job assignments and tools when
(5) when the crews have their job assignments

7. Sentence 3: **Erica started as the only female supervisor at Strong Landscapers, quickly gaining the respect of crew members in 1998.**

Which is the best way to write the underlined portion of the text? If the original is the best way, choose option (1).

(1) Landscapers quickly gaining the respect of crew members in 1998
(2) Landscapers, quickly gaining the respect in 1998 of crew members
(3) Landscapers in 1998 and quickly gained the respect of crew members
(4) Landscapers, and she quickly gained the respect of crew members in 1998
(5) Landscapers, in 1998 she quickly gained the respect of crew members

8. Sentence 5: **Erica also has a great reputation among our customers, representing Strong Landscapers proudly in the community.**

If you rewrote sentence 5 beginning with

Proudly representing Strong Landscapers,

the next words should be

(1) Erica also has
(2) a great reputation
(3) the community has
(4) customers have
(5) and having a great reputation

9. Sentence 6: **With pleasure, Erica Ortiz is recommended for a managerial position in the landscaping field.**

What correction should be made to sentence 6?

(1) change the comma to a period
(2) change Erica Ortiz is recommended to I recommend Erica Ortiz
(3) remove is
(4) insert a comma after recommended
(5) no correction is necessary

Answers start on page 275.

Directions: This is a ten-minute practice test. After ten minutes, mark the last question you finished. Then complete the test and check your answers. If most of your answers were correct, but you didn't finish, try to work faster next time. Choose the one best answer to each question.

Questions 1 through 4 refer to the following paragraphs.

Recycling

(A)

(1) Recycling has become a priority in this country because landfills are at capacity. (2) That's why residents are required to separate their trash in certain states. (3) Each household must separate bottles, cans, and paper in containers. (4) When left at the curb, residents help the recycling effort.

(B)

(5) Many companies in the recycling industry have found creative new uses for used products. (6) Industries with a promising future forming to help replace biodegradable items. (7) Factories create new glass and aluminum products from melted down cans and bottles. (8) One innovative shoe manufacturer makes soles and it uses worn-out tires to make them and the soles are for athletic shoes. (9) Publishing companies are trying to increase the amount of recycled paper in their products.

(C)

(10) With such continued efforts by both individuals and companies, the waste problem in this country can be greatly reduced.

1. Sentence 2: **That's why residents are required to separate their trash in certain states.**

   The most effective revision of sentence 2 would include which group of words?

   (1) separating trash in certain states
   (2) requirements in certain states
   (3) residents in certain states
   (4) separate in certain states
   (5) trash required in certain states

2. Sentence 4: **When left at the curb, residents help the recycling effort.**

   What correction should be made to sentence 4?

   (1) replace When with Being
   (2) replace When left with Left
   (3) insert these items are after When
   (4) remove the comma
   (5) change help to helping

3. Sentence 6: **Industries with a promising future forming to help replace biodegradable items.**

   What correction should be made to sentence 6?

   (1) replace Industries with a promising future with With a promising future, industries
   (2) replace with with have
   (3) insert are after future
   (4) insert a comma after forming
   (5) no correction is necessary

4. Sentence 8: **One innovative shoe manufacturer makes soles and it uses worn-out tires to make them and the soles are for athletic shoes.**

   The most effective revision of sentence 8 would include which group of words?

   (1) uses worn-out tires and is making soles for athletic shoes
   (2) out of worn-out tires makes soles for athletic shoes
   (3) is making using worn-out tires soles for athletic shoes
   (4) shoe and sole manufacturer uses worn-out tires for athletic shoes
   (5) makes soles for athletic shoes using worn-out tires

Questions 5 through 9 refer to the following paragraphs.

Buying a Used Car

(A)

(1) When looking to buy a used car, it can't be too carefully examined. (2) Know how to use your state's "lemon laws" against car-buying fraud.

(B)

(3) You should be cautious if you find a car with very low mileage at a used-car dealer. (4) The odometer shows the mileage and it may have been set back. (5) Look for a lot of wear on the foot pedals, that tells you the car was heavily driven. (6) Oily spots under a car may indicate further problems. (7) Excessive oil on the engine, too.

(C)

(8) Having the car inspected by a mechanic whom you trust is one way to avoid making a bad purchase. (9) If the dealer won't allow you to do this beware. (10) There seriously may be something wrong with the car.

5. Sentence 1: **When looking to buy a used car, it can't be too carefully examined.**

Which is the best way to write the underlined portion of the text? If the original is the best way, choose option (1).

(1) When looking to buy a used car, it
(2) When buying a used car, it
(3) When you're looking to buy a used car, it
(4) Looking to buy a used car? It
(5) Looking to buy a used car, it

6. Sentence 4: **The odometer shows the mileage and it may have been set back.**

What correction should be made to sentence 4?

(1) change shows to showing
(2) insert a comma after mileage
(3) remove and
(4) replace and with however
(5) remove have

7. Sentence 5: **Look for a lot of wear on the foot pedals, that tells you the car was heavily driven.**

Which is the best way to write the underlined portion of the text? If the original is the best way, choose option (1).

(1) pedals, that
(2) pedals that
(3) pedals yet that
(4) pedals, and that
(5) pedals. That

8. Sentences 6 and 7: **Oily spots under a car may indicate further problems. Excessive oil on the engine, too.**

The most effective combination of sentences 6 and 7 would include which group of words?

(1) problems, and excessive oil
(2) problems but also excessive oil
(3) An indication of further problems
(4) Oily spots under a car and excessive oil
(5) Further problems are indicated

9. Sentence 9: **If the dealer won't allow you to do this beware.**

What correction should be made to sentence 9?

(1) change If the dealer to The dealer
(2) change the spelling of won't to wo'nt
(3) insert a comma after you
(4) insert a comma after this
(5) no correction is necessary

Answers start on page 276.

GED SKILL **Parallel Structure**

parallel structure
writing in which all the
elements in a series
are written in the same
grammatical form

When a sentence contains a series of equal and related items, all the items should be in the same form. That is, each item should match grammatically with the others. This is called **parallel structure.** You will express your ideas more clearly if you use parallel structure.

RULE 1 Match items in a series in form and part of speech.

Not Parallel:	I hunted, searched, and was begging for an apartment.
Parallel:	I <u>hunted, searched,</u> and <u>begged</u> for an apartment.
Not Parallel:	My routine was to wake at six, to run for the paper, and checking every rental ad before breakfast.
Parallel:	My routine was <u>to wake</u> at six, <u>to run</u> for the paper, and <u>to check</u> every rental ad before breakfast.
Parallel:	My routine was <u>waking</u> at six, <u>running</u> for the paper, and <u>checking</u> every rental ad before breakfast.
Not Parallel:	A renter must look sensibly, carefully, and with caution at new apartments.
Parallel:	A renter must look <u>sensibly, carefully,</u> and <u>cautiously</u> at new apartments.

RULE 2 Match phrases with phrases.

Not parallel:	Look in the rooms, at the building, and the lease.
Parallel:	Look in the rooms, at the building, and <u>at</u> the lease.

RULE 3 Do not mix words or phrases with clauses.

Not Parallel:	Make sure that the building is clean, safe, and you can afford it.
Parallel:	Make sure that the building is clean, safe, and <u>affordable</u>.

Write *P* if a sentence has parallel structure. Write *N* if it does not.

_____ a. We love our pets because they live with us, know us well, but loving us anyway.

_____ b. We need them to charm, entertain, and comfort us.

_____ c. To eat enough, daily exercise, and a safe home are all they ask of us.

You were correct if you labeled only *option b* parallel. *Option a* should be *We love our pets because they live with us, know us well, but love us anyway. Option c* should be *Enough food, daily exercise, and a safe home are all they ask of us.*

When you notice that items in a series are connected by *and, but, or, nor, yet,* or *as well as,* check that the items are parallel.

A. Underline the items in a series in each sentence. Rewrite any series that is not in parallel form.

1. Many <u>infants, toddlers, and children not yet in school</u> carry around a "security blanket."

   infants, toddlers, and preschoolers

2. Children sleep under them, play with them, or talk to them.

   _____

3. If the blanket is removed, lost, or simply to be misplaced, the whole family will suffer.

   _____

4. As kids get older, growing tall, and wiser, they still secretly love their "blankies."

   _____

5. They may hide them under their pillows, in their bedding, or keep them under their beds.

   _____

6. Many adults fondly remember the security, warmth, and feeling happy their childhood blankets gave them.

   _____

B. Edit this paragraph for four more errors in parallel structure.

A typical American breakfast consists of a bowl of cereal, ~~drinking~~ a cup of coffee or tea, and a glass of orange juice. Maybe it's because breakfast eaters generally eat healthier foods, exercise more, or regular checkups, but eating breakfast seems to make people healthier. Breakfast eaters consume more fruits, more vegetables, and they eat less fat and oil than those who skip the first meal of the day. Breakfast eaters also seem to be more conscious of limiting their salt intake, which can raise blood pressure, dehydrate cells, and has lead to strokes. From all available evidence, it's clear that skipping an occasional lunch or to miss a dinner won't hurt you. However, don't forget to eat a healthy breakfast every day.

C. Write about the following topic.

What is your favorite meal? Write a paragraph describing that meal and what makes it your favorite. Then edit your paragraph for parallel structure and other errors.

Answers start on page 277.

GED Practice • Lesson 6

Questions 1 through 5 refer to the following paragraph.

Elevator Music

(1) You either love it, hate it, or ignore the music playing while you're shopping, riding in an elevator, or waiting for appointments. (2) The music that plays in the background of our lives is soft, vague, and we can recognize it. (3) It's well known that music can calm us, lower our heart rate, as well as reducing our blood pressure. (4) Businesses play so-called "elevator music" to affect our behavior in stores, at work, and while waiting in stressful situations. (5) Offices that use this music report less absenteeism better job performance, and less turnover of employees. (6) Stores think elevator music makes customers shop longer and buy more. (7) If you detest this background hum, you can try singing to yourself, wearing earplugs, or leaving.

1. Sentence 2: **The music that plays in the background of our lives is soft, vague, and we can recognize it.**

   What correction should be made to sentence 2?

   (1) change plays to can play
   (2) change soft to softly
   (3) change vague to vagueness
   (4) change and to so
   (5) replace and we can recognize it with and recognizable

2. Sentence 3: **It's well known that music can calm us, lower our heart rate, as well as reducing our blood pressure.**

   What correction should be made to sentence 3?

   (1) change can calm to calming
   (2) insert to before lower
   (3) remove as well as
   (4) change reducing to reduce
   (5) no correction is necessary

3. Sentence 4: **Businesses play so-called "elevator music" to affect our behavior in stores, at work, and while waiting in stressful situations.**

   Which is the best way to write the underlined portion of the text? If the original is the best way, choose option (1).

   (1) in stores, at work, and while waiting in stressful situations
   (2) in stores, while at work, and waiting in stressful situations
   (3) in stores, at work, and waiting in stressful situations
   (4) in stores, at work, and in stressful situations
   (5) in stores, working, and stressful situations

4. Sentence 5: **Offices that use this music report less absenteeism better job performance, and less turnover of employees.**

   What correction should be made to sentence 5?

   (1) insert a comma after music
   (2) change report to reporting
   (3) insert a comma after absenteeism
   (4) replace performance with performing
   (5) no correction is necessary

5. Sentence 7: **If you detest this background hum, you can try singing to yourself, wearing earplugs, or leaving.**

   What correction should be made to sentence 7?

   (1) remove the comma after hum
   (2) change singing with to sing
   (3) remove wearing
   (4) replace leaving with you can leave
   (5) no correction is necessary

Questions 6 through 10 refer to the following paragraph.

An Effective Interview

(1) Displaying interest, with a lot of experience, and carrying a good résumé are not enough for a successful job interview. (2) To get a good job, you should arrive at your interview on time and appropriately dressed. (3) You don't create a good impression when you arrive late, breathing hard, and loudly apologetic. (4) If you walk in wearing jeans, a sweatshirt, and sneakers, you won't impress anyone, either. (5) Wear clothes that are businesslike, conservative, and look serious. (6) If you are confident, professional, and be friendly, you stand a good chance of getting the job. (7) Even if you aren't hired at the very first interview, the experience of preparing for it should improve your chances at the next one.

6. Sentence 1: **Displaying interest, with a lot of experience, and carrying a good résumé are not enough for a successful job interview.**

   What correction should be made to sentence 1?

   (1) change Displaying to To display
   (2) remove the comma after interest
   (3) replace with a lot of with having
   (4) remove carrying
   (5) insert a comma after résumé

7. Sentence 3: **You don't create a good impression when you arrive late, breathing hard, and loudly apologetic.**

   If you rewrote sentence 3 beginning with

   By arriving late, breathing hard,

   the next words should be

   (1) and loudly apologetic
   (2) as if you were apologizing loudly
   (3) and to apologize loudly
   (4) and apologizing loudly
   (5) and with loud apologies

8. Sentence 4: **If you walk in wearing jeans, a sweatshirt, and sneakers, you won't impress anyone, either.**

   Which is the best way to write the underlined portion of the text? If the original is the best way, choose option (1).

   (1) and sneakers
   (2) and in sneakers
   (3) and with sneakers on
   (4) and wearing sneakers
   (5) and sneakers on your feet

9. Sentence 5: **Wear clothes that are businesslike, conservative, and look serious.**

   What correction should be made to sentence 5?

   (1) change Wear to Wearing
   (2) change Wear to To wear
   (3) remove the comma after businesslike
   (4) insert and before conservative
   (5) remove look

10. Sentence 6: **If you are confident, professional, and be friendly, you stand a good chance of getting the job.**

    Which is the best way to write the underlined portion of the text? If the original is the best way, choose option (1).

    (1) are confident, professional, and be friendly
    (2) are confident, a professional, and a friend
    (3) are confident, professional, and friendly
    (4) are confidently and professionally friendly
    (5) have confidence, professions, and friends

Answers start on page 277.

Directions: This is a ten-minute practice test. After ten minutes, mark the last question you finished. Then complete the test and check your answers. If most of your answers were correct, but you didn't finish, try to work faster next time. Choose the <u>one best answer</u> to each question.

<u>Questions 1 through 4</u> refer to the following memo.

Memorandum

To: All Project Members
From: Ken Lopez

(A)

(1) I evaluated Pinto Software in three areas: record of reliability, ease of installation, and how easy it is to use. (2) Pinto seems completely reliable. (3) Pinto users report their computers run for months without crashing and the program does not interfere with other applications. (4) Unfortunately, its installation process is not for the faint of heart. (5) I had to change my hard drive and I had to reconnect my mouse three times and I had to reinstall my Internet connection twice. (6) Finally, I'm afraid it's not easy to use either. (7) The graphics are complicated the commands are confusing.

(B)

(8) In conclusion, I recommend we keep searching for more appropriate software.

1. Sentence 1: **I evaluated Pinto Software in three areas: record of reliability, ease of installation, and how easy it is to use.**

   What correction should be made to sentence 1?

   (1) remove the comma after <u>reliability</u>
   (2) change <u>installation</u> to <u>being installed</u>
   (3) change <u>how easy it is to use</u> to <u>ease of use</u>
   (4) change <u>is</u> to <u>will be</u>
   (5) no correction is necessary

2. Sentence 3: **Pinto users report their computers run for months without crashing and the program does not interfere with other applications.**

   What correction should be made to sentence 3?

   (1) change <u>report</u> to <u>reporting</u>
   (2) change <u>run</u> to <u>running</u>
   (3) insert a <u>comma after crashing</u>
   (4) replace <u>and</u> with <u>without</u>
   (5) change <u>does not</u> to <u>don't</u>

3. Sentence 5: **I had to change my hard drive and I had to reconnect my mouse three times and I had to reinstall my Internet connection twice.**

   The most effective revision of sentence 5 would include which group of words?

   (1) Changing my hard drive and reconnecting my mouse three times and reinstalling
   (2) to change, to reconnect, and to reinstall
   (3) drive, reconnecting my mouse three times and reinstalling
   (4) drive, reconnect my mouse three times, and reinstall
   (5) drive, and I also had to reconnect my mouse three times, and I also had to reinstall

4. Sentence 7: **The graphics are <u>complicated the commands are confusing.</u>**

   Which is the best way to write the underlined portion of the text? If the original is the best way, choose option (1).

   (1) complicated the
   (2) complicated and the
   (3) complicated however the
   (4) complicated, the
   (5) complicated, and the

Questions 5 through 9 refer to the following paragraph.

Small Towns

(1) Small towns are back, according to new suburban planners and architects, in fashion. (2) A typical suburb used to be built with winding streets, ranch-style homes, and they had big backyards. (3) Many new suburban planners design straight streets, farm-style homes, and smaller yards. (4) The homes have front porches, they are set close to neighbors' homes. (5) All the new homes are within walking distance of a central square. (6) A neighborhood grocery store and other shops. (7) The main goal is to bring community spirit to the suburbs planners believe that homeowners who live closer together will talk and interact more with one another.

5. Sentence 1: **Small towns are back, according to new suburban planners and architects, in fashion.**

   The most effective revision of sentence 1 would begin with which group of words?

   (1) Back in fashion, according to
   (2) According to new suburban planners and architects,
   (3) Being back in fashion are small towns
   (4) Small towns are back, and according to
   (5) New suburban plans and architects

6. Sentence 2: **A typical suburb used to be built with winding streets, ranch-style homes, and they had big backyards.**

   Which is the best way to write the underlined portion of the text? If the original is the best way, choose option (1).

   (1) and they had big backyards
   (2) with big backyards
   (3) having big back yards
   (4) and had big backyards
   (5) and big backyards

7. Sentence 4: **The homes have front porches, they are set close to neighbors' homes.**

   What correction should be made to sentence 4?

   (1) remove the comma
   (2) insert and after the comma
   (3) remove are
   (4) change neighbors' to neighbors
   (5) no correction is necessary

8. Sentences 5 and 6: **All the new homes are within walking distance of a central square. A neighborhood grocery store and other shops.**

   The most effective combination of sentences 5 and 6 would include which group of words?

   (1) square that contains a
   (2) square and the square contains a
   (3) square, it contains a
   (4) With a square, a neighborhood grocery store, and other shops
   (5) Within walking distance are a square,

9. Sentence 7: **The main goal is to bring community spirit to the suburbs planners believe that homeowners who live closer together will talk and interact more with one another.**

   Which is the best way to write the underlined portion of the text? If the original is the best way, choose option (1).

   (1) suburbs planners
   (2) suburbs, planners
   (3) suburbs. Planners
   (4) suburbs and planners
   (5) suburbs but planners

Answers start on page 278.

GED WRITING LINK **Using Modifiers**

You have learned that modifiers describe words and phrases. They add detail to sentences. When used correctly and effectively, modifiers help your reader see more clearly what you are describing. As you practice your own writing skills, it's a good idea to be as specific as you can with your words. What are some ways to add descriptive details to your writing?

Read the following paragraph. How well can you understand what the writer is saying?

> I was on my way to work. This car swerved in front of me, cutting me off. I had to hit my brakes, and I almost skidded off the road. I was really mad. I just told myself not to let my anger get the better of me.

Now compare the above paragraph to the one that follows. Notice how modifiers make the writing come alive.

> Driving down a busy avenue one rainy morning, I was on my way to work. Suddenly, a red sports car zoomed up alongside me, then just as suddenly swerved in front of me and cut me off. Alarmed, I reflexively stomped on my brakes. My car almost skidded off the rain-slick road and onto the sidewalk. I was fuming mad. I just told myself that road rage can be even more dangerous than senseless drivers like the one in the red car.

To write this paragraph, the writer pictured the traffic incident in her head and thought of words and phrases that described the scene vividly. This method is called visualizing.

Visualize a person walking on the sidewalk at the moment the writer's car skidded toward it. On the lines below, jot down some ideas of your own that might describe him or her. You don't need to write complete sentences—just any words that pop into your head. There are no right or wrong answers.

_____

_____

_____

_____

Does your list include words that describe the way the person looked (for example, *young man, dressed in work clothes*) and moved (*stopped in his tracks* or *darted nervously back*)? If not, see if you can add some details like these.

The Personal Link

1. Write a short description of yourself when you get angry. Use plenty of modifying words and phrases, and be as specific as you can. For example, what kinds of things make you mad? How do you feel inside? How do you appear to other people?

_____

_____

_____

_____

_____

2. In your journal, write down some thoughts about a person or event that has made you angry recently. How did you express your anger? Was your reaction helpful to the situation? Did it improve the situation?

The GED Link

1. Read the following topic. On another sheet of paper, write as many thoughts as you can about the topic. Don't try to write complete sentences.

> Everyone feels angry at one time or another. What do you think is the best way to deal with anger? Give examples to support your opinion.

2. Use some of your ideas from the Personal Link and some of your ideas from this GED Link to write a short paragraph based on the topic above. Use only the ideas that support your point of view.

Edit

Read over what you have written, and correct any mistakes you find. Be sure to insert modifiers that help your reader picture what you are describing.

Portfolio Reminder

Put your paragraph about anger in your portfolio.

Answers start on page 279.

Unit 1 Cumulative Review **Sentence Structure**

Directions: Choose the <u>one best answer</u> to each question.

<u>Questions 1 through 5</u> refer to the following paragraph.

Drive-In Movies

(1) The drive-in movie was one of the ultimate expressions of Americans' love of cars. (2) In the heyday of the drive-in, families packed snacks and blankets, piled into the car, and would head for a movie under the stars. (3) The car of choice being the station wagon with a fold-down back gate. (4) Some families brought the entire makings of a picnic the barbecue grill, charcoal, cooler, and lawn chairs all were packed in with the kids. (5) Not even pesky mosquitoes, rowdy teenagers, or scratchy speakers dimmed the drive-in's appeal. (6) Nowadays, small cars and large multiplexes lure families. (7) Fading away, moviegoers seldom attend open-air cinemas anymore. (8) In fact, drive-ins hold more nostalgia than customers.

1. Sentence 2: **In the heyday of the drive-in, families packed snacks and blankets, piled into the car, and would head for a movie under the stars.**

   What correction should be made to sentence 2?

   (1) change <u>packed</u> to <u>would pack</u>
   (2) remove the comma after <u>blankets</u>
   (3) change <u>piled</u> to <u>piling</u>
   (4) change <u>would head</u> to <u>headed</u>
   (5) no correction is necessary

2. Sentence 3: **The car of choice being the station wagon with a fold-down back gate.**

   What correction should be made to sentence 3?

   (1) change <u>The</u> to <u>Everyone's</u>
   (2) insert a comma after <u>choice</u>
   (3) change <u>being</u> to <u>was</u>
   (4) replace <u>being</u> with a comma
   (5) no correction is necessary

3. Sentence 4: **Some families brought the entire makings of a <u>picnic the</u> barbecue grill, charcoal, cooler, and lawn chairs all were packed in with the kids.**

   Which is the best way to write the underlined portion of the text? If the original is the best way, choose option (1).

   (1) picnic the
   (2) picnic, the
   (3) picnic. The
   (4) picnic, even the
   (5) picnic and the

4. Sentence 5: **Not even pesky mosquitoes, rowdy teenagers, or scratchy speakers dimmed the drive-in's appeal.**

   What correction should be made to sentence 5?

   (1) replace <u>Not even</u> with <u>However</u>
   (2) remove the comma after <u>mosquitoes</u>
   (3) insert <u>listening to</u> after <u>or</u>
   (4) change <u>dimmed</u> to <u>dimming</u>
   (5) no correction is necessary

5. Sentence 7: **Fading away, moviegoers seldom attend open-air cinemas anymore.**

   What correction should be made to sentence 7?

   (1) change <u>Fading</u> to <u>As drive-ins fade</u>
   (2) remove the comma after <u>away</u>
   (3) insert <u>they</u> after <u>moviegoers</u>
   (4) change <u>attend</u> to <u>attending</u>
   (5) no correction is necessary

Questions 6 through 10 refer to the following paragraph.

Mars

(1) The planet Mars has always captured the imagination of scientists and writers. (2) Historically, by both groups the question asked was whether or not life existed on that planet. (3) When looking through a telescope lens, Mars appears to have waterways or canals crossing its surface. (4) Because there seemed to be waterways observers wondered for many years about possible life on that planet. (5) Writers like Edgar Rice Burroughs imagined a planet of exotic races, sharp swords, and strange creatures. (6) Another writer, H. G. Wells, and a Martian invasion of Earth he called "The War of the Worlds." (7) Some people had high expectations for the unmanned space flight to Mars. (8) These people were disappointed when it found no signs of life. (9) However, Earthlings' fascination with Mars still continues.

6. Sentence 2: **Historically, by both groups the question asked was whether or not life existed on that planet.**

Which is the best way to write the underlined portion of the text? If the original way is the best way, choose option (1).

(1) by both groups the question asked
(2) the question by both groups asked
(3) the question asked by both groups
(4) being asked by both groups
(5) both groups were asking

7. Sentence 3: **When looking through a telescope lens, Mars appears to have waterways or canals crossing its surface.**

What correction should be made to sentence 3?

(1) replace When with Whenever
(2) replace looking with one looks
(3) remove the comma after lens
(4) insert a comma after waterways
(5) no correction is necessary

8. Sentence 4: **Because there seemed to be waterways observers wondered for many years about possible life on that planet.**

Which is the best way to write the underlined portion of the text? If the original way is the best way, choose option (1).

(1) waterways observers
(2) waterways. Observers
(3) waterways so observers
(4) waterways, observers
(5) waterways observers,

9. Sentence 6: **Another writer, H. G. Wells, and a Martian invasion of Earth he called "The War of the Worlds."**

What correction should be made to sentence 6?

(1) replace the comma after writer with was
(2) replace and with described
(3) change Earth he to Earth. He
(4) insert that after Earth
(5) no correction is necessary

10. Sentences 7 and 8: **Some people had high expectations for the unmanned space flight to Mars. These people were disappointed when it found no signs of life.**

The most effective combination of sentences 7 and 8 would include which group of words?

(1) to Mars these people
(2) to Mars but they were
(3) to Mars, being disappointed
(4) to Mars, so they were
(5) to Mars and these disappointed people

To Our Valued Customers

(A)

(1) Elite Cleaners is a family-run business providing quality dry cleaning for those who want to look their best at all times. (2) Old-fashioned hand cleaning is available, and expert spot removal is available, too. (3) With our environmentally safe equipment, you are assured of top quality.

(B)

(4) Pampering your best dresses and sheerest silks, as well as your casual wear and heavy woolens. (5) Shirts and linens are done on state-of-the-art equipment. (6) This is how we offer the best quality laundering. (7) We provide special cleaning for wedding gowns and formal wear they will be stored in keepsake boxes fit for heirlooms.

(C)

(8) Are you too busy to visit our store, let us pick up and deliver for you. (9) Call us for a convenient pick-up time.

11. Sentence 2: **Old-fashioned hand cleaning is available, and expert spot removal is available, too.**

    If you rewrote sentence 2 beginning with

    We offer old-fashioned hand cleaning,

    the next words should be

    (1) such as expert spot removal
    (2) and expert spot removal
    (3) for example, such as expert spot removal
    (4) or expert spot removal
    (5) and we are expert

12. Sentence 4: **Pampering your best dresses and sheerest silks, as well as your casual wear and heavy woolens.**

    The most effective revision of sentence 4 would include which group of words?

    (1) Your best dresses are pampered
    (2) We will pamper your best dresses
    (3) Carefully pampering your best dresses
    (4) As we pamper your best dresses
    (5) Pampered will be your best dresses

13. Sentences 5 and 6: **Shirts and linens are done on state-of-the-art equipment. This is how we offer the best quality laundering.**

    Which is the best way to write the underlined portion of the text? If the original way is the best way, choose option (1).

    (1) equipment. This is how we offer
    (2) equipment. We offer
    (3) equipment, so we offer
    (4) equipment and we offer
    (5) equipment moreover, we offer

14. Sentence 7: **We provide special cleaning for wedding gowns and formal wear they will be stored in keepsake boxes fit for heirlooms.**

    What correction should be made to sentence 7?

    (1) replace We with Because we
    (2) insert a comma after gowns
    (3) insert a comma after wear
    (4) change wear they to wear. They
    (5) no correction is necessary

15. Sentence 8: **Are you too busy to visit our store, let us pick up and deliver for you.**

    Which is the best way to write the underlined portion of the text? If the original way is the best way, choose option (1).

    (1) store, let
    (2) store let
    (3) store then let
    (4) store so
    (5) store? Let

Questions 16 through 19 refer to the following paragraph.

Preventing Frozen Pipes

(1) To prevent your pipes from freezing, plumbers suggest allowing the faucet to drip slowly. (2) Slow dripping won't prevent an ice block. (3) Although it can prevent the pressure from building and bursting the pipes. (4) Don't close your faucet as soon as it stops dripping. (5) Pipes that run through unheated attics, damp crawl spaces, or walls that face the outside of your house are the most likely to freeze. (6) A pipe is usually frozen or near-frozen when a faucet isn't getting the necessary flow. (7) Or it could be an appliance such as a dishwasher or washing machine. (8) Cover water pipes with towels to insulate them. (9) Otherwise, you can use electric heat tape. (10) Surprisingly, burst pipes are a problem in the South because of the occasional subfreezing temperatures that harm plumbing.

16. Sentences 2 and 3: **Slow dripping won't prevent an ice block. Although it can prevent the pressure from building and bursting the pipes.**

    Which is the best way to write the underlined portion of the text? If the original way is the best way, choose option (1).

    (1) block. Although it
    (2) block. It
    (3) block, and it
    (4) block and
    (5) block, although it

Don't express too many ideas in one sentence. If a sentence on the GED Test is long and complicated, look for an option that separates the ideas correctly or reduces wordiness while keeping the meaning of the original.

17. Sentence 5: **Pipes that run through unheated attics, damp crawl spaces, or walls that face the outside of your house are the most likely to freeze.**

    What correction should be made to sentence 5?

    (1) remove that
    (2) remove the comma after attics
    (3) change walls that face the outside of your house to exterior walls
    (4) replace are with is
    (5) no correction is necessary

18. Sentences 6 and 7: **A pipe is usually frozen or near-frozen when a faucet isn't getting the necessary flow. Or it could be an appliance such as a dishwasher or washing machine.**

    The most effective combination of sentences 6 and 7 would include which group of words?

    (1) flow, or it could be
    (2) usually a faucet but sometimes a dishwasher or washing machine isn't
    (3) neither a faucet nor a dishwasher nor a washing machine
    (4) Not getting the necessary flow
    (5) a faucet, a dishwasher, or a washing machine isn't

19. Sentences 8 and 9: **Cover water pipes with towels to insulate them. Otherwise, you can use electric heat tape.**

    Which is the best way to write the underlined portion of the text? If the original way is the best way, choose option (1).

    (1) them. Otherwise, you can use
    (2) them, or use
    (3) them, use
    (4) them use
    (5) them or you use

Questions 20 through 22 refer to the following paragraph.

Saving ATM Fees

(1) Sometimes you need cash but aren't near your bank, here's a way you can avoid ATM fees. (2) Most large supermarket chains allow customers to make purchases and get cash back with an ATM card. (3) Fifty dollars is the average amount you can get, while some stores will give up to 100 dollars cash over the cost of a purchase. (4) Having enough in your account to cover both the purchase and the extra cash, you won't have to pay the extra fees that most banks charge. (5) Without those extra fees of one to five dollars, banking at a supermarket is more economical than at an ATM.

20. Sentence 1: **Sometimes you need cash but aren't near your bank, here's a way you can avoid ATM fees.**

    What correction should be made to sentence 1?

    (1) replace <u>you need</u> with <u>needing</u>
    (2) insert a comma after <u>cash</u>
    (3) remove the comma after <u>bank</u>
    (4) insert <u>so</u> after the comma
    (5) no correction is necessary

21. Sentence 3: **Fifty dollars is the average amount you can get, while some stores will give up to 100 dollars cash over the cost of a purchase.**

    The most effective revision of sentence 3 would begin with which group of words?

    (1) Giving up to 100 dollars over the cost of a purchase
    (2) Up to 100 dollars over the cost, while 50 dollars
    (3) While making a purchase, 50 dollars
    (4) You can get 50 dollars or up to 100 dollars cash
    (5) Fifty dollars is the average amount of cash you can get over the cost of a purchase

22. Sentence 4: <u>**Having**</u> **enough in your account to cover both the purchase and the extra cash, you won't have to pay the extra fees that most banks charge.**

    Which is the best way to write the underlined portion of the text? If the original way is the best way, choose option (1).

    (1) Having
    (2) Have
    (3) So have
    (4) If you have
    (5) Having had

Writing Links Review

Write a paragraph on the following topic. As you are writing, keep the following Writing Links topics in mind.

☑ Are my sentences complete? (Writing Link, pages 50–53)

☑ Am I including specific details? (Writing Link, pages 70–71)

☑ Am I including modifiers to add descriptive details to my writing? (Writing Link, pages 84–85)

> If you could give one piece of advice about life, what would it be? Give details and examples to support your ideas.

Answers start on page 279.

Cumulative Review Performance Analysis
Unit 1 ● Sentence Structure

Use the Answers and Explanations starting on page 279 to check your answers to the Unit 1 Cumulative Review. Then use the chart to figure out the skill areas in which you need more practice.

On the chart, circle the questions you answered correctly. Write the number correct for each skill area. Add the number of questions that you got correct on the Cumulative Review. If you feel that you need more practice, go back and review the lessons for the skill areas that were difficult for you.

Questions	Number Correct	Skill Area	Lessons for Review
2, 9, 12, 16	____/4	Sentence Fragments	1
10, 13, 19	____/3	Compound Sentences	2
8, 11, 18, 22	____/4	Subordination	3
3, 14, 15, 20	____/4	Run-on Sentences	4
5, 6, 7, 21	____/4	Misplaced Modifiers	5
1, 4, 17	____/3	Parallel Structure	6
TOTAL CORRECT	____/22		

Organization

As you learned in Unit 1, clear and correct sentences are critical to effective writing. This unit focuses on key elements that will help you organize your ideas. Organizing your ideas into paragraphs will help your reader understand your meaning. Paragraphs are groups of sentences that are organized around one main idea. The main idea of a paragraph is expressed in a topic sentence and supported by other sentences with examples, facts, and specific details. You can use transition words and phrases to show the relationship between sentences and between paragraphs.

Organization is an important content area on the GED Language Arts, Writing Test. Fifteen percent of the multiple-choice questions will be based on organization issues. Paying attention to the organization of the entire piece of writing will help you answer all the questions on the test.

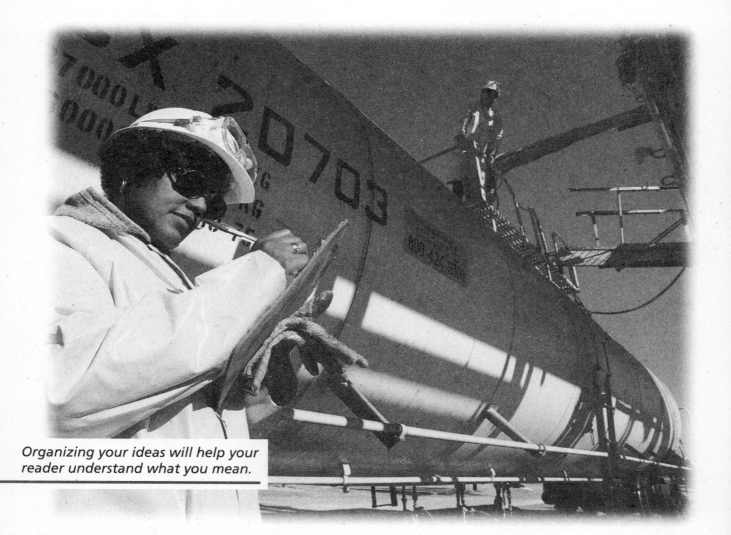

Organizing your ideas will help your reader understand what you mean.

The lessons in this unit include:

Lesson 7: **Effective Paragraphs**
A paragraph is a group of sentences about one main idea. The main idea is stated in the topic sentence and is supported by several sentences that supply details, examples, reasons, and facts.

Lesson 8: **Topic Sentences**
A topic sentence states the main idea of the paragraph. An effective topic sentence needs to be broad enough to unite the ideas in the paragraph and to help the reader see the big picture—the main idea.

Lesson 9: **Paragraphing**
Paragraphs help a reader understand the organization of written ideas. Each new paragraph tells the reader that the writer is moving on to another main idea.

Lesson 10: **Clear Transitions**
Transitions are words and phrases that tell the reader how ideas are related. The effective use of transitions allows writing to flow smoothly from idea to idea, from sentence to sentence, and from paragraph to paragraph.

> **WRITING LINKS**
>
> In this unit, you will practice these types of writing skills:
>
> - Writing Effective Paragraphs
> - Writing a Topic Sentence
> - Writing More Than One Paragraph
> - Making Transitions Between Ideas

To use the skills in this unit in your own writing, see the Writer's Checklist on page 315.

GED SKILL **Effective Paragraphs**

Paragraph Structure

An effective paragraph clearly develops an idea by presenting specific information in a logical order. A **paragraph** is a group of sentences about one main idea. It has a **topic sentence,** which states the main idea, as well as several sentences that supply supporting details. These **supporting details** help the reader understand the main idea of the paragraph by giving examples, facts, reasons, and specific details.

Read this paragraph from a letter in response to a help wanted ad. Notice how each of the other sentences helps explain and support the main idea stated in the topic sentence.

> I would be a knowledgeable and effective sales clerk at Handy Works Hardware. I have studied carpentry and advanced home repairs at Brookline Adult School, where I learned about electric and hand tools, paint mixing, and plumbing. I am also familiar with computerized registers, which I used at my summer job at Standard Stores. As my previous employer will confirm, I am friendly, polite, and helpful when dealing with the public. Finally, I am a quick learner and will be a great asset to your staff.

Look at these two paragraphs. Put a check mark by the one that has a clear paragraph structure.

_____ a. Every ten years the United States conducts a census. In a census, the government tries to count every person in the country. Every household receives a census questionnaire. Sometimes the government sends census workers to people's homes to collect information. It is important to have an accurate population count so that the 435 seats in the House of Representatives can be fairly distributed.

_____ b. Governments need to know how many people live within their borders. States need to know how many people live within their borders, too. Cities and towns like to post signs showing their populations. The current population of the United States is almost 300 million. Worldwide, it is over six billion.

You were correct if you chose *paragraph a.* Both paragraphs discuss population information. The first paragraph, however, is more effective because all the sentences in it support the main idea. The supporting sentences provide specific details, examples, and reasons. While all the sentences in *paragraph b* are about population, they do not connect to a topic sentence or main idea.

paragraph
a group of related sentences that develops a single main idea

topic sentence
states the main idea of a paragraph

supporting details
statements that explain the main idea of a paragraph by giving specific details, examples, and reasons

TIP

Remember to show the beginning of a paragraph by indenting. This tells your reader that you are moving on to a new idea.

A. Put a check mark next to the five sentences that belong in a paragraph with this topic sentence. Then write the topic sentence and supporting sentences in paragraph form.

Topic sentence: You can now buy stamps by mail.

_____ 1. A postage meter is very useful in business.

_____ 2. Buying by mail will save time.

_____ 3. Use an order form to pick the stamps you want to order.

_____ 4. The postage rates may change next year.

_____ 5. With mail orders, you have to buy stamps in rolls of 100.

_____ 6. A philatelist is a stamp collector.

_____ 7. Be sure to include a check or money order for the correct amount.

_____ 8. There are no extra fees for postage or handling.

_____

_____

_____

_____

_____

_____

B. Circle the topic sentence of this paragraph. Underline two details in other sentences that support the topic sentence.

Despite public radio's image as boring, it has a great variety of programs that appeal to many different listeners. You can hear international, national, and local news. Many celebrities refuse television or print interviews, yet they are willing to talk on public radio. There are comedy shows, automotive call-ins, and pop-music features. If you are willing to listen for one week, you are sure to find a program you like, regardless of your taste.

C. Write about the following topic.

The paragraph in Exercise B describes one place where people find out about the news. Write a paragraph that describes your favorite source for news and information. Make sure your paragraph has a topic sentence and other sentences with supporting details and examples.

Answers start on page 281.

Unity and Coherence

Unity and coherence are the results of good writing. A paragraph has **unity** when all the sentences support the main idea as stated in the topic sentence. When all the sentences are presented in a sensible, logical order, a paragraph has **coherence.** Irrelevant details or disorganized ideas make a paragraph seem sloppy and confusing.

For example, read this paragraph and notice the lack of unity and coherence:

> A lot of people want to own their homes, but owning can be expensive and stressful. Repairs can be costly, and you need to come up with a down payment. Repair companies can be unreliable. Our teenaged babysitter is pretty unreliable, too. All told, home ownership can be worrisome and costly. Property taxes are another hidden expense.

In contrast, read this edited paragraph. Pay attention to the changes in color. Notice how they make the ideas unified and coherent:

> A lot of people want to own their homes, but owning can be expensive and stressful. First, you need to come up with a down payment. Repairs can be costly, and repair companies can be unreliable. ~~Our teenaged babysitter is pretty unreliable, too.~~ Property taxes are another hidden expense. All told, home ownership can be worrisome and costly.

TIP

Be sure that every sentence in your paragraph is related to the main idea. Delete any unrelated sentences.

Put a check mark next to the sentence that could be used in this paragraph. Then indicate where you would place the sentence in the paragraph on the line below.

We have been having problems with sales reports. Some sales team members have been turning them in late or incomplete. Sales reports must be in your Team Folder each Thursday by 4:00. Inform your team leader if you have an unavoidable delay in turning in your reports.

_____ a. The promotion list is in the sales team office.

_____ b. Others have not been turning sales reports in at all.

_____ c. The sales team incentive program starts on Friday.

You were correct if you chose *option b.* It is the only sentence that relates to problems with turning in sales reports, the main idea. The other options mention sales teams, but they don't relate to the same main idea. The best place to add this detail in the paragraph is as the third sentence. The most logical relation of ideas is that some team members have been turning in reports late or incomplete and then that others have not been turning them in at all.

A. The first sentence in each paragraph is the topic sentence. One sentence that does not fit in each paragraph is crossed out. Cross out two more sentences in each paragraph that do not contribute to its unity or coherence.

1. A good way for employees to communicate with management is through a suggestion box. The purpose is for employees to offer suggestions relating to their jobs and the company. ~~Managers sometimes make suggestions, too.~~ Few people feel comfortable about expressing their opinions. Therefore, the suggestions are anonymous; that is, participants do not give their names. It is almost fun, like a secret ballot. That way, employees can participate honestly knowing their suggestions are confidential. Experts usually design surveys. Management can learn a lot about their workforce by responding to suggestions from employees.

2. There is new hope for anyone who hates the pain of an injection. ~~Of course, oral vaccines have always been painless.~~ New laser technology may soon allow doctors and nurses to inoculate patients without ever puncturing the skin with a needle. Many people cannot stand the sight of a needle. A rapid pulse from a laser temporarily opens the pores by creating stress waves in the skin. Small molecules of medicine enter the body through the opened pores. Then the medication is absorbed into the bloodstream. The skin is not broken, and there is no bleeding involved. When you bleed, a scab has to form on the skin. Soon the pores close themselves naturally, and unwanted bacteria remain sealed out.

3. Your local heating company offers these tips for saving energy and money this winter. ~~A wintry blast can cause heating prices to soar.~~ To prevent heat-loss through windows, open your curtains and drapes on sunny days to let in solar heat. Close them in the evening or on cloudy days. Taping window cracks or replacing broken windows also keeps heat in your house. Windows may crack if their sash cords snap. For good heat circulation, arrange your furniture so that it is not in front of radiators, vents, or baseboards. These can be painted, as well. If you have a furnace, check the water levels every other week or so during the heating season. If the water level drops too low, the whole system will shut down.

B. Write about the following topic.

Write a paragraph describing what you do to save energy in your home or workplace. Make sure all your sentences support the topic sentence and are presented in a logical order.

Answers start on page 281.

Directions: Choose the one best answer to each question.

Questions 1 through 3 refer to the following letter.

Dear Prospect HealthCare Subscriber:

(A)

(1) Some employers are switching from our health plan, Prospect HealthCare, to Park Plan. (2) Many employers are making changes to other employee benefits, too, including pensions and vacation time. (3) Since Prospect HealthCare accepts Park Plan insurance, we want to inform you that you may continue receiving your medical care from your current Prospect HealthCare doctors.

(B)

(4) On January 1, you will also have two options for purchasing prescription medication. (5) Option 1 allows you to use our network of pharmacy chains. (6) Option 2 allows you to continue using the Prospect HealthCare pharmacy housed within each of our medical offices. (7) The members of the network are Trust Drugs, Brook Pharmacies, PTR, and Best Stores. (8) We are also negotiating to add some independent pharmacies to our network. (9) Thank you for entrusting your care to Prospect HealthCare Associates' doctors and other caregivers.

(C)

(10) Please feel free to call us if you have any questions.

Thank you.
Prospect HealthCare

1. Which revision should be made to paragraph A?

   (1) remove sentence 2
   (2) move sentence 2 to the beginning of the paragraph
   (3) move sentence 2 to the end of the paragraph
   (4) move sentence 3 to the beginning of the paragraph
   (5) no revision is necessary

2. Which revision should be made to sentence 6?

   (1) remove sentence 6
   (2) move sentence 6 to follow sentence 3
   (3) move sentence 6 to follow sentence 8
   (4) move sentence 6 to the beginning of paragraph C
   (5) no revision is necessary

3. Which revision should be made to sentence 9?

   (1) move sentence 9 to the beginning of paragraph A
   (2) move sentence 9 to the end of paragraph A
   (3) remove sentence 9
   (4) move sentence 9 to the beginning of paragraph C
   (5) no revision is necessary

TIP

Be sure that you read the entire passage before you answer the questions. As you read, consider whether all the sentences support the main idea. Also, think about whether the sentences are in logical order.

The Whooping Crane

(A)

(1) The whooping crane, with its noisy songs and distinctive dances, has always fascinated observers. (2) Whooping cough, the common name for pertussis, was named after the sound the whooping crane makes. (3) This elegant, white, five-foot-tall bird is the largest native North American fowl. (4) In flight, whooping cranes have wingspans of over seven feet. (5) People travel miles to view these lovely creatures.

(B)

(6) In 1941, however, the whooping crane was nearly extinct. (7) Then, with federal assistance, a program was begun to rescue the species. (8) Today, there are almost 400 surviving "whoopers." (9) Thanks to scientist-inventors, eggs were hatched in incubators made to look like female whooping cranes. (10) In order to teach "whooping behavior" to young chicks, biologists dressed up like whooping cranes, waddled into marshes with the chicks, and pecked and scratched for food.

(C)

(11) If efforts to save the crane continue to succeed, these fascinating birds may be removed from the endangered species list soon. (12) Most wild animals don't get such personal attention. (13) The cranes' survival will be a natural success story.

TIP

When you are not sure if a sentence belongs in a paragraph, read the paragraph without it. Then decide whether the paragraph seems complete or whether the missing sentence helps to develop the main idea.

4. Which revision should be made to paragraph A?

  (1) remove sentence 1
  (2) move sentence 1 to the end of paragraph A
  (3) remove sentence 2
  (4) remove sentence 5
  (5) no revision is necessary

5. Which revision should be made to paragraph B?

  (1) move sentence 6 to the end of paragraph A
  (2) remove sentence 7
  (3) remove sentence 8
  (4) move sentence 8 to the end of the paragraph
  (5) move sentence 10 to the beginning of paragraph C

6. Which revision should be made to sentence 12?

  (1) move sentence 12 to the beginning of paragraph C
  (2) remove sentence 12
  (3) move sentence 12 to the end of paragraph C
  (4) replace sentence 12 with However, other wild animals will still be on the list.
  (5) no revision is necessary

7. Which revision should be made to sentence 13?

  (1) move sentence 13 to the end of paragraph A
  (2) move sentence 13 to the end of paragraph B
  (3) move sentence 13 to the beginning of paragraph C
  (4) remove sentence 13
  (5) no revision is necessary

Answers start on page 281.

Directions: This is a ten-minute practice test. After ten minutes, mark the last question you finished. Then complete the test and check your answers. If most of your answers were correct, but you didn't finish, try to work faster next time. Choose the <u>one best answer</u> to each question.

<u>Questions 1 through 4</u> refer to the following paragraphs.

Planning National Park Vacations

(A)

(1) To spend time in a national park during the summer, you need to make your plans early. (2) You should make them five months ahead of your trip at least for the twenty-two most popular camping areas in the National Parks System.

(B)

(3) For smooth processing, tour and camping reservation dates are staggered. (4) For example, if you want to see the Frederick Douglass Historic Site in Washington, D.C., touring reservations can be made on a certain date. (5) You can make them on the fifteenth of each month. (6) Most people attend the tours in Washington, D.C., as part of a school trip or course. (7) If you want to camp in California, campsites are open to reservations on the fifteenth of each month. (8) Sites in most other national parks reserved for camping after the twenty-fifth of each month. (9) Actually, campsites at little-used national parks are often available daily on a first-come, first-served basis.

1. Sentence 2: **You should make them five months ahead of your trip at least for the twenty-two most popular camping areas in the National Parks System.**

   The most effective revision of sentence 2 would include which group of words?

   (1) make them at least five months ahead
   (2) made them at least five months ahead
   (3) to make them five months ahead
   (4) will make them five months ahead
   (5) had made them five months ahead

2. Sentences 4 and 5: **For example, if you want to see the Frederick Douglass Historic Site in Washington, D.C., touring reservations can be made on a certain date. You can make them on the fifteenth of each month.**

   The most effective combination of sentences 4 and 5 would include which group of words?

   (1) For example, making reservations to tour
   (2) made, and you can
   (3) made on the fifteenth
   (4) Washington, D.C., on the fifteenth
   (5) The fifteenth of each month is an example

3. Sentence 6: **Most people attend the tours in Washington, D.C., as part of a school trip or course.**

   Which revision should be made to sentence 6?

   (1) remove sentence 6
   (2) move sentence 6 to follow sentence 3
   (3) replace sentence 6 with <u>Many tourists on tour in Washington, D.C., are students.</u>
   (4) move sentence 6 to the end of the paragraph
   (5) no revision is necessary

4. Sentence 8: **Sites in most other national <u>parks reserved</u> for camping after the twenty-fifth of each month.**

   Which is the best way to write the underlined portion of the text? If the original is the best way, choose option (1).

   (1) parks reserved
   (2) parks, reserved
   (3) parks. Reserved
   (4) parks can be reserved
   (5) parks, and are reserved

Questions 5 through 9 refer to the following paragraphs.

Winter Safety Tips

(A)

(1) Winter snow can be just as dangerous to children on sleds as it can be to adults in cars. (2) Here are some ideas for building safety into your children's sledding fun.

(B)

(3) Most important, choose a sled that can be steered so that your children won't crash into trees, rocks, or go smashing into other sledders. (4) If using last year's sled, make sure the steering mechanism hasn't rusted or broken. (5) The sledding area should not be too steep or icy, there must be a flat area at the bottom for slowing down. (6) Appearing frozen or not, your children shouldn't sled near or onto water. (7) Teach your children to wait their turn and to walk back to the top of the hill around, not up, the slopes.

(C)

(8) As for your children, have them wear helmets to avoid head injuries. (9) Gloves and boots are essential to protect them from cold and scrapes. (10) These you can buy at any store. (11) Finally, don't forget to bundle up yourself. (12) The top of a sledding hill can be very cold, windy, and bone-chilling for waiting parents.

5. Sentence 3: **Most important, choose a sled that can be steered so that your children won't crash into trees, rocks, or go smashing into other sledders.**

Which is the best way to write the underlined portion of the text? If the original is the best way, choose option (1).

(1) go smashing into other sledders
(2) smashing their sled into other sledders
(3) sliding into other sledders
(4) into other sledders
(5) other sledders

6. Sentence 5: **The sledding area should not be too steep or icy, there must be a flat area at the bottom for slowing down.**

What correction should be made to sentence 5?

(1) insert a comma after steep
(2) remove the comma
(3) insert and after the comma
(4) remove there must be
(5) no correction is necessary

7. Sentence 6: **Appearing frozen or not, your children shouldn't sled near or onto water.**

The most effective revision of sentence 6 would begin with which words?

(1) If appearing
(2) Should it be appearing
(3) While it appears
(4) Whether the water appears
(5) As it appears

8. Which revision would improve paragraph C?

(1) remove sentence 9
(2) remove sentence 10
(3) move sentence 11 to the beginning of the paragraph
(4) remove sentence 12
(5) no revision is necessary

9. Sentence 12: **The top of a sledding hill can be very cold, windy, and bone-chilling for waiting parents.**

What correction should be made to this sentence?

(1) insert it after hill
(2) replace can be with being
(3) remove the comma after cold
(4) insert it can be after and
(5) no correction is necessary

Answers start on page 282.

In Lesson 7 you learned that a paragraph is a group of sentences related to one main idea. A sentence that is not clearly related to the main idea of the paragraph can cause confusion. As both a reader and a writer, you can also appreciate the need for a paragraph to have enough supporting details so that the main idea is clearly explained.

For example, the writer of this paragraph did not clearly develop his main idea.

> The current minimum wage is not high enough. I used to earn $10 an hour at my landscaping job, but now I go to school. My wife has a minimum wage job. She works in a restaurant, and she doesn't earn enough money.

All the sentences in this paragraph have something to do with earning money. However, all the sentences do not support the main idea. They do not explain why the minimum wage is not high enough. There is even a sentence that does not belong at all—the one about what the writer used to earn at landscaping.

Now read this improved paragraph.

> The current minimum wage is not high enough, especially to support a family. My wife is paid minimum wage as a waitress while I am going to trade school. We are having trouble paying for our apartment, food, and child care. There is certainly no money left over for movies or restaurants. An additional dollar per hour would make paying our bills easier, and we would be able to relax and enjoy ourselves sometimes.

In this paragraph the writer clearly states his main idea about the minimum wage. Then he supports it with reasons and specific details—not enough money for bills and no money for extras. He also includes only details that support his main idea.

Read the topic sentence below, and add three sentences that support this statement.

There are many ways to cut costs when living on a budget.

_____

_____

_____

You might have included sentences like *Clipping coupons helps save on the grocery bill. Having a picnic is cheaper than going out to eat. Trading child care with other parents can save money.*

The Personal Link

1. **Write a paragraph on a separate sheet of paper explaining why work is important to you. Write a topic sentence stating your main idea. Then write supporting sentences that explain your main idea.** If you work, do you work just for the money, or are there other aspects of your job that are rewarding? If you are not currently working, imagine yourself working in a fast-food restaurant. Would a job like this fit your lifestyle and meet your needs? Think of specific reasons to support your view.

2. **In your journal, describe your dream job. What would you do? How much money would you earn? Why would you enjoy this job?**

The GED Link

1. **Read the following topic. On a separate sheet of paper, write as many thoughts as you can about the topic. Do not try to write complete sentences. Just let your ideas flow onto the page.**

    For some people money is the most important factor in job satisfaction. Do you agree? Why or why not? Use your personal observations, experience, and knowledge.

2. **Use your ideas from this GED Link to write a paragraph about the topic. If you like, use some of your ideas from the Personal Link, too. Make sure to state your main idea in a topic sentence and to support it.**

Edit

Read your paragraphs from the Personal Link and the GED Link, and correct any mistakes that you find. Be sure that all your sentences support one main idea.

Portfolio Reminder

Put your edited paragraph from the GED Link in your portfolio.

Answers start on page 282.

GED SKILL **Topic Sentences**

TIP

Try writing your topic sentence after deciding which supporting details to include in the paragraph.

A topic sentence states the main idea of a paragraph. It is a reader's guide to understanding the ideas in the paragraph. For that reason, many writers begin their paragraphs with the topic sentence, even though it may be placed anywhere in a paragraph.

Avoid writing topic sentences that are too specific or too general. If you are too specific, your reader will not see the big picture or main idea. A topic sentence that is too general will not help your reader focus on what you are saying about the topic. Every topic sentence should clearly answer the question, "What is the main point of this paragraph?"

RULE A topic sentence states the main idea of the entire paragraph without being too general or too specific.

For example, read this group of sentences. Then consider the possible topic sentences.

> Most air pollution is caused by forms of transportation. We flush polluting exhaust into the air every time we drive our cars. The diesel engine exhaust of commercial trucks is also very harsh. In addition, fuel combustion for heating our homes, offices, and factories contributes to pollution. Industrial processes such as oil refining do, too. Natural sources, such as volcanoes, contribute some pollutants, but not nearly as much as many people think.

Too general: The air is polluted.
Too specific: Most air pollution comes from cars and trucks.
Effective: Air pollution is most often caused by human activity.

The effective topic sentence sums up the details, which point to things done by humans that cause air pollution.

Put a check mark next to the best topic sentence for a paragraph on this topic.

Topic: How to obedience-train your puppy

_____ a. There are four major steps in obedience training.

_____ b. Reward good behavior with lots of praise.

_____ c. You can train your dog.

You were correct if you chose *option a* as the best topic sentence. It states the main idea and gives the reader clear information about what to expect. *Option b* is too specific. *Option c* is too general.

A. Write *OK* if the underlined topic sentence is effective for each letter to the editor. Write a new topic sentence if it is ineffective.

1. Dear Editor,
   <u>Despite all warnings, many people do not wear car safety belts.</u> Statistics show that passengers wearing seat belts have fewer injuries in car accidents. It is the law in our state, but the law is often ignored. It is not enforced consistently, either. I propose raising insurance rates for anyone who doesn't wear a seat belt. It's about time we became aggressive about safety.

   Alice Mayfield, M.D.

Topic sentence: _____

2. Dear Editor,
   <u>Highway funds are good for the economy.</u> My business is being hurt by the delay in building the Highway 41 extension. Instead of a one-hour direct trip from Sandy Point to Winslow, my trucks have to take winding local roads, which adds an additional hour to the trip. My business is not the only one affected by these long delays. Please pass the emergency funding today!

   Herbert J. Marshall, President, ShopRight Stores

Topic sentence: _____

3. Dear Editor,
   <u>We wish to thank Ms. Enders, announcer at the fundraiser for the high school band.</u> The fundraising committee's effort was a huge success. Every band member and his or her family participated, and everyone enjoyed a great evening of music and fun. Thanks also to the faculty, who always encourage our children's musical talents. Bravo!

   Mr. and Mrs. Green

Topic sentence: _____

B. Read this paragraph about working at home. Then write a topic sentence.

   Parents who work at home do not have to worry about reliable daycare for their children. On the other hand, their work is often interrupted by their children. People who work at home have more flexibility than workers on nine-to-five schedules. They often complain, however, that their work seeps into all their free time because there is no border between work and home. Finally, people who work at home may have the freedom to dress as they please, but they often miss the social interaction of working with others.

_____

_____

C. Write about the following topic.

   Write a paragraph explaining whether you would prefer working at home or at a workplace. Edit your topic sentence carefully and then correct your paragraph for other errors.

Answers start on page 282.

GED Practice • Lesson 8

Directions: Choose the one best answer to each question.

Questions 1 through 3 refer to the following letter.

Dear Seventh-Grade Parent,

(A)

(1) We will be attending the Winter Lights Show and "Mysteries of Ancient Mesopotamia." (2) The bus will leave the Middle School at 8:30 A.M. and will return at 2:30 P.M.

(B)

(3) The fee includes museum admission, a morning snack, and transportation. (4) Please make checks payable to the *Easton School Fund.* (5) Please do not send extra money because there will be no free time to go to the Museum Shop.

(C)

(6) There's a permission form attached. (7) If your child will need to be administered medication during the day, be sure to sign the attached medication form as well. (8) Your child's science teacher will collect the money and signed forms.

1. Which sentence below would be most effective at the beginning of paragraph A?

   (1) The seventh grade will visit the Science Museum on Monday, October 5.
   (2) Seventh-grade field trips are usually educational in nature.
   (3) This year the Cell Exhibit is temporarily closed, so the seventh grade will view other Science Museum offerings.
   (4) The seventh grade always takes one field trip a year.
   (5) Seventh graders learn a great deal from field trips to the Science Museum.

2. Which sentence below would be most effective at the beginning of paragraph B?

   (1) Parents will be notified of the cost of the trip.
   (2) The cost of the trip includes three items.
   (3) The cost of the trip is $8.00 payable in cash or check.
   (4) Most of the trip will be paid by the School Department, but parents will be asked to contribute a portion of the cost.
   (5) The cost to each student will be less than $10.

3. Sentence 6: **There's a permission form attached.**

   Which revision should be made to sentence 6?

   (1) replace sentence 6 with There's a permission form and a medication form, too.
   (2) replace sentence 6 with Please find the attached forms and sign the ones that apply.
   (3) replace sentence 6 with Sign any attached forms.
   (4) replace sentence 6 with You will need to sign the permission form that is attached.
   (5) no revision is necessary

TIP

On the GED Test, a question that asks for the most effective sentence to place at the beginning of a paragraph is asking for a topic sentence for the paragraph.

Questions 4 through 6 refer to the following article.

Change of Address Forms

(A)

(1) Every post office has Change of Address forms for your mail. (2) You can fill out this form at the post office, or take it home, fill it out, and pop it in any mailbox. (3) Postal workers recommend you turn in the form at least one month before you move so that your mail isn't delayed.

(B)

(4) Forwarded personal mail includes First Class, Priority, and Express Mail. (5) The post office will also forward newspapers and magazines free for 60 days. (6) It is your responsibility to notify those publications that you've moved.

(C)

(7) Most businesses can process your change of address within three months, so tell them early. (8) The post office won't deliver circulars, catalogs, or advertisements unless you specifically request it to do so.

4. Which sentence below would be most effective at the beginning of paragraph A?

(1) Moving is a very stressful experience.
(2) To keep receiving mail when you move, notify the post office of your new address.
(3) Change of Address forms take very little time to complete.
(4) The post office forwards your mail to your new address.
(5) There is a form called Change of Address.

5. Which revision should be made to paragraph B?

(1) insert at the beginning of the paragraph The post office will forward your personal mail and most packages for one year.
(2) remove sentence 4
(3) move sentence 4 to the end of the paragraph
(4) replace sentence 4 with Not all mail will be forwarded.
(5) no revision is necessary

6. Which sentence below would be most effective at the beginning of paragraph C?

(1) Then there's business mail.
(2) Many businesses send you mail, too.
(3) Some businesses send what people consider "junk mail."
(4) Many people forget to tell businesses that they are moving.
(5) Don't forget to notify businesses you deal with that you have moved.

TIP Once you choose a topic sentence for a paragraph on the GED Test, read the whole paragraph with the topic sentence at the beginning. That will help you "hear" whether the topic sentence that you chose is effective.

Answers start on page 282.

Directions: This is a ten-minute practice test. After ten minutes, mark the last question you finished. Then complete the test and check your answers. If most of your answers were correct, but you didn't finish, try to work faster next time. Choose the one best answer to each question.

Questions 1 through 5 refer to the following paragraph.

Nail Color

(1) White nails may indicate liver disease. (2) While half white and half pink may indicate kidney disease. (3) A heart condition may show up along with a red nail bed. (4) Nails that are thick, yellow, and have bumps may be telling you that your lungs are in trouble. (5) Pale nail beds show anemia. (6) Nails that are yellow with a slight pinkness at the base may indicate diabetes. (7) As for nail polish, it can dry nails out, especially the frequent use of nail polish remover. (8) You don't need to worry about white spots they seem to be caused by external damage rather than internal disease.

1. Which sentence below would be most effective at the beginning of the paragraph?

   (1) Sometimes nails change colors.
   (2) Some nails are white or pink; others are reddish or yellow.
   (3) Changes in the natural color of your nails can warn you of disease.
   (4) Examine your nails every day for disease.
   (5) Some nail color changes are serious, while others are not.

2. Which revision would improve the text?

   (1) remove sentence 3
   (2) move sentence 5 to the end of the paragraph
   (3) move sentence 6 to the end of the paragraph
   (4) remove sentence 7
   (5) move sentence 7 to the end of the paragraph

3. Sentences 1 and 2: **White nails may indicate liver disease. While half white and half pink may indicate kidney disease.**

   Which is the best way to write the underlined portion of the text? If the original is the best way, choose option (1).

   (1) disease. While
   (2) disease, while
   (3) disease and
   (4) disease,
   (5) disease, meaning that

4. Sentence 4: **Nails that are thick, yellow, and have bumps may be telling you that your lungs are in trouble.**

   Which correction should be made to sentence 4?

   (1) remove that
   (2) remove the comma after thick
   (3) insert they after and
   (4) change have bumps to bumpy
   (5) replace you that with you,

5. Sentence 8: **You don't need to worry about white spots they seem to be caused by external damage rather than internal disease.**

   Which is the best way to write the underlined portion of the text? If the original is the best way, choose option (1).

   (1) spots they
   (2) spots, they
   (3) spots because they
   (4) spots and they
   (5) spots in fact they

Questions 6 through 9 refer to the following paragraphs.

Going Through Customs

(A)

(1) Every day, thousands of international travelers enter the United States and go through customs. (2) When these travelers arrive at customs their luggage may be opened and inspected by customs officials searching for prohibited goods. (3) This includes carry-on luggage. (4) Carry-on luggage can vary from handbags or backpacks to briefcases and small overnight bags.

(B)

(4) Other than drugs and weapons, what are customs officials looking for? (5) Customs agents from the U.S. Department of Agriculture are responsible for making sure that no contaminated plant, food, or products that were made from animals are brought into the country. (6) USDA officers intercept about two million illegal products a year. (7) Imported fruits, vegetables, plants, and meat products are dangerous to U.S. agriculture they contain unwanted pests, such as fruit flies or parasites.

6. Sentence 2: **When these travelers arrive at customs their luggage may be opened and inspected by customs officials searching for prohibited goods.**

Which correction should be made to sentence 2?

(1) replace When these with These
(2) insert a comma after customs
(3) insert a comma after opened
(4) insert they are after officials
(5) no correction is necessary

7. Which revision should be made to paragraph A?

(1) replace sentence 1 with The United States has customs officials.
(2) remove sentence 1
(3) remove sentence 4
(4) replace sentence 4 with Many travelers bring carry-on luggage that is too large.
(5) no revision is necessary

8. Sentence 5: **Customs agents from the U.S. Department of Agriculture are responsible for making sure that no contaminated plant, food, or products that were made from animals are brought into the country.**

Which is the best way to write the underlined portion of the text? If the original is the best way, choose option (1).

(1) plant, food, or products that were made from animals
(2) plants and food and products made from animals
(3) plant products, food products, or products made from animals
(4) products having been produced from plants or food or animals
(5) plant, food, or animal products

9. Sentence 7: **Imported fruits, vegetables, plants, and meat products are dangerous to U.S. agriculture they contain unwanted pests, such as fruit flies or parasites.**

Which is the best way to write the underlined portion of the text? If the original is the best way, choose option (1).

(1) agriculture they
(2) agriculture, they
(3) agriculture if they
(4) agriculture. They
(5) agriculture in addition they

Answers start on page 283.

In Lesson 8 you learned the difference between an effective topic sentence and an ineffective one. Now that you have had some practice identifying effective topic sentences, you will have the opportunity to write some of your own.

To write an effective topic sentence, note each supporting detail in the paragraph. Then sum up those details in one clear, direct sentence.

For example, the following sentences supply the supporting details of a paragraph written in an accident report at work.

> First, we did not have enough safety monitors on the floor at the time. Second, we were in a hurry to complete the loading because we were already running late with the order. But probably the most important factor in the accident was the fact that we did not follow procedures and turn off the turning belt when it became jammed. As a result, two employees suffered hand injuries.

Those sentences give several factors, or reasons, for an accident. A topic sentence that tells the reader the main idea of the paragraph should point out that the accident happened for several reasons. Therefore, an effective topic sentence would be:

> There were several reasons for the accident that occurred on the job site today.

Write a topic sentence that tells the main idea of this paragraph about employees.

> Good attendance is important because you cannot be valuable to your company if you are not at work. In addition, a helpful and cooperative attitude is needed. Pleasant people make the workplace easier to deal with. Also, an employee's willingness to take on additional responsibilities is important to any company. All these characteristics make for a valuable employee.

_____

_____

You might have written a sentence like _To be a valuable employee, you have to have certain qualities._ Each sentence in the paragraph notes a particular characteristic or quality that makes an employee valuable. These sentences can be summed up in a topic sentence like the one above.

TIP

Be sure your topic sentence does not just state the topic of your paragraph. It must also include your main point about the topic.

The Personal Link

1. **Select a person that you admire—a friend, relative, co-worker, even a celebrity. Write one paragraph explaining why you admire the person.** Be sure you write a clear topic sentence that sums up your main idea. Then tell the reasons that you admire the person. Note specific details about his or her qualities and give examples of how he or she behaves.

2. **In your journal, write about both the qualities you like best about yourself and those that you would like to change.**

The GED Link

1. **Read the following topic. On a separate sheet of paper, write as many thoughts as you can about the topic. Do not try to write complete sentences. Just let your ideas flow onto the page.**

   Some people believe that the world no longer has any heroes. Do you agree, or do you think there are people who deserve our admiration? Use your personal observations, experience, and knowledge.

2. **Use your ideas from this GED Link to write a paragraph about the topic. If you like, use some of your ideas from the Personal Link, too. Make sure you state your main idea in a topic sentence and support it.**

Edit

Read your paragraphs from the Personal Link and GED Link again, and correct any mistakes you find. Be sure that each paragraph has an effective topic sentence.

Portfolio Reminder

Put your edited paragraph from the GED Link in your portfolio.

Answers start on page 283.

GED SKILL **Paragraphing**

Paragraphs are a way to organize your ideas. Each paragraph develops only one main idea. Also, writing is much easier to read when it is broken into paragraphs rather than in one long block of text.

RULE 1 Start a new paragraph when the main idea of a group of sentences shifts.

RULE 2 Both the introduction and conclusion are organized into paragraphs. The introduction is the first paragraph; the conclusion is the final paragraph.

Note where each paragraph starts in this article. The introduction is in a separate paragraph, but the conclusion is not.

TIP

Most paragraphs have a topic sentence and three or four supporting sentences. Introductory and concluding paragraphs may be shorter.

Introduction ⟶

> E-mail is fast becoming the most popular means of communication. E-mail users even predict that it will soon replace letters and stamps. Certainly, many individuals and companies use it on a daily basis.
>
> E-mail does have many advantages over regular mail. The speed of e-mail has made communication almost instantaneous. You can send messages to faraway places in almost no time at all. E-mail doesn't cost much, either. In fact, many people get free e-mail. A lot of people also like the informality of e-mails.
>
> Still, there are a lot of people who function without e-mail. Some people do not have access to or experience with computers. Others feel e-mails are too impersonal. They think less care and thought are put into an e-mail than a letter. Sooner or later, however, everyone will be getting e-mail. It's easy to imagine that within a few years, regular letters will go the way of manual typewriters. They will be seen as funny, old-fashioned antiques that your grandparents barely remember.

Conclusion ⟶

Put a check mark next to the sentence from the third paragraph that should begin the concluding paragraph.

_____ a. Sooner or later, however, everyone will be getting e-mail.

_____ b. It's easy to imagine that within a few years, regular letters will go the way of manual typewriters.

You were correct if you chose *option a*. The third paragraph is about people who function without e-mail. *Option a* introduces a new idea, the future of e-mail, which is the conclusion of the essay.

A. Read this page from an employee handbook. Mark where each new paragraph should begin with this symbol: ¶. Then explain why a new paragraph was needed. You can divide this passage into five paragraphs.

Introductory paragraph

Main idea shifts to what to do before first day of work

¶Welcome to the Bedford Company. We are proud of the manufacturing tradition we have here, and we know that you, as a new hire, will help contribute to the continuation of tradition. ¶When you report for your first day of work, you will be asked to read this Bedford Company Handbook in its entirety. Every employee must read and agree to its contents. When you are finished, please sign the card on page 25 and return it to the Human Resources Director. On your first day of work, you will need to arrive at 9:00 A.M. promptly, no matter what shift you are assigned. A company representative will meet you at the front desk and bring you to the Human Resources office, where you will have an identification photograph taken. You will complete personnel, payroll, and benefit forms. You will also see an orientation film about the Bedford Company and attend an orientation session. Your first afternoon will be spent on the manufacturing floor with your team leader. He or she will show you to your locker and to the uniform distribution station. You will meet your team and your teammate/mentor. Your mentor will demonstrate your work tasks, show you where to get your tools, and explain how to care for and store them. At 4:45 P.M., please return to the Human Resources office for your permanent identification card and a two-week shift schedule. Your first workday will end at 5:00 P.M.

B. Write about the following topic.

Write several paragraphs about how you spend a typical weekday. Tell what you do in the morning, in the afternoon, and at night. Begin a new paragraph for each time of the day. Then edit your paragraphs for errors.

Answers start on page 284.

Directions: Choose the <u>one best answer</u> to each question.

<u>Questions 1 and 2</u> refer to the following letter.

Dr. Eli Brownwood
Central Clinic
4201 Ashwood Avenue
Morris, OH 43201

Dear Dr. Brownwood:

(1) I am typing this letter with one hand because I broke my wrist last week when I fell on the ice in the parking lot at work. (2) I want to thank the staff members at Central Clinic for their extraordinary care, gentleness, and professionalism in treating my injury. (3) When I entered the clinic, I was almost fainting from pain and unable to remove the glove from my injured hand. (4) The first person I met was Marge Freeman at Reception, whose warmth and concern immediately calmed me down. (5) Next, Dr. Rayford managed to remove the glove from my swollen hand with care. (6) Then I moved on to Emergency Care. (7) Everyone I met was incredibly helpful. (8) Corey Clay administered the novocaine painlessly and efficiently. (9) The technician, Bill Stone, was extremely gentle and concerned. (10) Dr. Mayfield's surgery was professional, and she contacted me three times before my follow-up visit. (11) I am so grateful for my treatment at the hands of your staff. (12) I hope you will share this letter with all the people I mentioned and extend to them my deepest appreciation.

Sincerely,
Lupe Ortiz

1. Which revision would improve the text of this letter?

   Begin a new paragraph

   (1) with sentence 2
   (2) with sentence 3
   (3) with sentence 4
   (4) with sentence 5
   (5) with sentence 6

2. Which revision would improve the text of this letter?

   Begin a new paragraph

   (1) with sentence 8
   (2) with sentence 9
   (3) with sentence 10
   (4) with sentence 11
   (5) with sentence 12

TIP

Be careful not to create too many short paragraphs from individual sentences. An occasional short paragraph is acceptable when it is used for emphasis or as a transition between major points.

Evaluating a Student's Writing

(A)

(1) We use three levels of mastery to evaluate a student's writing. (2) The lowest level is novice, the middle level is proficient, and the highest level is superior. (3) The work of a novice may show flashes of quality, but it needs improvement in several important ways. (4) For example, a novice's description may be superficial or demonstrate incomplete understanding of the subject matter. (5) The writing may also contain serious errors in spelling, grammar, punctuation, or capitalization, or it may be poorly organized. (6) Overall, the final product may be untidy. (7) At the next level of mastery, the proficient student's writing is acceptable, but it could be improved in a few important ways. (8) For example, the writer's comprehension of the subject matter may seem at times incomplete or inaccurate. (9) The writing may contain several errors in grammar, punctuation, spelling, and/or capitalization. (10) The final product, however, is generally neat.

(B)

(11) Superior writers show an excellent understanding of their subject matter. (12) Specific, accurate details are plentiful. (13) The writing is well organized, words are well chosen, and mistakes in grammar, punctuation, spelling, and capitalization are generally avoided. (14) The final product is neat and professional. (15) Each student may submit two original pieces for competency evaluations per semester. (16) We suggest students who were evaluated as novices previously revise and resubmit those writings for re-evaluation.

3. Which revision would make the text more effective?

Begin a new paragraph

(1) with sentence 2
(2) with sentence 3
(3) with sentence 4
(4) with sentence 5
(5) with sentence 6

4. Which revision should be made to sentences 7 through 10?

Begin a new paragraph

(1) with sentence 7
(2) with sentence 8
(3) with sentence 9
(4) with sentence 10
(5) no revision is necessary

5. Which revision would make the text more effective?

Begin a new paragraph

(1) with sentence 12
(2) with sentence 13
(3) with sentence 14
(4) with sentence 15
(5) with sentence 16

Answers start on page 284.

Directions: This is a ten-minute practice test. After ten minutes, mark the last question you finished. Then complete the test and check your answers. If most of your answers were correct, but you didn't finish, try to work faster next time. Choose the one best answer to each question.

Questions 1 through 4 refer to the following paragraph.

A Family Health Tree

(1) Some facts about members of your family in order to make a family health tree. (2) The family members you need to know about are your parents, grandparents, siblings, children, grandchildren, aunts, and uncles. (3) More distant relatives, such as great-grandparents, cousins, nieces, and nephews, are added bonuses, the basic facts you need to know for each relative are date of birth and major diseases. (4) Also ask them for information about allergies, disabilities, weight or blood pressure problems, and general health habits such as diet or smoking. (5) Relatives who are overweight should diet, and smokers should definitely stop smoking. (6) For relatives who are deceased, record their ages and causes of death. (7) Give copies of your family health history to your doctor, your pediatrician, and other family members.

1. Which sentence below would be most effective if inserted at the beginning of the paragraph?

    (1) A family health tree shows medical histories.
    (2) Charting your family's health history may help save a life because heredity plays a role in many illnesses.
    (3) Illnesses such as allergies and diabetes should be listed on a family health tree.
    (4) Get your relatives to help you make a family health tree.
    (5) It's good to have information about your family's diseases.

2. Sentence 1: **Some facts about members of your family in order to make a family health tree.**

    What correction should be made to sentence 1?

    (1) replace Some with Need some
    (2) replace Some with You will need some
    (3) insert a comma after your family
    (4) insert for you after order
    (5) no correction is necessary

3. Sentence 3: **More distant relatives, such as great-grandparents, cousins, nieces, and nephews, are added bonuses, the basic facts you need to know for each relative are date of birth and major diseases.**

    Which is the best way to write the underlined portion of the text? If the original is the best way, choose option (1).

    (1) bonuses, the basic
    (2) bonuses the basic
    (3) bonuses although the basic
    (4) bonuses. The basic
    (5) bonuses because the basic

4. Which revision would improve the text?

    (1) move sentence 4 to follow sentence 2
    (2) remove sentence 5
    (3) move sentence 5 to the end of the paragraph
    (4) remove sentence 6
    (5) remove sentence 7

Questions 5 through 8 refer to the following notice.

From: The Desk of the Town Manager
To: The Residents of Oakland

(A)

(1) Town residents may now purchase at the Town Hall recycling permits. (2) They may also be purchased at the Recycling Station during normal operating hours. (3) Permits cost $10 and are valid for one year. (4) If you wish to obtain a permit you must appear in person with a valid vehicle registration certificate. (5) Permits will not be issued by mail, nor will they be issued without proof of registration. (6) Upon purchasing your permit, you must attach it to the rear driver's side window. (7) Permits are not valid unless they are permanently attached and visible. (8) Please remove permits from prior years.

(B)

(9) Yard waste can now be disposed of at the Recycling Station you can continue bringing it to the brush dump on E Street. (10) This area will be opened on Monday, Wednesday, and Saturday to coincide with the recycling division.

5. Sentence 1: **Town residents may now purchase at the Town Hall recycling permits.**

   What correction should be made to sentence 1?

   (1) change may now purchase to now purchasing
   (2) insert a comma after purchase
   (3) insert a comma after office
   (4) replace at the Town Hall recycling permits with recycling permits at the Town Hall
   (5) no correction is necessary

6. Sentence 4: **If you wish to obtain a permit you must appear in person with a valid vehicle registration certificate.**

   Which is the best way to write the underlined portion of the text? If the original is the best way, choose option (1).

   (1) permit you
   (2) permit. You
   (3) permit, you
   (4) permit so you
   (5) permit, therefore you

7. Which revision would improve the text of this notice?

   (1) begin a new paragraph with sentence 5
   (2) begin a new paragraph with sentence 6
   (3) remove sentence 6
   (4) remove sentence 8
   (5) move sentence 8 to the beginning of paragraph B

8. Sentence 9: **Yard waste can now be disposed of at the Recycling Station you can continue bringing it to the brush dump on E Street.**

   Which is the best way to write the underlined portion of the text? If the original is the best way, choose option (1).

   (1) Station you
   (2) Station, you
   (3) Station and you
   (4) Station even though you
   (5) Station, or you

Answers start on page 284.

GED WRITING LINK **Writing More Than One Paragraph**

When you write personal letters, you may begin writing without much planning. As you think of a new idea or topic, you begin a new paragraph. The new paragraph is a signal to your reader that you are going to be writing about something new.

When you write more formally—for example, a business letter, a letter to the editor, or a GED essay—you plan what you are going to say before you write. First you gather ideas and then group related ideas into paragraphs.

Read the following essay. Note how each paragraph talks about a different reason that some people think children should not be required to go to school in order to get an education.

Home schooling is a controversial topic. Supporters believe that school should not be required in the United States because there are many different ways to become educated. For example, a parent can be an excellent teacher for important life skills such as cooking and home repairs as well as for subjects such as reading, writing, and arithmetic.

Some home school advocates believe schools are not always effective places to learn. They maintain that children learn better in small, comfortable surroundings. They also cite the numbers of children who have brought weapons into schools.

Finally, they believe our country is founded on the ideas of choice and liberty. They feel that forcing kids to go to school is against the basic principles of freedom.

Read this letter to the editor about the same topic. Put a paragraph mark (¶) where a second paragraph should begin.

Dear Editor:

I just heard that some people are saying that kids should not be required to go to school. They think that their children can learn better at home. What they don't realize is that kind of thinking could lead to some children just sitting at home, unsupervised all day. Can you imagine ten-year-olds sitting in front of the TV with nothing to do? An additional result of not having mandatory education would be an unskilled workforce. Not enough people would be prepared to work as bankers, computer technicians, teachers, or mechanics. The economy would really suffer if school were not required.

You were correct if you put a paragraph symbol before the words *An additional.* That sentence begins a new main idea—the relationship between school and work.

The Personal Link

1. **Write a letter to a friend or relative who is in school. Explain why you think staying in school is important.** Try to give several reasons for staying in school. Use examples from your own life and the lives of other people you know. As you write about each new reason, begin a new paragraph.

2. **In your journal, write about your decision to study for and take the GED Test. How has this decision affected you?**

The GED Link

1. **Read the following topic. On a separate sheet of paper, write as many thoughts as you can about the topic. Do not try to write complete sentences. Just let your ideas flow onto the page.**

> Should formal school be required for all children up to age 18 in the United States? Why or why not? Use your personal observations, experience, and knowledge to support your view.

2. **On the same sheet of paper, write three or four paragraphs about the topic above. Use your ideas from this GED Link. Group related ideas, and write about each group in a paragraph with a topic sentence. If you like, use some of your ideas from the Personal Link, too.**

Edit

Read over your writing and make any changes you think would improve it. Pay special attention to how you have divided your writing into paragraphs.

Portfolio Reminder

Put your paragraphs from the GED Link into your portfolio.

Answers start on page 285.

Lesson 10

GED SKILL **Clear Transitions**

In Unit 1 you learned how certain words and phrases—coordinating conjunctions, subordinating conjunctions, and conjunctive adverbs—indicate that ideas are related in particular ways. These words and phrases are called **transitions.**

If you use transitions effectively, your writing will flow smoothly from idea to idea, from sentence to sentence, and from paragraph to paragraph. (To review transitional words and phrases with correct punctuation, see Lessons 2 and 3.)

RULE 1 Use transitions and punctuation to show the relationship between ideas in two sentences. A transition at the beginning of a sentence requires a comma after it. Within a sentence, it requires a comma before and after it.

No transition:	Small banks often discount fees. Average ATM fees are $1.25 at big banks, but 86¢ at small ones.
With transition:	Small banks often discount fees. <u>For example,</u> average ATM fees are $1.25 at big banks, but 86¢ at small ones.
With transition:	Small banks often discount fees. Average ATM fees, <u>for example,</u> are $1.25 at big banks, but 86¢ at small ones.

RULE 2 Use transitions and punctuation when moving from one paragraph to another to show how ideas are related.

A study of charges at big and small banks shows some interesting data. In almost every category, from checking account minimums to bounced check fees, small banks give consumers a better deal.

<u>Nevertheless,</u> consumers continue to put their money into big banks for several reasons. For instance, the big banks offer services that small banks cannot. . . .

Put a caret (^) where you would place the transitional word *However* in this short paragraph.

Wyoming's Devil's Tower was the first major monument named in the United States. South Dakota's Mt. Rushmore is much more famous. One reason it is more famous may be that it is close to Rapid City, an urban center.

You were correct if you chose to place *However* between the first and second sentences: *Wyoming's Devil's Tower was the first major monument named in the United States. However, South Dakota's Mt. Rushmore is much more famous.* The addition of the transition makes the relationship between the ideas clear.

---

transition
a word or phrase that signals the relationship from one idea to the next

Other common transitions are *in other words* (definition), *in the first place* (order), *as a matter of fact* (supporting detail), *on the other hand* (contrast), and *as a result* or *for this reason* (cause and effect).

A. Use the following transitions to fill in the blanks. Punctuate as needed.

therefore   for that reason   as a result   however   ~~of course~~

Dehydration is common in hot weather. To cool off, our bodies sweat and,

(1) _____*of course*_____ lose water. (2) _____ we become

thirsty. To quench our thirst, many of us drink soda. (3) _____ drinking

soda only adds to thirst. That is because soda often contains sodium.

(4) _____ health workers recommend water instead.

(5) _____ it is recommended that adults drink about two quarts of

water every day.

B. Read about people's attitudes toward change. The places where transitions could be used are underlined. Insert appropriate transitions and correct punctuation. Add other words if necessary to make the relationships clearer.

Furthermore, they believe that these

Most Americans believe social changes are happening faster than ever. ~~These~~ changes aren't

necessarily good ones. They believe things will turn out for the best eventually. Young people

are the most comfortable with change. People over 60 admit that changes are difficult.

In their personal lives, almost 50 percent of older people are happy with the way things

are. They wouldn't change their names, their friends, their spouses, their families, their homes,

or their looks. They don't want to change social class either, even if it would mean going to a

higher class. Many younger people would change all or some of those factors. Over 80 percent

of people polled believed that personal happiness is a matter of personal effort.

As for difficult changes, the death of a spouse is the hardest change to endure. Divorce is

the second hardest. Older folks tend to remember high school graduation as a pleasant

experience. More recent graduates disagree.

C. Write about the following topic.

Write a paragraph describing a change in your life that was either especially enjoyable or especially hard. Edit your work for effective transitions and then correct it for other errors.

Answers start on page 285.

Directions: Choose the <u>one best answer</u> to each question.

<u>Questions 1 through 4</u> refer to the following paragraph.

Child Care in the Workplace

(1) In some European countries, the government runs day-care centers for children. (2) In the United States, most parents who work are on their own. (3) Many find themselves late to work or even absent because of child-care problems, so more and more employers are providing child care for their employees. (4) One factory in Indiana runs a three-shift, on-site day-care center. (5) Grateful fathers and mothers can bring their children to work with them. (6) Lateness and absenteeism have been greatly reduced. (7) This program satisfies both employer and employee. (8) Employees don't have to worry about child care. (9) They tend to be far more productive than those who do worry.

1. Sentence 2: **In the United States, most parents who work are on their own.**

   Which revision should be made to sentence 2?

   (1) insert <u>however,</u> after the comma
   (2) insert <u>however,</u> after <u>parents</u>
   (3) insert <u>however</u> after <u>who</u>
   (4) insert <u>, however</u> after <u>work</u>
   (5) insert <u>however</u> after <u>own</u>

TIP

Before adding a transition, reread the previous sentence to choose the most appropriate transition.

2. Sentence 4: **One factory in Indiana runs a three-shift, on-site day-care center.**

   Which revision should be made to sentence 4?

   (1) replace <u>One factory</u> with <u>If one factory</u>
   (2) replace <u>One factory</u> with <u>For example, one factory</u>
   (3) replace <u>in Indiana</u> with <u>in, for example, Indiana</u>
   (4) insert <u>for example</u> after <u>center</u>
   (5) no revision is necessary

3. Sentence 6: **Lateness and absenteeism have been greatly reduced.**

   Which revision should be made to sentence 6?

   (1) replace <u>Lateness</u> with <u>Consequently, lateness</u>
   (2) insert <u>, consequently,</u> after <u>Lateness</u>
   (3) insert <u>, consequently,</u> after <u>and</u>
   (4) insert <u>consequently</u> after <u>absenteeism</u>
   (5) no revision is necessary

4. Sentences 8 and 9: **Employees don't have to worry about child care. They tend to be far more productive than those who do worry.**

   The most effective combination of sentences 8 and 9 would include which group of words?

   (1) for instance
   (2) as a result
   (3) even though
   (4) in the same way
   (5) in addition

Questions 5 through 8 refer to the following information.

Varnished Wood Furniture

(A)

(1) Wood that is varnished stands up well to normal wear and tear. (2) That's because varnish is a tough finish. (3) It protects for decades. (4) The major problem with varnished wood is that scratches show up very easily.

(B)

(5) Dust it regularly. (6) Wash it occasionally with paint thinner, which dissolves dirt. (7) Paint thinner may dull the finish, however, so be prepared to restore the shine with a good buffing. (8) A mild solution of a good detergent and water will also clean varnished furniture, but water should be used sparingly. (9) Polish isn't needed on varnished furniture. (10) Polish can build up and dull the finish. (11) It can even collect dirt.

(C)

(12) Follow this advice, and your varnished wood furniture will look good and last for a long, long time.

5. Sentence 4: **The major problem with varnished wood is that scratches show up very easily.**

   Which revision should be made to sentence 4?

   (1) replace The with Unfortunately, the
   (2) insert unfortunately, after wood
   (3) insert , unfortunately after scratches
   (4) insert unfortunately after up
   (5) no revision is necessary

TIP Select transitions that match the tone of the writing as well as its meaning. For example, with informal writing, *so* may be a better fit than the more formal *thus*.

6. Which sentence below would be most effective at the beginning of paragraph B?

   (1) Moreover, the following is advice for wood maintenance.
   (2) Most important, you can always clean the wood.
   (3) Fortunately, you can keep varnished wood looking good if you follow this advice.
   (4) Nevertheless, dusting wood is important, but polishing it isn't.
   (5) In contrast, rugs look good on clean, varnished floors.

7. Sentences 5 and 6: **Dust it regularly. Wash it occasionally with paint thinner, which dissolves dirt.**

   The most effective combination of sentences 5 and 6 would include which group of words?

   (1) and, of course,
   (2) and, in addition,
   (3) and, as a result,
   (4) and, for example,
   (5) and, in contrast,

8. Sentences 9 and 10: **Polish isn't needed on varnished furniture. Polish can build up and dull the finish.**

   Which is the best way to write the underlined portion of the text? If the original is the best way, choose option (1).

   (1) furniture. Polish
   (2) furniture, polish
   (3) furniture, so polish
   (4) furniture. In fact, polish
   (5) furniture, likewise polish

Answers start on page 285.

Directions: This is a ten-minute practice test. After ten minutes, mark the last question you finished. Then complete the test and check your answers. If most of your answers were correct, but you didn't finish, try to work faster next time. Choose the one best answer to each question.

Questions 1 through 4 refer to the following brochure.

Eastport Senior Council

(1) This is about the Eastport Senior Council. (2) Our mission is to provide emergency funds directly to people living in Eastport who are over age 64. (3) These direct payments are for basic needs such as medicine, transportation, buying heat, and food. (4) Social Security, a major source of income for many of our senior citizens, also helps with these needs. (5) In addition, we finance activities that improve the quality of life of seniors in Eastport. (6) Our program includes exercise groups as well as educational and cultural activities. (7) All activities are free to senior citizens. (8) The goal of helping ease loneliness and isolation.

1. Sentence 1: **This is about the Eastport Senior Council.**

   Which revision should be made to sentence 1?

   (1) replace sentence 1 with The Eastport Senior Council is an organization in Eastport.
   (2) replace sentence 1 with The Eastport Senior Council offers charitable programs.
   (3) replace sentence 1 with The Eastport Senior Council is not just a group of older people, you know; it is a group that works for them.
   (4) replace sentence 1 with The Eastport Senior Council is a nonprofit charitable organization dedicated to serving the elderly.
   (5) no revision is necessary

2. Sentence 3: **These direct payments are for basic needs such as medicine, transportation, buying heat, and food.**

   Which is the best way to write the underlined portion of the text? If the original is the best way, choose option (1).

   (1) medicine, transportation, buying heat, and food
   (2) medicine, transportation, heat, and food
   (3) medicine, transportation, buying heat and buying food
   (4) medical needs, getting rides, buying heat, and food
   (5) medical needs, transportation needs, heating needs, and for food

3. Which revision should be made to the text?

   (1) remove sentence 4
   (2) move sentence 5 to follow sentence 2
   (3) begin a new paragraph after sentence 6
   (4) remove sentence 6
   (5) replace sentence 7 with Never charging a fee.

4. Sentences 7 and 8: **All activities are free to senior citizens. The goal of helping ease loneliness and isolation.**

   The most effective combination of sentences 7 and 8 would include which group of words?

   (1) Free activities help ease
   (2) Being free, senior citizens in activities help
   (3) Free, and with a goal of helping
   (4) citizens, and to help
   (5) citizens, with the goal of helping ease

Questions 5 through 9 refer to the following paragraph.

Credit Checks

(1) You been turned down for a credit card or mortgage? (2) Here's how to check your credit rating to find out why. (3) You have the right to read your credit report and correct any errors, says the Fair Credit Reporting Act. (4) To do so, request the name and address of the credit bureau employed by the bank or credit card company that denied you a loan or credit. (5) The credit bureau must furnish you a copy of its report. (6) After examining the report, the credit bureau must correct or remove faulty information. (7) General credit information is kept for seven years, bankruptcy may be reported for ten years. (8) For more information, contact the National Foundation for Consumer Credit.

5. Sentence 1: **You been turned down for a credit card or mortgage?**

    What correction should be made to sentence 1?

    (1) replace You with Have you
    (2) replace You with So you
    (3) insert a comma after down
    (4) insert a comma after card
    (5) no correction is necessary

6. Sentence 3: **You have the right to read your credit report and correct any errors, says the Fair Credit Reporting Act.**

    The most effective revision of sentence 3 would begin with which words?

    (1) Says the Fair Credit Reporting Act,
    (2) Having the right to read
    (3) To read your credit report and correct
    (4) According to the Fair Credit Reporting Act,
    (5) You have, it says in the Fair Credit Reporting Act,

7. Sentence 4: **To do so, request the name and address of the credit bureau employed by the bank or credit card company that denied you a loan or credit.**

    Which is the best way to write the underlined portion of the text? If the original is the best way, choose option (1).

    (1) so, request
    (2) so. Request
    (3) so, requesting
    (4) so, in fact, request
    (5) so, therefore request

8. Sentence 6: **After examining the report, the credit bureau must correct or remove faulty information.**

    What correction should be made to sentence 6?

    (1) change After examining to After you examine
    (2) remove the comma after report
    (3) insert so after the comma
    (4) insert a comma after correct
    (5) no correction is necessary

9. Sentence 7: **General credit information is kept for seven years, bankruptcy may be reported for ten years.**

    Which is the best way to write the underlined portion of the text? If the original is the best way, choose option (1).

    (1) years, bankruptcy
    (2) years bankruptcy
    (3) years and bankruptcy
    (4) years. For example, bankruptcy
    (5) years, while bankruptcy

Answers start on page 286.

GED WRITING LINK Making Transitions Between Ideas

Transitions, or connections, between sentences and paragraphs help a reader understand the relationships between the ideas. Practice using transitions in your own writing to make your writing clear and interesting to your reader.

If you were the parent who received this note, you might have a little trouble understanding what the teacher is saying.

> Dear Mrs. Aboledo,
>
> Your son did not complete his reading assignment in class. He spent his time socializing with his classmates. He was required to stay inside during the recess period today.
>
> Respectfully,
> Mr. Morgan

The message would be easier to understand if the teacher used transitions to show the relationship between the ideas.

> Your son did not complete his reading assignment in class. **Instead,** he spent his time socializing with classmates. **Therefore,** he was required to stay inside during the recess period today.

Suppose you were Mrs. Aboledo and received that note. Complete the following letter to your son's teacher. Use the transitions to guide what you write.

Dear Mr. Morgan,

I'm sorry to hear that Alfredo caused trouble in class and did not get his work done. His father and I have talked with him. As a result,

_____

_____

In addition, _____

_____

_____

Sincerely,
Mrs. Aboledo

Your responses should follow logically from the transitions *As a result* and *In addition*. You might have written something like, *As a result, he promises to pay attention and work in class. In addition, he will do extra reading at home.*

The Personal Link

1. **Make a list of things you enjoy doing. Begin your list like this:**

   One thing I enjoy doing in my free time is _____

   _____

   In addition,

   _____

   _____

   _____

2. **Imagine you had a day that you could spend in any way you wished. In your journal, write down some thoughts about how you would use this time. Try to use transition words in and between sentences.**

The GED Link

1. **Read the following topic. On a separate sheet of paper, write as many thoughts as you can about the topic. Don't try to write complete sentences.**

   > If there were more hours in a day, do you think people would spend them working or relaxing? Give examples to support your opinion. Use your personal observations, experience, and knowledge.

2. **Use your ideas from this GED Link to write at least two paragraphs about the topic above. Group related ideas and write about each group in a paragraph with a topic sentence. If you like, use some of your ideas from the Personal Link, too. Include transitions between sentences and paragraphs.**

Edit

Read your paragraphs, and make sure you used transitions. Then check for other errors.

Portfolio Reminder

Put your edited paragraphs from the GED Link in your portfolio.

Answers start on page 286.

Unit 2 Cumulative Review **Organization**

Directions: Choose the <u>one best answer</u> to each question.

<u>Questions 1 through 3</u> refer to the following letter.

Dean Bowman
Accounting Director
KraftMade, Inc.
2001 Blue Mound Road
Milwaukee, WI 53202

Dear Mr. Bowman:

(A)

(1) Please consider my application for the entry-level bookkeeping position that you recently advertised in the Sunday *Heights*. (2) I check the help-wanted ads every week. (3) I believe that my skills fit the position very well.

(B)

(4) After obtaining my GED last March with the highest math test score recorded at Oakdale Night School, I completed three bookkeeping courses there. (5) In order to pay for my tuition, I worked in the night school office. (6) I gained valuable practical experience.

(C)

(7) Then in January, I was accepted at Hills Community College. (8) I am currently taking two courses at night in advanced math and basic accounting. (9) I plan to be an accounting major. (10) I look forward to meeting you and discussing the position further. (11) As you will see, I am very serious about becoming a successful bookkeeper. (12) I believe my skills, experience, and determination will be a valuable asset to your company.

Respectfully,
Joshua Rice

1. Which revision should be made to paragraph A?

   (1) move sentence 1 to the end of the paragraph
   (2) remove sentence 1
   (3) begin a new paragraph after sentence 2
   (4) remove sentence 2
   (5) no revision is necessary

2. Sentence 6: **I gained valuable practical experience.**

   The most effective revision of sentence 6 would begin with which group of words?

   (1) Valuable practical experience
   (2) Gaining valuable practical experience
   (3) As a result of my work, I
   (4) For instance, I gained
   (5) Even though I gained

3. Which revision should be made to paragraph C?

   (1) move sentence 7 to the end of paragraph B
   (2) remove sentence 8
   (3) begin a new paragraph with sentence 10
   (4) move sentence 11 to the end of the paragraph
   (5) remove sentence 12

TIP

Reading the entire GED passage is essential to understanding its organization. By understanding the piece as a whole, you can see the relationships between the sentences and the paragraphs.

Questions 4 through 7 refer to the following passage.

Home Furniture Repair

(A)

(1) Don't throw furniture away if you notice a mark or stain on a wooden table or desk. (2) Use the following techniques to repair it.

(B)

(3) A commercial furniture cleaner will usually make those marks disappear. (4) If the cleaner doesn't work, gently rub the area with a little lighter fluid until the spot is gone. (5) Very stubborn stains may require a solution of oxalic acid, applied with a sponge or brush.

(C)

(6) To remove ink, rub the stain with steel wool, sandpaper, or pumice. (7) Ink stains that have set require bleaching. (8) As with other stubborn stains, use oxalic acid. (9) For ink, an extra step is needed.

(D)

(10) When the oxalic acid is almost dry, dissolve borax in hot water, and apply the solution to the ink spot. (11) When that area dries, refinish the wood.

(E)

(12) Follow these techniques, and you won't have to worry when someone spills again.

TIP

When a GED question asks you to choose an effective topic sentence for a paragraph, be sure to read the whole paragraph. Then choose the option that includes all the ideas in the paragraph and that outlines or sums them up.

4. Sentences 1 and 2: **Don't throw furniture away if you notice a mark or stain on a wooden table or <u>desk. Use</u> the following techniques to repair it.**

Which is the best way to write the underlined portion of the text? If the original is the best way, choose option (1).

(1) desk. Use
(2) desk. Instead, use
(3) desk, using
(4) desk and use
(5) desk by using

5. Which sentence below would be most effective at the beginning of paragraph C?

(1) All different kinds of things can stain wood.
(2) Common household products are often all that you need.
(3) Some commercial cleaning products cost more than others.
(4) Go to the store and buy a commercial furniture cleaner.
(5) Some stains are quite easy to get out.

6. Sentence 9: **For ink, an extra step is needed.**

Which revision should be made to sentence 9?

(1) remove sentence 9
(2) move sentence 9 to follow sentence 6
(3) move sentence 9 to follow sentence 7
(4) replace <u>For</u> with <u>However, for</u>
(5) no revision is necessary

7. Which revision would improve the text, "Home Furniture Repair"?

(1) remove sentence 10
(2) remove sentence 11
(3) combine paragraphs C and D
(4) move sentence 12 to the end of paragraph D
(5) no revision is necessary

Questions 8 through 11 refer to the following memo.

Memo

To: Bell Company Staff
From: Aisha Smith, Director of Community Relations

(A)

(1) This year our employees collected a record 120 presents for the annual gift drive for Children's Hospital. (2) Last year, we didn't collect as many presents. (3) Every department participated, so congratulations are due all around! (4) Now we're looking for at least ten volunteers to wrap the presents. (5) It's faster and more fun with more people. (6) The present wrapping will start at 3 P.M. on Monday.

(B)

(7) Will you drive or distribute the presents on Tuesday? (8) We are especially eager for drivers with station wagons, vans, or trucks. (9) Even if you can't drive, you can help distribute gifts at the hospital. (10) Please sign up by this Friday, so we can assign everyone to a carpool.

(C)

(11) Bell Company—and the children at the hospital—will thank you for your effort! (12) For more information, or to volunteer for this wonderful opportunity, contact Paul at extension 3746.

8. Sentence 2: **Last year, we didn't collect as many presents.**

Which revision should be made to sentence 2?

(1) replace sentence 2 with Last year's collection organizers didn't do as well as we did.
(2) replace sentence 2 with Next year, we should try to double that number.
(3) move sentence 2 to follow sentence 3
(4) move sentence 2 to the end of paragraph A
(5) remove sentence 2

9. Which revision would improve the memo?

(1) begin a new paragraph with sentence 4
(2) begin a new paragraph with sentence 5
(3) begin a new paragraph with sentence 6
(4) combine paragraphs A and B
(5) no revision is necessary

10. Sentence 7: **Will you drive or deliver the presents on Tuesday?**

Which revision should be made to sentence 7?

(1) replace sentence 7 with We need some help Tuesday.
(2) replace sentence 7 with Let's not forget about Tuesday.
(3) replace sentence 7 with Can you distribute presents on Tuesday?
(4) replace sentence 7 with On Tuesday, we will need help delivering the presents.
(5) replace sentence 7 with The presents will need to be delivered, of course.

11. Sentence 11: **Bell Company—and the children at the hospital—will thank you for your effort!**

Which revision should be made to sentence 11?

(1) remove sentence 11
(2) move sentence 11 to the end of paragraph A
(3) move sentence 11 to the end of paragraph C
(4) replace sentence 11 with Thank you.
(5) no revision is necessary

Questions 12 through 14 refer to the following passage.

Child-Proofing Your Home

(A)

(1) Every year, millions of children are injured by hazards in their homes. (2) You can help prevent these injuries by installing child safety devices such as safety locks, latches, gates, and anti-scald devices.

(B)

(3) You can put safety locks and latches on cabinets and drawers. (4) They keep children from pulling drawers down on their heads. (5) They also keep knives and sharp tools out of reach. (6) A lock or latch can prevent children from getting into household cleaners or medicines, too.

(C)

(7) Safety gates help childproof a home, too. (8) Placed between rooms, gates can keep a child out of unsafe spaces. (9) The gates should also be installed at the top of stairs to prevent tumbles. (10) Gates that screw into the wall are more secure than pressure gates. (11) Anti-scald devices regulate water temperature in your home and can prevent burns. (12) A plumber can install them in showers and faucets. (13) Set the temperature to 120 degrees Fahrenheit, which is hot enough for washing but won't burn the skin.

(D)

(14) To find out about the reliability and cost of childproofing devices, talk to friends or look at consumer-oriented magazines. (15) Consumer magazines cover safety subjects ranging from alarm systems to liability insurance. (16) These safety devices can give you a new kind of security in your home.

12. Sentence 3: **You can put safety locks and latches on cabinets and drawers**.

    Which revision should be made to sentence 3?

    (1) replace sentence 3 with Safety locks and latches protect children in several ways.
    (2) replace sentence 3 with Install safety locks on drawers.
    (3) move sentence 3 to the end of paragraph A
    (4) remove sentence 3
    (5) no revision is necessary

13. Which revision should be made to paragraph C?

    (1) remove sentence 7
    (2) move sentence 7 to follow sentence 10
    (3) remove sentence 9
    (4) begin a new paragraph with sentence 11
    (5) begin a new paragraph with sentence 12

14. Sentence 15: **Consumer magazines cover safety subjects ranging from alarm systems to liability insurance.**

    Which revision should be made to sentence 15?

    (1) replace sentence 15 with In fact, consumer magazines can tell you about everything from alarm systems to liability insurance.
    (2) replace sentence 15 with You can get consumer magazines from the library, or you can subscribe to them.
    (3) move sentence 15 to the end of the paragraph
    (4) remove sentence 15
    (5) no revision is necessary

Upgrading Computers

(A)

(1) You can make your old computer last longer by upgrading its central processing unit (CPU), or "brain." (2) The CPU sends instructions to various programs and files on a computer. (3) An upgrade to the CPU will make your old computer send out instructions faster. (4) You can find the three kinds of upgrade kits in most computer stores. (5) The first is an internal plug-in to the motherboard. (6) The second is an external addition that stacks on top of your current CPU. (7) The last kind is a replacement CPU.

(B)

(8) Now you know that upgrades improve your computer's performance. (9) Don't expect it to work twice as fast, however. (10) Old computers have their limits, no matter how much you upgrade them.

15. Which revision would improve the text, "Upgrading Computers"?

(1) remove sentence 2
(2) begin a new paragraph with sentence 4
(3) move sentence 4 to the end of paragraph A
(4) begin a new paragraph with sentence 5
(5) no revision is necessary

16. Sentence 8: **Now you know that upgrades improve your computer's performance.**

Which revision should be made to sentence 8?

(1) replace sentence 8 with Any CPU upgrade is good for your computer.
(2) replace sentence 8 with Upgrades can be somewhat expensive, but they are necessary.
(3) replace sentence 8 with Upgrades improve your computer's performance.
(4) replace sentence 8 with My favorite, ONTIME, will improve your computer's performance.
(5) replace sentence 8 with As soon as you install the upgrade, you will notice an improvement in your computer's performance.

Writing Links Review

Write two or three paragraphs on the following topic. As you are writing, keep the following Writing Links topics in mind.

☑ Does each paragraph have enough supporting details? (Writing Link, pages 102–103)

☑ Does each paragraph have a clear topic sentence? (Writing Link, pages 110–111)

☑ Did I divide my writing into paragraphs correctly and effectively? (Writing Link, pages 118–119)

☑ Did I use transitions between my ideas? (Writing Link, pages 126–127)

There is an old saying, "Better safe than sorry." Do you agree or disagree with the idea that it is better to be cautious than to take risks? Use details and examples from your own knowledge, observation, and personal experiences to support your ideas.

Answers start on page 287.

Cumulative Review Performance Analysis
Unit 2 • Organization

Use the Answers and Explanations starting on page 287 to check your answers to the Unit 2 Cumulative Review. Then use the chart to figure out the skill areas in which you need more practice.

On the chart, circle the questions you answered correctly. Write the number correct for each skill area. Add the number of questions that you got correct on the Cumulative Review. If you feel that you need more practice, go back and review the lessons for the skill areas that were difficult for you.

Questions	Number Correct	Skill Area	Lessons for Review
1, 8, 11, 14	____/4	Unity and coherence	7
5, 10, 12, 16	____/4	Topic sentences	8
3, 7, 9, 13, 15	____/5	Paragraph divisions	9
2, 4, 6	____/3	Transitions	10
TOTAL CORRECT	____/16		

UNIT 3

Usage

As you studied in Unit 2, well-organized ideas are critical to effective writing. In this unit, you will learn how grammar and usage are applied correctly in sentences. Grammar is the rules of our language. Usage is the way we construct ideas and use our language. Usage concepts include subject-verb agreement, verb forms and tenses, and pronoun use and agreement. Mastery of grammar rules and usage concepts will help you to avoid some common errors to produce effective pieces of writing.

Usage is an important content area on the GED Language Arts, Writing Test. About 30 percent of the multiple-choice questions will be based on usage concepts.

Using correct grammar in your writing helps you construct your ideas in a meaningful way.

The lessons in this unit include:

Lesson 11: **Subject-Verb Agreement**
The subject and verb of a sentence must agree; that is, they must both be either singular or plural. In some cases, you may need to determine the form of the subject or what the subject is. You will learn a variety of rules and strategies to help you ensure subject-verb agreement.

Lesson 12: **Verb Forms**
Every verb has four principal parts. These parts make the different forms of verbs tell when something happens. Many of the verbs that we commonly use are called regular verbs. You will also learn the forms of special verbs, called irregular verbs.

Lesson 13: **Verb Tenses**
Verbs change their form to show when an action takes place—past, present, or future. These forms are called simple verb tenses. In addition to the simple tenses, there are three perfect tenses that show the time relationship between events.

Lesson 14: **Pronouns**
A pronoun is a word that can be used in place of the name of a person, place, or thing. Just as a subject and its verb must agree, a pronoun must agree with its antecedent, the word that it is replacing.

WRITING LINKS

In this unit, you will practice these types of writing skills:

○ Being Organized

○ Introducing and Concluding

○ Verbs in Your Writing

○ Point of View

To use the skills in this unit in your own writing, see the Writer's Checklist on page 316.

GED SKILL Subject-Verb Agreement

Agreement in Number

The subject and the verb in a sentence must both be singular (referring to one) or plural (referring to more than one). That is called **subject-verb agreement.** To check that these two parts of a sentence agree, first decide whether the subject is singular or plural. Then make the verb match the subject.

RULE 1 With a singular subject, use a singular verb.

Don't agree: Ms. Lopez plan the company party every year.
Agree: Ms. Lopez plans the company party every year.

The singular subject *Ms. Lopez* needs a singular verb, *plans.*

RULE 2 With a plural subject, use a plural verb.

Don't agree: Volunteers helps with the planning.
Agree: Volunteers help with the planning.

The plural subject *Volunteers* needs a plural verb, *help.*

RULE 3 With compound subjects joined by *and,* use a plural verb.

Don't agree: Pauline and Ray knows some fun activities.
Agree: Pauline and Ray know some fun activities.

The subject *Pauline and Ray* refers to two people. The plural verb *know* agrees with the compound subject.

TIP

Most verbs ending in *s* are singular: *she walks, he sings.* Most verbs not ending in *s* are plural: *we walk, they sing.* Verbs used with the pronouns *I* and singular *you* are exceptions: *I am, I walk, you are, you sing.*

If the subject is singular, write *S.* If it is plural, write *P.* If it is compound, write *C.*

_____ a. Often, hospital patients have lung problems when lying on their backs.

_____ b. Sometimes good medical solutions is very low tech.

_____ c. Lung problems and pneumonia improves when patients sit up in bed.

_____ d. Congestion is less likely to occur in this position.

You were correct if you wrote *P* for *sentences a* and *b, C* for *sentence c,* and *S* for *sentence d. Good medical solutions* is plural, so the verb should be *are* in *sentence b. Lung problems and pneumonia* is compound, so the verb should be *improve* in *sentence c.*

A. Choose and write the correct verb.

1. (mean, means) Fluoridated water _____ fewer Americans are toothless today.

2. (visit, visits) Grandparents and children alike _____ their dentist for regular check-ups.

3. (love, loves) Dentists _____ the fact that there is more awareness about dental hygiene.

4. (is, are) Despite the decrease in major dental work, dental careers _____ still popular.

5. (is, are) Dentistry _____ changing its focus to orthodontia, or correcting irregular teeth.

B. Edit the passage by making the verbs agree with the subjects. There are ten subject-verb agreement errors.

Say "Southern California vacation" to most people, and they ~~thinks~~ *think* of Hollywood, the ocean, or Disneyland. In reality, many people is skipping the usual tourist sites to visit the Mojave Desert, the most famous desert in the state.

The Mojave extend hundreds of miles east, jutting into Nevada. Spring and fall is the best times to see the desert, although many people go in other seasons, too. Winters isn't too bad, but summers can be fierce. Even in summer, the weather varies greatly, from scorching heat at midday to chilly nights.

The desert are filled with magnificent sights. Petroglyph Canyons, Fossil Falls, and Red Rock Canyon Park has fascinating natural spectacles. Death Valley is its own geology course. Perhaps most surprisingly, the exotic plants is varied, dramatic, and thriving. Beautiful flowers and cacti has adapted to the heat and dryness. The one part of the desert you won't see is the San Andreas Fault. It cross the Mojave outside of Los Angeles.

C. Write about the following topic.

The passage you edited in Exercise B described a fascinating place. Write a paragraph about a special place you know. Then edit it for subject-verb agreement and other errors.

Interrupting Phrases and Inverted Order

When a subject is separated from the verb by a word or phrase, it may be hard to decide which word is the subject. It also may be difficult to find the subject when it comes after the verb.

Decide on the subject of the sentence by asking yourself *who* or *what* the sentence is about. Then check for agreement between the subject and the verb.

RULE 1 Make the verb agree with the subject, not with the words or phrases that come between them.

Don't agree: Directions to the company party is easy.
Agree: Directions ~~to the company party~~ are easy.

If you didn't ask yourself what the sentence was about, you might think the subject is the singular *party,* not the plural *directions.*

RULE 2 Make the subject and verb agree even when the subject comes after the verb, as in a question or in a sentence that starts with *there* or *here.*

Don't agree: Is her assistant and Ms. Gross carpooling to the party?
Agree: Are her assistant and Ms. Gross carpooling to the party?

Don't agree: There are a map showing three different routes.
Agree: There is a map showing three different routes.
Agree: There are maps showing three different routes.

Put a check mark by the sentence in which the subject and the verb do not agree.

_____ a. There are three computer science courses still open for this semester.

_____ b. Students in one computer course learn how to search the Internet.

_____ c. Professor Hardy, along with his teaching assistants, have them surfing the Internet the first day of class.

You were correct if you chose *option c.* The subject of that sentence is *Professor Hardy,* so the verb should be the singular *has: Professor Hardy, along with his teaching assistants, has them surfing the Internet the first day of class.*

TIP

Interrupting phrases often begin with words showing relationships, such as *along with, as well as, among, at, between, of, in,* or *with.* Some interrupting phrases are set off by commas: *Sam, of all the brothers, is single.*

A. Underline the subject once and the verb twice in each sentence. If they do not agree, rewrite the sentence so that they do. If they already agree, write *Correct*.

1. Engagement <u>rings</u> for fiancées <u><u>is</u></u> not as popular as they used to be.

   Engagement rings for fiancées are not as popular as they used to be.

2. There is the problem of rising prices for the rings.

   _____

3. Have the price of engagement rings really risen that much?

   _____

4. A small diamond today cost an average of $550.

   _____

5. One of the famous jewelry houses says that prices will not go down.

   _____

6. Employed college graduates with a steady income buys about half of all engagement rings sold.

   _____

B. Edit this question-and-answer column for subject-verb agreement. There are six errors.

Q: What ~~are~~ *is* the status of the Land Bank bill in the state legislature?

A: The House and Senate has passed similar versions of the bill. The bill, officially named the Act for Preservation of Open Lands, allow individual towns to decide how best to preserve open land. The final versions of the House and Senate bill are due this week. There is still two major unresolved questions: Can towns vote to add a 1 percent tax on real estate purchases to fund land purchases? Do the state provide matching funds? State representatives and senators on both sides of the issue expects negotiations to continue all month.

C. Write about the following topic.

   The question-and-answer column you edited in Exercise B explained how one state is trying to preserve open land. Write a paragraph about an issue in your state that you think is important. Then edit the paragraph for subject-verb agreement and other errors.

Answers start on page 288.

Special Cases in Subject-Verb Agreement

collective noun
a word that refers to a group of people or things

RULE 1 A **collective noun** refers to a group of people or things. When the subject of a sentence is a collective noun in which the group is acting as one, use a singular verb.

Don't agree: The budget <u>committee</u> <u>are meeting</u> today.
Agree: The budget <u>committee</u> <u>is meeting</u> today.

A committee is made up of more than one person, but the people in the committee are acting together as one, so the subject is singular.

RULE 2 Some words do not refer to a specific person or thing. It is not always clear whether a word like this is singular or plural. Use this chart to help you determine subject-verb agreement.

Always Singular			Always Plural	Singular or Plural	
one	anybody	someone	several	all	any
each	anyone	something	few	some	part
much	anything	nobody	both	none	half
other	everybody	no one	many	most	
another	everyone	nothing			
either	everything				
neither	somebody				

Don't agree: <u>Everyone</u> <u>are</u> welcome!
Agree: <u>Everyone</u> <u>is</u> welcome!

RULE 3 When compound subjects are joined by *or, nor, either-or,* or *neither-nor,* make the verb agree with the nearest subject.

Don't agree: Neither the managers nor <u>Jay Holt</u> <u>are</u> planning to attend.
Agree: Neither the managers nor <u>Jay Holt</u> <u>is</u> planning to attend.

The compound subject is joined by *neither-nor,* so the verb should agree with the singular *Jay Holt,* which is the nearest subject.

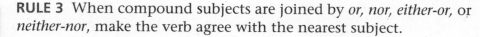

TIP

If you can substitute the pronoun *it* for a collective noun used as a subject, use a singular verb.

Write *A* if the subject and verb agree and *D* if they do not.

_____ a. My family has two vehicles: a van and a pick-up truck.

_____ b. Both has fairly low insurance rates.

_____ c. Neither my husband nor I has ever had an accident.

You were correct if you wrote *A* for *sentence a.* The collective noun *family* is singular. You were also correct if you wrote *D* for *sentences b* and *c.* The pronoun *Both* means two, so it is plural: *Both have fairly low insurance rates.* With the pair *neither-nor,* the verb should agree with the nearest subject: *Neither my husband nor I have ever had an accident.*

A. Write S if the subject is singular and P if it is plural. Then write the correct form of the verb.

1. __S__ (wish) Hills Learning Center _____wishes_____ to invite Governor Banks to speak at our GED ceremony.

2. _____ (open) Either one of the teachers or the director always _____ the ceremony.

3. _____ (receive) Everyone _____ his or her certificate from the director.

4. _____ (award) The learning center staff _____ outstanding students.

5. _____ (sponsor) Either the School Board or previous graduates _____ a buffet.

6. _____ (return) Many from former GED classes _____ for the ceremony.

7. _____ (miss) Nobody _____ the occasion if he or she can help it.

B. Edit this letter to the editor for subject-verb agreement errors. There are nine errors.

Dear Editor:

Neither the housing committee nor I ~~believes~~ *believe* that the land developers simply "forgot" to build affordable housing. Everyone know it is required as part of all large development projects. The town council are not allowed to grant waivers to developers, and nothing hurt the city more than neglect of the law.

Our great workforce make this town a dream town for business. But great workers won't stay without a place to live. Many needs affordable housing. The whole community agree that ignoring regulations decreases the quality of life for all of us. Our community are a desirable place to live because students, business people, and service workers live here.

At the council meeting next week, someone have to insist the town council choose between the community or the developers.

Janice Gold, Chair, Fair Housing Committee

C. Write about the following topic.

The letter you edited in Exercise B was about the conflict between affordable housing and real estate development. Write a paragraph about a conflict in your community that is important to you. Then edit your paragraph for subject-verb agreement problems and other errors.

Answers start on page 289.

Directions: Choose the <u>one best answer</u> to each question.

<u>Questions 1 through 5</u> refer to the following paragraph.

Houseplant Care

(1) Here are some advice for taking care of your houseplants if you need to be away for a period of time. (2) First, don't worry about fertilizing them. (3) Houseplants from the African violet to a zonal geranium lasts for months without needing fertilizer. (4) On the other hand, nothing survive without water. (5) To simplify watering, put the plants in a bathtub that gets light from a window. (6) Layers of paper protects the tub from getting scratched, so place them down first. (7) Then place bricks on the paper and the plants on the bricks. (8) Finally, fill the tub so that you cover all the bricks with water, but you don't cover the pots. (9) Then the roots can absorb the water through the holes in the bottoms of their pots.

1. Sentence 1: **Here are some advice for taking care of your houseplants if you need to be away for a period of time**.

   What correction should be made to sentence 1?

   (1) replace <u>Here are some</u> with <u>Some</u>
   (2) change <u>are</u> to <u>is</u>
   (3) insert a comma after <u>houseplants</u>
   (4) change <u>need</u> to <u>needs</u>
   (5) insert a comma after <u>away</u>

2. Sentence 3: **Houseplants from the African violet to a zonal geranium lasts for months without needing fertilizer.**

   What correction should be made to sentence 3?

   (1) insert a comma after <u>violet</u>
   (2) insert a comma after <u>geranium</u>
   (3) change <u>lasts</u> to <u>lasting</u>
   (4) change <u>lasts</u> to <u>last</u>
   (5) no correction is necessary

3. Sentence 4: **On the other hand, nothing survive without water.**

   What correction should be made to sentence 4?

   (1) replace <u>On the other hand, nothing</u> with <u>Not</u>
   (2) change <u>nothing</u> to <u>not one</u>
   (3) change <u>survive</u> to <u>survives</u>
   (4) change <u>survive</u> to <u>surviving</u>
   (5) no correction is necessary

4. Sentence 6: **Layers of paper <u>protects</u> the tub from getting scratched, so place them down first.**

   Which is the best way to write the underlined portion of the text? If the original is the best way, choose option (1).

   (1) protects
   (2) protect
   (3) protecting
   (4) is protecting
   (5) are protecting

5. Sentence 8: **Finally, fill the tub so that you cover all the bricks with water, but you don't cover the pots.**

   If you rewrote sentence 8 beginning with

   <u>Finally, fill the tub so that the bricks, but not the pots,</u>

   the next words should be

   (1) is covered
   (2) are covered
   (3) covered
   (4) covering
   (5) be covered

Questions 6 through 9 refer to the following warranty.

Fair Point Company

(A)

(1) Fair Point Company guarantee that the Excel Disk Player will be free from defects in materials and workmanship for a period of one year. (2) Occasionally, however, a defect occurs. (3) Then the company, at no charge to the owner for parts, have the option of replacing or repairing the machine. (4) The customer, because of misuse, might cause a defect, malfunction, or failure in which case this warranty becomes invalid.

(B)

(5) This warranty is valid only when the *Model JDS-23* is returned to a Fair Point Products dealer. (6) This warranty cover a period of one year from the date of purchase. (7) To establish that your warranty is valid, you must also submit a copy of the original sales slip.

6. Sentence 1: **Fair Point Company guarantee that the Excel Disk Player will be free from defects in materials and workmanship for a period of one year.**

   What correction should be made to sentence 1?

   (1) change guarantee to have guaranteed
   (2) change guarantee to guarantees
   (3) insert a comma after materials
   (4) insert a comma after workmanship
   (5) no correction is necessary

TIP

To check subject-verb agreement in a sentence with a phrase between the subject and verb, read the sentence without the phrase. For example, *The shed next to the apartments (is) (are) painted red.* Read the sentence without the phrase. *The shed (is) (are) painted red.* Now it's easy to see that the subject *shed* requires the singular verb *is.*

7. Sentence 3: **Then the company, at no charge to the owner for parts, have the option of replacing or repairing the machine.**

   Which is the best way to write the underlined portion of the text? If the original is the best way, choose option (1).

   (1) have
   (2) having
   (3) has
   (4) it has
   (5) is having

8. Sentence 4: **The customer, because of misuse, might cause a defect, malfunction, or failure in which case this warranty becomes invalid.**

   If you rewrote sentence 4 beginning with

   If a defect, malfunction, or failure

   the next words should be

   (1) are caused
   (2) might cause
   (3) will be caused
   (4) is caused
   (5) being caused

9. Sentence 6: **This warranty cover a period of one year from the date of purchase.**

   What correction should be made to sentence 6?

   (1) replace This with However, this
   (2) change cover to covers
   (3) change cover to covering
   (4) insert a comma after year
   (5) no correction is necessary

Answers start on page 289.

Directions: This is a ten-minute practice test. After ten minutes, mark the last question you finished. Then complete the test and check your answers. If most of your answers were correct, but you didn't finish, try to work faster next time. Choose the one best answer to each question.

Questions 1 through 4 refer to the following text.

Tips for Trip Preparation

(A)

(1) Families have different ways of planning for vacations or other trips. (2) Here's a way of getting the small tasks done, while stretching out the fun of anticipation.

(B)

(3) One member of the family records tasks as everyone call out his or her ideas. (4) Some examples from a typical planning session might include these tasks: find and clean out the cooler, cancel newspapers, have mail held at post office, check reservations, ask neighbor to feed cat. (5) Other people who might take care of your pet are relatives or friends. (6) When no one can think of any more ideas, assign a "must-be-completed-by" date to each item. (7) Then each family member initials the tasks he or she will be responsible to complete. (8) The tasks get completed. (9) Then they get checked off the list.

(C)

(10) This way, the whole family shares in the preparation. (11) Everyone gets excited as the day of departure approaches.

1. Which sentence below would be most effective at the beginning of paragraph B?

    (1) There are many things that must be done to prepare for a trip.
    (2) Preparing for a trip doesn't have to be a chore.
    (3) Don't forget to allow time for packing.
    (4) It's a good idea for everyone to help.
    (5) Together, make a list of things that must be done before the departure date.

2. Sentence 3: **One member of the family records tasks as everyone call out his or her ideas.**

    What correction should be made to sentence 3?

    (1) replace One with Next, one
    (2) change records to record
    (3) insert a comma after tasks
    (4) change call to calls
    (5) no correction is necessary

3. Which revision should be made to paragraph B?

    (1) remove sentence 4
    (2) remove sentence 5
    (3) move sentence 5 to follow sentence 6
    (4) move sentence 6 to follow sentence 3
    (5) no revision is necessary

4. Sentences 8 and 9: **The tasks get completed. Then they get checked off the list.**

    The most effective combination of sentences 8 and 9 would include which group of words?

    (1) completed, checking off the list
    (2) while completing each task
    (3) Getting completed, the tasks
    (4) As the tasks get completed,
    (5) Checking the tasks off the list,

Questions 5 through 8 refer to the following passage.

What Happens to That Old Car?

(A)

(1) Long after drivers have forgotten about the wrecked cars they left behind in the junkyard, most vehicles continue along the road to the steel mill. (2) In fact, the junkyard on the outskirts of town only one stop in the auto recycling process.

(B)

(3) Junk dealers flatten a car's frame. (4) Fluids and combustible parts are removed before that, though. (5) A car body that is flattened in this way is very valuable because it is mainly steel and iron. (6) The flattened car is then sold to a scrap dealer.

(C)

(7) The job of scrap dealers is to prepare material for reuse by the steel industry. (8) To do this, they first shred and crush the flattened hulk into small chunks. (9) Strong magnets separate out the steel and iron from these chunks, finally, aluminum, magnesium, fabric, plastic, and glass are sorted out and recycled, if possible.

5. Sentence 2: **In fact, the junkyard on the outskirts of town only one stop in the auto recycling process.**

What correction should be made to sentence 2?

(1) remove the comma after fact
(2) insert a comma after town
(3) insert is after town
(4) insert being after town
(5) insert a comma after stop

6. Sentences 3 and 4: **Junk dealers flatten a car's frame. Fluids and combustible parts are removed before that, though.**

The most effective combination of sentences 3 and 4 would include which group of words?

(1) frame, even though fluids
(2) flatten a car's frame and remove
(3) The removal of fluids and combustible parts
(4) After the fluids and combustible parts are removed,
(5) Although fluids and combustible parts

7. Sentence 7: **The job of scrap dealers is to prepare material for reuse by the steel industry.**

What correction should be made to sentence 7?

(1) change is to are
(2) remove is
(3) insert being after is
(4) insert a comma after reuse
(5) no correction is necessary

8. Sentence 9: **Strong magnets separate out the steel and iron from these chunks, finally, aluminum, magnesium, fabric, plastic, and glass are sorted out and recycled, if possible.**

Which is the best way to write the underlined portion of the text? If the original is the best way, choose option (1).

(1) chunks, finally,
(2) chunks. Finally,
(3) chunks finally,
(4) chunks, finally
(5) chunks finally

Answers start on page 290.

When you write, it's best to have an idea of what you want to say before you begin. Clear organization will help your reader understand your main idea.

Look at the following letter to a store manager from an unhappy customer. The writer did not take the time to organize her thoughts.

> I can't tell you how upset I am. Whenever I go to other stores, I receive good service and am treated like a welcome customer. I tried to buy a new couch at your store because our old one is torn and worn. I received very poor service. At first, I couldn't even find a salesperson to help me. Then the person who did come to "help" me was no help at all.

The customer did not mention the poor service she received until late in her letter. There are also ideas that are not relevant to the purpose of the letter, such as good service at other stores. Now look at how the customer could have organized the ideas in the letter.

1. Explain purpose of letter—why I'm writing
2. Describe poor service I received—no help, no answers
3. Tell how I would like to be helped

Can you see that this organization would help make the writer's main idea more clear? Here is an example of a letter that follows this organization.

> I can't tell you how upset I am because of the poor service I received at your store. I tried to buy a new couch, but at first, I couldn't even find a salesperson to help me. Then the person who did come to "help" was no help at all. He could not answer my questions about price or delivery time. I want to take advantage of your year-end sale, but would also like to receive better service. Would you be able to answer my questions?

Number these ideas to show how they should be organized in a response letter from the store manager to the unhappy customer.

_____ State how the situation will be handled

_____ Apologize for poor service

_____ Explain why poor service occurred—small staff due to illness, new employee

You were correct if you numbered the ideas *3, 1,* and *2.* That order of ideas would produce a well-organized response to the complaint letter.

The Personal Link

1. In your journal, write about a product you own or a service you receive with which you are particularly satisfied or dissatisfied.

2. Plan a letter to a company, store, or restaurant about that product or service. On a separate sheet of paper, organize your thoughts from your journal.

The GED Link

1. Read the following topic. On a separate sheet of paper, write as many thoughts as you can about the topic. You may want to use some of your ideas from the Personal Link.

> Why do so many customers complain about poor service in stores and restaurants? State your point of view. Use your experience, observations, and knowledge to support it.

2. Use the following plan to organize your thoughts.
    Customers complain about poor service because

    First reason: _____

    Second reason: _____

    Third reason: _____

3. On the same sheet of paper, write at least two paragraphs about the topic above. Use your ideas from the GED Link.

Edit

Read your paragraphs, and make sure the organization of your ideas is clear. Then check your writing for other errors.

Portfolio Reminder

Put your paragraphs from the GED Link in your portfolio.

Answers start on page 290.

GED SKILL Verb Forms

Regular Verbs

Every verb has four principal parts: present, present participle, past, and past participle. **Regular verbs** form these parts by adding *-d, -ed,* or *-ing* to their present forms. Most verbs are regular verbs.

regular verb
a verb that forms its principle parts by adding *-d, -ed,* or *-ing* to the present form

helping verb
(also called **auxiliary verb**) a form of the verb *be* or *have* used with the main verb to make participle forms

RULE 1 Form the present participle by adding *-ing* to the present form of the verb. The present participle always uses a **helping verb** in forms of the verb *be.*

Present: Scientists remind us to reduce the amount of trash right now.
Present participle: They are reminding us we must act immediately.

RULE 2 Form the past by adding *-d* or *-ed* to the present form of a verb. The past tense does not use a helping verb.

Present: Today, many towns require people to recycle paper, wood, and plastic.
Past: Years ago, towns required people to recycle paper only.

RULE 3 Form the past participle by adding *-d* or *-ed* to the present form of the verb and use a helping verb. The helping verbs used with the past participle are forms of the verb *be* or *have.*

Present: Today, towns recycle everything they can.
Past: In 2000 alone, my town recycled 178 tons of plastic.
Past participle: In fact, my town has recycled more plastic than any other town in the state.

Put a check mark next to the sentence in which a verb form is used incorrectly.

_____ a. Researchers have learned that optimistic people live longer.

_____ b. One study looked at over 800 Minnesotans for 30 years.

_____ c. About 20 percent more optimists than pessimists living today.

_____ d. Apparently, optimists watch out for themselves more carefully and are less prone to depression

You were correct if you chose *option c*. The sentence needs a helping verb to go along with the present participle *living*: *About 20 percent more optimists than pessimists are living today.*

TIP

A sentence with a present participle without a helping verb is often a sentence fragment: *About 20 percent more optimists than pessimists living today.*

A. Write a correct form of each verb. There may be more than one correct form.

1. (learn) Researchers have _____*learned*_____ that optimistic people live longer.

2. (confirm) "Our study has _____ our hypothesis," said one doctor.

3. (demonstrate) "It _____ that attitude is always important to health."

4. (look) "We have _____ at over 800 Minnesotans for 30 years."

5. (sort) Researchers _____ volunteers into three categories: optimists, pessimists, or combinations of the two.

6. (live) About 20 percent more optimists than pessimists are _____ today.

7. (watch) Apparently, they _____ out for themselves more carefully and are less prone to depression.

B. Edit the incorrect verb forms. There may be more than one way to correct some errors. There are eight errors.

Dear Customer,

In an effort to provide you with advanced Internet services, we have ~~upgrade~~ *upgraded* our network

to support higher bandwidth applications. Our records are indicating that you own a B-45

cable modem. Our upgraded network requiring a new modem for your system to avoid

interruptions in your high-speed Internet service. We are ordered a new modem for your

computer. The replacement modem providing all the same features and benefits as your

current modem.

Self-installation is designed to be fast and easy. We encouraging you to follow the

step-by-step instructions to complete the self-installation process. If you would like us

to install it for you, we are needing three to six weeks to schedule an appointment with

a technician. Customers who are agreeing to install the modem themselves will receive a

$50 credit.

C. Write about the following topic.

The letter you edited in Exercise B is from a business to a customer. Write a letter to a business as one of its customers. Ask about a product or service you are interested in. Then edit the letter for incorrect verb forms and other errors.

Answers start on page 290.

Irregular Verbs

irregular verb
a verb whose past forms are not made by adding -d or -ed to the simple present

Unlike regular verbs, **irregular verbs** usually change their spelling pattern in a variety of ways to form the past and past participle. Study the irregular verbs in these charts.

RULE 1: Form the past participle for some irregular verbs by adding -*en* or -*n* to the **present.**

Present	Past	Past Participle
blow	blew	blown
drive	drove	driven
eat	ate	eaten
fall	fell	fallen
give	gave	given

Present	Past	Past Participle
know	knew	known
rise	rose	risen
see	saw	seen
take	took	taken
write	wrote	written

RULE 2: Form the past participle for some irregular verbs by adding -*en* or -*n* to the **past.**

Present	Past	Past Participle
break	broke	broken
choose	chose	chosen

Present	Past	Past Participle
freeze	froze	frozen
speak	spoke	spoken

RULE 3: Form the past and past participle for some irregular verbs by changing the vowel from *i* in the present to *a* in the past and *u* in the **past participle.**

Present	Past	Past Participle
begin	began	begun
drink	drank	drunk
ring	rang	rung

Present	Past	Past Participle
sing	sang	sung
sink	sank	sunk
swim	swam	swum

RULE 4: Some irregular verbs do not follow a pattern.

Present	Past	Past Participle
buy	bought	bought
come	came	come
do	did	done

Present	Past	Past Participle
fly	flew	flown
go	went	gone
lose	lost	lost

Put a check mark next to the sentence that uses the irregular verb form incorrectly.

_____ a. It has begun snowing hard.

_____ b. I have drove my car into a snow bank.

You were correct if you chose *option b*. The correct past participle of *drive* is *driven: I have driven my car into a snow bank.*

A. Write a past form for each verb in parentheses.

1. (go) My wife and I _____*went*_____ to Puerto Rico last year.

2. We (drive) _____ around the island, (eat) _____ in wonderful

   restaurants, and (swim) _____ in warm Gulf waters.

3. My parents (give) _____ us airplane tickets for our anniversary.

4. My wife (is) _____ pregnant at the time, so we (know) _____

   it would be our last trip for a while.

5. We visited and (speak) _____ to cousins I had never (see)

   _____ before.

6. My parents (come) _____ from Puerto Rico over 25 years ago, when

   I (be) _____ just a baby.

B. Edit this conversation for correct verb forms. There are ten errors.

Anna: Hi! I haven't seen you in a while. You ^have^ done something to yourself, haven't you?

Kevin: Since I seen you last, I begun a special diet and workout routine.

Anna: What maked you do it?

Kevin: Ever since I been a teenager, I been overweight. Finally, I took my doctor's advice and

   gone on a serious diet. I breaked some bad habits, too. For instance, I haven't ate a

   late-night snack or fast food in months. Altogether, I losed 32 pounds.

Anna: You look great! Keep up the good work!

Kevin: Thanks! I certainly hope to!

C. Write about the following topic.

   In Exercise B you edited a conversation about changing behavior. Write a paragraph
describing something you have changed or would like to change about yourself. Then
edit it for incorrect verb forms and other errors.

Answers start on page 290.

Directions: Choose the one best answer to each question.

Questions 1 through 4 refer to the following letter.

Highland Park Delivery Service
304 Park Street
Highland Park, Missouri

Dear Mr. Brand:

(A)

(1) Please accept my application for the job of van driver that you listed in the *Hamlet News*. (2) I have driven a car for four years, and I have holded my category D license for six months. (3) In your ad, you mentioned that you need a driver in Highland Park. (4) I know the town well because I growed up in that area.

(B)

(5) I also have very suitable work experience. (6) I drived a delivery van for Economy Stores for two years. (7) In addition, I have been a substitute driver for Metro Service since May.

(C)

(8) Please consider me for the job. (9) I look forward to hearing from you.

Regards,
Jason May

1. Sentence 2: **I have driven a car for four years, and I have holded my category D license for six months.**

   What correction should be made to sentence 2?

   (1) remove have before driven
   (2) change driven to drove
   (3) remove the comma after years
   (4) change holded to held
   (5) insert a comma after license

2. Sentence 4: **I know the town well because I growed up in that area.**

   What correction should be made to sentence 4?

   (1) replace I know with Knowing
   (2) change know with knowed
   (3) remove because
   (4) change growed to grew
   (5) no correction is necessary

3. Sentence 6: **I drived a delivery van for Economy Stores for two years.**

   Which is the best way to write the underlined portion of the text? If the original is the best way, choose option (1).

   (1) drived
   (2) drove
   (3) done drove
   (4) driven
   (5) been driving

4. Sentence 7: **In addition, I have been a substitute driver for Metro Service since May.**

   Which is the best way to write the underlined portion of the text? If the original is the best way, choose option (1).

   (1) have been
   (2) has been
   (3) am been
   (4) am being
   (5) been

Questions 5 through 9 refer to the following article.

New Teenage Concern

(A)

(1) The priorities of teenagers been changed over the years. (2) Of course, many teens are still concerned about grades, friends, dates, and jobs. (3) In recent years, however, they have took on a new and very adult issue, the fear of violence.

(B)

(4) A major newspaper and television poll has indicated that teens thinking between 15 and 50 percent of their peers carry knives in school. (5) About 40 percent feeling personally afraid. (6) Yet over 80 percent also said that no one in their families was a victim of violence in the past two years. (7) Sadly, speaking about their fears is not something many teens have done with their parents.

5. Sentence 1: **The priorities of teenagers been changed over the years**.

   Which is the best way to write the underlined portion of the text? If the original is the best way, choose option (1).

   (1) been changed
   (2) have changed
   (3) has changed
   (4) changing
   (5) are changed

6. Sentence 3: **In recent years, however, they have took on a new and very adult issue, the fear of violence.**

   What correction should be made to sentence 3?

   (1) remove the comma after years
   (2) change have to has
   (3) change took to taken
   (4) insert they have after issue,
   (5) no correction is necessary

7. Sentence 4: **A major newspaper and television poll has indicated that teens thinking between 15 and 50 percent of their peers carry knives in school.**

   What correction should be made to sentence 4?

   (1) insert a comma after newspaper
   (2) change has indicated to indicating
   (3) insert be before thinking
   (4) change thinking to think
   (5) change carry to carries

8. Sentence 5: **About 40 percent feeling personally afraid.**

   Which is the best way to write the underlined portion of the text? If the original is the best way, choose option (1).

   (1) feeling
   (2) is feeling
   (3) been feeling
   (4) feeled
   (5) feel

9. Sentence 7: **Sadly, speaking about their fears is not something many teens have done with their parents.**

   If you rewrote sentence 7 beginning with

   Sadly, many teens

   the next words should be

   (1) not been speaking
   (2) have not spoke
   (3) have done speaking
   (4) have not spoken
   (5) not speaking

Answers start on page 291.

GED Mini-Test • Lesson 12

Directions: This is a ten-minute practice test. After ten minutes, mark the last question you finished. Then complete the test and check your answers. If most of your answers were correct, but you didn't finish, try to work faster next time. Choose the one best answer to each question.

Questions 1 through 4 refer to the following advice.

How to Foster Independence in Children

(A)

(1) Does your young child's behavior seem to be saying, "I want to do things for myself"? (2) Here's something you can do to help children when they begun to show their need for independence.

(B)

(3) Encourage them to dress themselves with some easy-on and easy-off clothes. (4) For example, buy pull-on pants with elastic waists. (5) Some parents has printed their child's name in permanent ink on the inside back of each garment. (6) This encourages children to learn the difference between the back and the front of clothes and to recognize their names. (7) Young children can also manage a zippered jacket with a large pull very well. (8) They need an adult to connect it at first.

(C)

(9) Learning to dress themselves being a big step for children, and they are justifiably proud when they accomplish it.

1. Sentence 2: **Here's something you can do to help children when they begun to show their need for independence.**

   What correction should be made to sentence 2?

   (1) change Here's to Here are
   (2) change do to to do. To
   (3) change children when to children. When
   (4) change begun to begin
   (5) change to show to showing

2. Sentence 5: **Some parents has printed their child's name in permanent ink on the inside back of each garment.**

   Which is the best way to write the underlined portion of the text? If the original is the best way, choose option (1).

   (1) has printed
   (2) have printed
   (3) are printed
   (4) to print
   (5) printing

3. Sentences 7 and 8: **Young children can also manage a zippered jacket with a large pull very well. They need an adult to connect it at first.**

   The most effective combination of sentences 7 and 8 would include which group of words?

   (1) although at first
   (2) more important, at first
   (3) at first, for instance,
   (4) whether or not the first
   (5) in the first case

4. Sentence 9: **Learning to dress themselves being a big step for children, and they are justifiably proud when they accomplish it.**

   What correction should be made to sentence 9?

   (1) change Learning to Learn
   (2) insert a comma after themselves
   (3) change being to is
   (4) remove the comma
   (5) change are to be

Asleep on the Job

(A)

(1) People in warm climates were knowing about the advantages of an afternoon rest for a long time. (2) Now corporate America is "waking up" to the advantages of a midday doze. (3) One reason for these revelations come from a study showing $18 billion was lost to poor job performance by an exhausted workforce. (4) To fight this waste, some companies have even opened "napping rooms" for their employees. (5) Both is pleased with the results. (6) When they wake up, workers are more alert, quicker to react, and they solve problems better than their sleepy co-workers. (7) Moreover, they spend more time on the job and less time at the coffee machine because they need less caffeine.

(B)

(8) It seems there are times when being asleep on the job pays off!

5. Sentence 1: **People in warm climates were knowing about the advantages of an afternoon rest for a long time**.

   What correction should be made to sentence 1?

   (1) insert a comma after climates
   (2) change were knowing to been knowing
   (3) change were knowing to have known
   (4) insert a comma after rest
   (5) no correction is necessary

6. Which revision would improve the text, "Asleep on the Job"?

   (1) move sentence 2 to follow sentence 3
   (2) remove sentence 2
   (3) begin a new paragraph with sentence 3
   (4) move sentence 5 to the end of paragraph A
   (5) move sentence 7 to the beginning of paragraph B

7. Sentence 3: **One reason for these revelations come from a study showing $18 billion was lost to poor job performance by an exhausted workforce.**

   What correction should be made to sentence 3?

   (1) change come to comes
   (2) change was lost to been lost
   (3) change was lost to were losed
   (4) insert a comma after performance
   (5) no correction is necessary

8. Sentence 5: **Both is pleased with the results.**

   Which is the best way to write the underlined portion of the text? If the original is the best way, choose option (1).

   (1) is pleased
   (2) are pleased
   (3) pleased
   (4) pleasing
   (5) being pleased

9. Sentence 6: **When they wake up, workers are more alert, quicker to react, and they solve problems better than their sleepy co-workers.**

   The most effective revision of sentence 6 would include which group of words?

   (1) and they are better at solving problems
   (2) being better problem solvers
   (3) and so solve problems better
   (4) and solve more problems better
   (5) and better at solving problems

Answers start on page 291.

When you write a piece with several paragraphs, it is important to include an introduction and a conclusion. An **introduction** at the beginning tells the reader what you plan to write about. A **conclusion** at the end restates what you have just written.

Suppose a supervisor wanted to write a memo about the goal of creating a safe workplace. Look at the notes he organized.

Safety procedures save—
1. time
2. money
3. lives

A good introduction to the memo should tell the workers what the memo will be about. Here is the introduction that the supervisor wrote:

A safe workplace is an extremely important goal here at Technosystems, Inc. If our workplace is not safe, we cannot do our jobs. Remember that safety can save time, money, and most importantly, lives.

Following this introduction, the supervisor gave examples of how time, money, and lives can be saved by following safety procedures. Then he wrote a conclusion to summarize the main points of his memo.

Put a check mark next to the better conclusion for the supervisor's memo.

_____ Conclusion 1

As you know, safety is our number one goal at Technosystems. When we are safe workers, we save time by not making mistakes. By following safety precautions, we also save money because workers are not getting injured. But most importantly, we can save lives just by following good safety practices.

_____ Conclusion 2

Safety is an important goal at Technosystems, but so is profit. If we work very hard and follow safety rules, we will be able to meet our sales and production goals, and our whole team will receive its maximum bonus.

You were correct if you chose *Conclusion 1*. It reviews the main points that the writer discussed in the memo.

The Personal Link

1. **In your journal, write about a goal that is important to you.** For example, maybe your goal is to organize your finances. Or, perhaps your goal is to raise money for a cause that you feel strongly about, such as cancer research, a local food pantry, or a toxic waste cleanup.

2. **On a separate sheet of paper, write a letter that tells a friend about your goal. Use your ideas from your journal. Include an introduction and a conclusion.**

The GED Link

1. **Read the following topic. On a separate sheet of paper, write as many thoughts as you can about the topic. You may want to use some of your ideas from the Personal Link.**

> How important is it to set goals in life? Explain your answer. Use your own observations, experiences, and knowledge.

2. **On the same sheet of paper, write at least three paragraphs about the topic above. Use your ideas from the GED Link.**

Edit

Read your paragraphs. Be sure you have included an introduction that tells what your writing will be about and a conclusion that reviews what you have written. Then check your writing for other errors.

Portfolio Reminder

Put your paragraphs from the GED Link in your portfolio.

Answers start on page 292.

Lesson 13

GED SKILL Verb Tenses

Simple and Perfect Tenses

Verbs change to show when an action takes place or when a condition is true. These are called **verb tenses.**

RULE 1 Use the simple tenses for actions or for conditions that are usually true.

- The **present tense** expresses that an action takes place now or that a condition is true now.
- The **past tense** expresses that an action took place or that a condition was true in the past.
- The **future tense** expresses that an action will take place or that a condition will be true in the future. Use the helping verbs *will* or *shall* with the present form.

Present: Mr. Gomez <u>advises</u> Paula to apply for another job.
Past: He <u>worked</u> with Paula on a special project last year.
Future: Paula <u>will bring</u> her résumé to the office next Thursday.

RULE 2 Use **perfect tenses** for more complex time relationships.

The perfect tenses always use a helping verb that is a form of the verb *have* plus the past participle.

- The **present perfect tense** expresses an action that began in the past and is already completed or continues into the present. Use *have* or *has* with the past participle.
- The **past perfect tense** expresses an action that was completed in the past before another past action began. Use *had* with the past participle.
- The **future perfect tense** expresses a future action that will begin and end before another future action begins. Use *will have* with the past participle.

Present perfect: I <u>have sent</u> along her application to Ms. Hall.
Past perfect: Previously, Ms. Hall <u>had considered</u> only graduates.
Future perfect: Paula <u>will have graduated</u> by June.

Put a check mark next to the correct sentence.

_____ a. The conference has ended before we arrived.

_____ b. The conference had ended before we arrived.

You were correct if you checked *option b.* In that sentence, the past perfect tense is correctly used because it describes a past action that was completed (*conference ended*) before the second action began (*we arrived*).

---

verb tense
tells when an action takes place or when a condition is true

TIP

In perfect tenses, only the helping verb, *have,* changes form. The past participle stays the same:
We have worked.
We had worked.
We will have worked.

A. Complete each sentence with a form of the verb in parentheses that shows an appropriate tense. Some verbs may have more than one correct form.

1. (vote) Last March the town _____*voted*_____ on the Allman Street site for the new fire station.

2. (start) Bell Contracting _____ the construction already.

3. (break) It _____ ground for the project in June.

4. (finish) It _____ erecting the station within the year.

5. (sign) The town _____ a contract with the company even before the March vote.

6. (provide) The state _____ some money for the project in the budget.

7. (expect) Everyone _____ the vote for a new sales tax to pass in November.

8. (raise) By next year, the town _____ the balance through the tax.

B. Edit this paragraph to correct the verb tenses. There are 11 errors.

Many major failures of the last century ~~happen~~ *happened* through folly, arrogance, or carelessness. Mistakes were made by individuals, enterprises, and nations alike. In mid-century, an aviator named Douglas Corrigan makes an incredible error. He was supposed to land in California on a trip from Brooklyn, but he flown to Ireland instead. Not surprisingly, that earns him the nickname "Wrong-Way Corrigan." The country of Chile also goes through hard times because of a careless mistake. A stockbroker accidentally typed "buy" instead of "sell," and an enormous chunk of the country's economy is destroyed. During the "Great Leap Forward," the Chinese government enforces a new "technological" agriculture. Instead of increasing the food supply, however, production fallen drastically. Widespread famine follows. There been even disasters in outer space. For example, an unmanned landing probe to Mars mysteriously disappears at a cost of several billion dollars.

C. Write about the following topic.

The paragraph in Exercise B discussed some major mistakes in history. Write a paragraph about a mistake you have made. It could be a funny mistake or a serious mistake. Then edit the paragraph for problems with verb tenses and for other errors.

Answers start on page 292.

Consistency and Sequence

The verb tenses within a sentence or paragraph should be consistent—all present, all past, or all future—unless the meaning requires a change in verb tense.

Clues in the sentence or paragraph often show which tense should be used. Sometimes other verbs in a sentence can tell you what tense you need. Other times you may have to read a whole paragraph to figure out the correct tense.

RULE 1 Avoid unnecessary shifts in verb tense within a sentence or paragraph.

Inconsistent: Last Wednesday, a woman from my office sat down next to me. She acts like she had never seen me before.

Consistent: Last Wednesday, a woman from my office sat down next to me. She acted like she had never seen me before.

In the first sentence, *Last Wednesday* indicates the past tense, so the verb *sat* is correct. Because the action in the second sentence takes place at the same time, it, too, should be the past tense, *acted.*

RULE 2 In a complex sentence, use the same verb tense in each clause unless the action in the second clause occurs at a different time.

Incorrect: When I said hello, she does not react.

Correct: When I said hello, she did not react.

Both actions occurred in the past, so both should be past tense. But look at this example:

Incorrect: If she behaves this rudely again, I become very upset.

Correct: If she behaves this rudely again, I will become very upset.

In the first sentence, the verbs *behave* and *become* are both in the present tense. However, the action in the second clause will occur *after* the action in the first clause, so the verb *become* should be changed to the future tense *will become.*

Put a check mark next to the sentence with an incorrect tense shift.

_____ a. Huan needs a job, so he goes to an employment agency.

_____ b. Huan got an application form and sat down to fill it out.

_____ c. He was interviewed after he completes the form.

_____ d. He was told that Mr. Fry will let him know next week.

You were correct if you chose *option c.* Both actions were completed in the past, so the verbs should be consistent: *He was interviewed after he completed the form.*

A. Underline the word or words in each sentence that are clues to the correct tense to use. Then complete the sentences with a form of the verb in parentheses.

1. (turn) When boys _____*turn*_____ 18, they <u>have</u> to register for the draft.

2. (state) The law _____*states*_____ that all male U.S. citizens and immigrant aliens have to register within 30 days of their eighteenth birthday.

3. (receive) Within 90 days of registering, men _____*will receive*_____ an acknowledgment in the mail.

4. (be) Registering for the draft does not mean you _____*are*_____ in the army, however.

5. (order) Congress and the president _____*ordered*_____ a draft call-up in the early 1970s for the Vietnam War.

6. (have, draft) The government _____*has*_____ not _____*drafted*_____ anyone into the military since 1973.

7. (call) It _____*will call*_____ up draftees again only if there is a war or national emergency.

B. Edit the errors in verb tense in this article on setting limits. There are 11 errors.

    Do
~~Did~~ you feel as if you say no to your children too often? Psychologists had some helpful

suggestions for setting limits. For instance, if your child will ask you for a new toy or a trip to

the ice cream store, say you need some time to decide. Saying "give me a minute" allows

you time to think about the situation before you will have answered. Your children must

understand that if they insist on an immediate answer, then the answer was no. If they have

given you time to think, however, your answer may be yes.

    Here's another tactic for setting limits. Tell your children they will have to convince you

that their request was valid. Your children learned how to negotiate, and you will make a fairer

decision. If you are upset or worn out, be clear that it had not been a good time for you to

make a decision. Tell them that you decide after you calm down. Distracted answers often are

poor ones, as your children soon has learned.

C. Write about the following topic.

    The article you edited in Exercise B gave advice about setting limits. Write a paragraph about advice you would give to people who feel they give in to others too often. Then edit the article for shifts in verb tense and other errors.

Answers start on page 292.

Directions: Choose the <u>one best answer</u> to each question.

<u>Questions 1 through 5</u> refer to the following letter.

Dear Customer:

(A)

(1) Thank you for shopping with Way More Sales. (2) We have been pleased to be your resource for quality home goods. (3) We regret that your order has been delayed. (4) We are waiting for the product from our vendors and will ship it within the next thirty days. (5) Upon arrival of this product at our warehouse, we will ship it to you.

(B)

(6) If you prefer to cancel your order, please be calling our service department at any time. (7) Credit card orders will not be charged until shipment is made. (8) We will appreciate your patience and look forward to serving you again.

1. Sentence 2: **We have been pleased to be your resource for quality home goods.**

   What correction should be made to sentence 2?

   (1) change <u>have</u> to <u>had</u>
   (2) change <u>have been</u> to <u>are</u>
   (3) change <u>be</u> to <u>have been</u>
   (4) insert a comma after <u>resource</u>
   (5) no correction is necessary

2. Sentence 4: **We are waiting for the product from our vendors and <u>will ship</u> it within the next thirty days.**

   Which is the best way to write the underlined portion of the text? If the original is the best way, choose option (1).

   (1) will ship
   (2) had shipped
   (3) are shipping
   (4) shipped
   (5) be shipping

3. Sentence 5: **Upon arrival of this product at our warehouse, we will ship it to you.**

   If you rewrote sentence 5 beginning with

   <u>We will ship the product as soon as it</u>

   the next word or words should be

   (1) will have arrived
   (2) were arriving
   (3) arrives
   (4) is arriving
   (5) arriving

4. Sentence 6: **If you prefer to cancel your order, please be calling our service department at any time.**

   What correction should be made to sentence 6?

   (1) change <u>prefer</u> to <u>are preferring</u>
   (2) remove the comma after <u>order</u>
   (3) replace <u>order, please</u> with <u>order. Please</u>
   (4) change <u>be calling</u> to <u>call</u>
   (5) no correction is necessary

5. Sentence 8: **We <u>will appreciate</u> your patience and look forward to serving you again.**

   Which is the best way to write the underlined portion of the text? If the original is the best way, choose option (1).

   (1) will appreciate
   (2) have appreciated
   (3) are appreciating
   (4) will have appreciate
   (5) appreciate

Safe Produce

(A)

(1) Consumers know for many years that growers treat produce with pesticides and other chemicals. (2) For example, a number of years ago consumers become angry when they learned about Alar, a chemical used to make apples and grapes larger and more colorful. (3) The problem, both then and today, is that consumers often choose produce that looked appealing. (4) Such consumer behavior only encourages growers to use chemicals that make fruits and vegetables more attractive.

(B)

(5) The Alar issue, however, did drive some consumers to organic groceries and farmer's markets instead. (6) As there is an increase in consumer demand for pesticide-free produce, there will be more produce growers focusing on organic growing methods. (7) Others may turn to genetic engineering of fruits and vegetables, which raises its own safety issues.

6. Sentence 1: **Consumers <u>know</u> for many years that growers treat produce with pesticides and other chemicals.**

Which is the best way to write the underlined portion of the text? If the original is the best way, choose option (1).

(1) know
(2) known
(3) knowed
(4) will know
(5) have known

TIP Use the passage as a whole to decide which tense is correct in a GED item. In some cases, a verb may be grammatically correct in the sentence but may not work with the meaning of the passage as a whole.

7. Sentence 2: **For example, a number of years ago consumers become angry when they learned about Alar, a chemical used to make apples and grapes larger and more colorful.**

What correction should be made to sentence 2?

(1) remove the comma after <u>example</u>
(2) change <u>become</u> to <u>became</u>
(3) insert a comma after <u>angry</u>
(4) insert <u>have</u> after <u>they</u>
(5) no correction is necessary

8. Sentence 3: **The problem, both then and today, is that consumers often choose produce that <u>looked</u> appealing.**

Which is the best way to write the underlined portion of the text? If the original is the best way, choose option (1).

(1) looked
(2) had looked
(3) has looked
(4) looks
(5) is looking

9. Sentence 6: **As there is an increase in consumer demand for pesticide-free produce, there will be more produce growers focusing on organic growing methods.**

If you rewrote sentence 6 beginning with

<u>As consumer demand for pesticide-free produce increases, more produce growers</u>

the next words should be

(1) will be focusing
(2) will have focused
(3) will focus
(4) are focusing
(5) focusing

Answers start on page 293.

Directions: This is a ten-minute practice test. After ten minutes, mark the last question you finished. Then complete the test and check your answers. If most of your answers were correct, but you didn't finish, try to work faster next time. Choose the <u>one best answer</u> to each question.

<u>Questions 1 through 4</u> refer to the following article.

Cleaning Tips for Clothes

(A)

(1) The dry cleaner at Acme Movie Studios offer these professional tips on ways to keep your clothes looking good after many wearings.

(B)

(2) First, never remove the fabric content or care labels from a garment. (3) Within a few months, you surely forget which clothes must be hand-washed and which must be dry-cleaned. (4) When you dry-clean your clothes, have matching pieces cleaned together. (5) Keep clothes away from deodorants, perfumes, and hair sprays, which are especially damaging to silks, wools, and garments made from synthetics. (6) Always tell your dry cleaner about stains because the more he or she knows about a stain, the more likely it can be removed. (7) When a piece of clothing is stained, wash it or take it to the cleaners as soon as possible. (8) If it stays in your laundry bag too long the stain will set and become permanent.

1. Sentence 1: **The dry cleaner at Acme Movie Studios offer these professional tips on ways to keep your clothes looking good after many wearings.**

   What correction should be made to sentence 1?

   (1) change offer to offers
   (2) change offer to offered
   (3) insert a comma after tips
   (4) replace tips on with tips. On
   (5) no correction is necessary

2. Sentence 3: **Within a few months, you surely forget which clothes must be hand-washed and which must be dry-cleaned.**

   Which is the best way to write the underlined portion of the text? If the original is the best way, choose option (1).

   (1) surely forget
   (2) had surely forgotten
   (3) had surely forgot
   (4) will surely forget
   (5) will have surely forgot

3. Sentence 5: **Keep clothes away from deodorants, perfumes, and hair sprays, which are especially damaging to silks, wools, and garments made from synthetics.**

   The most effective revision of sentence 5 would include which group of words?

   (1) silks, wool clothes, and garments made from synthetics
   (2) silks and wools and garments made from synthetics
   (3) silk clothes and woolen and synthetic garments
   (4) silks, wools, and garments that were made from synthetic materials
   (5) silks, wools, and synthetics

4. Sentence 8: **If it stays in your laundry bag too long the stain will set and become permanent.**

   What correction should be made to sentence 8?

   (1) change stays to is staying
   (2) replace stays with been
   (3) insert a comma after long
   (4) change will set to has set
   (5) insert a comma after set

Questions 5 through 9 refer to the following letter.

Dear Customer:

(A)

(1) The Bureau of Rates had approved a slight decrease in base rates for customers of Tower Electric Company last November 1. (2) This adjustment will reduce your electric bill between 3 and 4 percent over the next year. (3) The reduction is the result of two major factors. (4) First, Tower recently merged with Consolidated Electric Company. (5) This merger results in substantial savings by combining the supply sources and management costs of the two companies. (6) Second, the Bureau approved a very low increase in distribution rates last year these funds provided an upgrade of the Tower facility.

(B)

(7) Your charges are based on how much energy you use. (8) Also whether you are a residential or commercial customer. (9) If you have any questions about the charges on your bill, please call the Customer Service Number listed on your Tower Electric bill.

5. Sentence 1: **The Bureau of Rates had approved a slight decrease in base rates for customers of Tower Electric Company last November 1.**

What correction should be made to sentence 1?

(1) remove had
(2) change had approved to will approve
(3) insert a comma after rates
(4) insert a comma after Company
(5) no correction is necessary

6. Which revision would improve the letter?

Begin a new paragraph

(1) with sentence 2
(2) with sentence 3
(3) with sentence 4
(4) with sentence 6
(5) with sentence 9

7. Sentence 5: **This merger results in substantial savings by combining the supply sources and management costs of the two companies.**

What correction should be made to sentence 5?

(1) change results to will result
(2) change results to resulted
(3) insert a comma after savings
(4) replace savings by with savings. By
(5) no correction is necessary

8. Sentence 6: **Second, the Bureau approved a very low increase in distribution rates last year these funds provided an upgrade of the Tower facility.**

Which is the best way to write the underlined portion of the text? If the original is the best way, choose option (1).

(1) year these
(2) year, these
(3) year. These
(4) year and these
(5) year, however, these

9. Sentences 7 and 8: **Your charges are based on how much energy you use. Also whether you are a residential or commercial customer.**

The most effective combination of sentences 7 and 8 would include which group of words?

(1) Based on how your energy use,
(2) Your charges not only being based
(3) on energy use, also whether
(4) you use as well as whether you
(5) Residential or commercial customers are charged

Answers start on page 293.

You have just learned the importance of keeping verb tenses consistent within a piece of writing. It is also necessary to use the correct verb tense.

The verbs you choose have an effect on your writing. Verbs show action. When you use verbs that show strong and specific action, your writing becomes livelier and much more interesting to read.

Read the paragraph below. See whether you think the writer's ideas are vivid and interesting.

> Hard work is good. When people do not get handouts, but instead use their own abilities, they can do okay. My uncle, who was a Vietnam War veteran, is a good example. He did not have a leg because of a landmine. When he came home, he immediately started his own business. He was a husband, father, business owner, and citizen until he died last year. He will be remembered forever as someone who did not take help from others to make a life for himself.

Did the writer use descriptive, vivid verbs? No, the verbs in the paragraph include forms of verbs like *be, get, make, do,* and *take.* It is hard to picture the action or get a feel for the subject—the writer's uncle.

Now read the following paragraph. The underlined verbs paint a clearer picture of the writer's uncle and his life.

> Hard work pays off. When people do not beg or expect handouts, but instead develop and rely on their own abilities, they can succeed. My uncle, who fought in the Vietnam War, demonstrated this perfectly. Having lost his leg when a landmine exploded, he arrived home and immediately got to work building his own business. He married, fathered three children, thrived as a business owner, and served as a citizen until he died last year. He will live on in our memories forever as someone who did not rely on help from others to create a life for himself.

Now go back to the two stories again. Read just the underlined verbs in the first paragraph and then in the second. Can you see the difference that specific action verbs make?

Put a check mark next to the sentence with the more specific action verb.

_____ a. No one can do it completely on his or her own.

_____ b. No one can beat the odds on his or her own.

You were correct if you chose *option b.* The verb expression *beat the odds* is much more specific, active, and easy to visualize than *do.*

The Personal Link

1. **Write a paragraph about a time when you needed help from someone. Then write another paragraph about what you will do when someone you know needs help.** Remember that your first paragraph will be in the past tense. The second paragraph will be in the future tense. Use action verbs as much as possible.

2a. **In your journal, write about what it feels like to need help.** Are you the kind of person who is comfortable seeking help, or do you try to handle things on your own?

b. **In your journal, write these verbs: *run, ask, help*. Under each verb, write as many other verbs as you can think of that describe the same action.**

The GED Link

1. **Read the following topic. On a separate sheet of paper, write as many thoughts as you can about the topic. You may want to use some of your ideas from the Personal Link.**

> Who is more courageous—a person who asks for help when he or she needs it or a person who works things out alone? Answer the question, giving examples from your own experience, observations, and knowledge.

2. **On the same sheet of paper, write at least three paragraphs about the topic above. Use your ideas from the GED Link.**

Edit

Read your paragraphs. Be sure you have used specific action verbs and consistent and correct verb tenses. Then check your writing for other errors.

Portfolio Reminder

Put your paragraphs from the GED Link in your portfolio.

Answers start on page 294.

GED SKILL Pronouns

Subject and Object Pronouns

A **personal pronoun** is a word that can be used in place of the name of a person, place, or thing. Depending on the way you use it in a sentence, a personal pronoun can be a subject or an object.

personal pronoun
a word used in place of a noun, which names a person, place, or thing

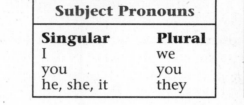

Subject Pronouns		Object Pronouns	
Singular	**Plural**	**Singular**	**Plural**
I	we	me	us
you	you	you	you
he, she, it	they	him, her, it	them

RULE 1 Use a subject pronoun as the subject of a sentence.

Correct:	<u>I</u> am writing about the nomination of Andy Walker for union representative.
Incorrect:	Andy and <u>me</u> work in the same department.
Correct:	Andy and <u>I</u> work in the same department.

RULE 2 Use a subject pronoun when the pronoun that refers to the subject follows a form of the verb *be*.

Incorrect:	The winner of the election will be <u>him</u>.
Correct:	The winner of the election will be <u>he</u>.

TIP

Pronouns in compound subjects with nouns can be tricky. To "hear" if a pronoun is correct, mentally cross out the noun. Which sounds better: ~~Andy and~~ *me work* or ~~Andy and~~ *I work*? *I work* sounds better.

RULE 3 Use an object pronoun as the object of a verb.

Correct:	Joe Burnitz also <u>knows him.</u>
Incorrect:	Andy <u>invited</u> Joe and <u>I</u> to run his campaign.
Correct:	Andy <u>invited</u> Joe and <u>me</u> to run his campaign.

RULE 4 Use an object pronoun as the object of a preposition—a word such as *in, on, of, for, with,* and *between.*

Correct:	Please vote <u>for him.</u>

Put a check mark next to the sentence that uses the correct personal pronoun.

_____ a. Mary asked my husband and I to visit her home.

_____ b. Mary asked my husband and me to visit her home.

You were correct if you checked *option b* because *my husband and me* is the object of the verb *asked.*

A. Write the correct pronouns in the sentences of this interview.

1. (I, me) Thank you for speaking with _____*me*_____, Ms. Dayton. _____*I*_____ understand you are Brooktown's only female motorcycle officer. Do you like the work?

2. (I, me) It was hard for _____ when _____ started five years ago.

3. (they, them) Some men in the division were unhappy. _____ didn't think I could keep up with _____.

4. (she, her) I had a good role model in Sergeant Donna Black. _____ was the first female motorcycle officer in town. The Police Department gave _____ its highest merit award before _____ retired three years ago.

5. (I, me) The men and _____ get along now, though. _____ think that women like Sergeant Black and _____ can bring something different to the job.

6. (we, us) I think _____ often take a different approach to problem solving. Maybe it's a little easier for _____ to avoid confrontations.

B. Change the underlined words in this invitation to pronouns. More than one pronoun is possible.

Dear Friends,

       We
The Wayland Firefighters wish to extend a cordial invitation to our friends to attend the

Annual Firefighters Dance. The dance will be held at the Oak River Club on Friday, May 4,

from 7 P.M. to midnight.

The Four Blue Notes will provide musical entertainment. We wish to thank The Four Blue

Notes for donating their time and talents to The Wayland Firefighters Association. A large

buffet and soft drinks will accompany the music and dancing. The dinner, drinks, and dancing

are all included in the price of the admission ticket.

Reservations are required. Please request your reservations by April 12. As our friends know,

proceeds from this event go to firefighters who are injured in the line of duty.

C. Write about the following topic.

   In Exercise B, you edited an invitation for a dinner and dance. Now write a letter of invitation to an event you would like to host. Then edit the letter for pronoun problems and other errors.

Answers start on page 294.

Possessive Pronouns

Personal pronouns can also be used to show possession.

Possessive Pronouns	
Singular	**Plural**
my, mine	our, ours
your, yours	your, yours
his, her, hers, its	their, theirs

Possession: Greta has <u>her</u> problems. I have <u>mine</u>.

Agreement with Antecedents

antecedent
the noun that a
pronoun takes
the place of

The noun that a pronoun stands for is its **antecedent.** A subject, object, or possessive pronoun must agree with its antecedent.

RULE 1 A pronoun must agree with its antecedent in **number—** singular or plural.

Agree: The <u>Greens</u> are in Room 1215. <u>They</u> love the view.

RULE 2 A pronoun must agree with its antecedent in **gender—** masculine, feminine, or neutral.

Agree: There's a <u>fax</u> for Ms. Vasquez. Bring <u>it</u> to Room 1580.

RULE 3 A pronoun must agree with its antecedent in **person.**

First person: I, we, me, us, my, mine, our, ours
Second person: you, your, yours
Third person: he, she, it, they, him, her, them, his, hers, its, their, theirs

Agree: <u>Martin and I</u> are meeting. <u>We</u> can be reached at home.

RULE 4 When compound antecedents are joined by *or, either-or,* or *neither-nor,* the pronoun should agree with the nearest antecedent.

Correct: Neither the <u>Livingstons</u> nor <u>Kevin</u> is happy with <u>his</u> room.

RULE 5 Use singular pronouns for collective nouns unless the meaning clearly expresses the individuals in the group.

As a unit: The <u>board</u> meets monthly. <u>It</u> is meeting now.
As individuals: The <u>board</u> put <u>their</u> signatures on the budget.

Put a check mark next to the correct sentence.

_____ a. The members of the audience leapt to their feet.

_____ b. The members of the audience leapt to its feet.

You were correct if chose *option a.* The pronoun refers to *members,* so it should be plural.

TIP

To determine which pronoun to use in a sentence, find its antecedent. Decide whether the antecedent is singular or plural or feminine, masculine, or neutral. Then choose a pronoun that agrees with its antecedent on both points.

A. Write an appropriate pronoun in each blank. Underline its antecedent. If there is more than one blank in a sentence, underline the second antecedent twice.

1. I discovered how to make extra-long knitting needles. _____*They*_____ are great for making afghans and large blankets.

2. My kids and I were at the hardware store. _____ were there because _____ was having a great sale.

3. My son Jake wanted to buy half-inch dowels to make a rack for _____ CDs.

4. I got the idea for making knitting needles from dowels, so I bought several of _____.

5. At home I put one of the dowels into a size 15 knitting gauge, and _____ fit perfectly.

6. I held the dowel and shaped one of _____ ends into a point. On its other end I tacked on a bottle cap.

7. I took all the other dowels and did the same to _____.

8. My son is pleased with _____ new rack, and I'm pleased with _____ new needles.

9. My knitting class will laugh when _____ see them.

10. Either my teacher or the other students will want some for _____ own.

B. Read this question to a home-repair advice column. Complete it with pronouns that agree with their antecedents.

My wife and I are fixing up _____*our*_____ new house. _____ is a "handyman's special." The wood floors are very dull. I think _____ were heavily waxed over the years. _____ both would like to remove the wax, and then varnish the wood. Mr. Oldham, the local hardware store owner, said _____ can't varnish over a waxed surface. _____ said that even if we try to get all the wax off, some of _____ will remain. Is he giving _____ good advice? Or do _____ have a better idea for _____ to try? This problem is really frustrating my wife and _____.

C. Write about the following topic.

In Exercise B you edited a question that was written to an advice column. Think about something you need advice on. Write a paragraph detailing your situation and asking for advice. Then edit it for errors in pronoun-antecedent agreement and other errors.

Answers start on page 294.

Pronoun Shifts and Clear References

A **pronoun shift** occurs when the person or number of a pronoun changes incorrectly within a sentence or paragraph.

RULE 1 Avoid shifts in pronoun person or number.

Incorrect: When you hear the shriek of a fire truck's siren, one should pull over and let it pass.

Correct: When you hear the shriek of a fire truck's siren, you should pull over and let it pass.

In the first sentence, there is a shift from the second person pronoun *you* to the third person pronoun *one*.

Incorrect: It makes an unbelievable amount of noise; in fact, they sometimes cause temporary deafness.

Correct: It makes an unbelievable amount of noise; in fact, it sometimes causes temporary deafness.

In the first sentence, the pronoun shifts from the singular *it* to the plural *they*.

An **unclear antecedent** means that a reader cannot be sure of the antecedent of a pronoun.

RULE 2 Avoid ambiguous pronouns with more than one possible antecedent.

Ambiguous: There are special devices firefighters use to open locked doors. They are helpful when a building is on fire.

A reader cannot be sure if *They* refers to *devices* or *firefighters*.

Clear: There are special devices firefighters use to open locked doors. The devices are helpful when a building is on fire.

RULE 3 Avoid vague pronouns without any antecedents.

Vague: Georgia wants to join the fire department because they are community heroes.

There is no antecedent for the pronoun *they*.

Clear: Georgia wants to join the fire department because firefighters are community heroes.

Underline two pronoun problems in these sentences.

I use a monthly bus pass. They say passes are good for public transportation. Some companies can buy passes for their workers at a discount. The passes make them happy.

You were correct if you underlined *They* in the second sentence (it has no antecedent) and *them* in the last sentence (it could refer to either *companies* or *workers*).

A. Rewrite each sentence to correct the underlined pronoun error. You may have to change the verb as well. There is more than one correct way to fix some unclear references.

1. Becky was pleased that she got several job offers because <u>it</u> gave her some choices.

   Becky was pleased that she got several job offers because they gave her some choices.

2. The company in St. Louis offered a great salary, and <u>they</u> would pay her moving costs.

   _____

3. When you move to a new city, <u>one</u> can always make new friends.

   _____

4. As Becky thought about starting a new job in a new city, she felt <u>it</u> was bound to be exciting.

   _____

5. Becky's friends urged her to take one of the local jobs, but she wasn't sure that <u>they</u> were right.

   _____

6. Then Becky's bosses offered her both a promotion and a raise. <u>They</u> made her change her mind.

   _____

B. Edit these paragraphs for pronoun shifts and unclear references. There are seven errors.

You might think "a nail is a nail is a nail," but in fact, there are differences between ~~one's~~ *your* toenails and fingernails. Also, if you are right-handed, our right-hand nails grow faster than our left. Podiatrists think nails grow faster in summer than in winter. They think that the change in their growth is due to changes in circulation.

To keep nail cells healthy, they have several suggestions. Cut them straight across, and use foot powder, not cornstarch, on your feet in the summer. Always wear sandals when one bathes in public places. Finally, be sure to change your socks or stockings every day.

C. Write about the following topic.

The paragraph you edited in Exercise B included health advice. Write a paragraph that describes a piece of health advice you think is important to follow. Then edit the paragraph for pronoun shifts, unclear references, and other errors.

Answers start on page 294.

Directions: Choose the <u>one best answer</u> to each question.

<u>Questions 1 through 4</u> refer to the following passage.

Avoiding Lyme Disease

(A)

(1) Summer is the time to watch for the symptoms of Lyme disease, a skin rash or flu-like symptoms. (2) The disease, which has become a major health problem, is caused by the bite of a deer tick.

(B)

(3) There are sensible things you can do to avoid it. (4) When you walk in tall grass, woodlands, or sand dunes, always wear long pants. (5) They say to tuck the bottom of your pants into your socks, too. (6) If you wear light colors, you will be able to see them and pull them off before they have a chance to bite you.

(C)

(7) There are tick collars that your pets— both cats and dogs, alike—can wear to protect themselves. (8) They are very important during tick season, which usually lasts from May until September.

1. Sentence 3: **There are sensible things you can do to avoid it.**

   What correction should be made to sentence 3?

   (1) replace <u>There are</u> to <u>There is</u>
   (2) change <u>you</u> to <u>one</u>
   (3) replace <u>you</u> with <u>I</u>
   (4) replace <u>it</u> with <u>the disease</u>
   (5) no correction is necessary

2. Sentence 5: **They say to tuck the bottom of your pants into your socks, too.**

   Which is the best way to write the underlined portion of the text? If the original is the best way, choose option (1).

   (1) They say to tuck
   (2) You should tuck
   (3) One advises tucking
   (4) We always tuck
   (5) Everyone should tuck

3. Sentence 6: **If you wear light colors, you will be able to see them and pull them off before they have a chance to bite you.**

   What correction should be made to sentence 6?

   (1) change <u>you wear</u> to <u>one wears</u>
   (2) remove <u>the comma after colors</u>
   (3) insert a comma after <u>see them</u>
   (4) replace <u>see them</u> with <u>see the ticks</u>
   (5) change <u>they have</u> to <u>it has</u>

4. Sentence 8: **They are very important during tick season, which usually lasts from May until September.**

   What correction should be made to sentence 8?

   (1) replace <u>They</u> with <u>Tick collars</u>
   (2) replace <u>tick season</u> with <u>it</u>
   (3) replace <u>season, which</u> with <u>season. Which</u>
   (4) change <u>lasts</u> to <u>is lasting</u>
   (5) no correction is necessary

TIP Read the entire passage when deciding which pronoun is the correct answer for a GED question.

Questions 5 through 9 refer to the following memo.

Memo

To: All Employees
From: Gene McKinney
RE: Carpooling

(1) Recently, Rick Fredericks informed my staff and I that 76 percent of the company's employees drive to work separately. (2) I am concerned that this statistic is so high. (3) We need to encourage more voluntary carpooling among ourselves. (4) For example, Rick and me realized we drive in separately from Kirkland Street every day. (5) We started carpooling on Monday. (6) Sharon Michaels has already offered to organize them for her department. (7) If you are interested in organizing your department or signing up for a carpool, give your name and phone number to Rick. (8) He will give it to me, and I will compile the information and get back to everyone shortly.

5. Sentence 1: **Recently, Rick Fredericks informed my staff and I that 76 percent of the company's employees drive to work separately.**

   What correction should be made to sentence 1?

   (1) insert he after Rick Fredericks
   (2) change I to me
   (3) change drive to drove
   (4) change drive to drives
   (5) no correction is necessary

6. Sentence 4: **For example, Rick and me realized we drive in separately from Kirkland Street every day.**

   Which is the best way to write the underlined portion of the text? If the original is the best way, choose option (1).

   (1) Rick and me
   (2) me and Rick
   (3) him and I
   (4) he and me
   (5) Rick and I

7. Sentence 6: **Sharon Michaels has already offered to organize them for her department.**

   What correction should be made to sentence 6?

   (1) replace Sharon Michaels with She
   (2) insert she after Michaels
   (3) change offered to been offering
   (4) replace them with carpool groups
   (5) replace her with their

8. Sentence 7: **If you are interested in organizing your department or signing up for a carpool, give your name and phone number to Rick.**

   What correction should be made to sentence 7?

   (1) change you are to one is
   (2) change are to be
   (3) insert a comma after department
   (4) remove the comma after carpool
   (5) no correction is necessary

9. Sentence 8: **He will give it to me, and I will compile the information and get back to everyone shortly.**

   The most effective revision of sentence 8 would include which group of words?

   (1) to me, compiling it and getting back
   (2) He will and I will compile all the information
   (3) give the information to me, and I will compile it
   (4) so that I can compile the information and get back
   (5) compile the information, and then I will get back

Answers start on page 295.

Directions: This is a ten-minute practice test. After ten minutes, mark the last question you finished. Then complete the test and check your answers. If most of your answers were correct, but you didn't finish, try to work faster next time. Choose the <u>one best answer</u> to each question.

<u>Questions 1 through 4</u> refer to the following article.

Women in the Marathon

(A)

(1) About 6,000 women competed in the last Boston Marathon, even though for decades women were not considered capable of the grueling race. (2) For several years, monetary prizes have been given to both male and female winners. (3) At one point, the male president of the International Olympic Committee even tried to have all female competitors banned from racing in the Olympic games. (4) The ban failed, but they did limit women's long-distance contests to 200 meters.

(B)

(5) In 1966, however, things began to change for female runners. (6) Roberta Gibb defied the marathon committee by sneaking into the crowd and finishing ahead of 291 "qualified" male runners to come in number 124. (7) Still, it took several more years to convince the marathon committee that they should be allowed to race. (8) In 1972, nine women entered. (9) Twenty years later, there were 1,893. (10) Today, we just about are stopping counting.

1. Which revision would improve the text, "Women in the Marathon"?

    (1) remove sentence 2
    (2) move sentence 2 to the beginning of paragraph A
    (3) move sentence 4 to the beginning of paragraph B
    (4) move sentence 5 to the end of paragraph A
    (5) no revision is necessary

2. Sentence 4: **The ban failed, but they did limit women's long-distance contests to 200 meters.**

What correction should be made to sentence 4?

    (1) replace The ban with It
    (2) remove the comma after failed
    (3) replace they with the committee
    (4) change did limit to have limited
    (5) no correction is necessary

3. Sentence 7: **Still, it took several more years to convince the marathon committee that they should be allowed to race.**

What correction should be made to sentence 7?

    (1) replace it with they
    (2) change to convince to convincing
    (3) change the marathon committee to them
    (4) replace committee that they with committee. They
    (5) change they to women

4. Sentence 10: **Today, we just about are stopping counting.**

Which is the best way to write the underlined portion of the text? If the original is the best way, choose option (1).

    (1) just about are stopping
    (2) are just about stopping
    (3) have just about stopped
    (4) will just about stop
    (5) just about stopped

Questions 5 through 9 refer to the following article.

Capuchins and Humans

(A)

(1) Capuchin monkeys are a lifeline to independent living for thousands of physically challenged people. (2) Capuchins make excellent home aides, with their sweet faces, lively dispositions, and they're intelligent, too.

(B)

(3) These agile primates can learn a wide range of tasks. (4) For example, a trained Capuchin can microwave food, bring it to the wheelchair, and feed their human partner. (5) Because these monkeys are so small, they fits easily in an apartment. (6) Moreover, if one jumps on its owner's shoulder, he won't get hurt. (7) Most important, they became precious companions, devoted to their owners. (8) Their human companions grow to treasure them.

5. Sentence 2: **Capuchins make excellent home aides, with their sweet faces, lively dispositions, and they're intelligent, too.**

   Which is the best way to write the underlined portion of the text? If the original is the best way, choose option (1).

   (1) they're intelligent, too
   (2) their intelligence
   (3) sharp intelligence
   (4) being intelligent
   (5) they can also be intelligent

6. Sentence 4: **For example, a trained Capuchin can microwave food, bring it to the wheelchair, and feed their human partner.**

   What correction should be made to sentence 4?

   (1) remove the comma after For example
   (2) remove the comma after food
   (3) change bring to bringing
   (4) replace their with its
   (5) no correction is necessary

7. Sentence 5: **Because these monkeys are so small, they fits easily in an apartment.**

   What correction should be made to sentence 5?

   (1) change are to is
   (2) remove the comma after small
   (3) replace they with it
   (4) replace they with he
   (5) replace fits with fit

8. Sentence 6: **Moreover, if one jumps on its owner's shoulder, he won't get hurt.**

   What correction should be made to sentence 6?

   (1) change one to they
   (2) replace its with their
   (3) remove the comma after shoulder
   (4) replace he with the owner
   (5) no correction is necessary

9. Sentence 8: **Their human companions grow to treasure them.**

   The most effective revision of sentence 8 would begin with which group of words?

   (1) On the other hand,
   (2) In turn,
   (3) Otherwise,
   (4) Next,
   (5) Nevertheless,

Answers start on page 296.

point of view
the perspective from which something is written

The **point of view** is the perspective from which you write. Sometimes you write from your own first-person point of view. Other times, you write from your reader's second-person point of view (as in this textbook) or from someone else's third-person point of view.

The personal pronouns used in a piece of writing are one clue to the writer's point of view. That is why the use of pronouns must be consistent. Read the paragraph below. Pay particular attention to the pronouns and their antecedents.

> People who put their own needs first are not selfish, but smart. When you take care of yourself, a person is better able to be helpful to others. For example, if I spend all my time and energy taking care of my family, and do nothing for myself, pretty soon you'd be a tired, grouchy, lousy wife and mother.
>
> On the other hand, if I take care of myself by doing some of the things I enjoy, like watching a movie or reading a book, a person has more energy and enthusiasm to do some of the things that your family wants or needs to do.

This writer has not been consistent in point of view. Look at the same writing with a consistent point of view.

> A woman who puts her own needs first is not selfish, but smart. When a woman takes care of herself, she is better able to be helpful to others. For example, if a woman spends all her time and energy taking care of her family, and does nothing for herself, pretty soon she'd be a tired, grouchy, lousy wife and mother.
>
> On the other hand, if she takes care of herself by doing some of the things she enjoys, like watching a movie or reading a book, she has more energy and enthusiasm to do some of the things that her family wants or needs to do.

When you write, there is no right or wrong point of view. The important thing is to be consistent by using the same point of view throughout your writing.

Rewrite the first two sentences in the example above using the point of view of the second person (*you*).

_____

_____

_____

You were correct if you wrote the following: *If you put your own needs first, you are not selfish, but smart. When you take care of yourself, you are better able to be helpful to others.*

The Personal Link

1. **Write a note of advice to someone having trouble meeting his or her needs. Use the second person *(you)* point of view.**

   _____

   _____

   _____

   _____

   _____

2. **In your journal, answer these questions. Notice that your writing naturally takes the first person *(I)* point of view.**

   * Do you think you take good care of yourself?
   * Does doing so help you take care of other people?
   * How do you find the right balance between your own needs and the needs of others?

The GED Link

1. **Read the following topic. On a separate sheet of paper, write as many thoughts as you can about the topic. You may want to use some of your ideas from the Personal Link.**

   > Do you agree or disagree that a person must look out for himself or herself before others? Support your opinion with personal observations, experience, and knowledge.

2. **On the same sheet of paper, write at least three paragraphs about the topic above. Use your ideas from the GED Link.**

Edit

Read your paragraphs. Pay special attention to your point of view. Then check your writing for other errors.

Portfolio Reminder

Put your paragraphs from the GED Link in your portfolio.

Answers start on page 296.

Unit 3 Cumulative Review Usage

Directions: Choose the one best answer to each question.

Questions 1 through 4 refer to the following letter.

To Whom It May Concern:

(A)

(1) I often fly Local Express Airlines.
(2) Recently, I have had an experience that is an example of the excellent service I always receive from Local Express Airlines.

(B)

(3) On my last flight, I left a library book at my seat. (4) I know I shouldn't travel with library books, but unfortunately, one does. (5) I didn't remember the book until I was at the baggage carousel, where I was waiting, and I told a clerk at the baggage desk. (6) She phoned the clerks at the gate, asking them to check the plane. (7) Sadly, they didn't find my book, nor did anyone else during the following week. (8) Finally, I called the library to say the book was lost. (9) The librarian said the book had came in the mail that morning!

(C)

(10) Bravo to the airline staff, who went the extra mile to return a book to its owner! (11) I will continue to recommend your airline to friends, relatives, and associates.

1. Sentence 2: **Recently, I have had an experience that is an example of the excellent service I always receive from Local Express Airlines.**

   What correction should be made to sentence 2?

   (1) change have had to had
   (2) change is to was
   (3) insert a comma after service
   (4) replace I always receive with one always receives
   (5) change receive to have received

2. Sentence 4: **I know I shouldn't travel with library books, but unfortunately, one does.**

   What correction should be made to sentence 4?

   (1) change know to knew
   (2) remove the comma after books
   (3) replace books, but with books. But
   (4) replace one does with you do
   (5) replace one does with I did

3. Sentence 5: **I didn't remember the book until I was at the baggage carousel, where I was waiting, and I told a clerk at the baggage desk.**

   If you rewrote sentence 5 beginning with

   As I was waiting at the baggage carousel, I

   the next word(s) should be

   (1) remember
   (2) have remembered
   (3) remembered
   (4) was remembering
   (5) had remembered

4. Sentence 9: **The librarian said the book had came in the mail that morning!**

   What correction should be made to sentence 9?

   (1) replace The librarian with They
   (2) change said to says
   (3) replace the book with it
   (4) change had came to had come
   (5) no correction is necessary

Questions 5 through 9 refer to the following article.

Island of the Sharks

(A)

(1) Out in the Pacific Ocean is an island of unmatched beauty called Cocos, "Island of the Sharks." (2) Its abundance of life are famous throughout the world. (3) Jewel-like fish circle the island's underwater reef, while hundreds of sharks have hunted them in packs.

(B)

(4) Cocos Island is actually the peak of an extinct volcano. (5) When deep ocean currents reach the volcano, they have been forced upward. (6) These currents bring cold water that is rich in plant life and food to the surface. (7) Minute plants and animals, collectively known as plankton, grows when they are exposed to the sunlight and food. (8) The plankton attracts small fish. (9) The small fish attract larger fish. (10) Finally, the largest fish in the chain attract the sharks that give Cocos its name.

5. Sentence 2: **Its abundance of life are famous throughout the world.**

   Which is the best way to write the underlined portion of the text? If the original is the best way, choose option (1).

   (1) are
   (2) is
   (3) has been
   (4) have been
   (5) being

6. Sentence 3: **Jewel-like fish circle the island's underwater reef, while hundreds of sharks have hunted them in packs.**

   What correction should be made to sentence 3?

   (1) change circle to circled
   (2) replace reef, while with reef. While
   (3) change have hunted to hunting
   (4) change have hunted to hunt
   (5) no correction is necessary

7. Sentence 5: **When deep ocean currents reach the volcano, they have been forced upward.**

   Which is the best way to write the underlined portion of the text? If the original is the best way, choose option (1).

   (1) have been
   (2) are
   (3) were
   (4) will be
   (5) been

8. Sentence 7: **Minute plants and animals, collectively known as plankton, grows when they are exposed to the sunlight and food.**

   What correction should be made to sentence 7?

   (1) change grows to grow
   (2) replace they are with it is
   (3) change are to be
   (4) change exposed to being exposed
   (5) replace the sunlight and food with them

9. Sentences 8 and 9: **The plankton attracts small fish. The small fish attract larger fish.**

   The most effective combination of sentences 8 and 9 would include which group of words?

   (1) fish, and it, in turn, attracts
   (2) fish, and them, in turn, attract
   (3) fish, and one, in turn, attracts
   (4) fish, and those there, in turn, attract
   (5) fish, and they, in turn, attract

 When you choose an answer option for a GED question, check it by going back and reading the sentence with that option in mind.

Questions 10 through 14 refer to the following article.

A Woman of Distinction

(A)

(1) Patricia Roberts Harris was the first African-American woman appointed to the U.S. Cabinet. (2) Her posts, under President Jimmy Carter, was Secretary of Housing and Urban Development and Secretary of Health, Education, and Welfare. (3) In addition to her cabinet positions, she was appointed the dean of Howard University's law school and served as the ambassador to Luxembourg.

(B)

(4) Harris had a humble background that did not prevent her from rising to great professional heights. (5) In honor of her public service, an image of Harris now appear on a commemorative postage stamp. (6) It is part of the prestigious Black Heritage stamp series. (7) This series, which honors distinguished African Americans, begun in 1978 with the image of abolitionist Harriet Tubman.

10. Sentence 2: **Her posts, under President Jimmy Carter, was Secretary of Housing and Urban Development and Secretary of Health, Education, and Welfare.**

    What correction should be made to sentence 2?

    (1) replace Her with Patricia Roberts Harris's
    (2) remove the comma after Carter
    (3) change was to were
    (4) remove the comma after Health
    (5) no correction is necessary

11. Sentence 3: **In addition to her cabinet positions, she was appointed the dean of Howard University's law school and served as the ambassador to Luxembourg.**

    What correction should be made to sentence 3?

    (1) change her to one's
    (2) replace was with been
    (3) insert a comma after school
    (4) insert her after and
    (5) no correction is necessary

12. Sentence 4: **Harris had a humble background that did not prevent her from rising to great professional heights.**

    If you rewrote sentence 4 beginning with

    Harris's background was humble, yet she

    the next word(s) should be

    (1) rises
    (2) is rising
    (3) will rise
    (4) rose
    (5) had risen

13. Sentence 5: **In honor of her public service, an image of Harris now appear on a commemorative postage stamp.**

    Which is the best way to write the underlined portion of the text? If the original is the best way, choose option (1).

    (1) appear
    (2) appears
    (3) have appeared
    (4) were appearing
    (5) do appear

14. Sentence 7: **This series, which honors distinguished African Americans, begun in 1978 with the image of abolitionist Harriet Tubman.**

    Which is the best way to write the underlined portion of the text? If the original is the best way, choose option (1).

    (1) begun
    (2) has begun
    (3) is beginning
    (4) was beginning
    (5) began

Questions 15 through 19 refer to the following paragraphs.

Checking Your Oil

(A)

(1) There is no better habit new drivers can learn than checking the oil level in one's car regularly. (2) Here is the steps you need to follow.

(B)

(3) First, open the hood and prop it up carefully. (4) Next, pull out the dipstick, wipe it clean, and then push the dipstick back down into its slot. (5) You have to make sure that it touch the bottom. (6) Then pull the dipstick straight up and check where the oil reaches on it. (7) If the level of the oil is within the range marked on the stick, it has sufficient oil. (8) If the level of oil is below that range, add a quart as soon as possible. (9) Check the level of the oil again once you have added oil to be sure it is within the necessary range. (10) If not, keep adding a quart and rechecking until it is.

15. Sentence 1: **There is no better habit new drivers can learn than checking the oil level in one's car regularly.**

    What correction should be made to sentence 1?

    (1) change is to are
    (2) change can learn to can have learned
    (3) insert a comma after learn
    (4) insert to be before checking
    (5) replace one's with their

16. Sentence 2: **Here is the steps you need to follow.**

    Which is the best way to write the underlined portion of the text? If the original is the best way, choose option (1).

    (1) is
    (2) are
    (3) be
    (4) being
    (5) will be

17. Sentence 5: **You have to make sure that it touch the bottom.**

    Which is the best way to write the underlined portion of the text? If the original is the best way, choose option (1).

    (1) touch
    (2) do touch
    (3) touches
    (4) touching
    (5) had touched

18. Sentence 7: **If the level of the oil is within the range marked on the stick, it has sufficient oil.**

    What correction should be made to sentence 7?

    (1) change is to was
    (2) replace stick, it with stick. It
    (3) remove the comma after stick
    (4) replace it with the car
    (5) no correction is necessary

19. Sentence 9: **Check the level of the oil again once you have added oil to be sure it is within the necessary range.**

    If you rewrote sentence 9 beginning with

    Once oil

    the next word(s) should be

    (1) has been added
    (2) been added
    (3) will be added
    (4) being added
    (5) be added

Questions 20 through 22 refer to the following warranty.

Automator IV

(1) This warranty is valid only when the *Automator IV* is returned to an authorized Highlight Products dealer. (2) Before you have returned your *Automator IV* telephone answering system, please call for a Return Authorization Number. (3) Please do not return it without a RAN. (4) We asks our customers to pack the *Automator IV* in its original carton, if possible. (5) To establish that your warranty is valid, please have submitted a copy of the original sales slip.

20. Sentence 2: **Before you have returned your *Automator IV* telephone answering system, please call for a Return Authorization Number.**

    What correction should be made to sentence 2?

    (1) replace you have with one has
    (2) change have returned to return
    (3) remove the comma after system
    (4) change call to have called
    (5) no correction is necessary

21. Sentence 4: **We asks our customers to pack the *Automator IV* carefully in its original carton, if possible.**

    Which is the best way to write the underlined portion of the text? If the original is the best way, choose option (1).

    (1) asks
    (2) have been asking
    (3) have asked
    (4) ask
    (5) had asked

22. Sentence 5: **To establish that your warranty is valid, please have submitted a copy of the original sales slip.**

    Which is the best way to write the underlined portion of the text? If the original is the best way, choose option (1).

    (1) have submitted
    (2) be submitting
    (3) submit
    (4) to submit
    (5) have submitted

Writing Links Review

Write at least three paragraphs on the following topic. As you are writing, keep the following Writing Links topics in mind.

☑ Are all my ideas clearly organized and relevant? (Writing Link, pages 146–147)

☑ Did I include an introduction and a conclusion? (Writing Link, pages 156–157)

☑ Did I include interesting action verbs in my paragraphs? (Writing Link, pages 166–167)

☑ Did I keep a consistent point of view? (Writing Link, pages 178–179)

If you could change one thing about human beings, what would it be? Explain your answer. Support your view with your personal observations, experiences, and knowledge.

Answers start on page 296.

Cumulative Review Performance Analysis
Unit 3 • Usage

Use the Answers and Explanations starting on page 296 to check your answers to the Unit 3 Cumulative Review. Then use the chart to figure out the skill areas in which you need more practice.

On the chart, circle the questions that you answered correctly. Write the number correct for each skill area. Add the number of questions that you got correct on the Cumulative Review. If you feel that you need more practice, go back and review the lessons for the skill areas that were difficult for you.

Questions	Number Correct	Skill Area	Lessons for Review
5, 8, 10, 13, 16, 21	____/6	Subject-verb agreement	11
4, 12, 14, 17, 19	____/5	Verb forms	12
1, 3, 6, 7, 20, 22	____/6	Verb tenses	13
2, 9, 11, 15, 18	____/5	Pronouns	14
TOTAL CORRECT	____/22		

UNIT 4

Mechanics

As you learned in Unit 3, grammar and usage are important for clear and correct writing. In this unit, you will learn how to apply different rules for mechanics and how to avoid some of the most common mistakes. Mechanics concepts include capitalization, punctuation, and spelling. Writing that is mechanically correct—that is, writing that has correct capitalization, punctuation, and spelling—always makes a better impression than writing that contains errors.

Mechanics is an important content area on the GED Language Arts, Writing Test. About 25 percent of the multiple-choice questions will be based on these topics.

You will use your writing skills in all areas of your life: personal, school, work.

The lessons in this unit include:

Lesson 15: Capitalization

You capitalize the first word of a sentence and the word *I*. You also capitalize the name of a specific person, place, or thing as well as specific holidays, days of the week, and months. It is also important to learn not to overcapitalize, that is, to use unnecessary capital letters.

WRITING LINKS

In this unit, you will practice these types of writing skills:

○ Writing a Longer Piece

○ Staying on Topic

Lesson 16: Commas

In the unit on sentence structure, you learned many uses of the comma, semicolon, and end punctuation. In this lesson, you will focus on using commas in a series and in other parts of a sentence—such as introductory elements and appositives.

Lesson 17: Spelling

This lesson focuses on the correct spelling of possessives, contractions, and homonyms. Homonyms are especially challenging because they are words that sound alike but have different spellings and different meanings.

To use the skills in this unit in your own writing, see the Writer's Checklist on page 317.

GED SKILL Capitalization

When to Capitalize

You probably already know that the first word in a sentence and the pronoun *I* are always capitalized. These additional rules will help you decide when to capitalize other words.

proper noun
a word that names a specific person, place, or thing

RULE 1 Capitalize a **proper noun,** a word that names a specific person, place, group, or thing.

> William Boyle invented the credit card in 1951.
> He lived on Spark Street in West Stead on Long Island.
> Mr. Boyle worked for the Franklin National Bank.

proper adjective
a descriptive word formed from a proper noun

RULE 2 Capitalize a **proper adjective,** a descriptive word that comes from the name of a specific person or place.

> Franklin's main competitor was First American Bank.

RULE 3 Capitalize a title that comes directly before a person's name.

> On the bank's board of directors was Mayor Graham.
> A depositor, Ms. Ailey, asked for credit to pay a big heating bill.

Titles and family names (for example, *mother, father, grandmother*) are capitalized when they are used to address a person directly.

> Ms. Ailey said, "How do you do, Mayor."
> "Mr. Boyle, Sir, I would appreciate a line of credit, just like you give to wealthy depositors and businesses."

RULE 4 Capitalize the names of holidays, days of the week, and months of the year.

> Statements were sent out on the first Monday of the month.
> By New Year's Day in January 1952, Franklin National Bank had set up over 700 credit card accounts for its customers.

Put a check mark by the sentence with an error in capitalization.

_____ a. Princess Caroline of Monaco is a descendant of the Grimaldi family from Genoa, Italy.

_____ b. Her mother was Grace Kelly, an American actress who retired from films when she married prince Rainier.

You were correct if you checked *option b.* The title *prince* should be capitalized because it comes directly before the name: *Prince Rainier.*

A. Complete this form with your own information. Capitalize words correctly.

Name: _____
        first   middle initial   last

Address: _____
            number & street   city, state

Birth Date and Place of Birth: _____
                                  month, day, year   city, state, country

What was the last school you attended? _____

Where do you work or want to work? _____

What language(s) do you speak? _____

B. Edit this letter for capitalization errors. There are 27 errors.

M
~~m~~arch 12, 2001

dr. martin allard

metropolitan hospital

3453 ridgefield road

oklahoma city, oklahoma 83346

Dear dr. martin,

    as we discussed last thursday, I am submitting an official request for a week of vacation

time from july 29 to august 5. I need that particular week because my family from virginia will

be visiting me.

    although I do not have much seniority, I appreciate your consideration of my request.

I have not taken any time off since thanksgiving. in addition, I will be working full shifts

on memorial day and the fourth of july.

sincerely,

matthew styles

C. Write about the following topic.

    The letter that you edited in Exercise B is a request for vacation time. Think of something that you would like to ask for at school or work, or from a business. Then write a letter of request. Edit your letter for capitalization and other errors.

Answers start on page 298.

When Not to Capitalize

Some writers overcapitalize; that is, they capitalize words that should not be capitalized. You need to learn to avoid using unnecessary capital letters.

RULE 1 A title or a family name that is preceded by *a, the,* or a possessive pronoun such as *my* is not capitalized.

Incorrect: Alice went to see the Dean.
Correct: Alice went to see the dean.
Correct: Alice went to see Dean Asher.

Incorrect: She went with her Uncle.
Correct: She went with her uncle.
Correct: She went with her Uncle William.

RULE 2 The names of the seasons are not capitalized.

Incorrect: Both are going back to school in the Fall.
Correct: Both are going back to school in the fall.

RULE 3 A school subject is not capitalized unless it is the name of a specific course or a language.

Incorrect: Alice wants to take a History course.
Correct: Alice wants to take a history course.
Correct: Alice wants to take American History 101 and Swahili.

RULE 4 A direction word is not capitalized unless it refers to a specific place, such as a region of the country.

Incorrect: They walked South to the administration building.
Correct: They walked south to the administration building.
Correct: Alice was born here, but William grew up in the South.

RULE 5 A geographic place is not capitalized unless it is part of a specific name you can find on a map.

Incorrect: The school is next to a huge Lake.
Correct: The school is next to a huge lake.
Correct: The school is next to Lake Ontario.

Put a check mark next to the sentence that has a capitalization error.

_____ a. Joe and his cousin, Hank, are taking geometry and English in school this summer.

_____ b. Hank is staying with his Aunt Carol on this side of the River, so he doesn't have a long commute from north of town.

You were correct if you checked *option b.* There is no reason to capitalize *river* because it is not part of a specific place name.

TIP

Proper nouns are sometimes abbreviated. When a word should be capitalized, its abbreviation should be capitalized too: *Mount Shasta, Mt. Shasta.*

A. Edit these sentences for overcapitalization.

1. I learned a lot about the ~~G~~geography of the United States in my American Studies 101 ~~C~~class.

2. On the East we are bordered by the Atlantic Ocean and on the West by the Pacific.

3. The States on the Gulf of Mexico have hot weather, but in the Great Lakes Region it can get freezing cold.

4. Going West from the Mississippi River, you see flat land and Cornfields.

5. West of the Great Plains are Deserts and Mountain Ranges.

6. To get to the most Northern State, Alaska, you have to cross the Country of Canada.

7. To get to the most Southern, Hawaii, you have to cross an Ocean.

8. My Professor, Dr. Reyes, has been to all fifty of the United States, but I have been to only two.

B. Edit this letter for errors in capitalization. Some words are capitalized that should not be; others are not capitalized but should be. There are 19 errors.

Dear ~~c~~Congresswoman Marks:

The debate between the two candidates for Senator begins at 6:30 this friday evening. The main issues on the agenda will be State property taxes and gun control. Two more debates will take place during the Winter. The primary will be held march 16.

The debate will be held in the auditorium of the Harold Brown Memorial library. The Mayor will attend, and Representative Jay Reynolds will preside over the debate.

Here are directions to the Library from the Airport. First, go North on Landover Highway all the way to Downtown. Turn Right onto Central Street. Go straight until you get to Morrow Drive. There will be a Courthouse on your Left. Turn North and drive two blocks. Brown Library will be on your Right on the East side of the Street. Parking is behind the building.

C. Write about the following topic.

The letter you edited in Exercise B included directions to a city library. Write a letter to a friend or co-worker giving directions from your home, school, or workplace to a library or other public building. Then edit the letter for overcapitalization and other errors.

Answers start on page 298.

Directions: Choose the <u>one best answer</u> to each question.

Questions 1 through 4 refer to the following paragraphs.

Elections

(A)

(1) Every four years in the Fall, Americans go to the polls on Election Day to elect a president. (2) The largest number of presidents have come from the South. (3) Interestingly, the nation's most populous State, California, has produced only two presidents, Richard Nixon and Ronald Reagan.

(B)

(4) Although the job of a vice president seems comparatively unimportant, it is a vital transitional position for the nation. (5) For example, after Nixon resigned from the White House, vice president Ford succeeded him. (6) Ford had been a representative in congress from the Midwest before Nixon named him to succeed Spiro Agnew. (7) Even though Ford was not returned to office by the voters, the country had been spared a serious gap in leadership.

1. Sentence 1: **Every four years in the Fall, Americans go to the polls on Election Day to elect a president.**

   What correction should be made to sentence 1?

   (1) change Fall to fall
   (2) change go to goes
   (3) change go to went
   (4) change president to President
   (5) no correction is necessary

2. Sentence 3: **Interestingly, the nation's most populous State, California, has produced only two presidents, Richard Nixon and Ronald Reagan.**

   What correction should be made to sentence 3?

   (1) change nation's to Nation's
   (2) change State to state
   (3) change has to have
   (4) insert they were after presidents,
   (5) change presidents to Presidents

3. Sentence 5: **For example, after Nixon resigned from the White House, vice president Ford succeeded him.**

   What correction should be made to sentence 5?

   (1) remove the comma after example
   (2) change White House to white house
   (3) remove the comma after House
   (4) change president to President
   (5) change vice president to Vice President

4. Sentence 6: **Ford had been a representative in congress from the Midwest before Nixon named him to succeed Spiro Agnew.**

   What correction should be made to sentence 6?

   (1) change had to has
   (2) change had been to was being
   (3) change representative to Representative
   (4) change congress to Congress
   (5) change Midwest to midwest

Questions 5 through 8 refer to the following paragraphs.

From Gifts to Gardens

(A)

(1) Many people throw out potted Easter lilies or mother's day plants soon after they bloom. (2) The National Lily foundation, however, claims that, with some care and rest in your garden, potted lilies can recover and bloom the next year.

(B)

(3) Wait until the last frost in your region. (4) In far northern areas, this usually means waiting until mid-june. (5) Knock the bulb out of its pot, keeping the leaves and stem because they provide food for the bulb. (6) Plant the bulb about eight inches deep in a sunny spot and feed it about once a month. (7) At the end of Summer when the leaves are dead, cut the plant back, and cover it with pine needles or mulch. (8) Your lily should blossom for many years.

5. Sentence 1: **Many people throw out potted Easter lilies or mother's day plants soon after they bloom.**

   What correction should be made to sentence 1?

   (1) change throw to threw
   (2) change Easter to easter
   (3) insert a comma after lilies
   (4) change mother's day to Mother's Day
   (5) insert a comma after plants

   TIP
   The names of many holidays and other proper nouns consist of more than one word. Be sure to capitalize all the relevant words in a proper noun.

6. Sentence 2: **The National Lily foundation, however, claims that, with some care and rest in your garden, potted lilies can recover and bloom the next year.**

   What correction should be made to sentence 2?

   (1) change National Lily to national lily
   (2) change foundation to Foundation
   (3) change claims to claim
   (4) replace potted lilies with they
   (5) change bloom to be blooming

7. Sentence 4: **In far northern areas, this usually means waiting until mid-june.**

   What correction should be made to sentence 4?

   (1) change northern to Northern
   (2) change means to meant
   (3) insert a comma after waiting
   (4) change mid-june to Mid-june
   (5) change mid-june to mid-June

8. Sentence 7: **At the end of Summer when the leaves are dead, cut the plant back, and cover it with pine needles or mulch.**

   What correction should be made to sentence 7?

   (1) change Summer to summer
   (2) remove the comma after dead
   (3) change dead, cut to dead. Cut
   (4) change pine to Pine
   (5) no correction is necessary

Answers start on page 299.

Directions: This is a ten-minute practice test. After ten minutes, mark the last question you finished. Then complete the test and check your answers. If most of your answers were correct, but you did not finish, try to work faster next time. Choose the <u>one best answer</u> to each question.

Questions 1 through 4 refer to the following announcement.

Civilian Complaints

(A)

(1) The men and women of the Ashland Police Department makes every effort to act legally and properly as they carry out their duties. (2) They attempt to treat all persons with fairness and respect. (3) Sometimes, however, they make mistakes or act in ways that citizens disapprove of or misunderstand.

(B)

(4) All complaints are investigated, but we cannot investigate a complaint until it has been filed. (5) Complaint forms are available at the department's headquarters on Ware road 24 hours a day. (6) Please be sure to fill out the form as completely as you can.

(C)

(7) All complaints are investigated by a supervisor or by the Internal Investigation Unit. (8) If you are still not satisfied, you may appeal that investigation to the town manager.

1. Sentence 1: **The men and women of the Ashland Police Department makes every effort to act legally and properly as they carry out their duties.**

   What correction should be made to sentence 1?

   (1) change <u>Police Department</u> to <u>police department</u>
   (2) change <u>makes</u> to <u>make</u>
   (3) insert a comma after <u>properly</u>
   (4) replace <u>they carry</u> with <u>it carries</u>
   (5) no correction is necessary

2. Which sentence below would be most effective at the beginning of paragraph B?

   (1) People often make complaints in person.
   (2) Try to include information such as a badge number or name of the officer.
   (3) Some complaints are serious.
   (4) Last year we had the fewest complaints filed in ten years.
   (5) If you have a complaint against an officer, we encourage you to bring it to our attention.

3. Sentence 5: **Complaint forms are available at the department's headquarters on Ware road 24 hours a day.**

   What correction should be made to sentence 5?

   (1) change <u>are</u> to <u>being</u>
   (2) change <u>department's</u> to <u>Department's</u>
   (3) change <u>headquarters</u> to <u>Headquarters</u>
   (4) change <u>road</u> to <u>Road</u>
   (5) insert a comma after <u>road</u>

4. Sentence 7: **All complaints are investigated by a supervisor or by the Internal Investigation Unit.**

   What correction should be made to sentence 7?

   (1) change <u>are</u> to <u>to be</u>
   (2) change <u>supervisor</u> to <u>Supervisor</u>
   (3) insert a comma after <u>supervisor</u>
   (4) change <u>Internal Investigation Unit</u> to <u>internal investigation unit</u>
   (5) no correction is necessary

Questions 5 through 9 refer to the following company notice.

Hiring Credentials

(1) In order to be hired at Southeast Framers, inc., you must provide one of the following proofs of identification. (2) We will accept a driver's license or an identification card, but only if a state issued it or Canada or Mexico. (3) A U.S. military I.D. is acceptable, as well as a Native american tribal document. (4) If you are under 18 and do not possess any of the documents already listed, you may submit an official school report or hospital record. (5) In addition to identification information, Southeast Framers also needs to verify employment eligibility before you can be hired. (6) For that purpose, you must submit one of the following documents. (7) You must show a birth certificate, a Social Security card, or we could accept a Certificate of Birth Abroad with an official seal issued by the Department of State.

5. Sentence 1: **In order to be hired at Southeast Framers, inc., you must provide one of the following proofs of identification.**

   What correction should be made to sentence 1?

   (1) insert a comma after hired
   (2) change inc. to Inc.
   (3) remove the comma after inc.
   (4) change provide to have provided
   (5) no correction is necessary

6. Sentence 2: **We will accept a driver's license or an identification card, but only if a state issued it or Canada or Mexico.**

   The most effective revision of sentence 2 would include which group of words?

   (1) in so far as it has been issued
   (2) If a state were to issue
   (3) accept by a state, Canada, or Mexico
   (4) as long as it was issued by
   (5) which have been got from

7. Sentence 3: **A U.S. military I.D. is acceptable, as well as a Native american tribal document.**

   What correction should be made to sentence 3?

   (1) change U.S. to u.s.
   (2) change military to Military
   (3) change Native american to Native American
   (4) change Native american to native American
   (5) no correction is necessary

8. Which revision would make the text more effective?

   Begin a new paragraph

   (1) with sentence 3
   (2) with sentence 4
   (3) with sentence 5
   (4) with sentence 6
   (5) with sentence 7

9. Sentence 7: **You must show a birth certificate, a Social Security card, or we could accept a Certificate of Birth Abroad with an official seal issued by the Department of State.**

   What correction should be made to sentence 7?

   (1) change show to have showed
   (2) remove the comma after certificate
   (3) change Social Security to social security
   (4) remove we could accept
   (5) change Department of State to department of state

Answers start on page 299.

Lesson 16

GED SKILL Commas

Items in Series and Compound Sentences

The comma is a guide for readers. It tells when to pause in a sentence or which elements in a sentence need to be separated in a meaningful way. Learning the rules for using commas will help you become a better writer and a better reader.

RULE 1 Use a comma to separate items in a series—a list of three or more. The items in the series may be words or phrases.

Correct: Cakes, pies, and cookies will be sold at the charity bake sale. Committees have helped with getting publicity, soliciting donations, and decorating booths.

When there are only two items, do not use a comma.

Correct: The advertising committee wants more posters and flyers.

When three or more items are all separated by the conjunction *and* or *or*, do not use commas.

Correct: The advertising committee wants more posters and flyers and mailings.

RULE 2 Use a comma between the clauses in a compound sentence. Remember that a compound sentence contains two or more complete thoughts, called independent clauses, joined by a coordinating conjunction: *and, but, or, for, nor, so,* or *yet.*

Everyone is helping, so the bake sale should be a hit.

Put a check mark next to the sentence with a comma error.

_____ a. Old-fashioned vending machines were usually filled with stale candy or sandwiches.

_____ b. Some newer vending machines contain rolls pizza coffee and fresh fruit.

_____ c. The newer ones also make change for bills in the denominations of ones, fives, or tens.

You were correct if you checked *option b.* The series needs commas: *Some newer vending machines contain rolls, pizza, coffee, and fresh fruit.*

TIP

A comma before the final *and* in a series is optional. However, using commas throughout the rest of a series is required.

TIP

Do not use a comma to separate two subjects in a compound subject or two verbs in a compound predicate: *Mary and Jim* fished. Liz *fished and swam.*

A. **Insert commas where needed. Write *NC* if a sentence does not need a comma.**

_____ 1. Here's a good recipe for pancakes griddlecakes or battercakes.

_____ 2. Sift together $1\frac{1}{2}$ cups of flour 1 teaspoon of salt 3 tablespoons of sugar and $1\frac{3}{4}$ teaspoons of baking powder.

_____ 3. Beat one or two egg whites in another bowl.

_____ 4. Add 1 cup of milk a few drops of vanilla and three tablespoons of butter to the egg mixture.

_____ 5. Combine the wet and dry ingredients together well but you can leave some lumps.

_____ 6. You will have the best and fluffiest batter you've ever mixed!

_____ 7. Your pancakes or griddlecakes will stack up high and fluffy and they will taste delicious too.

B. **Edit these paragraphs by inserting commas where they are needed and deleting unnecessary commas. The handwritten mark is an example of how to delete a comma. There are five missing commas and five unnecessary commas.**

What was life like for families in 1900? There was no electricity in a typical home in the rural Midwest the Deep South, or even Los Angeles. Artificial light was supplied by dim gas, or kerosene lamps. The first large electrical generating plant in the United States, had only just been built. People were still arguing that electricity would never be cheap available, or safe enough to use in the average home.

Hot water was a luxury bathtubs were kept in the kitchen and few homes had indoor plumbing. Heat was supplied by wood or coal stoves. Central heating was just beginning to be popular among prosperous city dwellers, and corporate magnates.

Some people consider that time the good old days but I am glad to be living now. Just consider how people howl, and scream when a storm knocks out their power for a few hours. I know because I am one of them!

C. **Write about the following topic.**

In Exercise B you edited a passage about life over 100 years ago. Pick another time in the past and describe some of the differences between then and now. Or choose a time in the future and write about differences you imagine. Then edit your description for comma mistakes and other errors.

Answers start on page 300.

Introductory Elements and Appositives

Words and phrases that introduce or interrupt the main idea of a sentence are usually set off from the rest of the sentence with commas.

RULE 1 Use a comma to separate introductory elements—words or phrases at the beginning of a sentence—from the rest of the sentence.

<u>No,</u> the bank is closed on Memorial Day.
<u>As a result of overspending,</u> Ron's funds are low.

RULE 2 Use a comma after a dependent clause that comes at the beginning of a sentence. Remember that a dependent clause contains a subject and a verb but is not a complete thought and cannot stand alone. It begins with a subordinating conjunction such as *before* or *if.*

| | <u>When all his bills came in,</u> he was stunned. |
| **But:** | He was stunned when all his bills came in. |

appositive
a noun phrase that adds information about a noun or pronoun

An **appositive** is a noun phrase that further explains or describes another noun or pronoun. If the appositive is necessary to identify the noun or pronoun, it is essential. If the appositive simply adds some information but is not necessary in order to identify the noun or pronoun, it is nonessential.

RULE 3 Use commas to separate a nonessential appositive from the rest of the sentence. Do not use commas for essential appositives.

Nonessential: Ron, <u>my friend,</u> has 13 credit cards.
Essential: He is reading the library book *Ten Ways to Get out of Debt.*

A **parenthetical expression** is a word or phrase that adds nothing essential to the meaning of a sentence. Many parenthetical expressions are transitions. Some common parenthetical expressions are *for example, incidentally, of course, however,* and *on the one hand.*

parenthetical expression
a word or phrase that adds nothing essential to the meaning of a sentence

RULE 4 Use commas to set off parenthetical expressions.

Ron has cards, <u>for example,</u> for most stores in the mall.

Put a check mark next to the sentence that uses commas correctly.

_____ a. In addition to skills, appearance is important at an interview.

_____ b. My job counselor, Della Rollins helped me pick an interview outfit.

You were correct if you checked *option a* because *In addition to skills* is an introductory phrase that should be followed by a comma. In *option b,* a second comma is needed after the nonessential appositive *Della Rollins.*

A. Add the comma that is missing in each sentence.

1. A county health expert, Hal Lahiff wanted to find out if county firefighters, paramedics, and ambulance drivers were aware of good nutrition.

2. Since it affects both reaction time and stamina good nutrition is critical in those jobs.

3. After he gathered data from 500 county employees Mr. Lahiff made some interesting observations.

4. Most workers got enough protein, an essential nutrient to sustain them well.

5. Almost one-third however, needed to cut down on fats and eat more fruits and vegetables.

6. According to several paramedics they frequently eat salads or fruits at home.

7. When they eat group meals on the job they tend to eat too much meat or fatty foods.

B. Edit this passage by inserting commas where needed. There are 11 missing commas.

The image of the wolf as a lone and vicious animal is a serious misconception. Contrary to popular myth wolves are very social and nurturing. In fact adult wolves spend many hours a day caring for and playing with their babies or pups.

Living in packs of from two to twelve animals adult wolves depend on each other for catching and sharing prey. The availability of prey, both small and large animals affects the size of the pack. When prey is scarce the pack decreases. When prey is plentiful the pack increases.

The myth that wolves hunt for sport or out of viciousness, however has been disproved. As part of a natural food chain wolves hunt the old, weak, or sick from herds. That allows the stronger animals in the herd to survive and reproduce. That in turn, helps strengthen the species.

Although wolves are predators they have also been prey for one species in particular. That species is humans.

C. Write about the following topic.

In Exercise B you edited a passage on misconceptions about wolves. Think about another popular belief that you know is a misconception. Write a paragraph explaining why the misconception is false. Then edit your paragraph for comma mistakes and other errors.

Answers start on page 300.

Directions: Choose the <u>one best answer</u> to each question.

<u>Questions 1 through 4</u> refer to the following memo.

Memo

TO: Staff
DATE: September 12, 2002
RE: Deli Opening

(A)

(1) Next Friday Saturday, and Sunday, the Four Corners Supermarket will hold an in-store sale to introduce our new deli department. (2) We will have tasty cooking demonstrations for customers. (3) All deli-made sandwiches, soups, and salads will be half-price. (4) In addition samples of our delicious smoked ham, roast beef, and tuna salad will be served throughout the store.

(B)

(5) Before the event, you will have the opportunity to meet all the new staff in the deli department. (6) The new deli manager, Sybil Howard expects that the new department will increase store sales by 50 to 75 percent during the special event. (7) You can help by encouraging your friends, and relatives to visit our new department.

1. Sentence 1: **Next Friday Saturday, and Sunday, the Four Corners Supermarket will hold an in-store sale to introduce our new deli department.**

   Which is the best way to write the underlined portion of the text? If the original is the best way, choose option (1).

   (1) Friday Saturday, and Sunday,
   (2) Friday Saturday and Sunday,
   (3) Friday, and Saturday and Sunday
   (4) Friday Saturday, and Sunday
   (5) Friday, Saturday, and Sunday,

2. Sentence 4: **In addition samples of our delicious smoked ham, roast beef, and tuna salad will be served throughout the store.**

   What correction should be made to sentence 4?

   (1) insert a comma after <u>In addition</u>
   (2) remove the comma after <u>ham</u>
   (3) insert a comma after <u>salad</u>
   (4) change <u>will be</u> to <u>was</u>
   (5) no correction is necessary

3. Sentence 6: **The new deli manager, Sybil Howard expects that the new department will increase store sales by 50 to 75 percent during the special event.**

   What correction should be made to sentence 6?

   (1) change <u>manager</u> to <u>Manager</u>
   (2) insert a comma after <u>Howard</u>
   (3) insert a comma after <u>sales</u>
   (4) change <u>expects</u> to <u>expected</u>
   (5) replace <u>the special event</u> with <u>it</u>

4. Sentence 7: **You can help by encouraging your friends, and relatives to visit our new department.**

   What correction should be made to sentence 7?

   (1) change <u>You</u> to <u>One</u>
   (2) change <u>help</u> to <u>be helping</u>
   (3) remove the comma after <u>friends</u>
   (4) insert a comma after <u>relatives</u>
   (5) no correction is necessary

Questions 5 through 9 refer to the following paragraphs.

Getting Your Calcium

(A)

(1) Calcium is a mineral needed for strong, healthy, and lasting, teeth and bones. (2) Doctors generally agree that 2000 milligrams of calcium a day is safe for most people.

(B)

(3) Although many people take calcium in pills nutritionists recommend eating foods naturally rich in calcium. (4) Dairy products are the foods richest in calcium and now many of them are also low-fat or non-fat. (5) For people with difficulty digesting milk there are now low-lactose alternatives. (6) In addition, foods such as orange juice can be fortified with calcium. (7) Non-dairy products that are rich in calcium, include broccoli, leafy green vegetables, and fortified bread and cereals.

5. Sentence 1: **Calcium is a mineral needed for strong, healthy, and lasting, teeth and bones.**

   What correction should be made to sentence 1?

   (1) change is to has been
   (2) insert a comma after mineral
   (3) remove the comma after lasting
   (4) insert a comma after teeth
   (5) no correction is necessary

6. Sentence 3: **Although many people take calcium in pills nutritionists recommend eating foods naturally rich in calcium.**

   What correction should be made to sentence 3?

   (1) change take to were taking
   (2) insert a comma after calcium
   (3) insert a comma after pills
   (4) change nutritionists to Nutritionists
   (5) no correction is necessary

7. Sentence 4: **Dairy products are the foods richest in calcium and now many of them are also low-fat or non-fat.**

   Which is the best way to write the underlined portion of the text? If the original is the best way, choose option (1).

   (1) calcium and
   (2) calcium
   (3) calcium. And
   (4) calcium, and
   (5) calcium and,

8. Sentence 5: **For people with difficulty digesting milk there are now low-lactose alternatives.**

   What correction should be made to sentence 5?

   (1) insert a comma after difficulty
   (2) insert a comma after milk
   (3) replace there are with they have
   (4) change are to is
   (5) no correction is necessary

9. Sentence 7: **Non-dairy products that are rich in calcium, include broccoli, leafy green vegetables, and fortified bread and cereals.**

   What correction should be made to sentence 7?

   (1) replace that with they
   (2) change are to have been
   (3) remove the comma after calcium
   (4) remove the comma after broccoli
   (5) insert a comma after bread

TIP Avoid unnecessary commas in a series by counting the items. For only two, do not use a comma. For three or more, subtract one from the number of items. That is the number of commas you need.

Answers start on page 301.

Directions: This is a ten-minute practice test. After ten minutes, mark the last question you finished. Then complete the test and check your answers. If most of your answers were correct, but you didn't finish, try to work faster next time. Choose the one best answer to each question.

Questions 1 through 4 refer to the following paragraphs.

Conserving Water

(A)

(1) Each American uses on average over 100 gallons of water per day, a precious natural resource for their personal needs. (2) Conservationists are concerned and have offered these ideas for conserving water in the home.

(B)

(3) To begin with, they suggest running washing machines and dishwashers with full loads, only. (4) Fix leaky faucets as soon as possible. (5) Leaking faucets can drip away dollars of water a day, but they cost only a few cents to fix. (6) The basin should be filled and plugged instead of leaving the tap running while shaving. (7) More than a gallon of water can be saved during a ten-minute shave. (8) Install a flow restrictor in your shower head to reduce the amount of water that runs down your drain. (9) Finally, water a flower or vegetable garden by using buckets to collect rainwater for watering them later.

1. Sentence 1: **Each American uses on average over 100 gallons of water a day, a precious natural resource for their personal needs.**

   Which is the best way to write the underlined portion of the text? If the original is the best way, choose option (1).

   (1) water a day, a precious natural resource
   (2) water a day a precious natural resource
   (3) water a day, a precious natural resource,
   (4) water a day a precious natural resource,
   (5) water a day. A precious natural resource

2. Sentence 3: **To begin with, they suggest running washing machines and dishwashers with full loads, only.**

   What correction should be made to sentence 3?

   (1) remove the comma after with
   (2) change suggest to will suggest
   (3) insert a comma after machines
   (4) remove the comma after loads
   (5) no correction is necessary

3. Sentence 6: **The basin should be filled and plugged instead of leaving the tap running while shaving.**

   If you rewrote sentence 6 beginning with

   Instead of leaving the tap running while you shave,

   the next words should be

   (1) the basin
   (2) one should
   (3) fill and plug
   (4) a filled basin
   (5) filling the basin

4. Sentence 9: **Finally, water a flower or vegetable garden by using buckets to collect rainwater for watering them later.**

   What correction should be made to sentence 9?

   (1) remove the comma after Finally
   (2) change have to had
   (3) remove the comma after garden
   (4) insert a comma after rainwater
   (5) replace them with it

Questions 5 through 9 refer to the following directions.

How to Make a Waterproof Cushion

(1) Here's a handy and inexpensive way to make a waterproof cushion. (2) For a 20-inch square cushion, you will need a piece of molded foam, two yards of waterproof vinyl some masking tape, and waterproof cement. (3) First, cut a piece of vinyl 25" by 25". (4) Place the foam facedown in the center of your vinyl square. (5) Fold up each side of the vinyl smooth the corners as you turn the cushion. (6) Cement the edges, press them down onto the vinyl, and then you need to tape them in place. (7) As soon as it is dry, you can attach another square of vinyl over the exposed foam. (8) You can make the cushion extra firm, too. (9) In that case, you should staple a square piece of plywood onto the foam before you cement the final square over the back of the cushion.

5. Sentence 2: **For a 20-inch square cushion, you will need a piece of molded foam, two yards of waterproof vinyl some masking tape, and waterproof cement.**

   What correction should be made to sentence 2?

   (1) remove the comma after cushion
   (2) change will need to needed
   (3) remove the comma after foam
   (4) insert a comma after yards
   (5) insert a comma after vinyl

6. Sentence 5: **Fold up each side of the vinyl smooth the corners as you turn the cushion.**

   Which is the best way to write the underlined portion of the text? If the original is the best way, choose option (1).

   (1) vinyl smooth
   (2) vinyl, smooth
   (3) vinyl, and having smoothed
   (4) vinyl, and smooth,
   (5) vinyl, smoothing

7. Sentence 6: **Cement the edges, press them down onto the vinyl, and then you need to tape them in place.**

   What correction should be made to sentence 6?

   (1) remove the comma after edges
   (2) insert and after edges,
   (3) remove you need to
   (4) insert a comma after tape them
   (5) no correction is necessary

8. Sentence 7: **As soon as it is dry, you can attach another square of vinyl over the exposed foam.**

   What correction should be made to sentence 7?

   (1) replace it with the cement
   (2) remove the comma after dry
   (3) change can to will
   (4) insert a comma after vinyl
   (5) no correction is necessary

9. Sentences 8 and 9: **You can make the cushion extra firm, too. In that case, you should staple a square piece of plywood onto the foam before you cement the final square over the back of the cushion.**

   The most effective combination of sentences 8 and 9 would include which group of words?

   (1) Extra firm cushions are stapled
   (2) For an extra firm cushion, staple
   (3) Stapling plywood onto the foam makes
   (4) They can make extra firm cushions by
   (5) Cushions that are extra firm make

Answers start on page 301.

Writing a Personal Narrative

In the Writing Links in this book, you have been learning about the components of good writing. You have looked at the smaller pieces—such as specific details and action verbs. You have also looked at the bigger picture—such as writing an effective paragraph, organizing your ideas, and adding an introduction and a conclusion.

In this Writing Link, you will have the opportunity to put all the components together. You will use what you have learned to write two full-length pieces of writing.

One kind of writing is the **personal narrative.** In a personal narrative, you tell a story about yourself. The writer of the personal narrative example below tells of a mistake she made. As you read the example, note how the events in the story are told in the order in which they happened.

> When I was 18 years old, I rushed into a marriage with a man whom I did not know well enough. Jim and I thought we loved each other, but it turned out that we were not well-matched at all.
>
> After high school graduation, I was eager to get out of my parents' house and start my life. I met Jim at a friend's party, and we really hit it off. We both liked biking, movies, and being with friends. When he wanted to move south after we had been dating for a few months, I went with him.
>
> Our lives looked promising after our move. We found decent jobs and nice apartments. We soon got married so that we would really feel settled. We couldn't have imagined being happier.
>
> Our happiness began to unravel when Jim decided he didn't like his job. He saw nothing wrong with quitting and spending all his time on the beach. I urged him to keep working so we could save money for a house, but he thought that I was being too conventional. We disagreed on a lot of important issues, including money, our relationships with our families, and lifetime goals.
>
> After a year of trying to work things out, we decided that we were too different to make our marriage work well. It was hard for us to admit we had made a mistake. Fortunately, we made our discovery before anyone was really hurt. After our divorce, I moved back home.

The Personal Link

Follow the steps below to write a personal narrative telling about a change in your life.

1. Think about a big change in your life. It could be a birth, a marriage, a divorce, a new job, or a new home. It could be a friend moving away or you moving away from a friend. Choose a topic and write it below.

   Topic _____

2. Write down the main events that happened before, during, and after the change.

   _____

   _____

   _____

   _____

   _____

   _____

   _____

3. Try to add more details to the events above. Include your feelings at the time. If you like, write about the change in your personal journal first.

4. Number the events in the order in which they happened. That is, the order in which you will write about them.

5. On a separate sheet of paper, write a personal narrative using your ideas from above. Add a short introductory paragraph and a short concluding paragraph.

Edit

Read your personal narrative. Make sure the events are in the order in which they happened. Then edit your narrative for errors.

 ## Portfolio Reminder

Put your personal narrative in your portfolio.

Writing an Essay

Like a personal narrative, an essay is a longer piece of writing. One kind of essay explains the writer's view on a topic.

Read this sample essay topic.

> People learn from their mistakes. Do you agree with this statement? Write an essay that explains your point of view. Use your observations, knowledge, and experience to support your view.

Now read the essay below. Note how the ideas are organized. The introduction states what the writer will say in the essay. The three middle paragraphs give three examples supporting her main idea. The conclusion summarizes what she has written.

> I believe that most people learn from their mistakes. I am aware of several mistakes that I have learned from, and I have watched my children learn and grow from their mistakes. In fact, I believe that most of the progress we have made in science and technology is the result of people learning from mistakes.
>
> When I was 18 years old, I rushed into a marriage with a man whom I did not know well enough. We thought we loved each other, but it turned out that we were not well-matched at all, and eventually we divorced. For the next several years, I was careful not to rush into any relationships. I took a long time to really get to know my current husband before I married him. We have been together for ten years and are very happy. I learned a lot from the mistake of rushing into my first marriage.
>
> My three-year-old son has also learned from his mistakes. Just the other day, he ate some soup that was too hot. I had warned him to wait, but he did not listen. As a result, he burned his tongue and cried. The next day I put some soup in front of him, and before I could say anything, he said, "I need to wait for it to cool off." He had learned to be more patient.
>
> Finally, I believe that scientific discoveries are all examples of people learning from mistakes. Thomas Edison did not invent the light bulb by following a plan straight from beginning to end. Instead, he tried different experiments based on what he knew. Sometimes, these experiments failed. But he did not quit; he learned what he did wrong and tried something different the next time. The more I read about technology, the more I understand that most inventions and discoveries came about after a long series of mistakes.
>
> Of course, there are some people who make mistakes and do not learn from them. But I think they are a small number compared to people like me, my son, and many scientists. Learning from mistakes is part of being human.

The GED Link

Follow the steps below to write an essay on this topic.

> It is difficult to make changes in one's life. Do you agree with this statement? State your view in an essay. Use your personal observations, experience, and knowledge.

1. Think about the topic. Write down any ideas you can think of about changes in people's lives. You may use ideas from the Personal Link on page 205 as well as your personal journal.

   _____

   _____

   _____

   _____

2. Look at your ideas. See what three main points you can make about the topic. Use the following plan to organize your ideas.

   Paragraph 1: Introduction

   Paragraph 2 will be about _____

   Paragraph 3 will be about _____

   Paragraph 4 will be about _____

   Paragraph 5: Conclusion

   Go back to the first question and number each idea you wrote down 2, 3, or 4 to show whether you will use it in body paragraph 2, 3, or 4.

3. On a separate sheet of paper, write an essay using your plan from above.

Edit

Read your essay. Make sure the ideas are organized and explained clearly. Then edit your essay for errors.

Portfolio Reminder

Put your essay from the GED Link into your portfolio.

Answers start on page 302.

Lesson 17

GED SKILL **Spelling**

Possessives

possessive
a word that shows
ownership

TIP

To check for
possession, try to
turn the words into
a phrase with *of*.
Possessive: *Bob's sister*
= *the sister of Bob*

Possessives are words that show ownership. You make a noun show possession by using an apostrophe (') and usually the letter *-s*. Plural nouns that do not show possession do not use an apostrophe.

RULE 1 Add *'s* to show the possessive for a singular noun and for a plural noun that does not end in *-s*.

Singular Possessive: John's sons are going fly-fishing next week.
Singular Possessive: Jess's old reel is oiled and ready.
Plural Possessive: The children's rods are stacked in the garage.

RULE 2 Add only an apostrophe to show the possessive for a plural noun ending in *-s*.

Plural Possessive: Both sons' fishing flies are already tied.
Plural Possessive: The flies' hooks have been carefully inserted.

RULE 3 Don't use an apostrophe with the possessive pronouns *his, hers, its, ours, yours, theirs,* and *whose*.

Incorrect: That big catch of trout is their's.
Correct: That big catch of trout is theirs.

Put a check mark by the sentence in which all possessives are spelled correctly.

_____ a. Here is Jills' picture in the photo album.

_____ b. Who's pictures are these?

_____ c. They are of my Grandmother Tess and her two younger sister's, Bess and Jess.

_____ d. Her brothers' names are Fess and Les Rimes.

You were correct if you checked *option d*. The possessive plural *brothers'* is spelled correctly. In *option a*, the singular possessive *Jills'* should be spelled *Jill's*. In *option b*, the possessive pronoun *Who's* should be spelled *Whose*. In *option c*, the plural noun *sister's* should be spelled *sisters*.

A. If the underlined word in a sentence is spelled correctly, write _C_. If it is incorrect, rewrite it correctly.

1. _____ The Maywood Park <u>Districts</u> catalog lists a course for youths who must stay home alone.

2. _____ The <u>youngsters's</u> class will be held every Saturday at 10:30 A.M.

3. _____ Rita Hall, <u>Maywood's</u> community health educator, will teach the children important skills.

4. _____ The idea for the class was all <u>her's</u>.

5. _____ <u>Topic's</u> include basic first aid and safety measures.

6. _____ They will be reinforced by the local Firemen and <u>Firewomens'</u> Community Service group.

7. _____ <u>Hall's</u> first class will be Telephone Rules for Safety.

8. _____ <u>Class's</u> are free, and registration is limited.

9. _____ At least one <u>parents'</u> signature is required on the registration form.

B. Edit the following guidelines for misspelled possessives. There are 11 errors.

Chat Room Rules of Behavior

A participants conduct in this chat room should be guided by common sense, basic etiquette, and the following chat rules:

Please be aware that this chat room is for adults'. It is not intended for individual's under the age of 18. It is the chat room administrators job to list members topic suggestions. We encourage you to be responsible and respectful of our communitys' participants. Please don't use this chat room to sell your product's or service's. We also ask that you respect everyone else's property rights and privacy. Please don't ask for other member's passwords. Please don't post personal information, such as your name, address, or phone number, or ask another member for his' or her's.

C. Write about the following topic.

In Exercise B you edited guidelines for rules of conduct for an Internet chat room. Think about a group or organization that you belong to, such as a social club, a bowling team, or a class. Write some guidelines to explain the rules that you and the members of your group follow. Then edit the guidelines for misspelled possessives and other errors.

Answers start on page 302.

Contractions

A **contraction** is a shortened way to write two words by combining them and omitting one or more letters. Like possessives, contractions use apostrophes.

RULE 1 Use an apostrophe to take the place of the missing letters in a contraction: *I + am = I'm*.

Incorrect: Do'nt put the apostrophe in the wrong place.
Correct: Don't put the apostrophe in the wrong place.

Most contractions combine a personal pronoun and a verb:

you've = you have   we're = we are
she'd = she had   he'd = he would
it's = it is   they'll = they will

Negative contractions combine a verb and the word *not*:

isn't = is not   wasn't = was not
aren't = are not   weren't = were not
don't = do not   didn't = did not
doesn't = does not   won't = will not
haven't = have not   hasn't = has not
can't = cannot   shouldn't = should not
couldn't = could not   wouldn't = would not

RULE 2 Do not confuse contractions with possessives that sound the same.

Incorrect: Its a common spelling problem.
Correct Contraction: It's a common spelling problem.

Incorrect: Make sure each word has it's apostrophe in the correct place.
Correct Possessive: Make sure each word has its apostrophe in the correct place.

To decide whether a word is a contraction or a possessive, mentally substitute the two words that form the contraction. If the sentence makes sense, the word is a contraction.

You can substitute *it is* in the first sentence, so that is a contraction and needs the apostrophe. You cannot substitute *it is* in the second sentence, so *its* is a possessive.

Put a check mark by the sentence that uses a contraction correctly.

_____ a. It's a library book.

_____ b. It's due date was last month.

You were correct if you checked *option a*. You can substitute *It is* in the sentence: *It is a library book.*

To check the spelling of a contraction, look at the placement of the apostrophe. An apostrophe replaces a letter or letters in one word of a contraction. For example: *We're = We are.* The apostrophe replaces the *a* in *are*.

A. Complete the sentences by writing the words in parentheses as contractions.

1. (I would) _____ like to learn more about the art of Japanese flower arranging.

2. (It is) _____ an ancient art called Ikebana.

3. (is not) There _____ anything cluttered in this art form.

4. (She is) My friend is Japanese. _____ giving me lessons.

5. (They are) The arrangements are asymmetrical. _____ also distinguished by gracefulness.

6. (would not) There's nothing I _____ do to perfect my skills.

B. Edit this business letter for misspelled contractions. There are seven contraction errors.

Dear Customer:

Its my pleasure to welcome you to Ocean Park Bank. Im writing to thank you for opening a new savings account with us.

Please read the enclosed pamphlet, "Ocean Park's Banking Guide," for a detailed description of all our services. On September 15, you're direct deposit option will begin. You wont have to do a thing. Your ATM card is enclosed. As soon as you activate your personal password, youl'l have access to 57 regional branches and more than 475 ATMs.

Thank you for giving us the opportunity to prove that Ocean Park is a smart choice for you. You're business is important to us, and wer'e working hard to exceed your expectations.

Very truly yours,

Clifford Rice

Vice President for Customer Relations

C. Write about the following topic.

In Exercise B you edited a letter from a business. Now write a letter to a business. It could be to complain, to praise good service, or to ask about a product. Then edit the letter for misspelled contractions and other errors.

Answers start on page 302.

Homonyms

homonyms
words that sound alike
but have different
spellings and meanings

To avoid errors with
homonyms, read
the entire sentence
before you decide
how to spell the
word. That way,
you will know the
intended meaning
of the word.

Homonyms are words that sound alike but have different
spellings and different meanings. There are no rules to help you write
homonyms. You simply have to learn how to spell the particular
homonym you want to use.

As you have learned, some contractions and possessives are
homonyms: *it's/its, you're/your, who's/whose.*

Here are some other commonly confused homonyms:

board (piece of wood)
bored (not interested)

brake (to stop)
break (to damage or destroy;
   rest period)

coarse (rough, textured)
course (path, track)

feat (achievement)
feet (plural of *foot*)

grate (to shred)
great (extremely good)

hear (to listen)
here (in this place)

hole (opening)
whole (entire)

knew (past tense of *know*)
new (latest, additional)

passed (went by)
past (a time before)

principal (main; head of a school)
principle (rule, belief)

right (correct; opposite of left)
write (to form words)

their (belonging to them)
there (in that place)
they're (contraction of *they are*)

to (in the direction of)
too (also)
two (the number 2)

way (path, direction)
weigh (to measure heaviness)

weak (not strong)
week (seven days)

wear (to have on clothing)
where (what place)

weather (climate)
whether (if)

wood (what trees are made of)
would (verb expressing a wish)

Some words are not actual homonyms, but they are often confused
because they sound so similar:

accept (to receive or get)   affect (to influence)   than (comparison)
except (excluding)   effect (a result)   then (after that)

Put a check mark by the sentence with no misspelling.

_____ a. The instructor's lesson will positively affect the class.

_____ b. The instructor's lesson will positively effect the class.

You were correct if you chose *option a.* The instructor's actions will
have a positive influence on the class.

A. Write the correct words to complete this dialog.

1. Al: _____ car is in my parking space?
   (Who's, Whose)

2. Ben: _____ Fred's.
   (It's, Its)

3. Al: _____, his car is red. It might be the Jones'.
   (Know, No)

4. Ben: _____ car is green. _____ come Bob and Tony.
   (Their, There, They're)   (Hear, Here)

   They'll _____.
   (know, no)

5. Tony: Hi! Isn't my _____ car _____?
   (knew, new)   (grate, great)

6. Al: _____ car!? That's my space!
   (You're, Your)

7. Tony: Oops. Please _____ my apology.
   (accept, except)

B. Edit this personal letter for homonym errors. There are 16 errors.

Dear Martha,

The whether hear has been awful! We are all so board that we are desperate to visit you. Can we come next weak? The breaks on the car will be fixed by then. Ray and his knew girlfriend want to come, two. Is that all write? Of coarse, if seven is to many, they'll just stay hear.

Won other thing. Can you send directions? You're uncle forgot the weigh. Please except our thanks for your open invitation. We're looking forward too a nice long visit.

Love,

Aunt Alison

C. Write about the following topic.

In Exercise B you edited a letter asking for a favor. Write a letter to a friend or relative asking for a favor. Then edit the letter for misspelled homonyms and other errors.

Answers start on page 303.

Directions: Choose the one best answer to each question.

Questions 1 through 4 refer to the following paragraphs.

How to Take Phone Messages

(A)

(1) In these days of voicemail and automated phone menus, the art of answering the telephone may be part of our past. (2) Yet some companies still recognize the value of personal contact. (3) Here are some great tips for receiving incoming calls and taking customer's messages.

(B)

(4) After greeting a customer, say the name of the company and "How may I help you?" as politely as possible. (5) Its important to listen carefully to callers and ask them to repeat any names or numbers you don't understand. (6) To take a message for an employee who isn't available, note the person's name who is getting the message and the time of the call. (7) Than write down the caller's name, company, phone number, and any message he or she wants to leave. (8) Verify both the name by spelling it back and the telephone number by repeating the numbers. (9) Finally, thank the caller and make sure the message gets to the right person promptly.

1. Sentence 1: **In these days of voicemail and automated phone menus, the art of answering the telephone may be part of our past.**

   What correction should be made to sentence 1?

   (1) insert a comma after voicemail
   (2) remove the comma after menus
   (3) change our to hour
   (4) change past to passed
   (5) no correction is necessary

2. Sentence 3: **Here are some great tips for receiving incoming calls and taking customer's messages.**

   What correction should be made to sentence 3?

   (1) change Here to Hear
   (2) change are to is
   (3) change great to grate
   (4) insert a comma after calls
   (5) change customer's to customers'

3. Sentence 5: **Its important to listen carefully to callers and ask them to repeat any names or numbers you don't understand.**

   What correction should be made to sentence 5?

   (1) change Its to It's
   (2) change callers to callers'
   (3) replace and with a comma
   (4) insert a comma after names
   (5) change don't to do'nt

4. Sentence 7: **Than write down the caller's name, company, phone number, and any message he or she wants to leave.**

   What correction should be made to sentence 7?

   (1) change Than to Then
   (2) change write to right
   (3) change caller's to callers
   (4) remove the comma after name
   (5) insert a comma after message

Questions 5 through 8 refer to the following letter.

Dear Thomas Peters:

(A)

(1) Don't miss this special renewal opportunity. (2) If you act now, you'll receive 48 weakly issues of *On-Line Emblem,* plus 12 monthly special reports for the great rate of only $18.95.

(B)

(3) Don't miss the only newsmagazine covering the people, local news, and community actions shaping the Internet economy. (4) Our magazines' coverage provides you with breaking news on e-mail, shopping discounts, jobs, and sports. (5) With your paid renewal, well send you an additional 12 monthly special reports covering exciting Internet issues.

(C)

(6) Don't wait another minute to continue the service that Professor Jane Notch of Dwyer University's School of Computer Science calls "the best, most accurate publication" covering the Internet today!

5. Sentence 2: **If you act now, you'll receive 48 weakly issues of *On-Line Emblem,* plus 12 monthly special reports for the great rate of only $18.95.**

What correction should be made to sentence 2?

(1) change you act to one acts
(2) remove the comma after now
(3) change receive to have received
(4) change weakly to weekly
(5) change great to grate

6. Sentence 4: **Our magazines' coverage provides you with breaking news on e-mail, shopping discounts, jobs, and sports.**

What correction should be made to sentence 4?

(1) change magazines' to magazine's
(2) change provides to provide
(3) change you to one
(4) change breaking to braking
(5) no correction is necessary

7. Sentence 5: **With your paid renewal, well send you an additional 12 monthly special reports covering exciting Internet issues.**

What correction should be made to sentence 5?

(1) change your to you're
(2) remove the comma
(3) change well to we'll
(4) change special reports to Special Reports
(5) no correction is necessary

8. Sentence 6: **Don't wait another minute to continue the service that Professor Jane Notch of Dwyer University's School of Computer Science calls "the best, most accurate publication" covering the Internet today!**

What correction should be made to sentence 6?

(1) change wait to weight
(2) insert a comma after service
(3) change Professor to professor
(4) change University's to Universities
(5) no correction is necessary

TIP

As you work through these exercises, note the homonyms that give you trouble. Study them and practice writing sentences with them. That way, you will know them when you take the GED Writing Test.

Answers start on page 303.

Directions: This is a ten-minute practice test. After ten minutes, mark the last question you finished. Then complete the test and check your answers. If most of your answers were correct, but you didn't finish, try to work faster next time. Choose the <u>one best answer</u> to each question.

<u>Questions 1 through 4 refer to the following</u> information.

The Flu

(A)

(1) This winter there's a new strain of flu. (2) Its worse than other recent flus, and more people are getting sicker.

(B)

(3) Flu victims are getting runny noses, watery eyes, and coughs. (4) Their also experiencing muscle aches, chills, and high fevers. (5) Visiting the emergency room is unnecessary, however, say many Doctors. (6) Instead, stay in bed, take acetaminophen, and drink liquids.

(C)

(7) Doctors also recommend flu shots. (8) In fact, get a flu shot early because a flu shot after you've gotten the flu won't help. (9) Bringing children and senior citizens for flu shots is important because the flu is especially dangerous for them, so do it before flu season starts. (10) Getting vaccinated in the fall means being healthier during the flu season.

1. Sentence 2: **Its worse than other recent flus, and more people are getting sicker.**

   What correction should be made to sentence 2?

   (1) change Its to It's
   (2) change than to then
   (3) remove the comma after flus
   (4) remove and
   (5) no correction is necessary

2. Sentence 4: **Their also experiencing muscle aches, chills, and high fevers.**

   What correction should be made to sentence 4?

   (1) change Their to They're
   (2) change Their to There
   (3) remove the comma after aches
   (4) insert a comma after high
   (5) no correction is necessary

3. Sentence 5: **Visiting the emergency room is unnecessary, however, say many Doctors.**

   What correction should be made to sentence 5?

   (1) change Visiting to Visit
   (2) change emergency to Emergency
   (3) remove the comma after unnecessary
   (4) change say to says
   (5) change Doctors to doctors

4. Sentence 9: **Bringing children and senior citizens for flu shots is important because the flu is especially dangerous for them, so do it before flu season starts.**

   If you rewrote sentence 9 beginning with

   <u>The flu is especially dangerous for children and senior citizens, so</u>

   the next words should be

   (1) bring them for flu shots before
   (2) doing it is important
   (3) it is important to be bringing
   (4) flu shots before flu season
   (5) the flu season starts

Questions 5 through 9 refer to the following paragraphs.

Credit Purchases

(A)

(1) Building a credit history with a department store card is easier than with a bank card. (2) What's more, department stores usually don't charge a yearly fee for use of there credit cards.

(B)

(3) On the whole, peoples experiences with department store cards are good except when they lose a card. (4) That can be nerve-wracking! (5) Losing a credit card, you learn something important. (6) You learn to keep track of your card numbers. (7) The principal thing to remember about a credit line is that it doesn't mean you have access to "free" money. (8) People whose credit card purchases add up to a huge sum every month get trapped. (9) Because they can't pay off the whole amount, high interest charges are adding to their accounts. (10) For them, it would be better to pay cash instead.

5. Sentence 2: **What's more, department stores usually don't charge a yearly fee for use of there credit cards.**

   What correction should be made to sentence 2?

   (1) change What's to Whats'
   (2) change department stores to Department Stores
   (3) change don't to do'nt
   (4) insert a comma after fee
   (5) change there to their

6. Sentence 3: **On the whole, peoples experiences with department store cards are good except when they lose a card.**

   What correction should be made to sentence 3?

   (1) change whole to hole
   (2) remove the comma
   (3) change peoples to people's
   (4) insert a comma after good
   (5) change except to accept

7. Sentences 5 and 6: **Losing a credit card, you learn something important. You learn to keep track of your card numbers.**

   The most effective combination of sentences 5 and 6 would include which group of words?

   (1) When you lose a credit card, you learn the importance of
   (2) and that important thing is
   (3) Learning how important it is to
   (4) Once someone, who has lost a credit card, learns
   (5) Losing a card and learning to keep track of your card numbers

8. Which revision would make the text more effective?

   Begin a new paragraph

   (1) with sentence 4
   (2) with sentence 5
   (3) with sentence 6
   (4) with sentence 7
   (5) with sentence 8

9. Sentence 9: **Because they can't pay off the whole amount, high interest charges are adding to their accounts.**

   Which is the best way to write the underlined portion of the text? If the original is the best way, choose option (1).

   (1) are adding
   (2) were added
   (3) adding
   (4) are added
   (5) been added

Answers start on page 304.

In Personal Writing

Like a conversation, some writing often changes topics. When you write in your journal, for example, you can change the topic as often as you like. Some personal letters may also go from topic to topic or contain ideas that are off the main topic.

Most writing, however, should focus on one main topic. You have learned that all sentences in a paragraph should support the topic sentence. In the same way, the topic sentence of each paragraph in a longer piece of writing should relate to the main idea of the piece.

Read the personal writing below. Can you find where the writer strays from the topic?

> The two qualities I am most proud of in myself are my objectivity and my determination. I try to always be open-minded in challenging situations and consider all sides involved. I also have more determination than most people so I have gotten along well most of my life.
>
> When my friends are having an argument, they often come to me to help them settle it. I listen carefully to all the facts, and without showing favoritism, I help both people see the other's point of view. I am not afraid to say what I think because I know I have thoroughly considered the issue. For example, when my brothers wanted to go to the movies without my sister, I listened to their side and helped them to see my sister's side. They thought about it and included her.
>
> Those who know me also admire my determination. This drive to succeed has enabled me to excel at many jobs. For example, I am always willing to work an extra hour or two at the construction site, which impresses my supervisor and co-workers. When performance reviews were given out, I was given special recognition for my ability to work beyond what was expected.
>
> At times my determination has gotten me into trouble. One day, for instance, I did not want to stop working at quitting time. I kept going without supervision, and unfortunately did the job all wrong! My boss was very upset that time.
>
> I am proud of my ability to be objective and my determination to succeed.

The writer began by introducing two qualities she liked in herself—objectivity and determination. She strayed from that topic in the fourth paragraph when she started to discuss how her determination caused a problem on the job. Although this paragraph discusses a quality about herself, it does not support the main idea of the essay.

The Personal Link

Follow the steps below to write a personal piece about yourself to a friend or relative.

1. It can be difficult to write about yourself—especially your good qualities. It may sound like boasting or bragging. However, it can help you know yourself better, as well as help the person to whom you are writing learn more about you.

   Make a list of good qualities about yourself. If you like, write your list in your journal instead. Remember that you don't have to show your journal to anyone.

   _____

   _____

   _____

2a. Choose two personal qualities from your list. Write examples of incidents when you showed those qualities.

   _____

   _____

   _____

   _____

   b. Review your examples to make sure they relate to the two qualities you chose. Cross out any that do not.

3. Use your list to write a description of your best qualities to a friend or relative. Add a short introductory paragraph and a short concluding paragraph.

Edit

Read your description of your personal qualities. Make sure you have stayed on the topic throughout. Then edit your description for errors.

Portfolio Reminder

Put your personal writing in your portfolio.

In General Writing

Staying on topic is essential in general writing such as business letters and essays.

Here are some good strategies for staying on topic to keep in mind:

- Plan your writing carefully. If you have a clear plan, you will be less likely to include irrelevant ideas.
- When you have finished your essay, reread it. Ask yourself whether each sentence relates to your main idea.

Read the essay below. See if you can find where the writer goes off topic.

> The personal qualities that can lead to successful relationships and successful careers are often the same. People with a sense of loyalty, mutual interests, and a personable manner are attractive both to an employer and a friend. It is not surprising that people who are effective employees also have many good friends.
>
> For example, consider the quality of loyalty. Surely an employer who is interviewing a candidate for a job wants to know that the person will be committed to the company. He or she hopes that the person will stay on the job and not always be looking for a better offer. Likewise, who wants a friend who is disloyal? A friendship cannot last if one person is constantly canceling commitments because he or she has other things to do. Friends need to know that both persons are committed to making it work.
>
> In addition, mutual interests are essential in both the workplace and in personal relationships. An employee might be smart, skilled, and loyal, but if he or she is interested in computers, and the job requires working with animals, the match will probably not be a good one. Similarly, a person who spends hours playing video games because he hates exercise will probably not be friends with someone who is a hiking fanatic and loves the outdoors.
>
> A personable manner is a quality that all people—whether employer or friend—find appealing. A perfect example is my friend Jane. She is the nicest person, the kindest person I know. When I need her, she is there for me, no matter what. Other friends may come and go, but Jane sticks by me. It is not surprising that Jane is a good employee as well as a good friend.

Did you see that the writer strays from the topic in the last paragraph? The essay is about the common qualities in a good employee and a good friend. The writer gives a general description of these qualities, but then strays off topic with a personal description of her friend.

The GED Link

Follow the steps below to write an essay on this topic.

> What qualities do you consider important in a person? Use your personal observations, experience, and knowledge to answer the question and support your point of view.

1. Think about the topic. Write down qualities you admire in people. Include examples and details. You may use ideas from the Personal Link on page 219 as well as your personal journal. Don't worry about writing complete sentences.

   _____

   _____

   _____

   _____

2. Look at your ideas. See what three main points you can make about the topic with them. Use the following plan to organize your ideas.

   Paragraph 1: Introduction

   Paragraph 2 will be about _____

   Paragraph 3 will be about _____

   Paragraph 4 will be about _____

   Paragraph 5: Conclusion

   Go back to the first question and number each idea you wrote down 2, 3, or 4 to show whether you will use it in body paragraph 2, 3, or 4.

3. On a separate sheet of paper, write an essay using your plan from above.

Edit

Read your essay. Make sure you have stayed on the topic throughout. Then edit your essay for errors.

Portfolio Reminder

Put your essay from the GED Link in your portfolio.

Answers start on page 304.

Unit 4 Cumulative Review Mechanics

Directions: Choose the <u>one best answer</u> to each question.

<u>Questions 1 through 4</u> refer to the following letter.

Dear Mr. and Mrs. Flowers:

(A)

(1) This letter is to inform you of Bayford Middle School's recommendation regarding your child's mathematics placement next year. (2) Jonathans current enrollment is in our general math course.

(B)

(3) Our recommendation is based on a combination of your child's grades and the Department's placement guidelines. (4) We believe it offers your child the best opportunity to increase his mathematical skills. (5) Therefore, we recommend placing Jonathan in Introduction to Algebra starting in the Fall semester.

(C)

(6) If you wish to discuss our recommendation, feel free to call his math teacher. (7) His math teacher is Mr. Porter, at extension 881.

Sincerely,
Bayford Middle School Math Department

1. Sentence 2: **Jonathans current enrollment is in our general math course.**

   What correction should be made to sentence 2?

   (1) change <u>Jonathans</u> to <u>Jonathan's</u>
   (2) insert a <u>comma</u> after <u>enrollment</u>
   (3) change <u>general math</u> to <u>General Math</u>
   (4) replace <u>course</u> with <u>coarse</u>
   (5) no correction is necessary

> **TIP**
> To decide if an appositive needs commas, say the sentence without the appositive. If you can still clearly identify the noun, put commas around the appositive.

2. Sentence 3: **Our recommendation is based on a combination of your child's grades and the Department's placement guidelines.**

   What correction should be made to sentence 3?

   (1) replace <u>Our</u> with <u>Hour</u>
   (2) change <u>is</u> to <u>being</u>
   (3) change <u>child's</u> to <u>childs'</u>
   (4) insert a comma after <u>grades</u>
   (5) change <u>Department's</u> to <u>department's</u>

3. Sentence 5: **Therefore, we recommend placing Jonathan in Introduction to Algebra starting in the Fall semester.**

   What correction should be made to sentence 5?

   (1) remove the comma after <u>Therefore</u>
   (2) change <u>recommend</u> to <u>recommended</u>
   (3) change <u>Introduction to Algebra</u> to <u>introduction to algebra</u>
   (4) insert a comma after <u>Algebra</u>
   (5) change <u>Fall</u> to <u>fall</u>

4. Sentences 6 and 7: **If you wish to discuss our recommendation, feel free to call his math teacher. His math teacher is Mr. Porter, at extension 881.**

   The most effective combination of sentences 6 and 7 would include which group of words?

   (1) call Mr. Porter, who is his math teacher at
   (2) teacher, Mr. Porter, at
   (3) Mr. Porter is his math teacher at
   (4) extension 881 for teacher discussions with Mr. Porter
   (5) Mr. Porter's extension 881

Questions 5 through 8 refer to the following information.

Saving Old Paint Brushes

(A)

(1) Do-it-yourself painters often find that old brushes have hardened with paint because they weren't properly cleaned after they were used. (2) Depending on how long the paint has dried these brushes can be saved. (3) Just follow these simple steps.

(B)

(4) To soften the dried paint, suspend the brush in a commercial softener, which is carried by most hardware stores. (5) Taking care, not to cut the bristles, scrape them with a putty knife. (6) If the dried paint reaches up to the handle, scrape it out with the knifes flat edge. (7) If any paint is still left, you can comb it out with a metal comb. (8) After that, soak the bristles overnight in the softener once again.

(C)

(9) Any remaining paint can be washed out with soap water, and a bit of turpentine. (10) Finally, rinse well with cold water. (11) For dirty brushes that have been seriously neglected, you may have to repeat the process.

5. Sentence 2: **Depending on how long the paint has dried these brushes can be saved.**

   Which is the best way to write the underlined portion of the text? If the original is the best way, choose option (1).

   (1) dried these
   (2) dried, yet these
   (3) dried, however these
   (4) dried, these
   (5) dried. These

6. Sentence 5: **Taking care, not to cut the bristles, scrape them with a putty knife.**

   What correction should be made to sentence 5?

   (1) change Taking to Take
   (2) remove the comma after care
   (3) replace to with too
   (4) remove the comma after bristles
   (5) no correction is necessary

7. Sentence 6: **If the dried paint reaches up to the handle, scrape it out with the knifes flat edge.**

   What correction should be made to sentence 6?

   (1) change reaches to reach's
   (2) replace to with too
   (3) remove the comma
   (4) insert a comma after out
   (5) change knifes to knife's

8. Sentence 9: **Any remaining paint can be washed out with soap water, and a bit of turpentine.**

   Which is the best way to write the underlined portion of the text? If the original is the best way, choose option (1).

   (1) soap water, and
   (2) soap water and
   (3) soap, water, and
   (4) soap, water, and,
   (5) soap, and water, and

Questions 9 through 12 refer to the following paragraphs.

Temporary Workers

(A)

(1) The use of temporary workers began slowly, but its now widespread and represents billions of dollars a year in wages. (2) If you include part-timers and freelancers among this group, it accounts for almost one-third of U.S. workers. (3) People "temp" because it sometimes leads to full-time employment. (4) A poll by a National Association of temporary workers has shown that almost 40 percent reported an offer of full-time work.

(B)

(5) American temps, unlike their european counterparts, are not unionized. (6) Only about a quarter of them receive any health benefits, vacation time, sick days, or job security. (7) In other Western countries, temporary workers receive national health care, workers compensation, and in some countries vacation and sick time.

(C)

(8) At present, the temporary workforce in this country is one of the strongest areas of employment growth. (9) That could mean more unionization of temps. (10) At least it could mean getting some of the benefits full-time workers enjoy.

9. Sentence 1: **The use of temporary workers began slowly, but its now widespread and represents billions of dollars a year in wages.**

What correction should be made to sentence 1?

(1) change began to begun
(2) remove the comma
(3) remove but
(4) replace slowly, but with slowly. But
(5) change its to it's

10. Sentence 4: **A poll by a National Association of temporary workers has shown that almost 40 percent reported an offer of full-time work.**

What correction should be made to sentence 4?

(1) replace poll with pole
(2) change National Association to national association
(3) insert a comma after workers
(4) change shown to showed
(5) no correction is necessary

11. Sentence 5: **American temps, unlike their european counterparts, are not unionized.**

What correction should be made to sentence 5?

(1) remove the comma after temps
(2) replace their with there
(3) replace their with they're
(4) change european to European
(5) remove the comma after counterparts

12. Sentences 9 and 10: **That could mean more unionization of temps. At least it could mean getting some of the benefits full-time workers enjoy.**

The most effective combination of sentences 9 and 10 would include which group of words?

(1) and it also could mean getting
(2) temps, getting some
(3) therefore leading to the getting
(4) or, at least, getting
(5) temps so that they get

Questions 13 through 15 refer to the following paragraph.

Tuna—A Surprising Fish

(1) There are more than 22,000 species of fish in the sea. (2) Yet only the tuna is warm-blooded. (3) It's normally high body temperature isn't affected by the water temperature in which it swims. (4) That's also why it is occasionally seen swimming on the surface during the summer. (5) Although you might think all tuna are small the bluefin is almost as big and as fast as a car. (6) It can way up to 1500 pounds, and its swimming speed is about 55 miles per hour.

13. Sentence 3: **It's normally high body temperature isn't affected by the water temperature in which it swims.**

    What correction should be made to sentence 3?

    (1) change It's to Its
    (2) change isn't to is'nt
    (3) replace affected with effected
    (4) insert a comma after water temperature
    (5) no correction is necessary

14. Sentence 5: **Although you might think all tuna are small the bluefin is almost as big and as fast as a car.**

    What correction should be made to sentence 5?

    (1) replace you with we
    (2) change are to is
    (3) insert a comma after think
    (4) insert a comma after small
    (5) insert a comma after big

15. Sentence 6: **It can way up to 1500 pounds, and its swimming speed is about 55 miles per hour.**

    What correction should be made to sentence 6?

    (1) replace way with weigh
    (2) remove the comma after pounds
    (3) change its to it's
    (4) change is to was
    (5) no correction is necessary

Writing Links Review

Write an essay on the following topic. As you are writing, keep the following Writing Links topics in mind.

☑ Do I have an introductory paragraph, middle paragraphs with examples and details, and a concluding paragraph? (Writing Link, pages 204–207)

☑ Do I stay on the topic throughout the essay? (Writing Link, pages 218–221)

Do you agree with the old saying "You can't teach an old dog new tricks"? Explain your answer. Support your view with your personal observations, experience, and knowledge.

Answers start on page 304.

Cumulative Review Performance Analysis
Unit 4 ● Mechanics

Use the Answers and Explanations starting on page 304 to check your answers to the Unit 4 Cumulative Review. Then use the chart to figure out the skill areas in which you need more practice.

On the chart, circle the questions that you answered correctly. Write the number correct for each skill area. Add the number of questions that you got correct on the Cumulative Review. If you feel that you need more practice, go back and review the lessons for the skill areas that were difficult for you.

Questions	Number Correct	Skill Area	Lessons for Review
2, 3, 10, 11	____/4	Capitalization	15
4, 5, 6, 8, 12, 14	____/6	Commas	16
1, 7, 9, 13, 15	____/5	Spelling	17
TOTAL CORRECT	____/15		

LANGUAGE ARTS, WRITING, PART I

Directions

The Language Arts, Writing Posttest is intended to measure your ability to use clear and effective English. It is a test of English as it should be written, not as it might be spoken.

This test consists of paragraphs with numbered sentences. Some of the sentences contain errors in sentence structure, organization, usage, or mechanics (spelling, punctuation, and capitalization). After reading the numbered sentences, answer the multiple-choice questions that follow. Some questions refer to sentences that are correct as written. The best answer for these questions is the one that leaves the sentence as originally written. The best answer for some questions is the one that produces a sentence that is consistent with the verb tense and point of view used throughout the paragraph.

You should spend no more than 75 minutes answering the 50 questions on this test. Work carefully, but do not spend too much time on any one question. Do not skip any items. Make a reasonable guess when you are not sure of an answer. You will not be penalized for incorrect answers.

When time is up, mark the last item you finished. This will tell you whether you can finish the real GED Test in the time allowed. Then complete the test.

Record your answers to the questions on a copy of the answer sheet on page 331. Be sure that all required information is properly recorded on the answer sheet.

To record your answers, mark the numbered space on the answer sheet that corresponds to the answer you choose for each question on the test.

Example:

Sentence 1: **We were all honored to meet governor Phillips.**

What correction should be made to sentence 1?

(1) change honored to honoring
(2) insert a comma after honored
(3) change meet to met
(4) change governor to Governor
(5) no correction is necessary   ① ② ③ ● ⑤

In this example, the word governor should be capitalized; therefore, answer space 4 would be marked on the answer sheet.

Do not rest the point of your pencil on the answer sheet while you are considering your answer. Make no stray or unnecessary marks. If you change an answer, erase your first mark completely. Mark only one answer space for each question; multiple answers will be scored as incorrect. Do not fold or crease your answer sheet.

When you finish the test, use the Performance Analysis Chart on page 244 to determine whether you are ready to take the real GED Test and, if not, which skill areas need additional review.

Directions: Choose the one best answer to each question.

Questions 1 through 7 refer to the following paragraphs.

Varieties of Life Insurance

(A)

(1) Life insurance can protect your family if you become disabled or die. (2) If you buy life insurance when you are young. (3) The cost is low. (4) It can also be a good investment. (5) In every state there is three basic kinds of life insurance—term, whole life, and universal life.

(B)

(6) The first kind, term insurance, is usually the most economical. (7) The reason it's cost is low is that it has no cash value. (8) Term insurance is also best when you have a temporary need. (9) The unfortunate thing about term insurance is that its annual premiums increase each year, meaning that as you get older it eventually becomes less economical.

(C)

(10) Because a whole life policy has a cash value, one can often stop making payments on it after a time. (11) Whole life insurance can also provide income when you retire. (12) It encourages regular saving, too.

(D)

(13) The last kind, universal life insurance, is a flexible plan that can accommodate anyone. (14) By changing the amount of insurance or the yearly premium you can adapt this kind of insurance to fit your changing needs. (15) Whatever kind of insurance you chose, shop carefully, and always buy from a reputable company.

1. Sentences 2 and 3: **If you buy life insurance when you are young. The cost is low.**

   Which is the best way to write the underlined portion of the text? If the original is the best way, choose option (1).

   (1) young. The
   (2) young the
   (3) young, the
   (4) young nevertheless the
   (5) young and the

2. Sentence 5: **In every state there is three basic kinds of life insurance—term, whole life, and universal life.**

   Which is the best way to write the underlined portion of the text? If the original is the best way, choose option (1).

   (1) is
   (2) was
   (3) are
   (4) have been
   (5) be

3. Sentence 7: **The reason it's cost is low is that it has no cash value.**

   What correction should be made to sentence 7?

   (1) change it's to its
   (2) insert a comma after low
   (3) change has to has had
   (4) replace no with know
   (5) no correction is necessary

4. Sentence 9: **The unfortunate thing about term insurance is that its annual premiums increase each year, meaning as you get older it eventually becomes less economical.**

   If you rewrote sentence 9 beginning with

   Unfortunately, annual premiums increase each year as you get older,

   the next words should be

   (1) and that means that eventually
   (2) eventually with term insurance becoming
   (3) economically becoming
   (4) so term insurance eventually becomes
   (5) making them become eventually

5. Which sentence below would be most effective at the beginning of paragraph C?

   (1) Some people buy whole life insurance.
   (2) Another kind is good, too.
   (3) The cash value varies in whole life insurance.
   (4) Whole life insurance is good for long-term investments.
   (5) The next kind is whole life, the most expensive insurance.

6. Sentence 10: **Because a whole life policy has a cash value, one can often stop making payments on it after a time.**

   What correction should be made to sentence 10?

   (1) replace Because with That's because
   (2) remove the comma after value
   (3) replace one with you
   (4) insert a comma after it
   (5) no correction is necessary

7. Sentence 14: **By changing the amount of insurance or the yearly premium you can adapt this kind of insurance to fit your changing needs.**

   Which is the best way to write the underlined portion of the text? If the original is the best way, choose option (1).

   (1) premium you
   (2) premium. You
   (3) premium then you
   (4) premium, you
   (5) premium so you

Tips for Successful Job Hunting
Reagan News Sunday Special

(A)

(1) Successful job hunting requires careful preparation. (2) Here are some useful steps those just entering the job market can take.

(B)

(3) First, list the kinds of jobs you been thinking you'd like to do. (4) You can determine the skills, training, and experience required by talking to workers. (5) That is, talk to people who have jobs you are interested in. (6) Next, list your qualifications and see if they match any of the jobs youve selected. (7) If not, you need to think again about the kinds of work you want. (8) For example, you can't start as a restaurant manager, but you may be able to start as a waiter or cashier and work your way up. (9) Once you select work that matches your qualifications and find a job opening in a company, you need to set up an interview. (10) Try to learn about the workplace before you go for the interview. (11) In order to make a good impression, you need to look, speak, and act your best. (12) Stress your qualifications, your positive work habits, and how interested you are in the job.

8. Sentence 3: **First, list the kinds of jobs you been thinking you'd like to do.**

   Which is the best way to write the underlined portion of the text? If the original is the best way, choose option (1).

   (1) been thinking
   (2) think
   (3) has thought
   (4) thinks
   (5) had been thinking

9. Sentences 4 and 5: **You can determine the skills, training, and experience required by talking to workers. That is, talk to people who have jobs you are interested in.**

   The most effective combination of sentences 4 and 5 would include which group of words?

   (1) workers, for example, having interesting jobs
   (2) workers who have jobs
   (3) workers, and talk to people
   (4) By talking to people who have the skills
   (5) Workers with the skills, training, and experience

10. Sentence 6: **Next, list your qualifications and see if they match any of the jobs youve selected.**

What correction should be made to sentence 6?

(1) remove the comma after Next
(2) change qualifications to qualification's
(3) remove and
(4) insert a comma after match
(5) change youve to you've

11. Sentence 9: **Once you select work that matches your qualifications and find a job opening in a company, you need to set up an interview.**

What correction should be made to sentence 9?

(1) insert a comma after qualifications
(2) change company to Company
(3) remove the comma after company
(4) replace company, you with company. You
(5) no correction is necessary

12. Which revision would improve the text, "How to Find a Job"?

Begin a new paragraph

(1) with sentence 6
(2) with sentence 7
(3) with sentence 8
(4) with sentence 9
(5) with sentence 10

13. Sentence 12: **Stress your qualifications, your positive work habits, and how interested you are in the job.**

The most effective revision of sentence 12 would include which group of words?

(1) be interested in the job
(2) the interesting job
(3) tell them you are interested in the job
(4) your interest in
(5) the job interests you

MEMORANDUM

TO: All Fitness Staff
FROM: Rick Benson
RE: Committee Report on Temporary Staff

(A)

(1) This is a summary of last month's report on Bellmore fitness centers' use of temporary staff. (2) Bellmore hires about 60 temporary office workers each season. (3) These temps help in various departments among our 36 fitness centers. (4) Temps cover reception desks complete filing order sportswear and equipment, and fill in for regular staff. (5) Bellmore hires temps so that various departments can complete projects as well as screen prospective permanent workers.

(B)

(6) In their report, the committee identified and explored the following issues. (7) Without direct fitness-center experience, problems for our clients are created by over one half of the temporary hires. (8) Because temps are hired for a maximum of three months, they receive very little training. (9) These workers are not motivated to solve problems. (10) Unresolved problems create a poor atmosphere for clients and staff alike. (11) In response to this report, Human Resources Director Jane Pierce and I are looking for volunteers to work on a brief and practical employee manual for temporary workers.

(C)

(12) Such a handbook would define roles, clarify procedures, and orient new workers quickly and efficiently. (13) If you wish to participate in this worthwhile project, please contact Jane or I. (14) I'm sure that this project will make everyone's job a little easier.

14. Sentence 1: **This is a summary of last month's report on Bellmore fitness centers' use of temporary staff.**

    What correction should be made to sentence 1?

    (1) change month's to months
    (2) change Bellmore to bellmore
    (3) change fitness centers' to Fitness Centers'
    (4) change centers' to center's
    (5) no correction is necessary

15. Sentence 4: **Temps cover reception desks complete filing order sportswear and equipment, and fill in for regular staff.**

    Which is the best way to write the underlined portion of the text? If the original is the best way, choose option (1).

    (1) desks complete filing order sportswear and equipment, and fill
    (2) desks, complete filing order sportswear and equipment, and fill
    (3) desks, complete filing, order sportswear, and equipment, and fill
    (4) desks complete filing order sportswear and equipment. And they fill
    (5) desks, complete filing, order sportswear and equipment, and fill

16. Sentence 6: **In their report, the committee identified and explored the following issues.**

    What correction should be made to sentence 6?

    (1) replace their with its
    (2) remove the comma after report
    (3) change committee to Committee
    (4) insert a comma after identified
    (5) no correction is necessary

17. Sentence 7: **Without direct fitness-center experience, problems for our clients are created by over one half of the temporary hires.**

    If you rewrote sentence 7 beginning with

    Because they have no direct fitness-center experience,

    the next words should be

    (1) over one half of the temporary hires create
    (2) problems are created for our clients by over one half
    (3) creating problems for our clients by over one half
    (4) and because they create problems for over one half
    (5) our clients have problems created by over one half

18. Sentences 9 and 10: **These workers are not motivated to solve problems. Unresolved problems create a poor atmosphere for clients and staff alike.**

    The most effective combination of sentences 9 and 10 would include which group of words?

    (1) These workers create a poor atmosphere
    (2) not solving unresolved problems creates
    (3) nevertheless unresolved problems create
    (4) Not motivated to solve problems,
    (5) solve problems, and unresolved

19. Which revision should be made to sentence 11?

    (1) move sentence 11 to the beginning of paragraph B
    (2) move sentence 11 to follow sentence 6
    (3) move sentence 11 to the beginning of paragraph C
    (4) move sentence 11 to the end of paragraph C
    (5) remove sentence 11

20. Sentence 12: **If you wish to participate in this worthwhile project, please contact Jane or I.**

    What correction should be made to sentence 12?

    (1) change wish to wishes
    (2) replace to with too
    (3) remove the comma
    (4) insert so after the comma
    (5) replace I with me

Road Rules: Change Your Tire Safely

Special Report to *Morning News*

(A)

(1) These safety rules are important to follow if you ever have a flat tire while driving. (2) The first thing you should do is to stop in a safe place. (3) Put on your hazard signal, and if you are on a multi-lane highway, move carefully into the far right lane. (4) Then slowly pull over to the curb or onto the shoulder and continue until you have drove to an area as free from traffic as possible.

(B)

(5) Try to park the car on firm, level ground, turn the ignition off, and set the parking brake. (6) If you have any passengers, let them out of the car on the passenger side.

(C)

(7) As you change the tire, remember these suggestions. (8) Never get under a car that is raised on a jack. (9) It is easy for a car to roll off the jack anyone underneath may be seriously injured. (10) After you have removed the flat, place it carefully on the ground with the outside surface up so that the wheel's finish won't be getting scratched. (11) Next, mount your spare tire and tighten the wheel nuts. (12) When the spare fit tightly against the hub, lower the car to the ground and remove the jack. (13) Tighten the wheel nuts as securely as you can, stow your tools safely, and store the flat.

(D)

(14) With your spare tire in place, your next stop should be at an auto repair shop. (15) Let mechanics there check the spare. (16) They may also be able to repair and replace the flat, so you can finally, be safely on your way.

21. Sentence 4: **Then slowly pull over to the curb or onto the shoulder and continue until you have drove to an area as free from traffic as possible.**

What correction should be made to sentence 4?

(1) change pull to pulling
(2) insert a comma after curb
(3) change drove to driven
(4) insert a comma after area
(5) no correction is necessary

22. Which revision would improve the text?

(1) move sentence 5 to the end of paragraph A
(2) combine paragraphs A and B
(3) remove sentence 6
(4) move sentence 7 to the end of paragraph B
(5) remove sentence 8

23. Sentence 9: **It is easy for a car to roll off the jack anyone underneath may be seriously injured.**

Which is the best way to write the underlined portion of the text? If the original is the best way, choose option (1).

(1) jack anyone
(2) jack, anyone
(3) jack which means anyone
(4) jack therefore anyone
(5) jack, and anyone

24. Sentence 10: **After you have removed the flat, place it carefully on the ground with the outside surface up so that the wheel's finish won't be getting scratched.**

Which is the best way to write the underlined portion of the text? If the original is the best way, choose option (1).

(1) be getting
(2) get
(3) got
(4) have gotten
(3) have been getting

25. Sentence 12: **When the spare fit tightly against the hub, lower the car to the ground and remove the jack.**

What correction should be made to sentence 12?

(1) change fit to fits
(2) insert a comma after tightly
(3) remove the comma after hub
(4) replace to with two
(5) no correction is necessary

26. Sentence 16: **They may also be able to repair and replace the flat, so you can finally, be safely on your way.**

What correction should be made to sentence 16?

(1) insert a comma after repair
(2) remove the comma after flat
(3) remove so
(4) remove the comma after finally
(5) change your to you're

History and You

Postal Delivery: Then and Now

(A)

(1) The U.S. Postal Service has come a long way since its founding by Ben Franklin in the late 1700s. (2) A multi-talented man, Franklin represented the new nation in Europe and gave us countless clever inventions. (3) Back then, it took weeks for mail to travel across the 13 states. (4) About 100 years later, the Pony Express took up to ten days to carry mail from Missouri West to California. (5) In this century, however, came the swift trains, the efficient trucks, and finally, fastest of all, came the speedy airplanes. (6) Today, according to the post office, most first-class mail within the 50 states is delivered within three days, while mail out of the country takes five to six days.

(B)

(7) In addition to speed, the cost of mailing a letter has also changed. (8) The cost of first class mail has rose dramatically since colonial days. (9) One ounce of first class mail cost less than 5 cents to mail in 1800. (10) By 2000, the cost was up to 33 cents. (11) Many people are upset by the cost of postage. (12) Costs relatively less now than in 1800. (13) The U.S. Postal Service, despite its faults, do the finest job in the world delivering mail fast and accurately.

27. Sentence 4: **About 100 years later, the Pony Express took up to ten days to carry mail from Missouri West to California.**

    What correction should be made to sentence 4?

    (1) remove the comma after later
    (2) change Pony Express to pony express
    (3) change took to been taken
    (4) insert a comma after days
    (5) change West to west

28. Sentence 5: **In this century, however, came the swift trains, the efficient trucks, and finally, fastest of all, came the speedy airplanes.**

    Which is the best way to write the underlined portion of the text? If the original is the best way, choose option (1).

    (1) came the speedy airplanes
    (2) we have the speedy airplanes
    (3) the speedy airplanes
    (4) the speedy airplanes came
    (5) the airplanes came speeding

29. Which revision should be made to paragraph A?

    (1) move sentence 1 to follow sentence 2
    (2) remove sentence 2
    (3) remove sentence 4
    (4) move sentence 6 to the beginning of the paragraph
    (5) no revision is necessary

30. Sentence 8: **The cost of first class mail has rose dramatically since colonial days.**

    What correction should be made to sentence 8?

    (1) change has to have
    (2) change rose to risen
    (3) insert a comma after dramatically
    (4) change colonial to Colonial
    (5) no correction is necessary

31. Sentences 11 and 12: **Many people are upset by the cost of postage. Costs relatively less now than in 1800.**

    Which is the best way to write the underlined portion of the text? If the original is the best way, choose option (1).

    (1) postage. Costs
    (2) postage, costs
    (3) postage, costing
    (4) postage costs
    (5) postage, yet it costs

32. Sentence 13: **The U.S. Postal Service, despite its faults, do the finest job in the world delivering mail fast and accurately.**

    Which is the best way to write the underlined portion of the text? If the original is the best way, choose option (1).

    (1) do
    (2) are doing
    (3) have done
    (4) will do
    (5) does

Ralph Yorita
Easy Systems, Inc.
One Fleet Street
Los Angeles, CA 90048

Dear Easy Systems Subscriber:

(A)

(1) In December, I wrote to say that the problems with our customer service operations had been solved. (2) However, service for a significant number of you, our valued customers, did not improve. (3) In fact, our service during the high volume of holiday calls were worse.

(B)

(4) I am writing once again to admit that Easy Systems let many of you down. (5) I apologize for any inconvenience or frustration. (6) We have been working diligently to resolve the remaining problems. (7) As a result, at this time we will be able to say with confidence that you can soon expect prompt, high-quality customer service.

(C)

(8) We are adding two new major features and they have been requested by our customers and these new features will make our service more convenient and efficient. (9) The first feature is a phone message that tells how long you will have to wait in order to speak to one of our customer service representatives. (10) The second feature is our new capacity to record a voicemail message or to receive a fax from you. (11) Both these features should be in place by June 1. (12) At Easy Service your continued support is important to us. (13) Our goal to deliver a superior level of service to all our customers. (14) Thank you for your patience and loyalty.

Sincerely,

Ralph Yorita
Vice President for Customer Services

33. Sentence 2: **However, service for a significant number of you, our valued customers, did not improve.**

Which is the best way to write the underlined portion of the text? If the original is the best way, choose option (1).

(1) you, our valued customers,
(2) you our valued customers,
(3) you, our valued customers
(4) you our valued customers
(5) you. Our valued customers

34. Sentence 3: **In fact, our service during the high volume of holiday calls were worse.**

What correction should be made to sentence 3?

(1) remove the comma after fact
(2) replace high with hi
(3) change holiday to Holiday
(4) insert a comma after calls
(5) change were to was

35. Sentence 7: **As a result, at this time, we will be able to say with confidence that you can soon expect prompt, high-quality customer service.**

Which is the best way to write the underlined portion of the text? If the original is the best way, choose option (1).

(1) will be
(2) have been
(3) are being
(4) were
(5) are

36. Sentence 8: **We are adding two new major features and they have been requested by our customers and these new features will make our service more convenient and efficient.**

The most effective revision of sentence 8 would include which group of words?

(1) Having been requested by our customers
(2) Two new features are being added that have been
(3) features, these having been requested,
(4) features requested by our customers to make
(5) We are adding for more convenient and efficient service

37. Which revision would make the letter more effective?

Begin a paragraph

(1) with sentence 9
(2) with sentence 10
(3) with sentence 11
(4) with sentence 12
(5) with sentence 13

38. Sentence 13: **Our goal to deliver a superior level of service to all our customers.**

What correction should be made to sentence 13?

(1) insert is after goal
(2) insert being after goal
(3) change deliver to be delivering
(4) insert a comma after service
(5) no correction is necessary

Safe Bunk Beds

(A)

(1) Bunk beds have long been a favorite space-saving solution for cramped quarters and children usually love the drama of climbing up the ladder to bed. (2) Unfortunately, for years these beds have also been a safety hazard. (3) Recently, the government issued strict standards to protect children from injury. (4) Here is some useful tips that can help every "bunker" have a safe night's sleep.

(B)

(5) First of all, find out whether your bunk bed was manufactured after the standards were issued. (6) Look for a permanent label with information about the bed's date of manufacture, company of distribution, and model. (7) Missing this label, you can assume the bed does not meet the standards. (8) You will probably want to buy a new one.

(C)

(9) If the bunk bed is up to standards, inspect its general condition. (10) Both bunks should have sturdy, full-length guardrails on the wall side. (11) The top bunk should also have a guardrail attached to the headboard and extending to within 15 inches of the footboard. (12) This is where the ladder to the upper bunk should be firmly attached. (13) The space between the bottom of a guardrail and the bed frame, should be no more than three and a half inches. (14) The top of it, moreover, must come to at least five inches above the mattress. (15) If necessary, add boards to close gaps. (16) Tighten any bolts or nails that are loose.

(D)

(17) Finally, for safety's sake, don't allow children younger than six on the upper bunk. (18) Never let babies and toddlers on either bunk.

39. Sentence 1: **Bunk beds have long been a favorite space-saving solution for cramped quarters and children usually love the drama of climbing up the ladder to bed.**

Which is the best way to write the underlined portion of the text? If the original is the best way, choose option (1).

(1) quarters and
(2) quarters, and
(3) quarters and,
(4) quarters. And
(5) quarters, and,

40. Sentence 4: **Here is some useful tips that can help every "bunker" have a safe night's sleep.**

What correction should be made to sentence 4?

(1) change is to are
(2) insert a comma after tips
(3) change have to has
(4) change night's to nights'
(5) change night's to nights

41. Sentence 7: **Missing this label, you can assume the bed does not meet the standards.**

The most effective revision of sentence 7 would begin with which group of words?

(1) You don't have the label
(2) Not having information labeling,
(3) If this label is missing,
(4) It doesn't have a label
(5) A label that is missing

42. Sentence 8: **You will probably want to buy a new one.**

Which revision should be made to sentence 8?

(1) move sentence 8 to follow sentence 5
(2) replace You with If that's the case, you
(3) replace You with Finally, you
(4) move sentence 8 to the beginning of paragraph C
(5) remove sentence 8

43. Sentence 13: **The space between the bottom of a guardrail and the bed frame, should be no more than three and a half inches.**

What correction should be made to sentence 13?

(1) insert a comma after guardrail
(2) remove the comma after frame
(3) insert it after the comma
(4) replace than with then
(5) no correction is necessary

44. Sentence 14: **The top of it, moreover, must come to at least five inches above the mattress.**

What correction should be made to sentence 14?

(1) replace it with the guardrail
(2) remove the comma after it
(3) remove the comma after moreover
(4) change come to have came
(5) replace the mattress with it

Josephine Waxman
Office of Consumer Assistance
23 NW Lincoln Street
Suite 500
Alexandria, VA 22314-2300

Dear Mr. and Ms. Sanders:

(A)

(1) In reply to your request, I have enclosed information about mortgage programs. (2) There are several programs available for families like your's. (3) These programs are for first-time home buyers who's income and credit history are satisfactory but who have little money for a down payment.

(B)

(4) Most of the programs have income and price limits. (5) Many also offer five-percent down payments, or they allow first-time buyers to borrow part of their down payment. (6) These kinds of programs, however, are typically limited to low-income buyers.

(C)

(7) Moderate-income buyers, on the other hand, can get Federal Housing Administration (FHA) loans. (8) FHA loans have no income limits, buyers can put less than five percent down. (9) One caution, however is that purchase price caps can reduce the value of FHA programs in areas where housing costs are high. (10) The Veterans Administration (VA) also has had loans without down payment requirements for buyers with moderate incomes.

(D)

(11) Once you have found a home you want, contact several lenders in the area you wish to buy. (12) Include small, local institutions. (13) I hope the enclosed chart will help you find local lenders who participate in these programs.

Sincerely,

Josephine Waxman

45. Sentence 2: **There are several programs available for families like your's.**

What correction should be made to sentence 2?

(1) change are to is
(2) change programs to program's
(3) insert a comma after available
(4) change families to family's
(5) change your's to yours

46. Sentence 3: **These programs are for first-time home buyers who's income and credit history are satisfactory but who have little money for a down payment.**

What correction should be made to sentence 3?

(1) insert a comma after buyers
(2) change who's to whose
(3) change are satisfactory to is satisfactory
(4) change have to has
(5) change for to four

47. Sentence 5: **Many also offer five-percent down payments, or they allow first-time buyers to borrow part of their down payment.**

Which is the best way to write the underlined portion of the text? If the original is the best way, choose option (1).

(1) payments, or they
(2) payments or they
(3) payments they
(4) payments. They
(5) payments, or

48. Sentence 8: **FHA loans have no income limits, buyers can put less than five percent down.**

Which is the best way to write the underlined portion of the text? If the original is the best way, choose option (1).

(1) limits, buyers
(2) limits. Buyers
(3) limits buyers
(4) limits so buyers
(5) limits and buyers

49. Sentence 10: **The Veterans Administration (VA) also has had loans without down payment requirements for buyers with moderate incomes.**

Which is the best way to write the underlined portion of the text? If the original is the best way, choose option (1).

(1) has had
(2) had
(3) is having
(4) has
(5) will have

50. Sentences 11 and 12: **Once you have found a home you want, contact several lenders in the area you wish to buy. Include small, local institutions.**

Which is the best way to write the underlined portion of the text? If the original is the best way, choose option (1).

(1) buy. Include
(2) buy, including
(3) buy and including
(4) buy and include
(5) buy. You should include

Answers start on page 305.

Posttest Performance Analysis Chart
Language Arts, Writing

This chart can help you determine your strengths and weaknesses on the content and skill areas of the Language Arts, Writing Test. Use the Answers and Explanations on pages 305–309 to check your answers to the test. Then circle on the chart the numbers of the test items you answered correctly. Put the total number correct for each content area and skill area in each row and column. If you answered fewer than 50 questions correctly, look at the total items correct in each column and row and decide which areas are difficult for you. Use the page references to study those areas. Use a copy of the Language Arts, Writing Study Planner on page 31 to guide your review.

Item Type / Content Area	Correction	Revision	Construction Shift	Number Correct	Page References
Sentence Structure *(Pages 32–91)*					
Sentences/Sentence Fragments	38	1, 31		____/3	34–41
Compound Sentences/ Combining Ideas		47	4, 18	____/3	42–49
Subordinating Ideas		50	9	____/2	54–61
Run-ons/Comma Splices		23, 48	36	____/3	62–69
Modifiers			17, 41	____/2	72–77
Parallel Structure		28	13	____/2	78–83
Organization *(Pages 92–133)*					
Paragraph Structure/ Unity and Coherence	19, 22, 29			____/3	94–101
Topic Sentences			5	____/1	104–109
Paragraph Division			12, 37	____/2	112–117
Transitions	42			____/1	120–125
Usage *(Pages 134–185)*					
Subject-Verb Agreement	25, 34, 40	2, 32		____/5	136–145
Verb Forms	21, 30	8		____/3	148–155
Verb Tenses		24, 35, 49		____/3	158–165
Pronouns	6, 16, 20, 44			____/4	168–177
Mechanics *(Pages 186–226)*					
Capitalization	14, 27			____/2	188–195
Commas	11, 26, 43	7, 15, 33, 39		____/7	196–203
Spelling	3, 10, 45, 46			____/4	208–217

1–40 → Use the Study Planner on page 31 to organize your review.
41–50 → You can get more practice with the Simulated Test on pages 245–262.

For additifonal help, see the *Steck-Vaughn GED Language Arts, Writing Exercise Book*.

LANGUAGE ARTS, WRITING, PART I

Directions

The Language Arts, Writing Simulated Test is intended to measure your ability to use clear and effective English. It is a test of English as it should be written, not as it might be spoken.

This test consists of paragraphs with numbered sentences. Some of the sentences contain errors in sentence structure, organization, usage, or mechanics (spelling, punctuation, and capitalization). After reading the numbered sentences, answer the multiple-choice questions that follow. Some questions refer to sentences that are correct as written. The best answer for these questions is the one that leaves the sentence as originally written. The best answer for some questions is the one that produces a sentence that is consistent with the verb tense and point of view used throughout the paragraph.

You should spend no more than 75 minutes answering the 50 questions on this test. Work carefully, but do not spend too much time on any one question. Do not skip any items. Make a reasonable guess when you are not sure of an answer. You will not be penalized for incorrect answers.

When time is up, mark the last item you finished. This will tell you whether you can finish the real GED Test in the time allowed. Then complete the test.

Record your answers to the questions on a copy of the answer sheet on page 331. Be sure that all required information is properly recorded on the answer sheet.

To record your answers, mark the numbered space on the answer sheet that corresponds to the answer you choose for each question on the test.

Example:

Sentence 1: **We were all honored to meet governor Phillips.**

What correction should be made to sentence 1?

(1) change honored to honoring
(2) insert a comma after honored
(3) change meet to met
(4) change governor to Governor
(5) no correction is necessary   ① ② ③ ● ⑤

In this example, the word governor should be capitalized; therefore, answer space 4 would be marked on the answer sheet.

Do not rest the point of your pencil on the answer sheet while you are considering your answer. Make no stray or unnecessary marks. If you change an answer, erase your first mark completely. Mark only one answer space for each question; multiple answers will be scored as incorrect. Do not fold or crease your answer sheet.

When you finish the test, use the Performance Analysis Chart on page 262 to determine whether you are ready to take the real GED Test and, if not, which skill areas need additional review.

Adapted with permission of the American Council on Education.

Directions: Choose the one best answer to each question.

Questions 1 through 7 refer to the following paragraphs.

The Oscars

(A)

(1) "May I have the envelope, please?" (2) Just hearing those words is enough to send a shiver of anticipation through the whole audience. (3) Soon a film nominee will receive an Oscar, the oldest and best known award of the academy of Motion Picture Arts and Sciences. (4) The statue is one of the most coveted awards. (5) Stands only ten inches high and weighs about seven pounds.

(B)

(6) Some of the awards are for artistic work, such as best picture, best director, best actor, or for the best song. (7) Other awards are also given in a number of technical categories, such as film editing or sound effects. (8) From time to time, the academy also presents a special prize called the Lifetime Achievement Award. (9) This prize is given to a member of the motion picture industry, based on his or her entire body of work rather than on a particular film.

(C)

(10) The Academy Awards ceremony has also become a popular television show each spring. (11) It is a showcase of talent, films, and personalities and talent in the entertainment industry. (12) Oscars are the most sought-after awards by actors and actresses because they are universally admired. (13) In addition, any film that wins one or more Oscars, is almost guaranteed to see its profits soar.

1. Sentence 3: **Soon a film nominee will receive an Oscar, the oldest and best known award of the academy of Motion Picture Arts and Sciences.**

   What correction should be made to sentence 3?

   (1) change nominee to Nominee
   (2) remove the comma
   (3) insert a comma after oldest
   (4) replace Arts and Sciences with arts and sciences
   (5) change academy to Academy

2. Sentences 4 and 5: **The statue is one of the most coveted awards. Stands only ten inches high and weighs about seven pounds.**

   Which is the best way to write the underlined portion of the text? If the original is the best way, choose option (1).

   (1) awards. Stands
   (2) awards, yet it
   (3) awards, it
   (4) awards, stands
   (5) awards stands

3. Which of the following would serve as an effective topic sentence for paragraph B?

(1) Oscars are awarded in many film categories.
(2) Most people are thrilled to be presented with the awards.
(3) Stars wear glamorous clothing to the ceremony.
(4) Some nominees do not attend the ceremony.
(5) Sometimes an entire group wins an Oscar.

4. Sentence 6: **Some of the awards are for artistic work, such as best picture, best director, best actor, or for the best song.**

What correction should be made to sentence 6?

(1) insert they after awards
(2) change are to is
(3) remove the comma after picture
(4) remove for the
(5) no correction is necessary

5. Sentence 9: **This prize is given to a member of the motion picture industry, based on his or her entire body of work rather than on a particular film.**

Which is the best way to write the underlined portion of the text? If the original is the best way, choose option (1).

(1) industry, based
(2) industry. Based
(3) industry based
(4) industry being based
(5) industry, and based

6. Sentence 12: **Oscars are the most sought-after awards by actors and actresses because they are universally admired.**

What correction should be made to sentence 12?

(1) change are to is
(2) insert a comma after awards
(3) change actors and actresses to actor's and actress's
(4) remove because
(5) change they to the awards

7. Sentence 13: **In addition, any film that wins one or more Oscars, is almost guaranteed to see its profits soar.**

What correction should be made to sentence 13?

(1) remove the comma after addition
(2) remove the comma after Oscars
(3) change is to are
(4) replace its with their
(5) change its to it's

West Star Insurance Company
570 West 47th Avenue
Port Grayson, FL 32007

Dear Ms. Santos:

(A)

(1) Thank you for doing business with West Star Insurance. (2) We certainly hope you never have damage or loss to you're car. (3) If you do, however, we at West Star is committed to settling your claim with the least inconvenience to you.

(B)

(4) In addition to providing speedy claim service, West Star offers top-quality workmanship on repairs done at any of our recommended body shops. (5) When replacing a cracked or broken windshield, our preferred list has the best glass shops in your area. (6) West Star also can negotiate special rates for car rentals.

(C)

(7) Please find enclosed a special kit that West Star provides for every new client it contains instructions on what to do if you are in an accident. (8) The kit also contains an accident information card on which to record important facts about an accident. (9) It is a good idea to keep the kit in the glove compartment of your car, so you have it on hand when you need it. (10) There's a list of toll-free numbers to call when reporting an accident, too.

(D)

(11) Everyone at West Star Insurance looks forward to serving you for many years to come. (12) We also wish you safe, accident-free driving.

Yours truly,

West Star Claims Department

8. Sentence 2: **We certainly hope you never have damage or loss to you're car.**

   What correction should be made to sentence 2?

   (1) insert will after certainly
   (2) change have to had
   (3) insert a comma after damage
   (4) change you're to your
   (5) no correction is necessary

9. Sentence 3: **If you do, however, we at West Star is committed to settling your claim with the least inconvenience to you.**

   Which is the best way to write the underlined portion of the text? If the original is the best way, choose option (1).

   (1) is committed
   (2) was committed
   (3) is committing
   (4) has committed
   (5) are committed

10. Sentence 5: **When replacing a cracked or broken windshield, our preferred list has the best glass shops in your area.**

    The most effective revision of sentence 5 would begin with which group of words?

    (1) A cracked or broken windshield needs replacing
    (2) When you need a cracked or broken windshield replaced,
    (3) With a cracked or broken windshield
    (4) Needing to repair a cracked or broken windshield
    (5) Upon cracking or breaking a windshield

11. Sentence 7: **Please find enclosed a special kit that West Star provides for every new client it contains instructions on what to do if you are in an accident.**

    Which is the best way to write the underlined portion of the text? If the original is the best way, choose option (1).

    (1) client it
    (2) client and it
    (3) client, while it
    (4) client. It
    (5) client, it

12. Sentence 10: **There's a list of toll-free numbers to call when reporting an accident, too.**

    Which revision should be made to sentence 10?

    (1) move it to the beginning of paragraph C
    (2) move it to follow sentence 8
    (3) move it to the beginning of paragraph D
    (4) remove sentence 10
    (5) no revision is necessary

13. Sentence 11: **Everyone at West Star Insurance looks forward to serving you for many years to come.**

    What correction should be made to sentence 11?

    (1) change looks to will look
    (2) change looks to look
    (3) change serving to serve
    (4) insert a comma after you
    (5) no correction is necessary

Tips to Jump-Start Your Car

(A)

(1) If you leave your automobile headlights on all night, you probably have a dead battery the next morning. (2) One way to start your car is by getting a jump-start following these steps from a friend's car.

(B)

(3) Before you begin, have your friend park his or her car facing or next to yours. (4) Open both car hoods, and secure them with support rods. (5) Turn off all electrical components. (6) Put both cars in neutral or park, and make sure both parking breaks are engaged.

(C)

(7) Connect one end of a jumper cable to the positive terminal of the car with the working battery. (8) Connect the other end of the jumper cable to the dead batteries positive terminal. (9) Next, connect a second jumper cable to the negative terminal of the working car. (10) Attach the other end of the jumper cable to the grounding strap. (11) Have your friend start his or her car's engine. (12) Then start your car. (13) Once your car is running, you can disconnect the cables. (14) First, disconnect the negative cable from your car. (15) Then remove the negative cable from your friend's car. (16) When you have took the positive cable from your car, remove the last connection from your friend's car.

(D)

(17) Let your car's engine run a few minutes to recharge your battery, now you can take your friend out to breakfast.

14. Sentence 1: **If you leave your automobile headlights on all night, you probably have a dead battery the next morning.**

Which is the best way to write the underlined portion of the text? If the original is the best way, choose option (1).

(1) have
(2) will have
(3) have had
(4) had
(5) are having

15. Sentence 2: **One way to start your car is by getting a jump-start following these steps from a friend's car.**

The most effective revision of sentence 2 would include which group of words?

(1) is by following these steps to get a
(2) get a jump-start for your car from a friend
(3) getting your friend to jump-start your car
(4) following these steps can jump-start
(5) following your friend who can jump-start

16. Sentence 6: **Put both cars in neutral or park, and make sure both parking breaks are engaged.**

What correction should be made to sentence 6?

(1) change Put to Putting
(2) insert a comma after neutral
(3) remove the comma
(4) replace breaks with brakes
(5) no correction is necessary

17. Sentence 8: **Connect the other end of the jumper cable to the dead batteries positive terminal.**

What correction should be made to sentence 8?

(1) replace Connect to As you connect
(2) replace the jumper cable with it
(3) insert a comma after cable
(4) change batteries to battery's
(5) no correction is necessary

18. Which revision would make the text more effective?

Begin a new paragraph

(1) with sentence 9
(2) with sentence 10
(3) with sentence 11
(4) with sentence 12
(5) with sentence 13

19. Sentence 16: **When you have took the positive cable from your car, remove the last connection from your friend's car.**

Which is the best way to write the underlined portion of the text? If the original is the best way, choose option (1).

(1) have took
(2) have taken
(3) taken
(4) took
(3) are taking

20. Sentence 17: **Let your car's engine run a few minutes to recharge your battery, now you can take your friend out to breakfast.**

Which is the best way to write the underlined portion of the text? If the original is the best way, choose option (1).

(1) battery, now
(2) battery. And now
(3) battery. Now
(4) battery now
(5) battery, as now

Reducing Cholesterol: Why and How

(A)

(1) The medical profession continues to stress the negative affects of fat in the diet. (2) Fat is the major cause of cholesterol in the blood. (3) Cholesterol is a significant factor in heart disease. (4) Experts do not agree on the level at which cholesterol becomes a risk factor. (5) In the 1990s, doctors were not concerned unless a cholesterol level reached 300. (6) Today, doctors are not concerned unless a cholesterol level is above 180.

(B)

(7) Studies show that about 70 percent of people can reduce their cholesterol 15 to 25 percent. (8) Eating less food that is high in fat and cholesterol. (9) The American public are encouraged to read labels and to choose products with low amounts of fat and cholesterol. (10) Doctors recommend replacing whole-milk products with those made with low-fat or skim milk. (11) Lean meat, beans, and oat bran in the diet helps reduce cholesterol levels in the bloodstream. (12) In addition, exercising keeps you fit and seems to help clear cholesterol from the arteries.

(C)

(13) According to the American Heart Association, keeping your cholesterol level low improves your chances of a long, healthy life. (14) Evidence is strong that your habits can affect your cholesterol level, and, therefore, your risk of heart disease. (15) As we've seen, these habits include eating and exercising.

21. Sentence 1: **The medical profession continues to stress the negative affects of fat in the diet.**

    What correction should be made to sentence 1?

    (1) change medical profession to Medical Profession
    (2) change continues to continue
    (3) change continues to have continued
    (4) replace affects with effects
    (5) no correction is necessary

22. Sentence 3: **Cholesterol is a significant factor in heart disease.**

    Which revision should be made to sentence 3?

    (1) move sentence 3 to the beginning of paragraph A
    (2) replace Cholesterol with In turn, cholesterol
    (3) move sentence 3 to follow sentence 4
    (4) remove sentence 3
    (5) move sentence 3 to the end of paragraph A

23. Sentences 7 and 8: **Studies show that about 70 percent of people can reduce their cholesterol 15 to 25 percent. Eating less food that is high in fat and cholesterol.**

    Which is the best way to write the underlined portion of the text? If the original is the best way, choose option (1).

    (1) percent. Eating
    (2) percent by eating
    (3) percent, and eating
    (4) percent, therefore, eating
    (5) percent even while eating

24. Sentence 9: **The American public are encouraged to read labels and to choose products with low amounts of fat and cholesterol.**

    Which is the best way to write the underlined portion of the text? If the original is the best way, choose option (1).

    (1) are encouraged
    (2) been encouraged
    (3) is encouraged
    (4) were encouraged
    (5) encouraged

25. Sentence 11: **Lean meat, beans, and oat bran in the diet helps reduce cholesterol levels in the bloodstream.**

    What correction should be made to sentence 11?

    (1) replace meat with meet
    (2) remove the commas after meat
    (3) insert a comma after diet
    (4) change helps to help
    (5) insert a comma after levels

26. Sentences 14 and 15: **Evidence is strong that your habits can affect your cholesterol level, and, therefore, your risk of heart disease. As we've seen, these habits include eating and exercising.**

    The most effective combination of sentences 14 and 15 would include which group of words?

    (1) disease, and as we've seen
    (2) Evidence about eating and exercising
    (3) It is evident that your habits affect
    (4) Your habits of eating and exercising
    (5) your eating and exercising habits can

Annual Report of
United Grain Operations, Inc.

(A)

(1) United Grain Operations (UGO) has much to celebrate in this, its centennial year. (2) It was one century ago that two grain magnates May Foods and Brans United, merged their rival firms. (3) In a stroke, they created the great UGO. (4) UGO's cereal products soon became household names and spawned an empire. (5) Today, not only does UGO continue to dominate the ready-to-eat cereal industry, but its other divisions compete strongly as well. (6) We were quite pleased with United Corn Oil's performance last year, and this was despite a tough business environment. (7) UCO listed record profits and begun negotiations with several Midwestern ethanol processors. (8) In addition, United Seed Company continues to dominate their market. (9) Sales have reached record levels for the third straight year. (10) Finally, United Mills was named one of the top 100 performers of the year by Investors magazine.

(B)

(11) The full annual report will detail UGO's on-going, as well as proposed, business ventures for its second century. (12) The report will be on your desks next week.

27. Sentence 2: **It was one century ago that two grain magnates May Foods and Brans United, merged their rival firms.**

    Which is the best way to write the underlined portion of the text? If the original is the best way, choose option (1).

    (1) magnates May Foods and Brans United,
    (2) magnates, May Foods and Brans United
    (3) magnates, May Foods and Brans United,
    (4) magnates May Foods and Brans United
    (5) magnates, May Foods, and Brans United,

28. Sentences 3 and 4: **In a stroke, they created the great UGO. UGO's cereal products soon became household names and spawned an empire.**

    The most effective combination of sentences 3 and 4 would include which group of words?

    (1) UGO, whose cereal
    (2) UGO, and their cereal
    (3) creating the great UGO cereal products
    (4) UGO, becoming household names
    (5) created cereal products and became

29. Sentence 6: **We were quite pleased with United Corn Oil's performance last <u>year, and this was despite</u> a tough business environment.**

Which is the best way to write the underlined portion of the text? If the original is the best way, choose option (1).

(1) year, and this was despite
(2) year and this despite
(3) year. And this despite
(4) year, despite
(5) year. This being despite

30. Sentence 7: **UCO listed record profits and <u>begun</u> negotiations with several Midwestern ethanol processors.**

Which is the best way to write the underlined portion of the text? If the original is the best way, choose option (1).

(1) begun
(2) began
(3) begin
(4) have began
(5) are beginning

31. Sentence 8: **In addition, United Seed Company continues to dominate their market.**

What correction should be made to sentence 8?

(1) remove the comma after <u>addition</u>
(2) change <u>Company</u> to <u>company</u>
(3) change <u>continues</u> to <u>continue</u>
(4) replace <u>to</u> with <u>too</u>
(5) replace <u>their</u> with <u>its</u>

32. Which revision would make this business report more effective?

Begin a new paragraph

(1) with sentence 5
(2) with sentence 6
(3) with sentence 7
(4) with sentence 8
(5) with sentence 10

Food and Fun

Barbecue Great Chicken Every Time
from *Sarah's Kitchen*

(A)

(1) Many people enjoy grilled chicken in the outdoors during the warm summer months. (2) Here are some handy tips for success with your barbecues.

(B)

(3) Before lighting up, it's always a good idea to brush or spray your grill with a little oil. (4) That way your chicken won't stick. (5) After the grill is fired up, let it get hot before you are putting on the chicken. (6) A hot grill will sear in the juices and keep the meat moist. (7) It will also make the pieces easier to turn.

(C)

(8) Once the meat is on the grill and seared, move the chicken slightly away from the flame. (9) Piercing the skin with the prongs of a fork will let the delicious juices escape. (10) Cooking best with just that single move, you should resist moving it again or picking it up to look under it. (11) Use long-handled tongs or a spatula instead of a fork to move the meat.

(D)

(12) To check whether the chicken is done, make a small cut into the thickest part. (13) It's ready if you didn't see any pinkness. (14) Another way to check the meat's readiness with a meat thermometer. (15) Whole chickens should be around 180°, and chicken parts should be around 170°.

(E)

(16) If you want great grilled chicken the next time don't forget to clean up when you're done. (17) A carefully scraped grate will prevent your next chicken from sticking to the grill.

33. Sentence 5: **After the grill is fired up, let it get hot before you <u>are putting</u> on the chicken.**

Which is the best way to write the underlined portion of the text? If the original is the best way, choose option (1).

(1) are putting
(2) put
(3) have put
(4) had put
(5) will put

34. Which revision should be made to paragraph C?

(1) move sentence 8 to the end of paragraph B
(2) remove sentence 9
(3) remove sentence 10
(4) move sentence 11 to follow sentence 8
(5) no revision is necessary

35. Sentence 10: **Cooking best with just that single move, you should resist moving it again or picking it up to look under it.**

The most effective revision of sentence 10 would begin with which group of words?

(1) A single move cooking it best, so you
(2) Resist moving it again or picking it up for best cooking
(3) The meat, moving only a single time, cooks best
(4) To singly move the meat will cook it best, so you
(5) The meat will cook best with just that single move, so you

36. Sentence 13: **It's ready if you <u>didn't see</u> any pinkness.**

Which is the best way to write the underlined portion of the text? If the original is the best way, choose option (1).

(1) didn't see
(2) don't see
(3) haven't seen
(4) weren't seeing
(5) aren't seeing

37. Sentence 14: **Another way to check the meat's readiness with a meat thermometer.**

What correction should be made to sentence 14?

(1) replace <u>way</u> with <u>weigh</u>
(2) change <u>meat's</u> to <u>meats</u>
(3) insert a comma after <u>readiness</u>
(4) insert is after <u>readiness</u>
(5) no correction is necessary

38. Sentence 16: **If you want great grilled chicken the next time don't forget to clean up when you're done.**

What correction should be made to sentence 16?

(1) replace <u>great</u> with <u>grate</u>
(2) insert a comma after <u>time</u>
(3) change <u>forget</u> to <u>have forgotten</u>
(4) change <u>you're</u> to <u>your</u>
(5) no correction is necessary

Ms. Elaine Stockwell, Hiring Manager
Fare Safe Hotels
Wilmington, IL 60100

Dear Ms. Stockwell:

(A)

(1) The customer service trainee position that you advertised in Sunday's Westwood Standard greatly interests me. (2) Fare Safe Hotels have always stood for comfortable accommodations with courteous service, and they are reasonably priced. (3) I would like to be part of Fare Safe's continued growth. (4) My aunt always stays at the Fare Safe Hotel when she visits, and she thinks it's great.

(B)

(5) As you seen from the resume I have attached, I possess the qualifications and determination needed for the trainee position. (6) In June, I received my high school equivalency certificate. (7) While I was attending school and studying to pass the GED Test, I have developed strong organizational skills. (8) Furthermore, my part-time job at the information desk of Westwood City hospital requires extensive interpersonal and public relations skills. (9) My supervisor gave me high scores on all my work reviews. (10) I received a commendation for exceptional service to patients. (11) I believe that these experiences are fine preparation for your training program in customer service.

(C)

(12) I would appreciate the opportunity to discuss my qualifications with you. (13) To set up an interview, please call me at 555-9091. (14) Thank you for your kind consideration.

Sincerely,

William Anson

39. Sentence 2: **Fare Safe Hotels have always stood for comfortable accommodations with courteous service, and they are reasonably priced.**

The most effective revision of sentence 2 would include which group of words?

(1) service at a reasonable price
(2) for accommodations that are comfortable
(3) for service with courtesy
(4) comfortable and courteous, and they
(5) Reasonably priced, Fare Safe Hotels

40. Sentence 5: **As you seen from the resume I have attached, I possess the qualifications and determination needed for the trainee position.**

Which is the best way to write the underlined portion of the text? If the original is the best way, choose option (1).

(1) seen
(2) will have seen
(3) have been seeing
(4) will be seen
(5) will see

41. Sentence 7: **While I was attending school and studying to pass the GED Test, I have developed strong organizational skills.**

What correction should be made to sentence 7?

(1) remove While
(2) insert a comma after school
(3) remove the comma after Test
(4) change Test to test
(5) change have developed to developed

42. Which revision would make the letter more effective?

(1) move sentence 1 to the end of paragraph A
(2) remove sentence 3
(3) remove sentence 4
(4) move sentence 5 to the end of paragraph A
(5) no revision is necessary

43. Sentence 8: **Furthermore, my part-time job at the information desk of Westwood City hospital requires extensive interpersonal and public relations skills.**

What correction should be made to sentence 8?

(1) remove the comma after Furthermore
(2) insert a comma after job
(3) change hospital to Hospital
(4) change requires to require
(5) change relations to relation's

44. Sentences 9 and 10: **My supervisor gave me high scores on all my work reviews. I received a commendation for exceptional service to patients.**

Which is the best way to write the underlined portion of the text? If the original is the best way, choose option (1).

(1) reviews. I
(2) reviews I
(3) reviews, I
(4) reviews and
(5) reviews, and I

Protect Yourself from Home-Repair Fraud

(A)

(1) Billions of dollars are wasted each year on home repairs that are shoddy, unfinished, or never started at all. (2) Here are some ways to avoid becoming a victim of such consumer fraud.

(B)

(3) First of all, recognize the warning signs. (4) Extravagant promises or free merchandise are usually cause for suspicion. (5) Another questionable tactic is an offer of a lower price if you refer potential customers, called a kickback. (6) Contracts should be free of tricky phrases or vague language, and them should match the promises of the sales pitch. (7) Take your time before signing, and resist pressure to sign right away.

(C)

(8) Once you have chosen a home-repair contractor, there are additional ways to protect your investment. (9) You should never pay in cash, and do not pay the whole amount before the work begins. (10) Reputable contractors rarely expect this kind of payment. (11) Instead, they usually agree to payments in thirds or quarters. (12) For example, the contractor will receive one third at the start one third halfway through the job, and the final third upon completion of the job. (13) Ask to see the licenses of the workmen that are hired. (14) Make sure written contracts clearly spell out the cost of materials and labor, as well as the start and finish dates.

(D)

(15) In summary, be alert to the warning signs when someone offers to repair your home. (16) Do'nt hesitate to refuse an offer that seems too good to be true. (17) Finally, contact the authorities if you believe that you have been a victim of fraud.

45. Sentence 4: **Extravagant promises or free merchandise are usually cause for suspicion.**

What correction should be made to sentence 4?

(1) change promises to promise's
(2) insert a comma after promises
(3) change are to is
(4) replace for with four
(5) no correction is necessary

46. Sentence 5: **Another questionable tactic is an offer of a lower price if you refer potential customers, called a kickback.**

The most effective revision of sentence 5 would begin with which group of words?

(1) Another questionable tactic for referring potential customers,
(2) Another questionable tactic, called a kickback,
(3) For referring potential customers, a questionable tactic
(4) A kickback for referring potential customers, known as a questionable tactic,
(5) Offering a lower price for a kickback is another

47. Sentence 6: **Contracts should be free of tricky phrases or vague language, and them should match the promises of the sales pitch.**

What correction should be made to sentence 6?

(1) change Contracts to Contracts'
(2) remove the comma after language
(3) change them to they
(4) change promises to promise's
(5) no correction is necessary

48. Sentence 9: **You should never pay in cash, and do not pay the whole amount before the work begins.**

Which is the best way to write the underlined portion of the text? If the original is the best way, choose option (1).

(1) cash, and
(2) cash
(3) cash. And
(4) cash and
(5) cash,

49. Sentence 12: **For example, the contractor will receive one third at the start one third halfway through the job, and the final third upon completion of the job.**

What correction should be made to sentence 12?

(1) remove the comma after example
(2) change will receive to received
(3) insert a comma after start
(4) insert a comma after final third
(5) replace upon completion of with when he completes

50. Sentence 16: **Do'nt hesitate to refuse an offer that seems too good to be true.**

What correction should be made to sentence 16?

(1) change Do'nt to Don't
(2) change hesitate to have hesitated
(3) replace seems with seams
(4) replace too with to
(5) no correction is necessary

Answers start on page 309.

Simulated Test Performance Analysis Chart
Language Arts, Writing

This chart can help you determine your strengths and weaknesses on the content and skill areas of the Language Arts, Writing Test. Use the Answers and Explanations on pages 309–313 to check your answers to the test. Then circle on the chart the numbers of the test items you answered correctly. Put the total number correct for each content area and skill area in each row and column. If you answered fewer than 50 questions correctly, look at the total items correct in each column and row and decide which areas are difficult for you. Use the page references to study those areas.

Item Type / Content Area	Correction	Revision	Construction Shift	Number Correct	Page References
Sentence Structure *(Pages 32–91)*					
Sentences/Sentence Fragments	37	2, 23		_____/3	34–41
Compound Sentences/ Combining Ideas		44		_____/1	42–49
Subordinating Ideas		29	26, 28	_____/3	54–61
Run-ons/Comma Splices		11, 20		_____/2	62–69
Modifiers			10, 15, 35, 46	_____/4	72–77
Parallel Structure	4		39	_____/2	78–83
Organization *(Pages 92–133)*					
Paragraph Structure/ Unity and Coherence	12, 34, 42			_____/3	94–101
Topic Sentences			3	_____/1	104–109
Paragraph Division			18, 32	_____/2	112–117
Transitions	22			_____/1	120–125
Usage *(Pages 134–185)*					
Subject-Verb Agreement	13, 25, 45	9, 24		_____/5	136–145
Verb Forms		19, 30, 40		_____/3	148–155
Verb Tenses	41	14, 33, 36		_____/4	158–165
Pronouns	6, 31, 47			_____/3	168–177
Mechanics *(Pages 186–226)*					
Capitalization	1, 43			_____/2	188–195
Commas	7, 38, 49	5, 27, 48		_____/6	196–203
Spelling	8, 16, 17, 21, 50			_____/5	208–217

1–40 → You need more review.
41–50 → Congratulations! You're ready for the GED!

For additional help, see the *Steck-Vaughn GED Language Arts, Writing Exercise Book*.

Answers and Explanations

1. **(3) change contains to contain**
(Usage/Subject-verb agreement) Option (3) is correct because *contain* agrees with the two subjects connected by *and*. Option (1) removes a necessary comma in a series. Option (2) inserts an unnecessary comma between the subject and verb. Option (4) incorrectly shifts the tense to the future. Option (5) uses an incorrect verb.

2. **(5) control it** (Usage/Verb tenses) Option (5) corrects the awkward, wordy tense shift of option (1) so that both verbs in the sentence are in the present simple tense. Option (2) incorrectly uses the present perfect tense. Option (3) incorrectly uses the future tense. Option (4) is the present tense but wordy.

3. **(2) insert a comma after relax**
(Mechanics/Commas in series) Option (2) is correct because a comma is needed to separate the items in the series *relax, unwind, and improve.* Option (1) is incorrect because it removes a comma after an introductory phrase. Option (3) incorrectly changes a possessive to a contraction. Option (4) inserts an unnecessary comma. Option (5) incorrectly changes the contraction for *you are* to a possessive.

4. **(3) job, such as pushing**
(Mechanics/Appositives) Option (3) effectively combines the sentences by making the second a nonessential appositive set off with a comma. Options (1), (2), (4), and (5) are wordy, use inappropriate connecting words, and are incorrectly punctuated.

5. **(1) Like most things, however, daydreaming can have a negative side as well.** (Organization/Topic sentences) Option (1) is the best topic sentence because it introduces the main idea of the paragraph. Option (2) is too general and does not closely relate to the details in the paragraph. Options (3), (4), and (5) are too specific and do not address the main point of the paragraph.

6. **(2) car, especially** (Sentence structure/Fragments) Option (2) is correct because it joins the fragment (sentence 11) to a complete thought and separates the two appropriately with a comma. Option (1) does not correct the sentence fragment. Option (3) omits the necessary comma that tells readers to pause between the two ideas. Options (4) and (5) use unnecessary and inappropriate connecting words.

7. **(1) change Spring to spring** (Mechanics/Capitalization) Option (1) is correct because seasons of the year are not capitalized. Option (2) removes a necessary comma after an introductory phrase. Option (3) incorrectly capitalizes the common noun *state*. Option (4) incorrectly shifts the verb tense to the future. Option (5) removes a necessary comma in a series.

8. **(5) change are to is** (Usage/Subject-verb agreement) Option (5) is correct because the singular verb *is* agrees with the singular subject *person*, not the interrupting phrase *digging with hand tools*. Option (1) incorrectly makes the verb *is digging*. Options (2) and (4) insert unnecessary commas. Option (3) incorrectly makes a plural noun possessive.

9. **(4) The building department** (Usage/Pronouns) Option (4) correctly replaces a vague pronoun with its antecedent. Option (1) is the pronoun with a vague antecedent. Options (2) and (3) are incorrect pronouns. Option (5) provides an incorrect antecedent.

10. **(4) Once the systems are marked,** (Sentence structure/Modifiers) Option (4) corrects a dangling modifier by inserting a subject and verb to create a subordinate clause. Options (1), (2), (3), and (5) do not correct the dangling modifier; it still has nothing to modify.

11. **(1) move sentence 8 to the end of paragraph B** (Organization/Unity and coherence) Option (1) correctly moves a detail to the paragraph it supports. Sentence 9 begins a whole new topic. Options (2) and (4) remove important details. Option (3) moves a supporting detail out of logical order.

12. **(2) remove the comma after signs**
(Mechanics/Unnecessary commas) Option (2) correctly removes an unnecessary comma between a subject and verb. Option (1) removes a necessary comma in a series. Option (3) is an incomplete verb form. Option (4) incorrectly changes the verb from plural to singular; the verb should agree with *signs*. Option (5) leaves an unnecessary comma.

13. **(3) tightening door screws** (Sentence structure/Parallelism) Option (3) is correct because it would make all the items in the series into similarly structured phrases. Options (1), (2), (4), and (5) do not correct the error in parallel structure.

14. **(4) remove sentence 4** (Organization/Unity and coherence) Option (4) correctly eliminates a sentence that does not support the main idea of the paragraph. Option (1) removes the topic sentence. Option (2) moves a detail to an illogical place in the paragraph. Option (3) removes an important supporting detail.

15. **(5) change there to their** (Mechanics/Homonyms) Option (5) is correct because the meaning of the sentence requires the possessive adjective *their,* not the adverb *there.* Option (1) is incorrect because the possessive *your* is needed in the sentence, not the contraction for *you are.* Option (2) incorrectly removes a necessary comma after an introductory clause. Option (3) incorrectly shifts the verb tense. Option (4) inserts an unnecessary comma.

16. **(2) change is to are** (Usage/Subject-verb agreement) Option (2) is correct because *are* agrees with the two subjects *oil-based paint* and *latex paint* connected by *and.* These are the subjects even though they come after the verb in this sentence. Option (1) incorrectly uses the singular verb. Option (3) uses an incomplete verb form. Options (4) and (5) incorrectly shift the verb tense.

17. **(3) You will also need an adequate** (Sentence structure/Fragments) Option (3) corrects the fragment by inserting a missing subject and verb. Options (1), (2), (4), and (5) do not correct the incomplete thought.

18. **(3) skills. The** (Sentence structure/Comma splices) Option (3) correctly makes two complete sentences to repair the comma splice. Option (1) is a comma splice. Option (2) is a run-on sentence. Option (4) does not include the comma that is needed to make a compound sentence with *and.* Option (5) uses an inappropriate connecting word and is incorrectly punctuated.

19. **(3) change johannes gutenberg to Johannes Gutenberg** (Mechanics/Capitalization) Option (3) is correct because all proper names are capitalized. Option (1) inserts an unnecessary comma. Option (2) is incorrect because there is no reason to capitalize *century.*

Option (4) incorrectly shifts the verb tense. Option (5) contains an error in capitalization.

20. **(3) replace All with Prior to the invention of the printing press, all** (Organization/Transitions) Option (3) is correct because it shows the time-order transition between ideas in the first paragraph and the second paragraph. Option (1) incorrectly moves a detail out of the paragraph it belongs with. Option (2) uses an inappropriate term to introduce the transition between paragraphs. Option (4) removes an important piece of information.

21. **(5) page and months** (Sentence structure/Fragments) Option (5) is correct because it uses an appropriate coordinating conjunction to join the idea in a fragment to an independent clause. Options (1) and (3) lead to sentence fragments. Option (2) creates a run-on sentence. Option (4) uses an inappropriate connecting phrase.

22. **(2) many copies of a page could be made quickly and easily** (Sentence structure/Modifiers) Option (2) correctly places the modifiers *of a page* and *quickly and easily* near the words they describe. Options (1), (3), (4), and (5) move, but do not eliminate, the misplaced modifiers.

23. **(3) This process meant** (Usage/Pronouns) Option (3) corrects the vague antecedent of the pronoun *it.* Option (1) contains a pronoun with a vague antecedent. Option (2) creates a sentence fragment. Options (4) and (5) do not clearly convey the relationship between ideas in sentence 9 and the sentence before it.

24. **(4) made except, perhaps, for the personal computer** (Sentence structure/Run-ons) Option (4) combines the ideas in the series of clauses into a clear, simple sentence without wordiness or repetition. Options (1), (2), (3), and (5) do not eliminate the run-on and wordiness.

25. **(3) felt** (Usage/Verb tenses) Option (3) corrects a tense shift because only the simple past is needed in the sentence. Options (1), (2), and (4) are perfect, not simple, forms of the past tense. Option (5) incorrectly uses the present tense.

26. **(5) went** (Usage/Verb tenses) Option (5) is the correct tense; the phrase "Yesterday morning" is a clue the simple past tense is needed. Option (1) is a present perfect tense. Option (2) is an incorrect verb form. Option (3) does not agree with the subject and is a present perfect tense. Option (4) is a continuous past tense, not the simple past required by the sentence.

27. **(3) replace they with she** (Usage/Pronouns) Option (3) correctly uses the singular *she* to refer to *clerk*. Option (1) uses an incorrect verb form. Option (2) removes the necessary comma after an introductory clause. Option (4) inserts an unnecessary comma. Option (5) uses an incorrect plural pronoun to refer to a singular noun.

28. **(1) Joe Forest, the supervisor, who said** (Sentence structure/Subordination) Option (1) eliminates repetition and wordiness by subordinating the detail about Joe Forest and making it an appositive. Options (2), (3), (4), and (5) do not eliminate the repetition or wordiness.

29. **(3) with sentence 11** (Organization/Paragraph divisions) Option (3) correctly begins a new paragraph with a time shift in ideas. The sentences in options (1), (2), (4), and (5) are details within paragraphs.

30. **(3) insert a comma after me** (Mechanics/Commas after introductory elements) Option (3) is correct because a comma is needed after an introductory clause. Option (1) would create a run-on sentence. Option (2) misspells the contraction for *had not*. Option (4) uses an incorrect verb form. Option (5) needlessly replaces a clearly understood pronoun.

31. **(4) remove the comma after radio** (Mechanics/Unnecessary commas) Option (4) is correct because it eliminates an unnecessary comma. Option (1) uses an incorrect verb form. Option (2) inserts an unnecessary comma. Option (3) incorrectly shifts the verb tense to the past perfect. Option (5) is incorrect because the word *right,* meaning *correct,* is appropriate for the sentence, not its homonym, the verb *write*.

32. **(5) change wont to won't** (Mechanics/Spelling contractions) Option (5) is correct because it inserts a needed apostrophe to take the place of the missing letter in *not*. Option (1) incorrectly inserts an unnecessary comma between the subject and verb. Option (2) uses an incomplete verb. Options (3) and (4) remove commas that are needed to set off the parenthetical word *however*.

33. **(4) has become** (Usage/Verb forms) Option (4) correctly adds a helping verb to complete the present perfect tense that indicates an action starting in the past and still continuing. Options (1) and (2) are incomplete verbs. Options (3) and (5) are past tense forms that are not appropriate in the sentence.

34. **(4) Everything from discount clothing to bus or train tickets** (Sentence structure/Subordination) Option (4) eliminates repetition and wordiness by combining related details in one smooth sentence. Options (1), (2), (3), and (5) do not lead to smooth, effective sentences.

35. **(3) insert , and after reliable** (Sentence structure/Run-ons) Option (3) fixes the run-on by inserting a comma and an appropriate coordinating conjunction between the independent clauses. Option (1) inserts an unnecessary comma. Option (2) is incorrect because the singular verb *is* agrees with the singular subject *delivery*. Option (4) inserts an unnecessary comma between two descriptive words, *shipping* and *handling*. Option (5) is a run-on sentence.

36. **(2) combine paragraphs B and C** (Organization/Paragraph divisions) Option (2) correctly combines two short paragraphs that contain details and information about one main idea. Options (1), (3), and (4) incorrectly move supporting details out of logical order. Option (5) removes an important piece of information.

37. **(2) change one to you** (Usage/Pronouns) Option (2) corrects a shift in pronouns from third person (one) to second person (you) to keep it consistent with the rest of the paragraph. Option (1) incorrectly removes a necessary comma after an introductory phrase. Option (3) uses an incorrect verb tense. Option (4) incorrectly replaces a plural noun with a singular possessive. Option (5) inserts an unnecessary comma.

38. **(2) insert a comma after careful** (Mechanics/Commas after introductory elements) Option (2) is correct because it inserts the comma needed after an introductory clause. Option (1) incorrectly shifts the pronoun from second person to third person. Option (3) incorrectly shifts the verb tense. Option (4) replaces a correctly spelled word with its homonym.

39. **(2) Unless you are describing a child** (Sentence structure/Modifiers) Option (2) corrects a dangling modifier by inserting a subject and complete verb to create a subordinate clause. Options (1), (3), (4), and (5) do not correct the dangling modifier.

40. **(5) no correction is necessary** (Usage/Verb forms) Sentence 3 is a correct sentence. Options (1) and (4) incorrectly change verb forms. Option (2) inserts an unnecessary comma. Option (3) is incorrect because the possessive

pronoun *their* is needed in the sentence, not the adverb *there*.

41. **(3) range, yet he** (Sentence structure/ Compound sentences) Option (3) is correct because it effectively combines two related independent thoughts with an appropriate connecting word and punctuation. Option (1) does not show the reader the relationship between the ideas in the two sentences. Option (2) uses an inappropriate connecting word. Option (4) creates a comma splice. Option (5) creates a run-on sentence.

42. **(4) fever, a** (Mechanics/Commas after introductory elements) Option (4) is correct because it inserts a necessary comma after the introductory phrase. Option (1) does not have the necessary comma. Option (2) makes the phrase a sentence fragment. Options (3) and (5) insert unnecessary and inappropriate connecting words.

43. **(4) move sentence 13 to the end of paragraph C** (Organization/Unity and coherence) Option (4) is correct because it places a detail in the most logical position in the paragraph. Option (1) moves a detail out of the paragraph where it belongs. Options (2) and (5) are incorrect because they remove important details. Option (3) moves a detail to an illogical position in the paragraph.

44. **(4) replace one's with his or her** (Usage/ Pronouns) Option (4) correctly uses the third person singular *his or her* to refer to *child*. Option (1) incorrectly removes the apostrophe from a possessive. Option (2) uses an incomplete verb form. Option (3) incorrectly replaces a possessive with a plural. Option (5) uses an incorrect pronoun.

45. **(4) is looking** (Usage/Verb tenses) Option (4) is correct because the continuous present tense is required in the sentence. Option (1) is the simple present. Options (2) and (5) are forms of the past tense. Option (3) is an incomplete verb form.

46. **(5) no revision is necessary** (Organization/ Unity and coherence) Option (5) correctly keeps the topic sentence at the beginning of the paragraph, where it belongs. Options (1), (3), and (4) move it to inappropriate positions. Option (2) removes the topic sentence.

47. **(5) pay attention to details** (Sentence structure/Parallelism) Option (5) is correct because it puts all the items in the series in the same form—verb phrases. Options (1), (2), (3), and (4) do not correct the error in parallel structure.

48. **(3) branches. Finally, the** (Sentence structure/ Comma splices) Option (3) corrects the comma splice by making the two independent clauses two complete sentences. Options (1) and (2) are comma splices. Option (4) is a run-on. Option (5) uses an inappropriate connecting word.

49. **(4) change it's to its** (Mechanics/Spelling possessives) Option (4) is correct because the possessive *its*, not the contraction for *it is,* is needed in the sentence. Options (1) and (3) insert unnecessary commas. Option (2) is incorrect because *high school* should not be capitalized unless it is part of a name.

50. **(3) starts** (Usage/Subject-verb agreement) Option (3) is correct because the verb should be singular to agree with the singular subject *salary level*. Option (1) is a plural verb. Options (2) and (5) incorrectly shift the tense of the verb. Option (4) is incorrect because it is plural and a shift in tense.

UNIT 1: SENTENCE STRUCTURE
Lesson 1
GED Skill Focus (Page 35)

A. 1. *I* This incomplete sentence is missing a verb.

2. *I* This incomplete sentence is not a complete thought.

3. *C*

4. *I* This incomplete sentence is missing a subject.

5. *C*

B. **Q:** I live in Los Angeles. How can I renew my passport?
A: You have several options. Can you wait seven to ten days for your passport? If so, getting a renewal form at the post office Fill it out and send it via overnight mail. With the necessary documentation You can also apply in person at the passport office. However, you'll probably have to wait in line.

Do you need the passport immediately? Then the same-day renewal service While you're at the passport office Finally, let me be the first to wish you a safe trip. Have a fabulous time!

C. After you write your paragraph and edit it for complete sentences and end punctuation, share your work with your instructor or another student.

GED Skill Focus (Page 37)

A. Sample answers:

1. Mothers used to cook for the family.

2. Today, many teens prepare dinner for the family because their working parents come home late.

3. Microwave cooking, take-out food, or packaged macaroni and cheese are easy favorites.

4. Teens feel they are accomplishing an important task, making them feel grown-up and valuable.

5. This is important to their self-esteem.

B.   Dry cleaning ~~costing~~ ^{costs} a lot of money. I know some good ways to remove stains from clothing without
~~clothing. Without~~ going to the dry cleaners. For example, I wasn't ~~upset. When~~ ^{upset when} my child came home with ink on her new sweater. First, I sprayed the ink with some hair ~~spray. That~~ ^{spray that} I keep around just for stains. When the stain was completely saturated, ^I wiped it off with a sponge. Fruit stains, too, will ~~disappear. If~~ ^{disappear if} you first soak them in cool water. Then ^use hot water with a few drops of ammonia. The stain must be gone before ~~washing. Because~~ ^{washing because} soap sets fruit stains. If you know of any other practical methods to remove stains, please let me know.

C. After you edit your paragraph for fragments and end punctuation, share your work with your instructor or another student.

GED Practice (Pages 38–39)

All items in this section are related to sentence fragments.

1. **(3) instead that** Option (3) is correct because it joins a fragment to a complete thought. Option (2) changes only the end punctuation; it does not eliminate the fragment. In option (4), the word *and* does not fit the meaning of the sentence. In option (5) the combination of *and* and *that* does not eliminate the fragment.

2. **(5) no correction is necessary** Options (1), (2), and (3) are incorrect because each creates a fragment. Option (4) creates two complete sentences without end punctuation.

3. **(1) insert It has been before 15** Option (1) is correct because it provides the fragment with a subject and verb. Options (2), (3), and (4) do not correct the fragment.

4. **(2) insert is after This** Option (2) corrects the fragments by inserting the missing verb. Option (1) removes the subject and does not eliminate the fragment. Option (3) creates an additional fragment. Options (4) and (5) do not eliminate the fragment.

5. **(3) account unless I receive an** Option (3) is correct because it provides the appropriate connecting word and a subject and verb for the fragment. Options (1), (2), (4), and (5) do not make sense.

6. **(5) no correction is necessary** The sentence is complete as is. Option (1) repeats the subject. Options (2), (3), and (4) create fragments.

7. **(2) cooking, which is one** Option (2) is correct because it joins the fragment (sentence 4) to a complete thought. Option (1) is incorrect because sentence 4 is a fragment. Options (3) and (5) do not correct the fragment. Option (4) does not make sense.

8. **(1) replace Less with Microwaves are less** Option (1) is correct because it gives this fragment both a subject and a verb. Options (2), (3), and (5) do not fix the fragment. Option (4) creates a new fragment.

9. **(4) are not worried because most** This option is correct because it provides the correct verb and connecting word *because* to join the fragment to the complete sentence. Options (1), (2), and (5) do not have complete verbs. Option (3) repeats the subject.

GED Mini-Test • Lesson 1 (Pages 40–41)

1. **(2) stomachs when** (Sentence fragments) Option (2) attaches the fragment to a complete thought. Options (1), (3), and (4) use incorrect punctuation without correcting the fragment. Option (5) does not make sense.

2. **(2) replace underestimating with they underestimate** (Sentence fragments) Option (2) is correct because it provides the sentence with a subject and verb. Option (1) changes the verb but doesn't provide the sentence with a subject. Option (3) misspells a word. Option (4) does not correct the fragment. Option (5) creates a new fragment.

3. **(3) He first measured** (Sentence fragments) Option (3) is correct because it supplies the

fragment with a needed subject. Options (1), (2), and (5) have no subjects. Option (4) supplies a subject, but *First* begins a fragment.

4. **(1) plate to show what** (Sentence fragments) Option (1) correctly combines the meanings of both the fragment and the complete sentence into one sentence. Options (2), (3), (4), and (5) would incorrectly or awkwardly combine the thoughts.

5. **(3) us, such as your** (Sentence fragments) Option (3) is correct because it joins a sentence fragment to a complete sentence. Option (1) is incorrect because it contains a fragment. Option (2) runs ideas together without correct punctuation. Options (4) and (5) use inappropriate words to connect the thoughts.

6. **(5) no correction is necessary** (Sentence fragments) Options (1), (2), and (3) all create fragments in a sentence that is already a complete thought. Option (4) misspells a word.

7. **(2) when you want to download** (Sentence fragments) Option (2) correctly joins a fragment to a complete thought and supplies a subject and verb. Options (1), (3), (4), and (5) would create awkwardly worded sentences or change the meaning of the text.

8. **(1) insert can be before updated** (Sentence fragments) Option (1) correctly completes the verb to eliminate the fragment. Option (2) is incorrect because it fails to complete the verb and eliminate the fragment. Option (3) creates another fragment. Option (4) does not correct the fragment. Option (5) does not complete the main verb of the sentence.

Lesson 2
GED Skill Focus (Page 43)
A. 1. People want their lawns to be insect-free, <u>so</u> many of them use chemical pesticides.

2. Chemical pesticides in grass can pose a hazard, <u>for</u> children often play on the grass.

3. Some thoughtful parents still use pesticides, <u>but</u> they follow instructions for use and <u>disposal</u> carefully.

4. Others prefer to use biodegradable sprays, <u>or</u> they choose natural bug repellents, like marigolds.

5. Professional exterminators must be certified, <u>and</u> they should apply pesticides properly.

B. Sample answers: (If you chose different words, show your work to your instructor or another

student to make sure that they signal the same relationship between ideas.)

The moon's gravitational pull affects the tides on <u>Earth, but some</u> people believe it affects humans more. People have been accused of behaving strangely under a full moon. The number of violent crimes seems to <u>rise, and accidents</u> are more frequent. Some people feel more <u>creative, yet others</u> feel depressed. Do you postpone a <u>haircut, or do</u> you fail to clip your nails during the full moon? Some people believe in these <u>superstitions, but they're</u> unlikely to admit to it in public.

C. After you write your paragraph and edit it for correct compound sentences, share your work with your instructor or another student.

GED Skill Focus (Page 45)
A. 1. ; moreover,

2. ; however,

3. ; for instance,

4. ; consequently,

5. ; nevertheless,

B. Sample answers: (There are many possible ways to combine these sentences, with just semicolons or with semicolons, conjunctive adverbs, and commas. If you chose different words, make sure that they signal a reasonable relationship between ideas.)

First, you should pick your color scheme; then, determine the kind and amount of paint you'll need. Most people use latex <u>paint; it</u> is easier to apply. Oil-based paint lasts <u>longer; however,</u> it is hard to apply and messy to <u>clean up</u>. Lightweight furniture can be moved to another <u>room;</u> heavy or bulky furniture can be dragged to the center of the room. Cover everything in the room with drop cloths. Remove hardware from doors, windows, and curtain <u>rods; likewise,</u> unscrew switch plates and electric outlet plates. Patch any cracks in the plaster or <u>ceiling; fill</u> small holes with plastic wood. Sand the walls with coarse sandpaper and the woodwork with fine sandpaper. Your room is now ready to paint.

C. After you edit your paragraph for compound sentences, share your work with your instructor or another student.

GED Practice (Pages 46–47)
All items in this section are related to compound sentences.

1. **(1) Internet, so your** Option (1) is correct because two complete, related thoughts are

correctly joined by a comma and an appropriate coordinating conjunction. Option (2) is incorrect because the two sentences are only joined by a comma without a coordinating conjunction. In option (3) the comma should be before *so*. In option (4), *so* is not preceded by a comma. Option (5) creates a fragment.

2. **(3) insert a comma after information** Option (3) is correct because compound sentences must be joined by a coordinating conjunction preceded by a comma. Option (1) removes the coordinating conjunction and forms a run-on sentence. Option (2) places the comma after instead of before the coordinating conjunction *and*. Option (4) removes the subject of the second sentence.

3. **(5) rejected, but the** Option (5) is correct because it correctly combines the two sentences with a comma followed by the appropriate coordinating conjunction. Option (1) contains no coordinating conjunction for the compound sentence. Option (2) uses incorrect punctuation. Option (3) contains no punctuation and an inappropriate connecting word. Option (4) contains the correct coordinating conjunction but is missing a comma.

4. **(2) insert or after the comma** Option (2) is correct because it provides an appropriate coordinating conjunction for the two clauses in the compound sentence. Options (1) and (5) are incorrect because the compound sentence needs a coordinating conjunction. Option (3) is incorrect because a conjunctive adverb needs a semicolon before it and a comma after it. Option (4) is incorrect because a comma is not needed.

5. **(3) insert so after the comma** Option (3) is correct because it provides the appropriate coordinating conjunction. Option (1) is incorrect because *Two months are combined* is not a complete independent clause. Option (2) contains an inappropriate conjunctive adverb punctuated incorrectly. Option (4) is incorrect because both a comma and a coordinating conjunction are needed to combine two sentences. Option (5) creates a comma splice.

6. **(5) month, but it** Option (5) is correct because it joins two complete sentences with a comma and an appropriate coordinating conjunction. Options (1) and (3) contain an inappropriate conjunctive adverb punctuated incorrectly. Option (2) lacks a comma. Option (4) uses an

inappropriate coordinating conjunction and is punctuated incorrectly.

7. **(1) change pick-up and, to pick-up, and** Option (1) moves the comma to its correct place before the coordinating conjunction. Option (2) uses an inappropriate connecting word and is punctuated incorrectly. Option (3) removes the necessary coordinating conjunction. Option (4) removes the comma from the wrong place but does not reinsert it correctly. Option (5) puts the punctuation in the wrong place.

8. **(2) calls, but** Option (2) is correct because it joins two complete sentences with a comma and an appropriate coordinating conjunction. Option (1) lacks a comma. Option (3) requires a semicolon before the conjunctive adverb *however*. Option (4) lacks a comma. Option (5) is incorrect because it separates the related clauses into two sentences.

9. **(5) no correction is necessary** The clauses in the sentence are correctly combined and punctuated. Option (1) uses an inappropriate contrasting conjunctive adverb. Option (2) uses an inappropriate coordinating conjunction and is incorrectly punctuated. Option (3) removes a necessary comma. Option (4) uses an unnecessary comma because the coordinating conjunction *and* is not linking two independent clauses.

GED Mini-Test • Lesson 2 (Pages 48–49)

1. **(2) designs such as maps** (Sentence fragments) Option (2) corrects the fragment by combining it with the sentence before. Option (1) connects the fragment as if it were an independent clause. Options (3), (4), and (5) do not connect the fragment and do not keep the meaning of the original text.

2. **(1) patches, or they** (Compound sentences) The sentence is correct because two complete, related thoughts are joined by a comma and an appropriate coordinating conjunction. Option (2) is missing the necessary comma. Option (3) creates a fragment. Option (4) misplaces the comma. Option (5) has a second, unnecessary comma.

3. **(5) uniform, yet** (Compound sentences) Option (5) is correct because two complete, related thoughts are correctly joined by a comma and a contrasting coordinating conjunction. Option (1) lacks the necessary comma. Option (2) uses an inappropriate conjunctive

adverb and is incorrectly punctuated. Option (3) creates a fragment. Option (4) misplaces the comma.

4. **(2) change Became to It became** (Sentence fragments) Option (2) corrects the fragment by adding a subject. Option (1) incorrectly changes the form of the verb and does not add a subject. Option (3) inserts an unnecessary comma. Option (4) capitalizes a word unnecessarily. Option (5) is a sentence fragment.

5. **(5) section that is filled** (Sentence fragments) Option (5) is correct because it uses the word *that* to connect the fragment appropriately to the independent clause. Option (1) creates a compound sentence but uses an inappropriate coordinating conjunction. Options (2), (3), and (4) change the meaning of the original text.

6. **(2) insert or after the comma** (Compound sentences) Option (2) correctly includes a coordinating conjunction in the compound sentence. Option (1) removes the necessary comma. Option (3) inserts an unnecessary comma. Option (4) uses an inappropriate connecting word and does not supply the semicolon and comma that would be needed with such a conjunctive adverb. Option (5) inserts an unnecessary comma.

7. **(2) help, but** (Compound sentences) Option (2) is correct because it combines two complete sentences with a comma and an appropriate coordinating conjunction. Option (1) omits the necessary comma. Option (3) creates a sentence fragment. Option (4) misplaces the comma. Option (5) omits the necessary coordinating conjunction and the comma.

8. **(5) patrons who** (Sentence fragments) Option (5) correctly fixes a fragment by attaching it to a complete sentence. Option (2) creates a compound sentence but uses an inappropriate coordinating conjunction and changes the meaning. Option (3) creates two sentences but makes the meaning unclear. Option (4) uses an inappropriate coordinating conjunction and does not supply a second subject, so it sounds as if libraries "don't have other access to these devices."

9. **(4) insert for after the comma** (Compound sentences) Option (4) adds an appropriate and necessary coordinating conjunction to join the two sentences. Option (1) creates a fragment by removing part of the verb. Option (2) adds an

unnecessary comma. Option (3) removes a comma needed to separate the clauses in the compound sentence. Option (5) is a comma splice.

GED Writing Link (Pages 50–53)
Personal Link (Page 51)
Share your work with your instructor or another student.

Personal Link (Page 52)
Your journal writing is for your eyes only. You do not need to show it to your instructor or another student unless you want to.

GED Link (Page 53)
1. **a.** general essay
   b. personal essay
   c. general essay

2. Share your work with your instructor or another student.

Lesson 3
GED Skill Focus (Page 55)
A. Sample sentences:
   1. When Bob quit smoking, he gained weight.

   2. Even though people may put on pounds, they still should quit smoking.

   3. People tend to gain weight for several years after they kick the habit.

   4. Because smoking represses hunger, the heaviest smokers put on the most weight.

   5. People need to exercise so that weight gain can be limited.

B.   Although many would deny it, judges and juries are swayed by a witness's appearance. Even though justice is supposed to be impartial, juries tend to believe attractive people more often. That is why lawyers hire jury consultants to advise witnesses. When a witness is more believable, he or she is more valuable to a client. Witnesses are told to dress as they would for a job interview or business meeting. While fashionable clothing isn't forbidden, a plain suit with a white blouse or shirt is the best choice. Whether they're male or female, people who wear sandals can expect to be ignored. In a suit, you're seen as a trustworthy person. It also satisfies a jury because you give the appearance of understanding and following society's rules.

C. After you write your paragraph and edit it for complex sentences, share your work with your instructor or another student.

GED Skill Focus (Page 57)

A. Sample sentences:
  1. You will need milk, cocoa, and sugar.
  2. Put 8 ounces of milk, $2\frac{1}{2}$ tablespoons of cocoa, and 2 tablespoons of sugar in a saucepan.
  3. Stir the mixture constantly while you heat it.
  4. The mixture should be piping hot, but not boiling.
  5. Serve the cocoa plain, or top it with marshmallows.

B. There is more than one correct way to combine the details. A sample notice follows:

The Zoning Board announces a public hearing for Tuesday, November 30, at 8:10 P.M. in the East Lake City Hall.

Allied Hardware wants a building variance to construct a parking lot in a residential neighborhood. Parking lots are not usually permitted in residential neighborhoods. Allied Hardware's petition and plans are on file with the Zoning Board and can be inspected in the Office of City Zoning.

Residents who wish to comment on the variance request can register their names on the Comments Roster posted in the Office of City Zoning.

C. After you write your announcement and edit it for short, choppy sentences and other errors, share your work with your instructor or another student.

GED Practice (Pages 58–59)

All items in this section are related to subordinating ideas.

1. **(2) insert a comma after enter** Option (2) is correct because an introductory subordinate clause is always followed by a comma. Option (1) is incorrect because it uses an inappropriate subordinating conjunction. Option (3) creates a fragment. Options (4) and (5) insert unnecessary commas.

2. **(3) buys such as magazines, candy, and** Option (3) combines all the details into one smooth sentence by listing them. Option (1) would not produce a sentence or keep the meaning of the original text. Option (2) combines the subjects but not all the other details. Option (4) creates a compound sentence missing a coordinating conjunction. Option (5)

repeats a form of the verb *see* and does not combine the details.

3. **(5) milk, we'll** Option (5) fixes the subordinate-clause fragment in the original text (option 1) by attaching it to the beginning of an independent clause and adding a comma. Options (2) and (3) make compound sentences with inappropriate coordinating conjunctions. Option (4) omits the necessary comma.

4. **(4) if we understand** Option (4) combines the thoughts into a complex sentence by making the second sentence a subordinate clause. Options (1) and (2) create compound sentences but use inappropriate coordinating conjunctions. Options (3) and (5) would create complex sentences but do not keep the meaning of the original text.

5. **(2) books and commercial exercise programs are** Option (2) is correct because it combines the subjects into one sentence. Option (1) omits the coordinating conjunction needed for a compound sentence. Option (3) does not combine the ideas smoothly. Option (4) uses an inappropriate coordinating conjunction. Option (5) omits a verb.

6. **(3) insert a comma after shape** Option (3) is correct because a comma is needed after an introductory subordinate clause. Option (1) creates a compound sentence with no coordinating conjunction. Option (2) inserts the comma in the middle of the subordinate clause. Option (4) creates a fragment out of the subordinate clause.

7. **(5) a good pair of walking shoes** Option (5) combines the detail from the second clause into the first. The revised sentence would be *You can simply buy a good pair of walking shoes and take a brisk walk in them several times a week.* Options (1) and (4) do not combine the details as smoothly. Options (2) and (3) do not keep the meaning of the original text.

8. **(3) feel since you've** Option (3) fixes the subordinate-clause fragment by attaching it to the independent thought before it. Option (2) inserts an unnecessary comma and coordinating conjunction; the relationship between the two thoughts is subordinate, not equal. Option (4) uses an inappropriate subordinating conjunction. Option (5) removes the connecting word that shows how the ideas in the two clauses are related.

GED Mini-Test • Lesson 3 (Pages 60–61)

1. **(3) insert a comma after due**
(Subordination) Option (3) correctly punctuates the complex sentence with a comma after the introductory subordinate clause. Option (1) uses an inappropriate subordinate conjunction and omits the necessary comma. Option (2) replaces a correctly spelled word with a misspelling. Option (4) omits the necessary comma. Option (5) is a run-on sentence.

2. **(5) removed and replaced** (Subordination) Option (5) is correct because it combines details by making two verbs and reduces the repetitiveness of the original text. Option (2) is incorrect because it connects two independent clauses without a coordinating conjunction. Option (3) is incorrect because it connects two independent clauses without a comma and coordinating conjunction. Option (4) is incorrect because it uses an inappropriate coordinating conjunction.

3. **(1) Because removing and installing machines** (Subordination) Option (1) is correct because it combines the details in two independent clauses into one subordinate clause. The revised sentence would be *Because removing and installing machines is a slow process, the copy machine service will probably be interrupted next week*. Options (2) and (3) do not combine the details as smoothly. Option (4) does not keep the meaning of the original text. Option (5) leaves out information.

4. **(2) insert a comma after long** (Compound sentences) Option (2) is correct because it inserts a needed comma into the compound sentence. Option (1) makes the first clause subordinate but omits the necessary comma after it. Option (3) uses an inappropriate coordinating conjunction and omits the necessary comma. Option (4) removes the subject from the second clause. Option (5) inserts an unnecessary comma because *for* is not a coordinating conjunction in this sentence.

5. **(3) country, moving** (Sentence fragments) Option (3) is correct because it fixes a subordinate-clause fragment by attaching it to the independent clause that follows it and includes a comma after the subordinate clause. Option (1) creates a fragment. Option (2) omits the comma after the introductory subordinate clause. Option (4) is incorrect because it uses an inappropriate coordinating conjunction.

Option (5) uses an inappropriate subordinating conjunction before the independent clause, making a sentence fragment.

6. **(2) insert a comma after time** (Subordination) Option (2) is correct because it inserts a comma after the introductory subordinate clause. Option (1) uses an inappropriate subordinating conjunction and does not include the comma after the clause. Option (3) incorrectly changes the verb to the past tense. Option (4) inserts an unnecessary comma. Option (5) is a run-on sentence.

7. **(5) address and** (Subordination) Option (5) is correct because it combines related details smoothly and reduces repetition. Option (1) creates a fragment. Option (2) joins two independent clauses without a coordinating conjunction. Option (3) is incorrect because it doesn't combine the details smoothly. Option (4) creates a fragment.

8. **(3) survival kit containing** (Subordination) Option (3) is correct because it smoothly combines the details into one sentence. Option (1) does not combine the details smoothly and repeats words. Option (2) uses an inappropriate connecting term between *kit* and the listed items. Option (4) leaves out necessary information about the kit. Option (5) creates a sentence fragment with an incomplete verb.

9. **(5) no correction is necessary** (Compound sentences) The sentence is a compound sentence correctly linked with a comma and the coordinating conjunction *so*. Option (1) inserts an unnecessary comma. Option (2) removes the comma between the independent clauses. Option (3) uses an inappropriate coordinating conjunction. Option (4) replaces a correctly spelled word with a misspelling.

Lesson 4
GED Skill Focus (Page 63)

A. Sample answers:

1. *R* Consumers need help buying used cars if they want to avoid overpriced ones.

2. *C*

3. *R* The cars look fine because they have cosmetic repairs.

4. *C*

5. *R* Moveable parts of the car should line up with each other; for example, the seams should be straight and even.

Answers and Explanations

6. *R* The car should have an in-state license plate. Badly damaged cars are often moved between states.

B. Sample answers:

It's not often a child rescues his mother; however, it did happen recently. A mother-son team of Southern Right whales was trapped in shallow water off the coast of Argentina because an out-going tide had confused them. Human volunteers doused them with water to keep the whales' skin safely wet. At the first high tide, the calf swam into deeper water, but he wouldn't leave his mother, who seemed half-asleep. The calf and the volunteers slowly moved the mother toward deeper water. The volunteers pushed, and the calf bumped the mother's head with its tail. Eventually the mother woke up from her drowsy state. Then she and her calf were able to swim back to the ocean. Apparently, their ordeal left them with only minor bruises.

C. After you edit your paragraph for run-on sentences and other errors, share your work with your instructor or another student.

GED Skill Focus (Page 65)

A. Sample answers:

1. Muscles are tough elastic tissue. They enable other body parts to move.

2. Americans lose only about 15 percent of muscle strength before the age of 50. After that, they lose almost twice as much muscle strength. After 70, the rate of loss falls even faster.

3. This can lead to many health problems. People may fall frequently, become obese, or have brittle bones.

4. Strength training seems to help. Lifting light weights or doing pushups rebuilds muscles fast.

5. If you are over 45, visit your doctor before you start strength training. People of any age who haven't exercised in many years should also get a checkup, and anyone who has high blood pressure or is taking medications should go to their doctor first.

B. It may come as a surprise, but snug pajamas are the safest kind of sleepwear for small children. Snug-fitting cotton pajamas seem to be the safest. Loose-fitting T-shirts or nightgowns have air pockets that may speed up a fire. Less oxygen fits under snug clothing. Synthetic or polyester material must be treated with chemicals. Snug-

fitting cotton pajamas don't have to be treated; that's why they cost less. Many people feel that cotton is more comfortable than polyester anyway. Children shouldn't sleep in bathrobes either because robes catch on fire more easily than pajamas. Bathrobe belts can also be a problem, for they can get caught around a sleeping child's neck. Finally, be sure to wash flame-resistant pajamas according to the instructions; otherwise, the chemicals that make them safe could be washed away.

C. After you edit your paragraph for run-ons, comma splices, and other errors, share your work with your instructor or another student.

GED Practice (Pages 66–67)

All items in this section are related to run-on sentences.

1. **(4) City Hospital. You are correct** Option (4) is correct because it uses a period to separate the independent clauses of the run-on into two sentences. Option (1) is a run-on sentence. Option (2) is a comma splice and capitalizes incorrectly. Option (3) is also a comma splice. Option (5) omits the necessary comma in a compound sentence.

2. **(5) no correction is necessary** Option (1) inserts an unnecessary comma because *for* is not a coordinating conjunction in this sentence. Option (2) removes the comma needed in a compound sentence. Option (3) inserts a second, unnecessary coordinating conjunction. Option (4) creates a comma splice.

3. **(5) insert but after the comma** Option (5) adds the necessary coordinating conjunction to fix the comma splice. Option (1) makes the first clause subordinate, but with an inappropriate subordinating conjunction. Option (2) creates a run-on. Option (3) creates a compound sentence without the necessary comma. Option (4) inserts an appropriate conjunctive adverb but without the semicolon and comma it requires.

4. **(1) programs, and almost all fail to comply in one or more areas. Total** Option (1) is correct because it creates a compound sentence and a simple sentence. Options (2), (3), (4), and (5) do not clearly separate the clauses and keep the meaning of the original text.

5. **(5) equipment. Some** Option (5) is correct because it uses a period to separate the independent clauses of the comma splice into two sentences. Option (2) is incorrect because it creates a run-on. Option (3) uses an

inappropriate conjunctive adverb with incorrect punctuation. Option (4) uses an inappropriate subordinating conjunction.

6. **(3) syndrome. Their** Option (3) is correct because it uses a period to separate the independent clauses of the run-on into two sentences. Option (2) is a comma splice. Options (4) and (5) create compound sentences with coordinating conjunctions that are not preceded by commas.

7. **(5) no correction is necessary** Option (1) creates a fragment. Option (2) inserts an unnecessary comma because *and* is not separating two independent clauses in this sentence; it is joining two subjects in a compound subject. Option (3) removes the necessary word *and*. Option (4) creates a fragment by taking away the verb of the sentence.

8. **(4) jobs; for example,** Option (4) is correct because it separates the two clauses of the comma splice with an appropriate connecting word and punctuation. Option (1) creates a compound sentence, but with an inappropriate coordinating conjunction. Option (2) creates a subordinate clause from the first independent clause, but with an inappropriate subordinating conjunction. Option (3) creates a subordinate clause from the second independent clause, but with an inappropriate subordinating conjunction. Option (5) omits information from the original text.

9. **(4) replace <u>common workers with</u> <u>common. Workers</u>** Option (4) correctly separates the two independent clauses into two sentences. Option (1) creates a subordinate clause from the first independent clause, but with an inappropriate subordinating conjunction and without the necessary comma after the introductory clause. Option (2) creates a comma splice. Option (3) creates a compound sentence without the necessary comma between the two clauses.

GED Mini-Test • Lesson 4 (Pages 68–69)

1. **(5) application, and everything** (Run-on sentences) Option (5) fixes the run-on by separating the independent clauses with a comma and an appropriate coordinating conjunction. Option (2) creates a comma splice. Option (3) uses an inappropriate conjunctive adverb and incorrect punctuation. Option (4) omits the necessary comma in a compound sentence.

2. **(3) change the comma to a period** (Comma splices) Option (3) is correct because it fixes the comma splice by making the two clauses into two sentences. Option (1) is incorrect because it separates an idea from the clause it belongs with. Option (2) creates a run-on sentence. Option (4) uses an inappropriate coordinating conjunction. Option (5) connects the ideas inappropriately.

3. **(1) insert <u>I can</u> after the comma** (Sentence fragments) Option (1) correctly adds a subject to fix the sentence fragment. Option (2) does not fix the fragment; it only changes the form of the verb. Option (3) adds an inappropriate subject and removes the verb. Option (4) inserts an unnecessary comma because *or* is not separating two independent clauses in this sentence.

4. **(4) letter and include my name,** (Compound sentences) Option (4) is correct because it fixes the lack of a comma between the independent clauses and removes unnecessary words by combining two verbs in one main clause. The other options do not lead to smoothly combined ideas in one sentence.

5. **(3) car, do** (Sentence fragments) Option (3) fixes the subordinate-clause fragment by attaching it to the next sentence and includes the necessary comma. Option (2) does not fix the fragment; in fact, it removes the subject (the understood *you*) from the independent clause. Option (4) treats the subordinate clause as if it were an independent clause and adds a comma and coordinating conjunction to incorrectly create a compound sentence. Option (5) creates a run-on sentence.

6. **(4) recommends, and keep** (Comma splices) Option (4) correctly adds the appropriate coordinating conjunction to repair the comma splice. Option (2) creates a run-on sentence. Option (3) changes the meaning of the original text. Option (5) uses an inappropriate conjunctive adverb and omits the necessary punctuation of a semicolon before and a comma after it.

7. **(5) no correction is necessary** (Run-on sentences) The sentence is a correct complex sentence. Options (1) and (2) create a fragment. Option (3) inserts an unnecessary comma because no comma is needed before the subordinate clause. Option (4) inserts an unnecessary comma because *and* is not separating two independent clauses in this sentence.

8. (1) When you bring your car in, don't insist (Run-on sentences) Option (1) combines all the details in the three independent clauses of the run-on into one complex sentence. The revised sentence would be *When you bring your car in, don't insist on a diagnosis.* The other options do not help create sentences that smoothly and effectively combine all the necessary information.

9. (4) insert so that after number (Run-on sentences) Option (4) correctly links the related thoughts in the run-on by making the second independent clause subordinate to the first. Option (1) inserts *you* unnecessarily because it is the understood subject of the first clause, and the option does not fix the run-on. Option (2) merely changes the verb form in the first clause but does nothing to fix the run-on. Option (3) creates a comma splice. Option (5) merely changes the verb in the second clause but does nothing to fix the run-on.

GED Writing Link (Pages 70–71)
Share your work for the Personal Link and GED exercises with your instructor or another student.

Lesson 5
GED Skill Focus (Page 73)
A. 1. *M* When customers buy clothes, one size does not fit all.

2. *C*

3. *M* A new three-dimensional sizing database of 8,000 volunteers is being developed of all shapes, sizes, ages, and ethnicities.
A new three-dimensional sizing database is being developed of 8,000 volunteers of all shapes, sizes, ages, and ethnicities.

4. *M* The project managers promise when the database is finished that a customer will be able to trust the size on a label.
When the database is finished, the project managers promise that a customer will be able to trust the size on a label.

5. *C*

6. *M* Of course, high-end fashion designers will still want women to believe that their clothes are smaller who buy expensive designer dresses.
Of course, high-end fashion designers will still want women who buy expensive designer dresses to believe that the clothes they wear are smaller.

B. Sample answers:
Vitamins and iron can reach starving people around the world in scientifically enriched "golden rice". In poor countries, almost 400 million people who are deficient in vitamin A risk suffering from infections and blindness. Additionally, millions of people suffer from iron deficiency. Causing anemia and retarded development in children, iron-poor blood in pregnant women is a special problem. Hoping for a major improvement in the health of millions around the world, scientists believe this golden rice might be the answer.

C. After you write your paragraph and edit it for modifiers, share your work with your instructor or another student.

GED Practice (Pages 74–75)
All items in this section are related to misplaced and dangling modifiers.

1. (1) replace By installing with If you install Option (1) is correct because it inserts a subject and verb into the dangling modifier, transforming the phrase into a subordinating clause. Option (2) removes a comma needed after an introductory phrase and does not fix the dangling modifier. Option (3) treats the sentence as if it were compound, with two independent clauses, but it is not. Option (4) merely changes the verb form in the main clause and does not fix the dangling modifier.

2. (1) Costing about $20 Option (1) is correct because it moves the wrongly placed phrase near the word it modifies, *way.* The revised sentence would be *Costing about $20, the best way to save money is by etching your vehicle identification number into the windows.* The other options do not create a sentence in which the modifier is placed correctly and the meaning of the original text is kept.

3. (4) hard for car thieves to break Option (4) is correct because it moves the wrongly placed phrase near the word it modifies, *hard.* The revised sentence would be *Etched windows make it hard for car thieves to break a car down into sellable pieces.* The other options do not create a sentence in which all modifiers are placed correctly.

4. (5) no correction is necessary The sentence is correct because all the modifiers are placed correctly. Option (1) unnecessarily replaces the introductory subordinate clause. Option (2) removes the comma needed after an introductory subordinate clause. Option (3) replaces the subject of the main clause with a subject *and* a verb. Option (4) inserts an unnecessary comma because the *and* is not separating two independent clauses in this sentence.

5. **(1) As senior crew supervisor, Erica Ortiz** Option (1) is correct because the modifying phrase is placed correctly in the sentence. Option (2) creates a fragment. Option (3) creates a sentence with two verbs—*is* and *supervises*. Option (4) is wordy and requires commas around the modifying phrase. Option (5) creates a sentence with two subjects—*Erica Ortiz* and *she*.

6. **(4) sure that the crews have their job assignments and tools when** Option (4) is correct because it moves the modifying clause near the noun it modifies—*crews*. Option (1) would not create an effective revision or keep all the information in the sentence. Option (2) makes the clause modify *Erica*, not *crew*. Options (3) and (5) change the meaning of the sentence.

7. **(3) Landscapers in 1998 and quickly gained the respect of crew members** Option (3) is correct because it moves the wrongly placed phrase *in 1998* closer to the idea it modifies and removes wordiness by giving the sentence two verbs—*started* and *gained*. Option (1) is a run-on sentence. Options (2) and (4) do not move the phrase *in 1998* to the best location in the sentence. Neither does option (5), which also creates a comma splice.

8. **(1) Erica also has** Option (1) is correct because it gives the opening modifying phrase the correct subject to modify—*Erica*. The revised sentence would be *Proudly representing Strong Landscapers, Erica also has a great reputation among our customers in the community.* Options (2), (3), and (4) create a dangling modifier by not supplying the correct subject. Option (5) leaves out the verb to be used in the main clause.

9. **(2) change Erica Ortiz is recommended to I recommend Erica Ortiz** Option (2) is correct because it uses the subject that the phrase *With pleasure* modifies—*I*. Option (1) creates a fragment. Option (3) creates a fragment by making the verb incomplete. Option (4) inserts an unnecessary comma because the word *for* is not a coordinating conjunction in this sentence. Option (5) creates a dangling modifier.

GED Mini-Test • Lesson 5 (Pages 76–77)

1. **(3) residents in certain states** (Misplaced modifiers) Option (3) is correct because it moves the wrongly placed phrase near the word it

modifies. The other options do not lead to sentences that smoothly and clearly state the information.

2. **(3) insert these items are after When** (Dangling modifiers) Option (3) is correct because it inserts a subject and verb into the dangling modifier, transforming the phrase into a subordinating clause. Options (1) and (2) do not fix the dangling modifier. Option (4) removes the comma needed after the introductory phrase and does not fix the dangling modifier. Option (5) merely changes the verb form in the main clause and does not fix the dangling modifier.

3. **(3) insert are after future** (Sentence fragments) Option (3) is correct because it fixes the fragment by completing the verb. Option (1) merely rearranges the modifying phrase and the word it modifies. By inserting a verb into the first part of the sentence, option (2) creates another misplaced modifier. Option (4) inserts an unnecessary comma. Option (5) is missing a complete verb.

4. **(5) makes soles for athletic shoes using worn-out tires** (Run-on sentences) Option (5) is correct because it combines all the details in the three independent clauses into one clause and places them correctly. The other options lead to sentences that are wordy or repetitive or that contain misplaced modifiers.

5. **(3) When you're looking to buy a used car, it** (Dangling modifiers) Option (3) is correct because it inserts a subject and completes the verb in the dangling modifier, transforming the phrase into a subordinating clause. Option (2) changes the meaning and does not fix the dangling modifier. Option (4) creates a fragment. Options (1) and (5) do not fix the dangling modifier.

6. **(2) insert a comma after mileage** (Compound sentences) Option (2) is correct because it inserts the comma needed between independent clauses in a compound sentence. Option (1) makes the verb in the first clause incomplete. Option (3) creates a run-on sentence. Option (4) does not use the correct punctuation—a semicolon and comma—with the conjunctive adverb *however*. Option (5) makes the verb in the second clause incomplete.

7. **(5) pedals. That** (Comma splices) Option (5) is correct because it turns a comma splice, option (1), into two complete sentences. Option (2) creates a run-on sentence. Options (3)

and (4) add inappropriate coordinating conjunctions. Option (3) also omits a necessary comma.

8. **(4) Oily spots under a car and excessive oil** (Sentence fragments) Option (4) is correct because it fixes the fragment by taking the detail in the fragment and making it part of the subject. Options (1) and (2) do not clearly and effectively eliminate the wordiness and repetition. Options (3) and (5) create wordy, unclear sentences.

9. **(4) insert a comma after this** (Subordination—Complex sentences) Option (4) is correct because it inserts a comma after an introductory subordinate clause. The independent clause is short—*beware*—but it is the main clause of the sentence. Options (1) and (5) create run-on sentences. Option (2) leads to a misspelled word. Option (3) inserts the comma in the middle of the subordinate clause.

Lesson 6
GED Skill Focus (Page 79)
A. 1. Many infants, toddlers, and children not yet in school
   Many infants, toddlers, and preschoolers carry around a "security blanket."

2. Children sleep under them, play with them, or talk to them.

3. removed, lost, or simply to be misplaced
   If the blanket is moved, lost, or simply misplaced, the whole family will suffer.

4. get older, growing tall, and wiser
   As kids grow older, taller, and wiser, they still secretly love their "blankies."

5. under their pillows, in their bedding, or keep them under their beds
   They may hide them under their pillows, in their bedding, or under their beds.

6. security, warmth, and feeling happy
   Many adults fondly remember the security, warmth, and happiness their childhood blankets gave them.

B. Sample answers:
   A typical American breakfast consists of a bowl of cereal, a cup of coffee or tea, and a glass of orange juice. Maybe it's because breakfast eaters generally eat healthier foods, exercise more, or get regular checkups, but eating breakfast seems to make people healthier. Breakfast eaters consume more fruits, more vegetables, and less fat and oil than those who skip the first meal of

the day. Breakfast eaters also seem to be more conscious of limiting their salt intake, which can raise blood pressure, dehydrate cells, and lead to strokes. From all available evidence, it's clear that skipping an occasional lunch or missing a dinner won't hurt you. However, don't forget to eat a healthy breakfast every day.

C. After you edit your paragraph for parallel structure and other errors, share your work with your instructor or another student.

GED Practice (Pages 80–81)
All items in this section are related to parallel structure.

1. **(5) replace and we can recognize it with and recognizable** Option (5) is correct because it changes a clause into a single-word adjective, like the others in the series—*soft, vague, recognizable*. Option (1) changes the form of the verb but does not correct the error in parallel structure. Options (2) and (3) change the other adjectives in the series to further the error in parallel structure. Option (4) changes the subordinate conjunction but does not keep the meaning of the original text.

2. **(4) change reducing to reduce** Option (4) is correct because it puts all the verbs in the series in the same form—*calm, lower, reduce*. Options (1) and (5) do not correct the non-parallel structure. Option (2) furthers the non-parallel structure by changing the middle verb to a different form. Option (3) changes the meaning of the original sentence.

3. **(4) in stores, at work, and in stressful situations** Option (4) is correct because it creates a series of parallel prepositional phrases. In options (1) and (3), the third phrase in each series is not parallel. In options (2) and (5), all the phrases are in different forms.

4. **(3) insert a comma after absenteeism** Option (3) is correct because a comma is necessary between the items in a series. Option (1) inserts an unnecessary comma. Option (2) creates a fragment with an incomplete verb. Option (4) creates a non-parallel structure. Option (5) creates a run-on sentence.

5. **(5) no correction is necessary** Option (5) is correct because three words ending in *-ing* are in parallel structure. Option (1) is incorrect because the comma is needed after the introductory subordinate clause. Option (2) is incorrect because it changes the parallel *-ing* form to a non-parallel form. Option (3) is incorrect because leaving *earplugs* alone would create non-parallel structure. Option (4) is incorrect because

replacing the -ing form with a clause would create non-parallel structure.

6. **(3) replace <u>with a lot of</u> with <u>having</u>** Option (3) is correct because it matches the other -ing endings in the series. Option (1) changes the parallel form to a non-parallel form (*to*). Option (2) removes a necessary comma between items in the series. Option (4) changes a parallel form to a non-parallel form. Option (5) inserts an unnecessary comma.

7. **(4) and apologizing loudly** Option (4) is correct because the phrases are parallel when each contains an -*ing* word and an adverb. Option (1) contains no -*ing* word. Option (2) uses a subordinate clause. Option (3) uses the *to* form of the verb. Option (5) uses a phrase.

8. **(1) and sneakers** Option (1) is correct because the three nouns—*jeans, sweatshirt*, and *sneakers*—are in parallel structure. Options (2) and (3) are incorrect because they use phrases. Option (4) uses the -*ing* form. Option (5) uses a phrase after the noun. All these create non-parallel structures.

9. **(5) remove <u>look</u>** Option (5) is correct because it removes the verb and allows *serious* to match the other adjectives in this series. Options (1) and (2) create fragments. Option (3) removes the comma that is needed between items in a series. Option (4) inserts an unnecessary coordinating conjunction. The comma is all that is necessary to separate the items.

10. **(3) are confident, professional, and friendly** Option (3) is correct because it removes the verb *be* and allows *friendly* to match the other adjectives in the series. Option (2) lists an adjective with two nouns. Options (4) and (5) change the meaning of the original sentence. Option (1) does not correct the non-parallel structure.

GED Mini-Test • Lesson 6 (Pages 82–83)

1. **(3) change <u>how easy it is to use</u> to <u>ease of use</u>** (Parallel structure) Option (3) is correct because it creates a phrase that matches the other phrases in the series. Option (1) removes the comma needed between items in a series. Option (2) changes a parallel word into a non-parallel phrase. Option (4) merely changes the verb in the clause that is causing the non-parallel structure. Option (5) does not correct the non-parallel structure.

2. **(3) insert a comma after <u>crashing</u>** (Compound sentences) Option (3) inserts the comma needed between independent clauses in a compound sentence. Option (1) makes the verb in the first clause incomplete. Option (2) incorrectly changes a verb form. Option (4) incorrectly replaces a needed coordinating conjunction *and*. Option (5) changes the verb in the second independent clause from *does not* to *do not*.

3. **(4) drive, reconnect my mouse three times, and reinstall** (Subordination—Combining details) Option (4) combines the information in the three independent clauses into one sentence: *I had to change my hard drive, reconnect my mouse three times, and reinstall my Internet connection twice.* The other options do not eliminate the wordiness or repetition. Option (2) leaves out important information.

4. **(5) complicated, and the** (Run-on sentences) Option (5) fixes the run-on by inserting the comma and coordinating conjunction needed between the independent clauses. Option (2) omits the necessary comma. Option (3) uses an inappropriate conjunctive adverb without correct punctuation. Option (4) creates a comma splice. Option (1) is a run-on sentence.

5. **(2) According to new suburban planners and architects,** (Misplaced modifiers) Option (2) is correct because it moves an unclear modifier to a position in the sentence that clarifies it. Options (1), (3), (4), and (5) do not clarify the meaning of the sentence by moving the modifier.

6. **(5) and big backyards** (Parallel structure) Option (5) is correct because it fixes the original error in parallel structure by making the final clause an adjective-noun phrase. Options (1), (2), (3), and (4) do not correct the non-parallel structure.

7. **(2) insert <u>and</u> after the comma** (Comma splices) Option (2) correctly adds a coordinating conjunction to fix the comma splice. Option (1) creates a run-on sentence. Option (3) uses a wrong verb. Option (4) uses a misspelled word. Option (5) is a comma splice.

8. **(1) square that contains a** (Sentence fragments) Option (1) correctly joins the fragment to the independent clause. Option (2) creates a compound sentence missing the

necessary comma and is also repetitive. Option (3) creates a comma splice. Options (4) and (5) change the meaning of the original text.

9. **(3) suburbs. Planners** (Run-on sentences) Option (3) correctly divides a run-on sentence into two complete sentences. Option (2) creates a comma splice. Options (4) and (5) are missing commas before the coordinating conjunctions. Option (1) is a run-on sentence.

GED Writing Link (Pages 84–85)
Share your work for the Personal Link and GED Link exercises with your instructor or another student.

Unit 1 Cumulative Review (Pages 86–91)

1. **(4) change would head to headed** (Parallel structure) Option (4) puts all the verbs (*packed, piled, headed*) in the same form. Option (1) makes the first and third verbs match but not the second. Option (2) removes the comma needed between items in a series. Option (3) furthers the non-parallel structure by changing the form of the second verb.

2. **(3) change being to was** (Sentence fragments) Option (3) gives this fragment a complete verb. Option (1) does not fix the fragment. Option (2) inserts an unnecessary comma. Option (4) removes the verb totally from the fragment. Option (5) is a fragment.

3. **(3) picnic. The** (Run-on sentences) Option (3) corrects the run-on by dividing the two independent clauses into two complete sentences. Option (2) is a comma splice. Option (4) does not correct the run-on and shows a contrast that is not meant. Option (5) lacks the comma before the coordinating conjunction.

4. **(5) no correction is necessary** (Parallel structure) The sentence is complete, parallel, and correctly punctuated. Option (1) changes the meaning of the sentence and is incorrectly punctuated. Option (2) removes the comma needed between items in a series. Option (3) removes the parallel structure. Option (4) creates a fragment without a complete verb.

5. **(1) change Fading to As drive-ins fade** (Misplaced modifiers) Option (1) turns the dangling modifier into a subordinate clause by adding a subordinating conjunction, a subject, and a complete verb. Option (2) removes a necessary comma after the introductory phrase. Option (3) adds a second, repetitive subject. Option (4) creates a fragment with an incomplete verb.

6. **(3) the question asked by both groups** (Misplaced modifiers) Option (3) moves the phrase next to the word it modifies, *question*. In options (1), (2), (4), and (5), the modifier is still misplaced and unclear.

7. **(2) replace looking with one looks** (Dangling modifiers) Option (2) adds a subject and a verb into the dangling modifier, making a subordinate clause. Option (1) still leaves a dangling modifier. Option (3) removes the comma needed after an introductory subordinate clause. Option (4) inserts an unnecessary comma; the word *or* is not connecting two independent clauses in this sentence.

8. **(4) waterways, observers** (Subordination—Complex sentences) Option (4) correctly inserts a comma after the introductory subordinate clause. Option (2) creates a fragment. Option (3) uses an inappropriate coordinating conjunction to connect the subordinate and independent clauses. Option (5) misplaces the comma. Option (1) is a run-on sentence.

9. **(2) replace and with described** (Sentence fragments) Option (2) gives this fragment a verb. Option (1) creates an independent clause at the beginning, but the last part of the sentence is unclearly attached to it. Option (3) creates a second fragment. Option (4) does not fix the fragment because it needs a verb. Option (5) is a fragment.

10. **(4) to Mars, so they were** (Compound sentences) Option (4) uses a coordinating conjunction to establish a relationship between the two independent clauses and make a compound sentence. Option (1) is a run-on sentence. Option (2) uses an inappropriate coordinating conjunction and omits the necessary comma. Options (3) and (5) do not clearly and effectively combine the ideas of the two sentences.

11. **(2) and expert spot removal** (Subordination—Combining details) Option (2) combines the information in the two independent clauses clearly and removes wordiness and repetition. Options (1) and (3) relate incorrect relationships between the ideas in the clauses—expert spot removal is in addition to the hand cleaning, not an example of it. Option (4) changes the meaning of the original. Option (5) leads to a wordy sentence.

12. **(2) We will pamper your best dresses** (Sentence fragments) Option (2) inserts a subject and complete verb to fix the sentence fragment. Option (1) leads to a wordy sentence. Options (3) and (4) do not fix the fragment. Option (5) is awkwardly worded.

13. **(3) equipment, so we** (Compound sentences) Option (3) correctly uses a comma and coordinating conjunction to create a compound sentence with the independent clauses. Option (1), is wordy and not most effective way to relate the ideas in the clauses. Option (2) does not show the relationship between the ideas. Option (4) omits the necessary comma and uses an inappropriate coordinating conjunction. Option (5) uses an inappropriate conjunctive adverb with incorrect punctuation.

14. **(4) change wear they to wear. They** (Run-on sentences) Option (4) correctly divides the two independent clauses in the run-on into two complete sentences. Option (1) inserts an inappropriate subordinating conjunction at the beginning of the first clause and omits the necessary comma. Option (2) inserts an unnecessary comma because the coordinating conjunction *and* is not connecting two independent clauses in this sentence. Option (3) creates a comma splice. Option (5) is a run-on sentence.

15. **(5) store? Let** (Comma splices) Option (5) correctly divides the two independent clauses into a question and a statement. Options (2) and (3) create run-ons. Option (4) uses an inappropriate coordinating conjunction and omits the necessary comma before it.

16. **(5) block, although it** (Sentence fragments) Option (5) fixes a subordinate-clause fragment by attaching it to an independent clause. Option (2) does not show the relationship between the two ideas. Options (3) and (4) use an inappropriate coordinating conjunction. Option (1) does not connect the subordinate clause to the independent clause.

17. **(3) change walls that face the outside of the house to exterior walls** (Parallel structure) Option (3) is correct because it makes all the items in the series parallel adjectives and nouns—*unheated attics, damp crawl spaces, exterior walls*. Option (1) changes the meaning of the original text. Option (2) removes the comma needed between items in a series. Option (4)

changes the verb incorrectly—the verb *are* agrees with the subject *pipes*. Option (5) is not the best choice for making the items in the series parallel.

18. **(5) a faucet, a dishwasher, or a washing machine isn't** (Subordination—Combining details) Option (5) is correct because it combines the details in the two sentences clearly and effectively: *A pipe is usually frozen or near-frozen when a faucet, a dishwasher, or a washing machine isn't getting the necessary flow.* Option (1) merely makes a compound sentence. Options (2), (3), and (4) do not combine the details in a clear way that would still keep the meaning of the original.

19. **(2) them, or use** (Compound sentences) Option (2) creates a compound sentence with a comma and shows the relationship between the two independent clauses with the coordinating conjunction *or*. Option (1), the original, is wordy. Option (3) creates a comma splice. Option (4) creates a run-on sentence. Option (5) omits the necessary comma and uses an unnecessary word.

20. **(4) insert so after the comma** (Comma splices) Option (4) corrects the comma splice by inserting a coordinating conjunction after the comma to create a compound sentence. Option (1) makes the verb in the first clause incomplete. Option (2) inserts an unnecessary comma. Option (3) creates a run-on sentence. Option (5) is a run-on sentence.

21. **(5) Fifty dollars is the average amount of cash you can get over the cost of a purchase** (Misplaced modifiers) Option (5) correctly moves an unclear modifier to a place in the sentence that makes the meaning of the sentence clear. Options (1), (2), (3), and (4) would produce unclear, wordy sentences.

22. **(4) If you have** (Subordination—Complex sentences) Option (4) makes the meaning clear by using the subordinating conjunction *if*. Options (2) and (3) create comma splices. Option (5) uses the wrong verb for the meaning of the sentence. Option (1) is a dangling modifier.

Writing Links Review

Ask your instructor or another student to review your paragraph. Ask them to give you feedback on the following:

- Complete sentences
- Detailed sentences
- Use and placement of modifiers

Revise your paragraph as needed.

UNIT 2: ORGANIZATION

Lesson 7

GED Skill Focus (Page 95)

A. Check sentences 2, 3, 5, 7, 8.

You can now buy stamps by mail. Buying by mail will save time. Use an order form to pick the stamps you want to order. With mail orders, you have to buy stamps in rolls of 100. Be sure to include a check or money order for the correct amount. There are no extra fees for postage or handling.

B. You were correct if you circled the first sentence and underlined any two of the details underlined here:

Despite public radio's image as boring, it has a great variety of programs that appeal to many different listeners. You can hear international, national, and local news. Many celebrities refuse television or print interviews, yet they are willing to talk on public radio. There are comedy shows, automotive call-ins, and pop-music features. If you are willing to listen for one week, you are sure to find a program to your liking, regardless of your taste.

C. After you edit your paragraph for a topic sentence and supporting details, share your work with your intructor or another student.

GED Skill Focus (Page 97)

A. These three sentences should be crossed out:

1. Managers sometimes make suggestions, too.
   It is almost fun, like a secret ballot.
   Experts usually design surveys.

2. Of course, oral vaccines have always been painless.
   Many people cannot stand the sight of a needle.
   When you bleed, a scab has to form on the skin.

3. A wintry blast can cause heating prices to soar.
   Windows may crack if their sash cords snap.
   These can be painted, as well.

B. After you edit your paragraph for unity and coherence and other errors, share your work with your instructor or another student.

GED Practice (Pages 98–99)

All items in this practice are related to paragraph unity and coherence.

1. **(1) remove sentence 2** Option (1) correctly eliminates a sentence that does not support the main idea. Options (2) and (3) move this information but do not eliminate it. Option (4) suggests that a supporting detail is the topic of the paragraph.

2. **(3) move sentence 6 to follow sentence 8** Option (3) is correct because it reorders the sentences more logically, putting the mention of the second pharmacy option after all the details of the first are discussed. Option (1) is incorrect because it removes an important piece of information. Option (2) is incorrect because it places information about the second pharmacy option before the choices for the first option are given. Option (4) is incorrect because it suggests that a secondary detail is the topic sentence of the last paragraph.

3. **(4) move sentence 9 to the beginning of paragraph C** Option (4) is correct because it moves a concluding remark to introduce the final, concluding paragraph. Option (1) incorrectly places the remark as if it were the topic sentence of the whole letter. Option (2) incorrectly moves the concluding remark to the introductory paragraph. Option (3) incorrectly removes the effective and polite concluding remark.

4. **(3) remove sentence 2** Option (3) correctly eliminates a sentence that doesn't support the main idea. Option (1) incorrectly removes a topic sentence. Option (2) would misplace the topic sentence at the end of the paragraph. Option (4) incorrectly removes a supporting detail from the paragraph.

5. **(4) move sentence 8 to the end of the paragraph** Option (4) correctly moves a supporting detail to its logical place in the paragraph. It concludes the description of how the birds were saved. Option (1) moves a topic sentence from its most effective position. Options (2) and (3) remove important supporting details. Option (5) moves a detail supporting the main idea of paragraph B to paragraph C.

6. **(2) remove sentence 12** Option (2) is correct because it removes an irrelevant detail. Options (1) and (3) merely move the irrelevant detail. Option (4) replaces the irrelevant detail with another irrelevant detail.

7. **(5) no revision is necessary** This sentence is an appropriate conclusion to the paragraph and the passage. Options (1), (2), and (3) move the sentence to where it would make no sense. Option (4) removes the conclusion to the passage.

GED Mini-Test • Lesson 7 (Pages 100–101)

1. **(1) make them at least five months ahead** (Misplaced modifiers) Option (1) correctly places the modifier *at least* by the word it modifies, *five*. Option (2) moves the modifier but uses the wrong verb tense. Options (3), (4), and (5) do not solve the misplaced modifier problem and use the wrong verb tense as well.

2. **(3) made on the fifteenth** (Subordination) Option (3) is correct because it effectively combines the important details from sentence 5 into sentence 4. Options (1), (4), and (5) do not create a clear, concise sentence that accurately restates the information in the original sentences. Option (2) creates a wordy, repetitive compound sentence.

3. **(1) remove sentence 6** (Paragraph unity) Option (1) correctly eliminates a sentence that doesn't support the main idea. Options (2) and (4) move the irrelevant detail. Option (3) restates the irrelevant detail.

4. **(4) parks can be reserved** (Sentence fragments) Option (4) fixes the fragment by completing the verb. Option (2) uses an inappropriate comma and does not fix the fragment. Option (3) creates two fragments. Option (5) uses punctuation and a coordinating conjunction appropriate for a compound sentence.

5. **(5) other sledders** (Parallel structure) Option (5) is correct because it changes a long phrase into a short adjective and noun, making it parallel with *trees* and *rocks*. Options (1), (2), (3), and (4) do not correct the error in parallel structure.

6. **(3) insert <u>and</u> after the comma** (Comma splices) Option (3) correctly adds the coordinating conjunction *and* to repair a comma splice. Option (1) inserts an unnecessary comma. Option (2) creates a run-on. Option (4) ignores the relationship between the ideas.

7. **(4) Whether the water appears** (Dangling modifiers) Option (4) correctly inserts a subordinating conjunction and a subject into the dangling modifier, changing the phrase into a subordinating clause. Option (1) does not supply a noun for the phrase to modify. Options (2), (3), and (5) create unclear sentences.

8. **(2) remove sentence 10** (Paragraph unity) Option (2) correctly eliminates a sentence that doesn't support the main idea of the paragraph.

Options (1) and (4) eliminate supporting details. Option (3) incorrectly moves a supporting detail out of logical order.

9. **(5) no correction is necessary** The sentence is correct as written. Option (1) inserts a second, unnecessary subject. Option (2) creates a fragment. Option (3) removes a comma needed in a parallel series. Option (4) creates an error in parallel structure.

GED Writing Link (Pages 102–103)

Share your work for the Personal Link and GED Link exercises with your instructor or another student.

Lesson 8
GED Skill Focus (Page 105)

A. Sample answers:
   1. OK

   2. I would like the funds for the Highway 41 extension to be restored as soon as possible.

   3. We wish to thank the entire committee and Ms. Enders for the recent fundraiser for the high school band.

B. Sample answer: Working at home has both advantages and disadvantages.

C. After you edit your paragraph for a topic sentence and other errors, share your work with your instructor or another student.

GED Practice (Pages 106–107)

All items in this practice are related to topic sentences.

1. **(1) The seventh grade will visit the Science Museum on Monday, October 5.** Option (1) is the best topic sentence because it introduces the main idea of the paragraph. Options (2), (4), and (5) are too general to be effective topic sentences. Option (3) is too specific to be an effective topic sentence.

2. **(3) The cost of the trip is $8.00 payable in cash or check.** Option (3) introduces the main idea of the paragraph and provides essential information to which all the sentences that follow relate. Option (1) provides inaccurate information. Option (2) does not provide specific enough information. Option (4) provides unnecessary information. Option (5) is too vague.

3. **(4) replace sentence 6 with <u>You will need to sign the permission form that is attached.</u>** Option (4) is an effective revision of the topic sentence because it introduces the topic of forms and clearly communicates essential information. Option (1) is too general.

Option (2) is not clear. Option (3) does not have a tone that matches the rest of the letter.

4. **(2) To keep receiving mail when you move, notify the post office of your new address.** Option (2) is correct because it introduces the main idea of the paragraph and provides a topic to which all the sentences that follow relate. Options (1), (3), (4), and (5) are too general to be effective topic sentences.

5. **(1) insert at the beginning of the paragraph The post office will forward your personal mail and most packages for one year.** Option (1) inserts a clear, effective topic sentence for the paragraph. Option (2) removes a supporting detail. Option (3) moves the sentence to an illogical place. Option (4) substitutes a general, unclear statement for a clear statement.

6. **(5) Don't forget to notify businesses you deal with that you have moved.** Option (5) is correct because it introduces the main idea of the paragraph and provides a topic to which all the sentences that follow relate. Options (1) and (2) are too general. Option (3) is an irrelevant detail. Option (4) does not effectively state the main idea of the paragraph.

GED Mini-Test • Lesson 8 (Pages 108–109)

1. **(3) Changes in the natural color of your nails can warn you of disease.** (Topic sentences) Option (3) is correct because it introduces the main idea of the paragraph and provides a topic to which all the sentences that follow relate. Options (1) and (2) are too general. Option (4) makes an inaccurate, misleading statement. Option (5) does not clearly and effectively state the main idea of the paragraph.

2. **(4) remove sentence 7** (Paragraph unity) Option (4) correctly eliminates a sentence that is irrelevant and does not support the main idea. Option (1) removes an important supporting detail. Options (2) and (3) incorrectly move supporting details out of logical order. Option (5) moves an irrelevant sentence that should be eliminated.

3. **(2) disease, while** (Subordination/Complex sentences) Option (2) is correct because it connects a subordinate-clause fragment to an independent clause. Option (1) contains a sentence fragment. Option (3) joins rather than contrasts the ideas and lacks the necessary comma in a compound sentence. Option (4)

creates a comma splice. Option (5) creates a sentence that gives an inaccurate reason.

4. **(4) change have bumps to bumpy** (Parallel structure) Option (4) correctly changes a verb-noun phrase into a single word (an adjective) that is parallel to *thick* and *yellow*. Option (1) removes a necessary word. Option (2) removes the comma needed in a parallel series. Option (3) creates a new error in parallel structure. Option(5) creates a comma splice.

5. **(3) spots because they** (Run-on sentences) Option (3) correctly fixes the original run-on by making the second clause subordinate to the first. Option (2) creates a comma splice. Option (4) uses an inappropriate coordinating conjunction and lacks the comma needed in a compound sentence. Option (5) uses an inappropriate conjunctive adverb and is incorrectly punctuated.

6. **(2) insert a comma after customs** (Subordination/ Complex sentences) Option (2) correctly inserts a comma after an introductory subordinate clause. Option (1) creates a run-on sentence. Option (3) inserts an unnecessary comma because *and* is not joining two independent clauses. Option (4) creates a run-on.

7. **(3) remove sentence 4** (Paragraph unity) Option (3) is correct because it eliminates a sentence that doesn't support the main idea. Option (1) replaces an effective opening statement with a general, vague statement. Option (2) removes the effective opening statement. Option (4) replaces one irrelevant sentence with another.

8. **(5) plant, food, or animal products** (Parallel structure) Option (5) is correct because it changes a long clause into a noun phrase that is parallel to the two other items in the series. Options (1), (2), (3), and (4) do not correct the error in parallel structure.

9. **(3) agriculture if they** (Run-on sentences) Option (3) is correct because it fixes the original run-on sentence by making the second clause subordinate with the appropriate subordinating conjunction *if*. Option (2) creates a comma splice. Option (4) fails to explain the relationship between the ideas in the clauses. Option (5) uses an inappropriate conjunctive adverb and is incorrectly punctuated.

GED Writing Link (Pages 110–111)
Share your work for the Personal Link and GED Link exercises with your instructor or another student.

Lesson 9

GED Skill Focus (Page 113)

A. These sentences start new paragraphs:
   Welcome to the Bedford Company. (Introduction)

   When you report for your first day of work, you will be asked to read this Bedford Company Handbook in its entirety. (Shift to new idea)

   On your first day of work, you will need to arrive at 9:00 A.M. promptly, no matter what shift you are assigned. (Shift to new time)

   Your first afternoon will be spent on the manufacturing floor with your team leader. (Shift to later time; breaks up a dense paragraph)

   At 4:45 P.M., please return to the Human Resources office for your permanent identification card and a two-week shift schedule. (Shift to a later time; Conclusion)

B. After you edit your writing for paragraph divisions and errors, share your work with your instructor or another student.

GED Practice (Pages 114–115)

All items in this practice are related to paragraph divisions.

1. **(2) with sentence 3** Option (2) is correct because the sentence shifts from the introduction to a new idea. Option (1) breaks apart the introductory paragraph. Options (3), (4), and (5) break apart the second paragraph, about the events at the hospital.

2. **(4) with sentence 11** Option (4) is correct because the sentence shifts to the conclusion. Options (1), (2), and (3) would break apart the second paragraph, about events at the hospital. Option (5) would create a single-sentence conclusion.

3. **(2) with sentence 3** Option (2) is correct because the sentence shifts from the introduction to a new idea. Option (1) breaks apart the introductory paragraph. Option (3) separates a topic sentence about novice writers from the details about that main idea. Options (4) and (5) break apart what should be the second paragraph, about novice writers.

4. **(1) with sentence 7** Option (1) is correct because the sentence shifts to the second of three ideas about proficient student writing. Options (2), (3), and (4) break apart what should be the third paragraph.

5. **(4) with sentence 15** Option (4) is correct because the sentence shifts to the conclusion.

Option (1) separates a topic sentence about superior writers from the details about that main idea. Options (2) and (3) break apart what should be the fourth paragraph. Option (5) breaks apart what should be the concluding paragraph.

GED Mini-Test • Lesson 9 (Pages 116–117)

1. **(2) Charting your family's health history may help save a life because heredity plays a role in many illnesses.** (Topic sentences) Option (2) is the best choice for a topic sentence because it introduces the overall subject of the paragraph and tells the main idea about that topic. Options (1), (4), and (5) are too general; they don't address the main point of the paragraph. Option (3) is too specific.

2. **(2) replace Some with You will need some** (Sentence fragments) Option (2) is correct because it adds a subject and verb that makes the original fragment into a complete sentence. Option (1) supplies only a partial verb. Option (3) inserts an unnecessary comma. Option (4) does not eliminate the fragment.

3. **(4) bonuses. The basic** (Comma splices) Option (4) correctly fixes the original comma splice by dividing the two independent clauses into two complete sentences. Option (2) creates a run-on sentence. Options (3) and (5) combine the two sentences with inappropriate subordinating conjunctions.

4. **(2) remove sentence 5** (Unity and coherence) Option (2) correctly eliminates a sentence that does not support the main idea. Option (1) incorrectly moves a supporting detail to an illogical place. Option (3) merely moves the irrelevant information. Options (4) and (5) remove important supporting details.

5. **(4) replace at the Town Hall recycling permits with recycling permits at the Town Hall** (Misplaced modifiers) Option (4) correctly moves a modifying phrase so that it does not interrupt a verb and its object. Option (1) creates a fragment with an incomplete verb. Options (2) and (3) insert unnecessary commas.

6. **(3) permit, you** (Subordination/Complex sentences) Option (3) is correct because it inserts a comma after an introductory subordinate clause. Option (1) is missing the comma. Option (2) creates a fragment. Option (4) uses an inappropriate subordinate conjunction and lacks the necessary comma. Option (5) uses an inappropriate conjunctive adverb and is incorrectly punctuated.

7. **(2) begin a new paragraph with sentence 6** (Paragraph divisions) Option (2) is correct because the sentence shifts to a new idea about what happens after you have purchased a permit. Option (1) breaks apart the first paragraph, about buying a permit. Options (3) and (4) remove important supporting details. Option (5) incorrectly suggests that a detail from one paragraph should become part of another paragraph.

8. **(5) Station, or you** (Run-on sentences) Option (5) is correct because it inserts a comma and an appropriate coordinating conjunction between the two complete sentences in the original run-on sentence. Option (2) creates a comma splice. Option (3) uses an inappropriate coordinating conjunction and lacks the necessary comma. Option (4) uses an inappropriate subordinate conjunction.

GED Writing Link (Pages 118–119)
Share your work for the Personal Link and GED Link exercises with your instructor or another student.

Lesson 10
GED Skill Focus (Page 121)

A. Sample answers:
1. To cool off in hot weather, our bodies sweat and, of course, lose water.

2. As a result, we become thirsty. To quench our thirst, many of us drink soda.

3. However, drinking soda only adds to thirst. That is because soda often contains sodium.

4. For that reason, health workers recommend water instead.

5. Therefore, it is recommended that adults drink about two quarts of water every day.

B. Sample answers:

Most Americans believe social changes are happening faster than ever. Furthermore, they believe that these changes aren't necessarily good ones. However, they still believe things will turn out for the best eventually. Young people are the most comfortable with change, while people over 60 admit that changes are difficult.

In their personal lives, almost 50 percent of older people are happy with the way things are. For example, they wouldn't change their names, their friends, their spouses, their families, their homes, or their looks. They don't want to change social class either, even if it would mean going to a higher class. On the other hand, many younger people would change all or some of those factors. Additionally, over 80 percent of people polled believed that personal happiness is a matter of personal effort.

As for difficult changes, the death of a spouse is the hardest change to endure, whereas divorce is the second hardest. Older folks tend to remember high school graduation as a pleasant experience. In contrast, more recent graduates disagree.

C. After you edit your paragraph for transitions and other errors, share your work with your instructor or another student.

GED Practice (Pages 122–123)
All items in this practice are related to transitions.

1. **(1) insert however, after the comma** Option (1) is correct because it adds a transition showing contrast between the ideas in sentences 1 and 2. Options (2), (3), (4), and (5) insert the transition in places where the relationship between the ideas is not clearly shown. They are also incorrectly punctuated.

2. **(2) replace One factory with For example, one factory** Option (2) is correct because it adds a transition that shows the idea in sentence 4 is an example of the idea in sentence 3. Option (1) uses an inappropriate subordinating conjunction and creates a fragment. Options (3) and (4) misplace the transition.

3. **(1) replace Lateness with Consequently, lateness** Option (1) is correct because it adds a transition that shows the idea in sentence 6 is a result of the idea in sentence 5. Options (2), (3), and (4) insert the transition in places where the relationship between the ideas is not clearly shown.

4. **(2) as a result** Option (2) is correct because it suggests combining two related sentences with a transition that shows cause and effect. Option (1) incorrectly suggests that the idea in sentence 9 is an example of the idea in sentence 8. Option (3) incorrectly suggests that the idea in sentence 9 contrasts with the idea in sentence 8. Options (4) and (5) incorrectly suggest that the idea in sentence 9 is an addition to the idea in sentence 8.

5. **(1) replace The with Unfortunately, the** Option (1) is correct because it inserts a transition that suggests the idea in sentence 4 contrasts with the idea in sentence 3. Options (2), (3), and (4) insert the transition in places where the relationship between the ideas is not clearly shown; in addition, they are incorrectly punctuated.

6. **(3) Fortunately, you can keep varnished wood looking good if you follow this advice.** Option (3) is correct because it provides an effective topic sentence for paragraph B and includes a transition between the main ideas in paragraphs A and B. Options (1), (2), (4), and (5) use inappropriate transitions that do not contain the main idea of paragraph B.

7. **(2) and, in addition,** Option (2) is correct because it suggests combining two related sentences with a transition that shows the addition of a detail. Option (1) does not show this relationship. Option (3) suggests that the idea in sentence 6 is a result of the idea in sentence 5. Option (4) suggests that the idea in sentence 6 is an example of the idea in sentence 5. Option (5) suggests that the idea in sentence 6 is a contrast to the idea in sentence 5.

8. **(4) furniture. In fact, polish** Option (4) correctly combines a sentence and a supporting detail with an appropriate transition. Options (1) and (2) are incorrect because they fail to show the relationship between the ideas in the two sentences. Option (2) also creates a comma splice. Option (3) incorrectly suggests that the idea in sentence 9 causes the idea in sentence 10. Option (5) incorrectly suggests that the idea in sentence 10 is the same as the idea in sentence 9.

GED Mini-Test • Lesson 10 (Pages 124–125)

1. **(4) replace sentence 1 with The Eastport Senior Council is a nonprofit, charitable organization dedicated to serving the elderly.** (Topic sentences) Option (4) is the best topic sentence because it introduces the main idea of the paragraph and corrects a topic sentence that is too informal and general. Options (1), (2), and (3) are too general and vague.

2. **(2) medicine, transportation, heat, and food** (Parallel structure) Option (2) is correct because it puts the four nouns in parallel structure. Options (1), (3), (4), and (5) do not correct the error in parallel structure.

3. **(1) remove sentence 4** (Unity and coherence) Option (1) correctly eliminates a sentence that doesn't support the main idea. Option (2) moves a supporting detail to an illogical position. Option (3) splits a paragraph where the main idea does not change. Option (4) removes a supporting detail. Option (5) replaces a supporting sentence with a fragment.

4. **(5) citizens, with the goal of helping ease** (Sentence fragments) Option (5) corrects a fragment by combining the detail in it with the previous sentence. Options (1), (2), (3), and (4) do not lead to effective sentences that fix the fragment and accurately restate the information in the original.

5. **(1) replace You with Have you** (Sentence fragments) Option (1) corrects the original fragment by completing the verb. Option (2) does not fix the fragment. Options (3) and (4) insert unnecessary commas and do not fix the fragment.

6. **(4) According to the Fair Credit Reporting Act,** (Transitions) Option (4) is correct because it adds a transition at the beginning of the sentence that explains the relationship between the ideas in sentences 2 and 3. It also has the correct tone. Options (1) and (5) create awkwardly worded sentences. Options (2) and (3) do not lead to effective sentences that accurately restate the meaning of the original text.

7. **(1) so, request** (Transitions) The original is the best way to express the idea because it uses an appropriate transitional phrase and is correctly punctuated. Options (2) and (3) create fragments. Options (4) and (5) insert unnecessary and inappropriate transitions. Option (5) is also incorrectly punctuated.

8. **(1) change After examining to After you examine** (Dangling modifiers) Option (1) fixes a dangling modifier by inserting a subject and correct verb form to create a subordinate clause. Option (2) removes a necessary comma. Option (3) creates a fragment. Option (4) inserts an unnecessary comma.

9. **(5) years, while bankruptcy** (Comma splices) Option (5) is correct because it fixes the comma splice by inserting a subordinate conjunction, making the last clause dependent on the first and showing the appropriate relationship of time order. Option (2) creates a run-on sentence. Option (3) uses an inappropriate coordinating conjunction and is incorrectly punctuated. Option (4) uses an inappropriate transition.

GED Writing Link (Pages 126–127)
Share your work for the Personal Link and GED Link exercises with your instructor or another student.

Unit 2 Cumulative Review (Pages 128–133)

1. **(4) remove sentence 2** (Unity and coherence) Option (4) correctly eliminates a sentence that does not support the main idea. Option (1) moves the topic sentence, creating a lack of coherence. Option (2) removes the topic sentence. Option (3) puts a supporting detail in the wrong paragraph.

2. **(3) As a result of my work, I** (Transitions) Option (3) shows the cause-effect relationship between the ideas in sentences 5 and 6. The other options do not lead to effective restatements that show a relationship between the sentences.

3. **(3) begin a new paragraph with sentence 10** (Paragraph divisions) Option (3) is correct because it creates a new paragraph when the main idea shifts from school to the meeting. Option (1) incorrectly moves the topic sentence of paragraph C to paragraph B. Option (2) removes a supporting detail. Option (4) moves a supporting detail to a place where it makes no sense. Option (5) removes an effective concluding statement.

4. **(2) desk. Instead, use** (Transitions) Option (2) shows the contrasting relationship between the ideas in sentences 1 and 2. Option (1) does not connect the ideas. Options (3), (4), and (5) do not lead to sentences that show the correct relationship.

5. **(2) Common household products are often all that you need.** (Topic sentences) Option (2) is correct because it introduces the main idea of the paragraph and provides a topic to which all the sentences relate. Option (1) does not state the main idea of the paragraph. Options (3) and (4) are irrelevant ideas about a supporting detail. Option (5) is too specific and does not directly state the main idea.

6. **(4) replace For with However, for** (Transitions) Option (4) is correct because it shows the contrasting relationship between the ideas in sentences 8 and 9. Option (1) removes a supporting detail. Options (2) and (3) move the detail to illogical positions within the paragraph.

7. **(3) combine paragraphs C and D** (Paragraph divisions) Option (3) is correct because it combines the two short paragraphs that relate to the same main idea about removing ink stains. Options (1) and (2) remove supporting details. Option (4) moves an effective, general, concluding statement to a paragraph that relates specifically to removing ink stains.

8. **(5) remove sentence 2** (Unity and coherence) Option (5) is correct because it removes a sentence that does not support the main idea. Option (1) just restates the nonessential detail. Option (2) replaces it with another irrelevant detail. Options (3) and (4) move the sentence, creating a lack of coherence.

9. **(1) begin a new paragraph with sentence 4.** (Paragraph divisions) Option (1) correctly creates a second paragraph when the main idea shifts to wrapping the presents. Options (2) and (3) begin the new paragraph at inappropriate places, separating details that belong together. Option (4) incorrectly makes one long paragraph out of three distinct main ideas and their supporting details.

10. **(4) replace 7 with On Tuesday, we will need help delivering the presents.** (Topic sentences) Option (4) correctly substitutes an effective topic sentence that states the main idea of the paragraph and includes a transition from the previous paragraph. Option (1) is too general. Options (2) and (5) are too vague, and their word choice creates too informal a tone. Option (3) is too specific.

11. **(3) move sentence 11 to the end of paragraph C** (Unity and coherence) Option (3) is correct because it moves an effective concluding statement to the end of the memo. Option (1) incorrectly removes the statement. Option (2) places the statement in a paragraph with a different main idea. Option (4) substitutes an ineffective and inappropriate concluding statement.

12. **(1) replace sentence 3 with Safety locks and latches protect children in several ways.** (Topic sentences) Option (1) is correct because it replaces an ineffective topic sentence with one that states the main idea of the paragraph and leads into the supporting details. Option (2) substitutes a supporting detail for the topic sentence. Option (3) moves the topic sentence to the previous paragraph, where it does not relate directly to the main idea, leaving paragraph B without a topic sentence. Likewise, option (4) removes the topic sentence from paragraph B.

13. **(4) begin a new paragraph with sentence 11** (Paragraph divisions) Option (4) correctly begins a new paragraph where the main idea shifts from safety gates to anti-scald devices. Option (1) removes an effective topic sentence for paragraph C. Option (2) moves the topic

sentence to an ineffective position. Option (3)
removes a supporting detail. Option (5)
incorrectly begins a new paragraph, separating a
topic sentence (sentence 11) from its supporting
details.

14. **(4) remove sentence 15** (Unity and coherence)
Option (4) is correct because the sentence
includes a point that is not relevant to the main
idea of the passage. Option (1) just restates the
irrelevant idea. Option (2) replaces it with
another irrelevant idea. Option (3) merely moves
the irrelevant idea.

15. **(2) begin a new paragraph with
sentence 4** (Paragraph divisions) Option (2) is
correct because it divides one long paragraph
into two paragraphs where the main idea shifts
from a general discussion of upgrades to the
three kinds of upgrades. Option (1) removes an
important piece of information from the first,
introductory paragraph. Option (3) moves the
topic sentence from what should be the
beginning of paragraph B to an ineffective
position at the end of paragraph A. Option (4)
begins the new paragraph in an inappropriate
place, separating a topic sentence from its
supporting details.

16. **(5) replace sentence 8 with As soon as you
install the upgrade, you will notice an
improvement in your computer's
performance.** (Topic sentences) Option (5)
replaces an ineffective topic sentence with one
that has a transition from the preceding
paragraph into the new one. Option (1) is too
general and not supported. Option (2) introduces
new, unrelated ideas. Option (3) is a general
restatement of a supporting detail from the first
paragraph. Option (4) is too specific.

Writing Links Review
Ask your instructor or another student to review your
paragraphs. Ask them to give you feedback on the
following:
• Sufficient supporting details
• Clear topic sentences
• Paragraph divisions
• Transitions
Revise your paragraphs as needed.

UNIT 3: USAGE
Lesson 11
GED Skill Focus (Page 137)
A. 1. means

2. visit

3. love

4. are

5. is

B.   Say "Southern California vacation" to most
people, and they <u>think</u> of Hollywood, the ocean,
or Disneyland. In reality many people <u>are</u>
skipping the usual tourist sites to visit the Mojave
Desert, the most famous desert in the state.

The Mojave <u>extends</u> hundreds of miles east,
jutting into Nevada. Spring and fall <u>are</u> the best
times to see the desert, although many people go
in other seasons, too. Winters <u>aren't</u> too bad, but
summers can be fierce. Even in summer, the
weather varies greatly, from scorching heat at
midday to chilly nights.

The desert <u>is</u> filled with magnificent sights.
Petroglyph Canyons, Fossil Falls, and Red Rock
Canyon Park <u>have</u> fascinating natural spectacles.
Death Valley <u>is</u> its own geology course. Perhaps
most surprisingly, the exotic plants <u>are</u> varied,
dramatic, and thriving. Beautiful flowers and
cacti <u>have</u> adapted to the heat and dryness. The
one part of the desert you won't see is the San
Andreas Fault. It <u>crosses</u> the Mojave outside of
Los Angeles.

C.   After you edit your paragraph for subject-verb
agreement and other errors, share your work with
your instructor or another student.

GED Skill Focus (Page 139)
A. 1. Engagement <u>rings</u> for fiancées <u>are</u> not as
popular as they used to be.

2. There <u>is</u> the <u>problem</u> of rising prices for the
rings. Correct

3. <u>Has</u> the <u>price</u> of engagement rings really risen
that much?

4. A small <u>diamond</u> today <u>costs</u> an average of
$550.

5. <u>One</u> of the famous jewelry houses <u>says</u> that
prices will not go down. Correct

6. Employed college <u>graduates</u> with a steady
income <u>buy</u> about half of all engagement
rings sold.

B. **Q:** What <u>is</u> the status of the Land Bank bill in the
state legislature?
A: The House and Senate <u>have</u> passed similar
versions of the bill. The bill, officially named the
Act for Preservation of Open Lands, <u>allows</u>
individual towns to decide how best to preserve
open land. The final versions of the House and
Senate bill are due this week. There <u>are</u> still two

major unresolved questions. Can towns vote to add a 1 percent tax on real estate purchases to fund land purchases? Does the state provide matching funds? State representatives and senators on both sides of the issue expect negotiations to continue all month.

C. After you edit your paragraph for subject-verb agreement and other errors, share your work with your instructor or another student.

GED Skill Focus (Page 141)

A. 1. S wishes

2. S opens

3. S receives

4. S awards

5. P sponsor

6. P return

7. S misses

B. Dear Editor:

Neither the housing committee nor I believe that the land developers simply "forgot" to build affordable housing. Everyone knows it is required as part of all large development projects. The town council is not allowed to grant waivers to developers, and nothing hurts the city more than neglect of the law.

Our great workforce makes this town a dream town for business. But great workers won't stay without a place to live. Many need affordable housing. The whole community agrees that ignoring regulations decreases the quality of life for all of us. Our community is a desirable place to live because students, business people, and service workers live here.

At the council meeting next week, someone has to insist the town council choose between the community or the developers.

C. After you edit your paragraph for subject-verb agreement and other errors, share your work with your instructor or another student.

GED Practice (Pages 142–143)

All items in this practice are related to subject-verb agreement.

1. **(2) change are to is** Option (2) is correct because *is* agrees with the singular subject *advice*. Option (1) is incorrect because it creates a fragment without a verb. Option (3) is incorrect because dependent clauses following independent clauses generally do not need a comma. Option (4) makes the subject and verb

disagree in the dependent clause. Option (5) inserts an unnecessary comma.

2. **(4) change lasts to last** Option (4) is correct because *last* agrees with the plural subject *houseplants*. Options (1) and (2) insert unnecessary commas. Option (3) creates a sentence fragment because the verb is incomplete.

3. **(3) change survive to survives** Option (3) is correct because *survives* agrees with the singular subject *nothing*. Option (1) is incorrect because it removes an important transition. Option (2) does not correct the subject-verb disagreement. Option (4) creates a sentence fragment because the verb is incomplete.

4. **(2) protect** Option (2) is correct because the plural verb *protect* agrees with the subject *Layers*. Options (1) and (4) are incorrect because they are singular verbs. Option (3) creates a sentence fragment because the verb is incomplete. Option (5) is incorrect because only the plural verb *protect* is needed in the sentence.

5. **(2) are covered** Option (2) is correct because the plural verb *are covered* is needed with the plural subject *bricks*. Option (1) is incorrect because it is a singular verb. Options (3) and (5) are incorrect verb forms for the sentence. Option (4) creates a sentence fragment because the verb is incomplete.

6. **(2) change guarantee to guarantees** Option (2) is correct because *guarantees* agrees with the singular subject *Fair Point Company*. Option (1) incorrectly changes the verb tense. Options (3) and (4) insert unnecessary commas.

7. **(3) has** Option (3) is correct because *has* needs to agree with the singular subject *company*, not the interrupting phrase between the subject and the verb. Option (1) is incorrect because *company* and *have* do not agree. Option (2) creates a sentence fragment because the verb is incomplete. Option (4) repeats the subject. Option (5) is an incorrect verb form for the sentence.

8. **(4) is caused** Option (4) is correct because the verb agrees with the last subject after *or*. Option (1) is incorrect because it is a plural verb and the subject is singular. Options (2), (3), and (5) are incorrect verb forms for the sentence.

9. **(2) change cover to covers** Option (2) is correct because the singular verb *covers* agrees with the singular subject *warranty*. Option (1)

inserts an unnecessary transition. Option (3) creates a sentence fragment with an incomplete verb. Option (4) inserts an unnecessary comma.

GED Mini-Test • Lesson 11 (Pages 144–145)

1. **(5) Together, make a list of things that must be done before the departure date.** (Organization/topic sentence) Option (5) is the best choice of topic sentence because it introduces the overall subject of the paragraph. Options (1), (2), and (4) are too general; they do not address the main point of the paragraph. Option (3) does not relate to the details in the paragraph.

2. **(4) change call to calls** (Subject-verb agreement) Option (4) is correct because *calls* agrees with the singular indefinite subject *everyone*. Option (1) does not fix the subject-verb disagreement and inserts an inappropriate transition. Option (2) changes a singular verb that agrees with the singular subject *member* to a plural verb. Option (3) incorrectly inserts a comma between an independent clause and a dependent clause.

3. **(2) remove sentence 5** (Unity and coherence) Option (2) correctly eliminates a sentence that does not support the main idea. Option (1) removes an important supporting detail. Options (3) and (4) move sentences out of logical order.

4. **(4) As the tasks get completed,** (Subordination/ Complex sentences) Option (4) correctly subordinates the idea in the first sentence to create a smooth complex sentence. Options (1), (2), (3), and (5) do not lead to smooth, effective sentences.

5. **(3) insert is after town** (Sentence fragments) Option (3) is correct because it inserts the correct missing verb. Option (1) removes a necessary comma. Options (2) and (5) insert unnecessary commas. Option (4) inserts an incomplete verb form.

6. **(4) After the fluid and combustible parts are removed,** (Subordination/Complex sentences) Option (4) correctly subordinates the idea in the second sentence to show the correct time order and create a smooth complex sentence. Options (1), (2), (3), and (5) do not lead to smooth, effective sentences.

7. **(5) no correction is necessary** (Subject-verb agreement) Option (5) is correct because the singular subject *job* agrees with the singular verb

is. Option (1) is incorrect because it changes the verb to a plural form. Option (2) removes the verb, creating a sentence fragment. Option (3) uses an incorrect verb form for the sentence. Option (4) inserts an unnecessary comma.

8. **(2) chunks. Finally,** (Run-on sentences) Option (2) correctly divides a run-on sentence into two complete sentences with correct punctuation. Options (1), (3), (4), and (5) do not correct the run-on.

GED Writing Link (Pages 146–147)

Share your work for the Personal Link and GED Link exercises with your instructor or another student.

Lesson 12

GED Skill Focus (Page 149)

A. 1. learned

 2. confirmed

 3. demonstrates *or* demonstrated *or* has demonstrated

 4. looked

 5. sorted *or* have sorted

 6. living

 7. watch *or* watched *or* have watched

B. Dear Customer,

 In an effort to provide you with advanced Internet services, we have <u>upgraded</u> our network to support higher bandwidth applications. Our records <u>indicate</u> that you own a B-45 cable modem. Our upgraded network <u>requires</u> a new modem for your system to avoid interruptions in your high-speed Internet service. We <u>have</u> ordered a new modem for your computer. The replacement modem <u>provides</u> all the same features and benefits as your current modem.

 Self-installation is designed to be fast and easy. We <u>encourage</u> you to follow the step-by-step instructions to complete the self-installation process. If you would like us to install it for you, we <u>need</u> three to six weeks to schedule an appointment with a technician. Customers who <u>agree</u> to install the modem themselves will receive a $50 credit.

C. After you edit your letter for incorrect verb forms and other errors, share your work with your instructor or another student.

GED Skill Focus (Page 151)

A. 1. went

 2. drove, ate, swam

 3. gave

4. was, knew

5. spoke, seen

6. came, was

B. Anna: Hi! I haven't seen you in a while. You <u>have done</u> something to yourself, haven't you?

Kevin: Since I <u>saw</u> you last, I <u>began</u> a special diet and workout routine.

Anna: What <u>made</u> you do it?

Kevin: Ever since I <u>was</u> a teenager, I <u>have been</u> overweight. Finally, I took my doctor's advice and <u>went</u> on a serious diet. I <u>broke</u> some bad habits, too. For instance, I haven't <u>eaten</u> a late-night snack or fast food in <u>months.</u> Altogether, I <u>lost</u> 32 pounds.

Anna: You look great! Keep up the good work!

Kevin: Thanks! I certainly hope to!

C. After you edit your paragraph for incorrect verb forms and other errors, share your work with your instructor or another student.

GED Practice (Pages 152–153)

All items in this practice relate to verb forms.

1. **(4) change holded to held** Option (4) is correct because the past participle of *hold* is *held*. Option (1) is incorrect because the helping verb *have* is needed before *driven*. Option (2) is incorrect because a past participle is required with the helping verb *have*. Option (3) is incorrect because a comma is needed when two independent clauses are joined with a coordinating conjunction. Option (5) inserts an unnecessary comma.

2. **(4) change growed to grew** Option (4) is correct because *grew* is the past form of *grow*. Option (1) creates a sentence fragment because the independent clause would lack a subject. Options (2) and (5) use incorrect verb forms. Option (3) creates a run-on sentence.

3. **(2) drove** Option (2) correctly supplies the past form of *drive*. Options (1), (3), and (5) are incorrect verb forms. Option (4) is a past participle without a helping verb.

4. **(1) have been** Option (1) is correct because the original, *have been*, is the correct past participle form of the verb *be*. Option (2) does not agree with the subject *I*. Options (3), (4), and (5) are not correct verb forms.

5. **(2) have changed** Option (2) is correct because *have* is the correct helping verb to go with the past participle *changed*. Option (1) uses an incorrect helping verb. Option (3) is a singular verb with a plural subject. Option (4) creates a sentence fragment with an incomplete verb. Option (5) uses an incorrect helping verb.

6. **(3) change took to taken** Option (3) is correct because *taken* is the past participle of the verb *take*. Option (1) removes a necessary comma. Option (2) is a singular verb with a plural subject. Option (4) creates a comma splice by making the ending phrase an independent clause with its own subject and verb.

7. **(4) change thinking to think** Option (4) is correct because the present participle *thinking* requires a helping verb. *Think* is the correct verb form to use with *teens*. Option (1) inserts an unnecessary comma. Option (2) creates a sentence fragment with an incomplete verb. Option (3) is an incorrect verb form. Option (5) would break the subject-verb agreement *50 percent . . . carry*.

8. **(5) feel** Option (5) is the correct form of the verb *feel*. Option (1) is a present participle without the needed helping verb. Option (2) is a singular verb with a plural subject. Options (3) and (4) are incorrect verb forms.

9. **(4) have not spoken** Option (4) supplies the correct form of the helping verb and past participle of *speak*. Options (1), (2), and (5) are incorrect verb forms. Option (3) does not accurately restate the meaning of the original sentence and is an incorrect verb form.

GED Mini-Test • Lesson 12 (Pages 154–155)

1. **(4) change begun to begin** (Irregular verbs) Option (4) supplies the correct verb form; there is no helping verb, so the past participle *begun* is incorrect. Option (1) breaks the subject-verb agreement between *thing* and *is*. Options (2) and (3) create sentence fragments. Option (5) is an incorrect verb form.

2. **(2) have printed** (Subject-verb agreement) Option (2) correctly uses a plural verb with a plural subject. Option (1) incorrectly uses a singular verb. Option (3) uses an incorrect tense. Options (4) and (5) create sentence fragments with incomplete verbs.

3. **(1) although at first** (Subordination/Complex sentences) Option (1) is correct because it subordinates the idea in the second sentence and connects it with an appropriate conjunction to the first sentence. Options (2), (3), (4), and (5) do not smoothly combine the two sentences.

4. **(3) change being to is** (Verb forms) Option (3) is correct because the sentence requires the present form *is*. Option (1) is incorrect because *Learning* is actually the subject and should not be in the present form. Option (2) inserts an unnecessary comma. Option (4) incorrectly removes the comma needed between two independent clauses in a compound sentence. Option (5) is an incorrect verb form for the sentence.

5. **(3) change were knowing to have known** (Verb forms) Option (3) is correct because it supplies the appropriate helping verb and past participle. Options (1) and (4) insert unnecessary commas. Options (2) and (5) use incorrect verb forms.

6. **(3) begin a new paragraph with sentence 3** (Organization/Paragraph divisions) Option (3) is correct because sentence 3 shifts to a new idea that supports the main idea given in the next sentences. Options (1) and (4) suggest moving sentences out of logical order. Option (2) removes an important idea. Option (5) incorrectly moves a detail that supports the main idea of the second paragraph into the concluding paragraph.

7. **(1) change come to comes** (Subject-verb agreement) Option (1) is correct because the singular verb *comes* agrees with the subject *reason*. Options (2), (3), and (5) use incorrect verb forms. Option (4) inserts an unnecessary comma.

8. **(2) are pleased** (Subject-verb agreement) Option (2) is correct because the word *Both* is always plural and takes a plural verb. Option (1) is incorrect because it is singular. Options (3), (4), and (5) create sentence fragments with incomplete verb forms.

9. **(5) and better at solving problems** (Parallel structure) Option (5) is correct because it makes the third phrase parallel with the first two. Options (1), (2), (3), and (4) do not fix the problem in parallel structure.

GED Writing Link (Pages 156–157)
Share your work for the Personal Link and GED Link exercises with your instructor or another student.

Lesson 13
GED Skill Focus (Page 159)
A. 1. voted

2. has started *or* started

3. broke

4. will finish

5. had signed *or* signed

6. had provided *or* provided

7. expects

8. will have raised

B.   Many major failures of the last century <u>happened</u> through folly, arrogance, or carelessness. Mistakes were made by individuals, enterprises, and nations alike. In mid-century, an aviator named Douglas Corrigan <u>made</u> an incredible error. He was supposed to <u>land</u> in California on a trip from Brooklyn, but he <u>flew</u> to Ireland instead. Not surprisingly, that <u>earned</u> him the nickname "Wrong-Way Corrigan." The country of Chile also <u>went</u> through hard times because of a careless <u>mistake</u>. A stockbroker accidentally typed "buy" instead of "sell," and an enormous chunk of the country's economy <u>was</u> destroyed. During the "Great Leap Forward," the Chinese government <u>enforced</u> a new "technological" agriculture. Instead of increasing the food supply, however, production <u>fell</u> drastically. Widespread famine <u>followed</u>. There <u>were</u> even disasters in outer <u>space</u>. For <u>example</u>, an unmanned landing probe to Mars mysteriously <u>disappeared</u> at a cost of several billion dollars.

C. After you edit your paragraph for incorrect verb tenses and other errors, share your work with your instructor or another student.

GED Skill Focus (Page 161)
A. 1. turn, <u>have</u>

2. states, <u>have</u>

3. <u>Within 90 days of registering,</u> will receive

4. <u>does not mean,</u> are

5. ordered, <u>in the 1970s</u>

6. has . . . drafted, <u>since 1973</u>

7. will call . . . <u>again, only if there is</u>

B.   Do you feel as if you say no to your children too often? Psychologists <u>have</u> some helpful suggestions for setting limits. For instance, if your child <u>asks</u> you for a new toy or a trip to the ice cream store, say you need some time to decide. Saying, "Give me a minute" allows you time to think about the situation before you <u>answer</u>. Your children must understand that if they insist on an immediate answer, then the answer <u>will be</u> no. If they <u>give</u> you time to think, however, your answer may be yes.

  Here's another tactic for setting limits. Tell your children they will have to convince you that their request is valid. Your children will learn how to negotiate, and you will make a fairer decision. If you are upset or worn out, be clear that it is not a good time for you to make a decision. Tell them that you will decide after you calm down. Distracted answers often are poor ones, as your children soon will learn.

C. After you edit your paragraph for verb-tense shifts and other errors, share your work with your instructor or another student.

GED Practice (Pages 162–163)
All items in this practice relate to verb tenses.

1. **(2) change have been to are** Option (2) is correct because it fixes an unnecessary verb tense shift; the present tense is consistent with the rest of the paragraph. Option (1) incorrectly changes the verb to the past perfect tense, which is inconsistent with the rest of the paragraph. Option (3) incorrectly changes another verb in the sentence to the present perfect. Option (4) inserts an unnecessary comma. Option (5) used the wrong verb tense.

2. **(1) will ship** Option (1) is correct because *within the next thirty days* indicates that the verb should be in the future tense. Options (2) and (4) are past tenses. Option (3) is the present tense. Option (5) is missing the helping verb *will* and so creates a sentence fragment.

3. **(3) arrives** Option (3) is correct because *as soon as* is a clue that the simple present tense is needed. Option (1) is the future perfect. Option (2) is a plural past tense, so it does not agree in time or in number with the subject. Option (4) is incorrect because *is arriving* suggests the action is going on now. Option (5) is an incomplete verb form and would create a fragment.

4. **(4) change be calling to call** Option (4) correctly uses a present tense verb in the second clause because the verb in the first clause is in the present tense. Option (1) uses an incorrect present tense because the action is not ongoing. Option (2) removes a necessary comma after an introductory dependent clause. Option (3) creates a fragment out of the clause.

5. **(5) appreciate** Option (5) is correct because the present tense is consistent with the other verb in the sentence, *look*. Options (1), (2), (3), and (4) are all incorrect shifts in verb tense.

6. **(5) have known** Option (5) is correct because the time phrase *for many years* indicates a past action that continues into the present, which

requires the present perfect tense. Option (1) is the simple present tense. Option (2) is the past participle without a helping verb. Option (3) is an incorrect verb form for the past tense. Option (4) is the future tense.

7. **(2) change become to became** Option (2) is correct because the phrase *a number of years ago* is a clue that the simple past is needed. Option (1) removes a necessary comma. Option (3) inserts an unnecessary comma. Option (4) changes a correct past tense verb to the past perfect. Option (5) leaves an incorrect verb tense.

8. **(4) looks** Option (4) is correct because the words *today* and *often choose* are clues that the simple present tense is needed. Options (1), (2), (3), and (5) are incorrect shifts in verb tense.

9. **(3) will focus** Option (3) is correct because the simple future tense is needed in the second, main clause. The introductory clause (*As consumer demand . . . increases*) sets up a condition that continues into the future. Options (1), (2), and (4) are incorrect shifts in verb tense. Option (5) is an incomplete verb form.

GED Mini-Test • Lesson 13 (Pages 164–165)

1. **(1) change offer to offers** (Subject-verb agreement) Option (1) is correct because the verb should be singular to agree with the subject *dry cleaner*, not the interrupting phrase *Acme Movie Studios*. Option (2) incorrectly shifts the verb to the past tense. Option (3) inserts an unnecessary comma. Option (4) creates a sentence fragment out of the last part of the sentence.

2. **(4) will surely forget** (Verb tenses) Option (4) is correct because *Within a few months* implies future time, and the future tense is formed by adding *will* to the present form *forget*. Option (1) is missing the necessary helping verb. Option (2) is the past perfect tense and creates a tense shift. Options (3) and (5) are incorrect verb forms in inappropriate tenses.

3. **(5) silks, wools, and synthetics** (Parallel structure) Option (5) is correct because it changes a phrase into a single word, *synthetics*, so that it is parallel with *silks* and *wools*. Options (1), (2), (3), and (4) do not correct the error in parallel structure.

4. **(3) insert a comma after long** (Sentence structure/ Complex sentences) Option (3) is correct because a comma is needed after the introductory clause. Options (1) and (4) change correct verbs to an incorrect tense. Option (2)

uses an incorrect verb form. Option (5) inserts an unnecessary comma.

5. **(1) remove had** (Verb tenses) Option (1) correctly changes the verb to the simple past because the phrase *Last November* implies past tense. Option (2) would be a tense shift to the future. Options (3) and (4) insert unnecessary commas. Option (5) incorrectly used past perfect tense.

6. **(2) with sentence 3** (Paragraph divisions) Option (2) is correct because sentence 3 shifts from the introduction to a new idea. Option (1) splits the introductory paragraph. Options (3) and (4) would split details within the new second paragraph. Option (5) would split the concluding paragraph.

7. **(2) change results to resulted** (Verb tenses) Option (2) is correct because it supplies the simple past form to be consistent with the previous sentence. Option (1) incorrectly uses the future tense. Option (3) inserts an unnecessary comma. Option (4) creates a sentence fragment.

8. **(3) year. These** (Run-on sentences) Option (3) is correct because it splits the original run-on sentence, option (1), into two complete sentences. Option (2) creates a comma splice. Option (4) is missing the necessary comma between two independent clauses. Option (5) incorrectly uses a connecting word and punctuation.

9. **(4) you use as well as whether you** (Sentence fragments) Option (4) effectively fixes the fragment by combining the thoughts in a parallel form. Options (1), (2), (3), and (5) do not lead to smooth, effective sentences that accurately restate the meaning of the original text.

GED Writing Link (Pages 166–167)
Share your work for the Personal Link and GED Link exercises with your instructor or another student.

Lesson 14
GED Skill Focus (Page 169)
A. 1. me, I

2. me, I

3. They, them

4. She, her, she

5. I, I, I

6. we, us

B. Dear Friends,
We wish to extend a cordial invitation to you to attend the Annual Firefighters Dance. It will be held at the Oak River Club on Friday, May 4, from 7 P.M. to midnight.
The Four Blue Notes will provide musical entertainment. We wish to thank them for donating their time and talents to us. A large buffet and soft drinks will accompany the music and dancing. They [It is] are all included in the price of the admission ticket.
Reservations are required. Please request yours [or them] by April 12. As you know, proceeds from this event go to firefighters who are injured in the line of duty.

C. After you edit your invitation for pronoun mistakes and other errors, share your work with your instructor or another student.

GED Skill Focus (Page 171)
A. 1. needles, They

2. kids and I, we; hardware store, it

3. son Jake, his

4. dowels, them

5. one, it

6. dowel, its

7. dowels, them

8. son, his; I, my

9. class, they

10. students, their

B. My wife and I are fixing up our new house. It is a "handyman's special." The wood floors are very dull. I think they were heavily waxed over the years. We both would like to remove the wax, and then varnish the wood. Mr. Oldham, the local hardware store owner, said we can't varnish over a waxed surface. He said that even if we try to get all the wax off, some of it will remain. Is he giving us good advice? Or do you have a better idea for us to try? This problem is really frustrating my wife and me.

C. After you edit your paragraph for mistakes in pronoun-antecedent agreement and other errors, share your work with your instructor or another student.

GED Skill Focus (Page 173)
A. 1. Becky was pleased that she got several job offers because they gave her some choices.

2. The company in St. Louis offered a great salary, and it would pay her moving costs.

3. When you move to a new city, you can always make new friends.

4. Sample answer: As Becky thought about starting a new job in a new city, she felt the changes were bound to be exciting.

5. Sample answer: Becky's friends urged her to take one of the local jobs, but she wasn't sure that her friends were right.

6. Sample answer: Then Becky's bosses offered her both a promotion and a raise. Those offers made her change her mind.

B. You might think "a nail is a nail is a nail," but in fact, there are differences between your toenails and fingernails. Also, if you are right-handed, your right-hand nails grow faster than your left. Podiatrists think nails grow faster in summer than in winter. They think that the change in nail growth is due to changes in circulation.

To keep nails cells healthy, podiatrists have several suggestions. Cut nails straight across, and use foot powder, not cornstarch, on your feet in the summer. Always wear sandals when you bathe in public places. Finally, be sure to change your socks or stockings every day.

C. After you edit your paragraph for mistakes in pronoun usage and other errors, share your work with your instructor or another student.

GED Practice (Pages 174–175)
All the items in this practice relate to pronouns.

1. **(4) replace it with the disease** Option (4) is correct because it makes the antecedent of *it* clear; it could have referred to *disease, bite,* or *tick*. Option (1) is incorrect because the plural subject *things* requires a plural verb, *are*. Options (2) and (3) are incorrect because they are pronoun shifts. Option (5) has an unclear antecedent.

2. **(2) You should tuck** Option (2) corrects the vague antecedent of the original, option (1). Option (3) uses another pronoun with a vague antecedent. Options (4) and (5) create pronoun shifts from the second person pronoun *you* used in the passage.

3. **(4) replace see them with see the ticks** Option (4) is correct because it makes the antecedent of *them* clear; it could have referred to *ticks* or *colors*. Option (1) creates a pronoun shift from *you* to *one*. Option (2) removes the necessary comma after an introductory clause. Option (3)

inserts an unnecessary comma. Option (5) creates a pronoun shift from *them* to it.

4. **(1) replace They with Tick collars** Option (1) is correct because it makes the antecedent of *They* clear; it could refer to *tick collars* or *pets*. Option (2) replaces a noun with an unclear pronoun. Option (3) creates a sentence fragment. Option (4) replaces a correct present-tense verb with an incomplete verb form. Option (5) has an unclear antecedent.

5. **(2) change I to me** Option (2) is correct because an object pronoun is needed for a direct object of the verb *informed*. Option (1) inserts an unneeded subject pronoun after the noun subject. Option (3) incorrectly changes the verb tense from present to past. Option (4) incorrectly uses a verb that does not agree with the subject of the clause. Option (5) incorrectly uses a subject pronoun.

6. **(5) Rick and I** Option (5) is correct because *I* is a subject pronoun. Options (1) and (2) are incorrect because *me* is an object pronoun regardless of the order it appears in a compound subject. Option (3) is incorrect because *him* is an object pronoun. Option (4) is incorrect because it is unclear who *he* refers to and *me* is an object pronoun.

7. **(4) replace them with carpool groups** Option (4) is correct because it makes the antecedent of *them* clear; *them* could refer to *carpool groups* or *employees*. Options (1) and (5) create unclear antecedents. Option (2) is incorrect because it inserts an unnecessary subject pronoun after a noun subject. A pronoun that follows immediately after its antecedent is unnecessarily repetitive. Option (3) incorrectly changes the tense of the verb.

8. **(5) no correction is necessary** Option (1) is incorrect because it would create a pronoun shift. Option (2) replaces a correct helping verb with an incorrect one. Option (3) inserts an unnecessary comma. Option (4) removes a necessary comma after an introductory clause.

9. **(3) give the information to me, and I will compile it** Option (3) is correct because it makes the antecedent of *it* clear by switching the order of the pronoun and its antecedent in the sentence. None of the other options leads to a smooth, effective sentence that makes the antecedent clear and accurately restates the meaning of the original sentence.

GED Mini-Test • Lesson 14 (Pages 176–177)

1. **(1) remove sentence 2** (Unity and coherence) Option (1) correctly eliminates a sentence that is irrelevant to the main idea. Option (2) moves but does not eliminate the irrelevant sentence. Options (3) and (4) incorrectly change where paragraph B begins.

2. **(3) replace they with the committee** (Pronouns) Option (3) corrects a vague antecedent and a pronoun shift in person. Option (1) creates an unclear antecedent. Option (2) removes a necessary comma between two independent clauses in a compound sentence. Option (4) causes an incorrect shift in verb tense.

3. **(5) change they to women** (Pronouns) Option (5) is correct because it makes the antecedent of *they* clear; it could refer to *committee* or *women*. Options (1) and (3) are incorrect because each inserts another unclear pronoun into the sentence. Option (2) uses an incorrect verb form. Option (4) unnecessarily splits the sentence into two complete sentences, making the relationship between the two clauses unclear.

4. **(3) have just about stopped** (Verb tenses) Option (3) is correct because the present perfect tense is needed for actions that started in the past and continue into the present. The remaining options are incorrect verb tenses for the sentence.

5. **(3) sharp intelligence** (Parallel structure) Option (3) is correct because it changes a clause into a phrase—a noun modified by an adjective—to match the form of the other two elements in the series. None of the other options fixes the error in parallel structure.

6. **(4) replace their with its** (Pronouns) Option (4) is correct because it makes the possessive pronoun singular to agree with its singular antecedent, *a trained Capuchin*. Option (1) is incorrect because it removes a necessary comma. Option (2) removes a necessary comma between the items in a series. Option (3) creates an error in parallel structure of the three verbs—*microwave, bring, feed*. Option (5) incorrectly uses a plural pronoun with a singular antecedent.

7. **(5) replace fits with fit** (Subject-verb agreement) Option (5) is correct because the plural subject *they* needs the plural verb *fit*. Option (1) is incorrect because it would create another error in subject-verb agreement.

Option (2) removes the comma necessary after an introductory clause. Option (3) uses the singular pronoun *it* to refer to the plural *monkeys*. Option (4) is incorrect because it uses the singular pronoun *he* for the plural antecedent *monkeys*.

8. **(4) replace he with the owner** (Pronouns) Option (4) is correct because it makes the antecedent of *he* clear; it could refer to the monkey or the monkey's owner. Option (1) creates a pronoun shift as well as disagreement between the subject and verb in the dependent clause (*they jumps*). Option (2) is incorrect because the antecedent *one* needs the singular pronoun *its*. Option (3) removes a necessary comma after an introductory clause. Option (5) creates an unclear antecedent.

9. **(2) In turn,** (Transitions) Option (2) is correct because it adds a transition to show the correct sequence of ideas. Options (1), (3), (4), and (5) are transitions that do not show a logical relationship between the ideas.

GED Writing Link (Pages 178–179)

Share your work for the Personal Link and GED Link exercises with your instructor or another student.

Unit 3 Cumulative Review (Pages 180–185)

1. **(1) change have had to had** (Verb tenses) *Recently* implies past tense, so option (1) is correct. Options (2) and (5) are incorrect because *always* tells you the condition happens regularly, so the present tense is needed for both *is* and *receive*. Option (3) inserts an unnecessary comma. Option (4) creates a pronoun shift.

2. **(5) replace one does with I did** (Pronouns) Option (5) corrects a pronoun shift, using the first person *I*, as the rest of the passage does, instead of the third person *one*. Option (1) is incorrect because a regular condition needs the present tense. Option (2) removes a necessary comma between independent clauses in a compound sentence. Option (3) creates a sentence fragment. Option (4) does not correct the pronoun shift because it replaces the third person *one* with the second person *you*.

3. **(3) remembered** (Verb tenses) Option (3) is correct because the past tense would be needed in the reconstructed sentence: *As I was waiting at the baggage carousel, I remembered the book and told a clerk at the baggage desk.* The other options use incorrect tenses for the sentence.

4. **(4) change had came to had come** (Verb forms) Option (4) is correct because *had come* is

the correct form of the past perfect tense of *come; came* is the simple past tense. Options (1) and (3) create vague pronoun references. Option (2) incorrectly uses the present tense when the past tense is needed. Option (5) incorrectly uses the simple past tense.

5. **(2) is** (Subject-verb agreement) Option (2) is correct because *is* agrees with the singular subject *abundance*. Options (1) and (4) are plural verbs. Option (3) is singular but the wrong tense. Option (5) is an incomplete verb.

6. **(4) change <u>have hunted</u> to <u>hunt</u>** (Verb tenses) Option (4) corrects a tense shift so that *hunt* is consistent with the other present-tense verbs in the passage. Option (1) incorrectly changes the first verb in the sentence to the past tense. Option (2) would make the last clause a sentence fragment. Option (3) is an incomplete verb form. Option (5) uses an incorrect verb tense.

7. **(2) are** (Verb tenses) Option (2) corrects a tense shift so that *are* is consistent with the other simple present tense verb in the sentence, *reach*. Options (1), (3), and (4) would make the verb tense inconsistent with *reach*. Option (5) is an incomplete verb form.

8. **(1) change <u>grows</u> to <u>grow</u>** (Subject-verb agreement) Option (1) is correct because *grow* agrees with the compound subject *plants and animals*, not the interrupting phrase *collectively known as plankton*. Option (2) changes a correct plural pronoun referring to the subject with an incorrect singular one. Option (3) is an incorrect verb form. Option (4) creates a shift in verb tenses by using a continuous form of the present perfect tense. Option (5) creates a vague pronoun reference.

9. **(5) fish, and they, in turn, attract** (Pronouns) Option (5) is correct because it combines the sentences smoothly to make one compound sentence and replaces the repetitive *small fish* with the correct plural pronoun *they*. Options (1), (2), (3), and (4) use incorrect pronouns for the antecedent *fish*.

10. **(3) change <u>was</u> to <u>were</u>** (Subject-verb agreement) Option (3) is correct because the plural verb *were* agrees with the plural subject *posts*, not the interrupting phrase *under President Jimmy Carter*. Option (1) is an unnecessary change because the antecedent of *Her* is clear from the previous sentence. Option (2) removes a necessary comma. Option (4) removes a

necessary comma between the items in a series. Option (5) uses a singular verb for a plural subject.

11. **(5) no correction is necessary** (Pronouns) The sentence is correct and clear as written. Option (1) creates a pronoun shift. Option (2) is an incorrect verb form. Option (3) inserts an unnecessary comma between the two verbs in the sentence. Option (4) would incorrectly create a compound sentence without a necessary comma and use an object pronoun as the subject of the second clause.

12. **(4) rose** (Verb forms) Option (4) correctly provides the past tense form of the irregular verb *rise* because the tense of the first verb in the reconstructed sentence, *was*, is past tense. The other options are verbs in the wrong tense for the sentence.

13. **(2) appears** (Subject-verb agreement) Option (2) is correct because the singular subject *image* needs a singular verb. The other options are incorrectly plural. Options (3) and (4) also represent unnecessary tense shifts.

14. **(5) began** (Verb forms) Option (5) is the correct form of the past tense of the verb. Option (1) is an incomplete verb form. Options (2), (3), and (4) are incorrect tenses for the sentence because *in 1978* indicates that the simple past tense should be used.

15. **(5) replace <u>one's</u> with <u>their</u>** (Pronouns) Option (5) corrects the pronoun shift from singular third person (*one*) to plural third person (*their*). Option (1) creates an error in subject-verb agreement because the subject *habit* is singular. Option (2) uses an inappropriate tense. Option (3) inserts an unnecessary comma. Option (4) incorrectly changes the form of the verb *checking*.

16. **(2) are** (Subject-verb agreement) Option (2) is correct because the plural subject *steps* needs the plural verb *are*. Option (1) uses a singular verb for a plural subject. Options (3) and (4) use incorrect verb forms. Option (5) is incorrect because the future tense is inappropriate for the sentence.

17. **(3) touches** (Verb forms) Option (3) is correct because it is the simple present tense of *touch*, matching the other present tense verbs in the passage. Option (1) is an incorrect verb form. Option (2) is an incorrect verb form as well as plural. Option (4) is an incomplete verb form. Option (5) is incorrect because the past perfect tense is inappropriate for the sentence.

18. (4) replace it with the car (Pronouns) Option (4) correctly replaces an unclear pronoun with its antecedent. Option (1) creates a shift in verb tense because the second verb in the sentence, *has*, is present, so the first verb should be, too. Option (2) creates a sentence fragment from the introductory clause. Option (3) removes the necessary comma after the introductory clause.

19. (1) has been added (Verb forms) Option (1) is the correct verb form and tense to use in the reconstructed sentence: *Once oil has been added, check the level again to be sure it is within the necessary range.* Options (2), (4), and (5) are incorrect verb forms. Option (3) is the incorrect tense.

20. (2) change have returned to return (Verb tenses) Option (2) corrects a tense shift so that *return* is consistent with the other simple present tense verbs in the warranty. Option (1) creates a pronoun shift. Option (3) removes a necessary comma after the introductory clause. Option (4) makes the verb tense inconsistent with the rest of the warranty.

21. (4) ask (Subject-verb agreement) Option (4) is correct because the plural subject *We* needs a plural verb. Option (1) is incorrect because the singular verb does not agree with the plural subject. Options (2), (3), and (5) create shifts in the verb tense because the rest of the warranty is in the present.

22. (3) submit (Verb tenses) Option (3) is correct because the simple present is consistent with other tenses in the warranty. Options (1), (2), and (5) create shifts in the verb tense. Option (4) uses an incorrect form of the verb.

Writing Links Review

Ask your instructor or another student to review your paragraphs. Ask them to give you feedback on the following:

- Organization of ideas
- Introduction and conclusion
- Action verbs
- Point of view

Revise your paragraphs as needed.

UNIT 4: MECHANICS
Lesson 15
GED Skill Focus (Page 189)

A. Ask your instructor or another student to check your capitalization.

B. March 12, 2001

Dr. Martin Allard
Metropolitan Hospital
3453 Ridgefield Road
Oklahoma City, Oklahoma 83346

Dear Dr. Martin,

As we discussed last Thursday, I am submitting an official request for a week of vacation time from July 29 to August 5. I need that particular week because my family from Virginia will be visiting me.

Although I do not have much seniority, I appreciate your consideration of my request. I have not taken any time off since Thanksgiving. In addition, I will be working full shifts on Memorial Day and the Fourth of July.

Sincerely,
Matthew Styles

C. After you edit your letter for capitalization and other errors, share your work with your instructor or another student.

GED Skill Focus (Page 191)

A. 1. I learned a lot about the geography of the United States in my American Studies 101 class.

2. On the east we are bordered by the Atlantic Ocean and on the west by the Pacific.

3. The states on the Gulf of Mexico have hot weather, but in the Great Lakes region it can get freezing cold.

4. Going west from the Mississippi River, you see flat land and cornfields.

5. West of the Great Plains are deserts and mountain ranges.

6. To get to the most northern state, Alaska, you have to cross the country of Canada.

7. To get to the most southern, Hawaii, you have to cross an ocean.

8. My professor, Dr. Reyes, has been to all fifty of the United States, but I have been to only two.

B. Dear Congresswoman Marks:

The debate between the two candidates for senator begins at 6:30 this Friday evening. The main issues on the agenda will be state property taxes and gun control. Two more debates will take place during the winter. The primary will be held March 16.

The debate will be held in the auditorium of the Harold Brown Memorial Library. The mayor will attend, and Representative Jay Reynolds will preside over the debate.

Here are directions to the library from the airport. First, go north on Landover Highway all the way to downtown. Turn right onto Central Street. Go straight until you get to Morrow Drive. There will be a courthouse on your left. Turn north and drive two blocks. Brown Library will be on your right on the east side of the street. Parking is behind the building.

C. After you edit your letter for overcapitalization and other errors, share your work with your instructor or another student.

GED Practice (Pages 192–193)

All items in this practice are related to capitalization.

1. **(1) change Fall to fall** Option (1) is correct because seasons of the year are not capitalized. Option (2) is incorrect because *goes* does not agree with the subject *Americans*. Option (3) incorrectly changes the verb tense. Option (4) is incorrect because a title is not capitalized unless it is followed by a name.

2. **(2) change State to state** Option (2) is correct because *state* is not a proper noun and therefore should not be capitalized. For the same reason, option (1) is incorrect; *Nation's* should not be capitalized. Option (3) is incorrect because the verb *have* does not agree with the subject *state*. Option (4) creates a comma splice. Option (5) is incorrect because a title is not capitalized unless it is followed by a name.

3. **(5) change vice president to Vice President** Option (5) is correct because a title is capitalized when it is followed by a name. Option (1) incorrectly removes a comma after an introductory phrase. Option (2) is incorrect because *White House* is a proper noun naming a specific building. Option (3) incorrectly removes a comma after an introductory clause. Option (4) capitalizes only part of the title.

4. **(4) change congress to Congress** Option (4) is correct because *Congress* is a proper noun naming a specific organization. Options (1) and (2) incorrectly change the verb tense. Option (3) incorrectly capitalizes a title that is not followed by a name. Option (5) is incorrect because *Midwest* is a proper noun naming a specific region of the country.

5. **(4) replace mother's day with Mother's Day** Option (4) is correct because holidays

are capitalized. Option (1) incorrectly changes the verb tense. Option (2) is incorrect because *Easter* is a holiday and should be capitalized. Options (3) and (5) insert unnecessary commas.

6. **(2) change foundation to Foundation** Option (2) is correct because *foundation* is part of the name of a specific organization and should be capitalized. For the same reason, option (1) incorrectly makes a proper name lowercase. Option (3) is incorrect because the verb *claim* does not agree with the singular subject *Foundation*. Option (4) incorrectly uses a pronoun with an unclear antecedent. Option (5) incorrectly changes the verb form.

7. **(5) change mid-june to mid-June** Option (5) is correct because months of the year should be capitalized. Option (1) is incorrect because *northern* is a direction and does not name a specific region of the country. Option (2) incorrectly changes the verb tense. Option (3) inserts an unnecessary comma. Option (4) incorrectly capitalizes the wrong part of the phrase *mid-June*.

8. **(1) change Summer to summer** Option (1) is correct because seasons are not capitalized. Option (2) removes a comma after an introductory clause. Option (3) creates a sentence fragment out of the introductory clause. Option (4) is incorrect because there is no reason to capitalize the adjective *pine*.

GED Mini-Test • Lesson 15 (Pages 194–195)

1. **(2) change makes to make** (Subject-verb agreement) Option (2) is correct because *make* agrees with the plural subject *men and women*. Option (1) is incorrect because the *Ashland Police Department* names a specific organization and should be capitalized. Option (3) inserts an unnecessary comma. Option (4) is incorrect because it changes a correct pronoun to one that does not match the antecedent *men and women*.

2. **(5) If you have a complaint against an officer, we encourage you to bring it to our attention.** (Topic sentences) Option (5) is the best topic sentence because it introduces the main idea of the paragraph. Options (1) and (3) are too general; they do not address the main point of the paragraph. Option (2) has too many specific details to be an effective topic sentence. Option (4) does not relate to the main idea of the paragraph.

3. **(4) change road to Road** (Capitalization) Option (4) is correct because *Ware Road* is the

name of a specific place and should be capitalized. Option (1) incorrectly uses an incomplete verb and creates a sentence fragment. Options (2) and (3) are incorrect because they capitalize words that are not proper nouns. Option (5) inserts an unnecessary comma.

4. **(5) no correction is necessary** (Capitalization) The sentence is correct as written. Option (1) uses an incorrect verb form. Option (2) incorrectly capitalizes a title that is not followed by a name. Option (3) inserts an unnecessary comma. Option (4) is incorrect because the name of a specific group should be capitalized.

5. **(2) change <u>inc.</u> to <u>Inc.</u>** (Capitalization) Option (2) correctly capitalizes an abbreviation that is part of the name of a company. Option (1) inserts an unnecessary comma. Option (3) removes a comma after an introductory phrase. Option (4) incorrectly changes the verb tense.

6. **(4) as long as it was issued by** (Subordination) Option (4) is correct because it smoothly combines the ideas by making a complex sentence. Options (1), (2), (3), and (5) do not lead to smooth, effective sentences that keep the meaning of the original sentence.

7. **(3) change <u>Native american</u> to <u>Native American</u>** (Capitalization) Option (3) is correct because the name of a specific nation or ethnic group should be capitalized as proper nouns. Option (1) is incorrect because *U.S.* is an abbreviation of the proper noun *United States*. Option (2) is incorrect because *military* is not part of a specific name. Option (4) is incorrect because it does not capitalize the entire name of the group.

8. **(3) with sentence 5** (Paragraph divisions) Option (3) correctly divides the text when the main idea shifts from kinds of I.D.s to other types of documents that are needed for employment eligibility. Options (1) and (2) divide the first paragraph unnecessarily, splitting off supporting details. Options (4) and (5) do the same with the second paragraph.

9. **(4) remove <u>we could accept</u>** (Parallel structure) Option (4) creates parallel structure with noun phrases. Option (1) incorrectly changes the verb tense. Option (2) incorrectly removes the comma needed in a parallel series. Option (3) is incorrect because *Social Security* is a proper noun. For the same reason, option (5) is incorrect.

Lesson 16
GED Skill Focus (Page 197)
A. 1. Here's a good recipe for pancakes, griddlecakes, or battercakes.

2. Sift together $1\frac{1}{2}$ cups of flour, 1 teaspoon of salt, 3 tablespoons of sugar, and $1\frac{3}{4}$ teaspoons of baking powder.

3. NC

4. Add 1 cup of milk, a few drops of vanilla, and three tablespoons of butter to the egg mixture.

5. Combine the wet and dry ingredients together well, but you can leave some lumps.

6. NC

7. Your pancakes or griddlecakes will stack up high and fluffy, and they will taste delicious too.

B. What was life <u>like for</u> families in 1900? There was no electricity in a typical home in the rural <u>Midwest, the</u> Deep South, or even Los Angeles. Artificial light was supplied by dim <u>gas or</u> kerosene lamps. The first large electrical generating plant in the United States <u>had</u> only just been built. People were still arguing that electricity would never be <u>cheap, available</u>, or safe enough to use in the average home.

Hot water was a <u>luxury, bathtubs</u> were kept in the <u>kitchen, and</u> few homes had indoor plumbing. Heat was supplied by wood or coal stoves. Central heating was just beginning to be popular among prosperous city <u>dwellers and</u> corporate magnates.

Some people consider that time the good old <u>days, but</u> I am glad to be living now. Just consider how people <u>howl and</u> scream when a storm knocks out their power for a few hours. I know because I am one of them!

C. After you edit your description for comma mistakes and other errors, share your work with your instructor or another student.

GED Skill Focus (Page 199)
A. 1. A county health expert, Hal <u>Lahiff</u>, wanted to find out if county firefighters, paramedics, and ambulance drivers were aware of good nutrition.

2. Since it affects both reaction time and <u>stamina</u>, good nutrition is critical in those jobs.

3. After he gathered data from 500 county <u>employees</u>, Mr. Lahiff made some interesting observations.

4. Most workers got enough protein, an essential nutrient, to sustain them well.

5. Almost one-third, however, needed to cut down on fats and eat more fruits and vegetables.

6. According to several paramedics, they frequently eat salads or fruits at home.

7. When they eat group meals on the job, they tend to eat too much meat or fatty foods.

B. The image of the wolf as a lone and vicious animal is a serious misconception. Contrary to popular myth, wolves are very social and nurturing. In fact, adult wolves spend many hours a day caring for and playing with their babies, or pups.

Living in packs of from two to twelve animals, adult wolves depend on each other for catching and sharing prey. The availability of prey, both small and large animals, affects the size of the pack. When prey is scarce, the pack decreases. When prey is plentiful, the pack increases.

The myth that wolves hunt for sport or out of viciousness, however, has been disproved. As part of a natural food chain, wolves hunt the old, weak, or sick from herds. That allows the stronger animals in the herd to survive and reproduce. That, in turn, helps strengthen the species.

Whereas wolves are predators, they have also been prey for one species in particular. That species is humans.

C. After you edit your paragraph for comma mistakes and other errors, share your work with your instructor or another student.

GED Practice (Pages 200–201)
All items in this practice are related to commas.

1. **(5) Friday, Saturday, and Sunday,**
Option (5) is correct because *Friday* is the first item in a series of three days. Options (1), (2), (3), and (4) do not correctly punctuate the series.

2. **(1) insert a comma after In addition**
Option (1) correctly inserts a comma after an introductory phrase. Option (2) incorrectly removes a comma in a series. Option (3) inserts an unnecessary comma at the end of the series. Option (4) incorrectly changes the verb tense.

3. **(2) insert a comma after Howard** Option (2) is correct because *Sybil Howard* is a nonessential appositive that identifies the noun *manager* and should be set off by commas before and after. Option (1) is incorrect because *manager* is not a proper noun. Option (3) inserts an unnecessary

comma. Option (4) incorrectly changes the verb tense. Option (5) uses a pronoun with a vague antecedent.

4. **(3) remove the comma after friends**
Option (3) is correct because a comma is not needed between two items. Option (1) incorrectly creates a pronoun shift. Option (2) uses an incorrect verb form. Option (4) inserts an unnecessary comma.

5. **(3) remove the comma after lasting**
Option (3) is correct because it removes an unnecessary comma at the end of a series. Option (1) incorrectly changes the verb tense. Options (2) and (4) insert unnecessary commas.

6. **(3) insert a comma after pills** Option (3) is correct because it inserts a comma after the introductory clause. Option (1) incorrectly changes the verb tense. Option (2) inserts an unnecessary comma. Option (4) incorrectly capitalizes a noun that is not proper.

7. **(4) calcium, and** Option (4) is correct because it inserts a comma before the coordinating conjunction that connects two independent clauses in a compound sentence. Options (1), (2), (3), and (5) do not use the correct combination of commas and conjunctions.

8. **(2) insert a comma after milk** Option (2) is correct because it inserts a comma after the introductory phrase. Option (1) is incorrect because it inserts the comma too early in the sentence; *digesting milk* is part of the introductory phrase. Option (3) is incorrect because it incorrectly changes the verb. Option (4) is incorrect because *is* does not agree with the plural subject *alternatives*.

9. **(3) remove the comma after calcium**
Option (3) is correct because it removes an unnecessary comma separating the subject from the verb. Option (1) replaces *that* with a pronoun. Option (2) incorrectly changes the verb tense. Option (4) removes a comma needed in a series. Option (5) inserts an unnecessary comma because the pair *bread and cereals* is the last item in the series.

GED Mini-Test • Lesson 16 (Pages 202–203)
1. **(3) water, a precious natural resource,**
(Commas) Option (3) is correct because it places commas before and after the nonessential appositive. Options (1), (2), (4), and (5) do not.

2. **(4) remove the comma after loads**
(Commas) Option (4) is correct because it

removes an unnecessary comma. Option (1) is incorrect because introductory phrases should be followed by a comma. Option (2) incorrectly changes the verb tense. Option (3) inserts an unnecessary comma between two items.

3. **(3) fill and plug (Misplaced modifiers)**
Option (3) is correct because it uses the understood *you* as the subject of the sentence, together with the compound predicate *fill and plug*. Options (1), (4), and (5) provide subjects that leave the modifier *Instead of leaving the tap water running while you shave* dangling. Option (2) creates a pronoun shift.

4. **(5) replace them with it** (Pronouns)
Option (5) is correct because it uses the correct pronoun *it* for the antecedent *garden*. Option (1) incorrectly removes the comma after the introductory element. Option (2) uses the incorrect verb tense. Option (3) incorrectly removes the comma after the introductory clause. Option (4) inserts an unnecessary comma.

5. **(5) insert a comma after vinyl** (Commas)
Option (5) is correct because it inserts the comma needed in a series of three or more. Option (1) incorrectly removes a comma after the introductory phrase. Option (2) incorrectly changes the verb tense. Option (3) incorrectly removes a comma needed in the series. Option (4) incorrectly inserts an unnecessary comma because the second item in the series is *two yards of waterproof vinyl*.

6. **(5) vinyl, smoothing** (Run-on sentences/ Subordination) Option (5) corrects the run-on sentence by subordinating the idea in the second clause. Option (1) is a run-on sentence. Option (2) creates a comma splice. Option (3) does not lead to a smooth, effective sentence. Option (4) incorrectly uses a comma after *smooth*.

7. **(3) remove you need to** (Parallel structure) Option (3) correctly creates parallel structure by making a series of short verb phrases. Option (1) incorrectly removes the comma after the first item in the series. Option (2) inserts an unnecessary coordinating conjunction between the first and the second item in the series. Option (4) inserts an unnecessary comma.

8. **(1) replace it with the cement** (Pronouns)
Option (1) corrects an unclear antecedent. Option (2) is incorrect because it removes the comma after the introductory clause. Option (3) incorrectly changes the verb tense. Option (4) inserts an unnecessary comma.

9. **(2) For an extra firm cushion, staple** (Subordination) Option (2) subordinates the information in the first sentence and reduces the wordiness to produce a smooth, more effective sentence. Options (1), (3), (4), and (5) do not lead to smooth, effective sentences that accurately restate the meaning of the original sentences.

GED Writing Link (Pages 204–207)
Share your work for the Personal Link and GED Link exercises with your instructor or another student.

Lesson 17
GED Skill Focus (Page 209)
A. 1. District's

2. youngsters'

3. C

4. hers

5. Topics

6. Firewomen's

7. C

8. Classes

9. parent's

B.   A participant's conduct in this chat room should be guided by common sense, basic etiquette, and the following chat rules:

  Please be aware that this chat room is for adults. It is not intended for individuals under the age of 18. It is the chat room administrator's job to list members' topic suggestions. We encourage you to be responsible and respectful of our community's participants. Please don't use this chat room to sell your products or services. We also ask that you respect everyone else's property rights and privacy. Please don't ask for other members' passwords. Please don't post personal information, such as your name, address, or phone number, or ask another member for his or hers.

C. After you edit your paragraph for misspelled possessives and other errors, share your work with your instructor or another student.

GED Skill Focus (Page 211)
A. 1. I'd

2. It's

3. isn't

4. She's

5. They're

6. wouldn't

B. Dear Customer:

It's my pleasure to welcome you to Ocean Park Bank. I'm writing to thank you for opening a new savings account with us.

Please read the enclosed pamphlet, "Ocean Park's Banking Guide," for a detailed description of all our services. On September 15, your direct deposit option will begin. You won't have to do a thing. Your ATM card is enclosed. As soon as you activate your personal password, you'll have access to 57 regional branches and more than 475 ATMs.

Thank you for giving us the opportunity to prove that Ocean Park is a smart choice for you. Your business is important to us, and we're working hard to exceed your expectations.

Very truly yours,
Clifford Rice
Vice President for Customer Relations

C. After you edit your letter for misspelled contractions and other errors, share your work with your instructor or another student.

GED Skill Focus (Page 213)

A. 1. Whose

2. It's

3. No

4. Their, Here, know

5. new, great

6. Your

7. accept

B. The weather here has been awful! We're all so bored that we're desperate to visit you. Can we come next week? The brakes on the car will be fixed by then. Ray and his new girlfriend want to come, too. Is that all right? Of course, if seven is too many, they'll just stay here.

One other thing. Can you send directions? Your uncle forgot the way. Please accept our thanks for your open invitation. We're looking forward to a nice long visit.

C. After you edit your letter for misspelled homonyms and other errors, share your work with your instructor or another student.

GED Practice (Pages 214–215)

All items in this practice are related to spelling.

1. (5) no correction is necessary The sentence is correct as written. Option (1) inserts an unnecessary comma. Option (2) incorrectly removes a comma after an introductory phrase.

Options (3) and (4) replace correctly spelled words with their homonyms.

2. (5) change customer's to customers' Option (5) corrects the misspelled plural possessive. Options (1) and (3) replace correctly spelled words with their homonyms. Option (2) is incorrect because *is* does not agree with the plural subject *tips*. Option (4) inserts an unnecessary comma.

3. (1) change Its to It's Option (1) is correct because the contraction of *It is* is needed in the sentence. Option (2) incorrectly replaces a plural with a plural possessive. Option (3) creates a comma splice. Option (4) inserts an unnecessary comma. Option (5) misspells a contraction.

4. (1) change Than to Then Option (1) is correct because the word meaning "at that time" is needed in the sentence. Option (2) replaces a correctly spelled word with its homonym. Option (3) replaces a correctly spelled singular possessive with a plural. Option (4) removes a necessary comma in a series. Option (5) inserts an unnecessary comma at the end of the series.

5. (4) change weakly to weekly Option (4) is correct because the homonym meaning "once every seven days" is needed in the sentence. Option (1) incorrectly creates a pronoun shift. Option (2) incorrectly removes a comma after an introductory clause. Option (3) incorrectly changes the verb tense. Option (5) replaces a correctly spelled word with its homonym.

6. (1) change magazines' to magazine's Option (1) is correct because the possessive is singular, not plural. Option (2) is incorrect because *provides* agrees with the singular subject *coverage*. Option (3) incorrectly creates a pronoun shift. Option (4) replaces a correctly spelled word with its homonym.

7. (3) change well to we'll Option (3) is correct because the contraction of *we will* needs an apostrophe. Option (1) incorrectly replaces the possessive pronoun *your* with the contraction of *you are*. Option (2) incorrectly removes a comma after the introductory phrase. Option (4) is incorrect because *special reports* is not a proper noun.

8. (5) no correction is necessary The sentence is correct as written. Option (1) replaces a correctly spelled word with its homonym. Option (2) inserts an unnecessary comma. Option (3) is incorrect because a title followed by a name should be capitalized. Option (4) incorrectly replaces a possessive with a plural.

GED Mini-Test • Lesson 17 (Pages 216–217)

1. **(1) change Its to It's** (Spelling) Option (1) is correct because the contraction of *It is* is needed in the sentence, not the possessive pronoun. Option (2) replaces a correctly spelled word with its homonym. Option (3) incorrectly removes a comma between independent clauses in a compound sentence. Option (4) creates a comma splice.

2. **(1) change Their to They're** (Spelling) Option (1) is correct because the contraction *They are* is needed in the sentence, not a possessive pronoun. Option (2) incorrectly uses a homonym for *They're*. Option (3) incorrectly removes the comma from a series. Option (4) inserts an unnecessary comma.

3. **(5) change Doctors to doctors** (Capitalization) Option (5) is correct because a title is not capitalized unless it is followed by a name. Option (1) uses an incorrect verb form. Option (2) incorrectly capitalizes a common noun. Option (3) incorrectly removes a comma before a parenthetical comment. Option (4) is incorrect because the verb *say* agrees with the plural subject *doctors*.

4. **(1) bring them for flu shots before** (Subordination) Option (1) is correct because it leads to a smooth, effective sentence by removing wordiness. Options (2), (3), (4), and (5) do not lead to smooth, effective restatements.

5. **(5) change there to their** (Spelling) Option (5) is correct because the possessive pronoun is needed in the sentence, not the homonym meaning "in that place." Option (1) incorrectly changes the position of the apostrophe in the contraction for *What is*. Option (2) incorrectly capitalizes a noun that is not proper. Option (3) incorrectly changes the position of the apostrophe in the contraction for *do not*. Option (4) inserts an unnecesary comma.

6. **(3) change peoples to people's** (Spelling) Option (3) is correct because the possessive of a plural that does not end in -s requires 's. Option (1) replaces a correctly spelled word with its homonym. Option (2) incorrectly removes a comma after an introductory phrase. Option (4) inserts an unnecessary comma. Option (5) replaces a correctly spelled word with a word that it is commonly confused with.

7. **(1) When you lose a credit card, you learn the importance of** (Subordination) Option (1) is correct because it provides a logical way to combine the ideas of the two sentences into a smooth, effective complex sentence. Options (2), (3), (4), and (5) do not lead to smooth, effective restatements.

8. **(4) with sentence 7** (Paragraph divisions) Option (4) correctly begins a new paragraph when the main idea shifts to using a credit card inappropriately. Options (1), (2), and (3) split supporting details away from paragraph B. Option (5) does the same in what should be paragraph C.

9. **(4) are added** (Verb forms) Option (4) correctly supplies the past participle form of *add*. Option (2) is an incorrect verb tense. Options (1), (3), and (5) are incorrect verb forms.

GED Writing Link (Pages 218–221)

Share your work for the Personal Link and GED Link exercises with your instructor or another student.

Unit 4 Cumulative Review (Pages 222–226)

1. **(1) change Jonathans to Jonathan's** (Possessives) Option (1) is correct because the possessive for the singular noun *Jonathan* is made by adding 's. Option (2) is incorrect because it would separate the subject from the verb with an unnecessary comma. Option (3) is incorrect because school subjects are not capitalized. Option (4) replaces a correctly spelled word with its homonym.

2. **(5) change Department to department** (Capitalization) Option (5) is correct because *department* is not a proper noun and should not be capitalized. Option (1) replaces a correctly spelled word with its homonym. Option (2) uses an incomplete verb form. Option (3) incorrectly changes the singular possessive. Option (4) inserts an unnecessary comma.

3. **(5) change Fall to fall** (Capitalization) Option (5) is correct because seasons are not capitalized. Option (1) is incorrect because it removes the comma after the introductory element. Option (2) incorrectly changes the verb tense. Option (3) is incorrect because the name of a specific course should be capitalized. Option (4) inserts an unnecessary comma.

4. **(2) teacher, Mr. Porter, at** (Commas) Option (2) most effectively combines the sentences by including all the information in the nonessential appositive set off by commas.

UNIT 4

Options (1), (3), (4), and (5) do not lead to smooth, effective combinations of the original sentences.

5. **(4) dried, these** (Commas) Option (4) is correct because it inserts a comma after the introductory element. Option (1) does not. Options (2) and (3) use inappropriate connecting words. Option (5) creates a sentence fragment.

6. **(2) remove the comma after care** (Commas) Option (2) correctly removes an unnecessary comma. Option (1) creates a comma splice. Option (3) replaces a correctly spelled word with its homonym. Option (4) incorrectly removes a comma after an introductory phrase.

7. **(5) change knifes to knife's** (Possessives) Option (5) correctly includes an apostrophe in the singular possessive. Option (1) misspells the verb as if it were a possessive. Option (2) replaces a correctly spelled word with its homonym. Option (3) incorrectly removes the comma after the introductory clause. Option (4) inserts an unnecessary comma.

8. **(3) soap, water, and** (Commas) Option (3) correctly separates the items in the series with commas. Options (1), (2), (4), and (5) do not.

9. **(5) change its to it's** (Contractions) Option (5) is correct because the contraction *it is* is needed in the sentence. Option (1) uses an incorrect verb form. Option (2) incorrectly removes a comma needed before a coordinating conjunction in a compound sentence. Option (3) creates a comma splice. Option (4) creates a sentence fragment.

10. **(2) change National Association to national association** (Capitalization) Option (2) is correct because *national association* is not a proper noun and should not be capitalized. Option (1) replaces a correctly spelled word with its homonym. Option (3) inserts an unnecessary comma. Option (4) uses an incorrect verb form.

11. **(4) change european to European** (Capitalization) Option (4) is correct because *European* is a proper adjective and should be capitalized. Option (1) removes a comma that is needed before a parenthetical expression. Options (2) and (3) are incorrect because the homonym needed in this sentence is the possessive *their*. Option (5) removes a comma needed after a parenthetical expression.

12. **(4) or, at least, getting** (Commas) Option (4) leads to the most effective combination of the sentences by including a short parenthetical

phrase set off by commas. Options (1), (2), (3), and (5) do not lead to smooth, effective sentences.

13. **(1) change It's to Its** (Possessives) Option (1) is correct because a possessive, not the contraction for *it is*, is needed in the sentence. Option (2) misspells a contraction. Option (3) replaces a correctly spelled word with a word that it is commonly confused with. Option (4) inserts an unnecessary comma.

14. **(4) insert a comma after small** (Commas) Option (4) is correct because it inserts a comma after the long introductory clause. Option (1) creates a pronoun shift. Option (2) is incorrect because *is* does not agree with the plural subject *all tuna*. Options (3) and (5) insert unnecessary commas.

15. **(1) replace way with weigh** (Homonyms) Option (1) corrects the homonym error because the meaning of the sentence relates to measurement, not a method. Option (2) incorrectly removes the comma between independent clauses in a compound sentence. Option (3) is incorrect because a possessive, not the contraction for *it is*, is needed in the sentence. Option (4) incorrectly shifts the verb tense.

Writing Links Review
Ask your instructor or another student to review your essay. Ask them to give you feedback on the following:
- Organization of an introductory paragraph, middle paragraphs with details and examples, and a concluding paragraph
- Staying on topic

Revise your essay as needed.

POSTTEST (Pages 227–242)
1. **(3) young, the** (Sentence structure/Fragments) Option (3) is correct because it joins a dependent-clause fragment (sentence 2) to an independent clause with the correct punctuation, a comma. Option (1) contains a sentence fragment. Option (2) omits the necessary comma after the introductory clause. Options (4) and (5) use inappropriate connecting words and omit the necessary punctuation.

2. **(3) are** (Usage/Subject-verb agreement) Option (3) is correct because the plural verb *are* agrees with the plural subject *kinds*. Option (1) is incorrect because it is singular. Option (2) is incorrect because it is singular and past tense. Option (4) is the wrong tense. Option (5) is an incomplete verb form.

3. **(1) change it's to its** (Mechanics /Spelling possessives) Option (1) is correct because a possessive, not the contraction for *it is,* is needed in the sentence. Option (2) inserts an unnecessary comma. Option (3) incorrectly shifts the tense of the verb. Option (4) misspells the homonym *no,* meaning negative. Option (5) leaves the uncorrected contraction.

4. **(4) so term insurance eventually becomes** (Sentence structure/Compound sentences) Option (4) corrects the awkward sentence structure by creating a compound sentence. Options (1), (2), (3), and (5) create additional wordiness.

5. **(5) The next kind is whole life, the most expensive insurance.** (Organization/Topic sentences) Option (5) is the best topic sentence because it introduces the main idea of the paragraph. Options (1) and (2) are too general to be topic sentences. Options (3) and (4) are too specific; they give details.

6. **(3) replace one with you** (Usage/Pronouns) Option (3) corrects the shift in pronoun from *you* to *one; you* is used in the rest of the passage. Option (1) changes the meaning of the sentence. Option (2) removes the necessary comma after the introductory dependent clause. Option (4) inserts an unnecessary comma. Option (5) uses an incorrect pronoun.

7. **(4) premium, you** (Mechanics/Commas after introductory elements) Option (4) is correct because it inserts the comma needed after an introductory dependent clause. The comma is missing in option (1). Option (2) makes the dependent clause a sentence fragment. Options (3) and (5) use inappropriate connecting words and omit necessary punctuation.

8. **(2) think** (Usage/Verb forms) Option (2) is correct because the simple present tense is needed in the sentence. Option (1) is an incorrect verb form of a perfect tense. Option (3) is an incorrect verb form. Option (4) uses the incorrect form of the present tense. Option (5) is the correct tense but does not agree with the subject *you.*

9. **(2) workers who have jobs** (Sentence structure/ Subordination) Option (2) effectively combines the sentences, placing the new details from the second sentence in a clause and eliminating the repetition and wordiness. Options (1), (3), (4), and (5) do not lead to smooth, effective sentences.

10. **(5) change youve to you've** (Mechanics/ Spelling contractions) Option (5) is correct because an apostrophe is needed to take the place of the missing letters in the contraction for *you have.* Option (1) removes a helpful, necessary comma after an introductory element. Option (2) incorrectly changes a plural to a possessive. Option (3) creates a run-on sentence. Option (4) inserts an unnecessary comma.

11. **(5) no correction is necessary** (Mechanics/ Commas) The sentence is correct as written. Option (1) inserts an unnecessary comma. Option (2) is incorrect because *company* is capitalized only when it is part of a name. Option (3) incorrectly removes the comma needed after the introductory dependent clause. Option (4) makes the dependent clause a sentence fragment.

12. **(4) with sentence 9** (Organization/Paragraph divisions) Option (4) is correct because sentence 9 shifts to a new main idea and so should begin a new paragraph. Options (1), (2), and (3) involve sentences that are details about the main idea of paragraph B. Option (5) is a detail that relates to the idea in sentence 9, so it should follow it in the new paragraph.

13. **(4) your interest in** (Sentence structure/ Parallelism) Option (4) is correct because it puts all the items in the series in the same form— *your + noun.* Options (1), (2), (3), and (5) do not correct the error in parallel structure.

14. **(3) change fitness centers' to Fitness Centers'** (Mechanics/Capitalization) Option (3) is correct because all elements of the name of a specific organization should be capitalized and by reading the entire piece you see that there are 36 fitness centers. Option (1) incorrectly replaces a singular possessive with a plural. Option (2) is incorrect because it changes part of a name to lowercase. Option (4) incorrectly replaces a plural possessive with a singular possessive.

15. **(5) desks, complete filing, order sportswear and equipment, and fill** (Mechanics/Commas in series) Option (5) is correct because a comma is needed to separate the items in a series of three or more. Options (1), (2), (3), and (4) do not correctly separate the items with commas.

16. **(1) replace their with its** (Usage/Pronouns) Option (1) is correct because the antecedent is the collective noun *committee,* so the pronoun should be the singular *its.* Option (2) incorrectly

removes a comma after an introductory element. Option (3) is incorrect because *committee* is a common noun and should not be capitalized. Option (4) incorrectly inserts a comma between the two verbs of a compound predicate. Option (5) does not correct the error in pronoun usage.

17. **(1) over one half of the temporary hires create** (Sentence structure/Modifiers) Option (1) has the correct subject (*one half of temporary hires*) next to the modifier (*Because they have . . .*). Options (2), (3), (4), and (5) do not lead to sentences in which it is clear what the modifier is modifying.

18. **(5) solve problems, and unresolved** (Sentence structure/Compound sentences) Option (5) eliminates repetition and wordiness by combining information in the two sentences into one compound sentence. Options (1), (2), and (4) do not lead to smooth, effective sentences that restate the meaning of the two sentences. Option (3) would create a run-on.

19. **(3) move sentence 11 to the beginning of paragraph C** (Organization/Unity and coherence) Option (3) correctly moves the topic sentence to the beginning of the paragraph it introduces. Option (1) moves the topic sentence to the beginning of the wrong paragraph. Option (2) moves it to an illogical place in the same paragraph. Option (4) moves the topic sentence to the end of the paragraph it should introduce. Option (5) removes the topic sentence altogether.

20. **(5) replace I with me** (Usage/Pronouns) Option (5) is correct because it provides the correct objective pronoun *me* as an object of the verb *contact*. Option (1) leads to a disagreement between subject and verb. Option (2) misspells the homonym *to*. Option (3) removes the comma needed after the introductory clause. Option (4) inserts an unnecessary connecting word.

21. **(3) change drove to driven** (Usage/Verb forms) Option (3) correctly inserts the participle form of the verb *drive* needed with the helping verb *have*. Option (1) uses an incomplete verb form. Options (2) and (4) insert unnecessary commas. Option (5) uses an incorrect verb form.

22. **(2) combine paragraphs A and B** (Organization/ Paragraph structure) Option (2) correctly combines two paragraphs that contain details on one main idea. Option (1) moves only one of the details to the first paragraph and leaves a one-sentence paragraph. Options (3)

and (5) remove important supporting details. Option (4) incorrectly moves a topic sentence from the paragraph it introduces.

23. **(5) jack, and anyone** (Sentence structure/ Run-ons) Option (5) fixes the run-on by separating the independent clauses with a comma and an appropriate coordinating conjunction. Option (1) is a run-on. Option (2) is a comma splice. Option (3) leads to an awkward, wordy, and incorrectly punctuated sentence. Option (4) uses an inappropriate connecting word and is incorrectly punctuated.

24. **(2) get** (Usage/Verb tenses) Option (2) is correct because the simple future tense (*will not get* or *won't get*) is required in the last clause of the sentence, where an action is being described that has not yet happened. Options (1), (3), (4), and (5) use incorrect tenses.

25. **(1) change fit to fits** (Usage/Subject-verb agreement) Option (1) is correct because the singular verb *fits* matches the singular subject *spare*. Option (2) inserts an unnecessary comma into the introductory clause. Option (3) removes the comma needed after the introductory clause. Option (4) replaces the correctly spelled preposition *to* with its homonym, the number *two*.

26. **(4) remove the comma after finally** (Mechanics/ Commas) Option (4) is correct because it eliminates an unnecessary comma. Option (1) inserts an unnecessary comma. Option (2) removes the comma needed between two independent clauses in a compound sentence. Option (3) leads to a comma splice. Option (5) is incorrect because the sentence requires the possessive *your*, not its homonym, the contraction for *you are*.

27. **(5) change West to west** (Mechanics/ Capitalization) Option (5) is correct because directions should not be capitalized. Option (1) removes a necessary comma after an introductory element. Option (2) is incorrect because the name of a specific organization such as Pony Express should be capitalized. Option (3) uses an incomplete verb form. Option (4) inserts an unnecessary comma.

28. **(3) the speedy airplanes** (Sentence structure/ Parallelism) Option (3) is correct because it gives all the items in the series the same structure— adjective + noun—*swift trains, efficient trucks, speedy airplanes*. Options (1), (2), (4), and (5) do not correct the error in parallel structure.

29. **(2) remove sentence 2** (Organization/Unity and coherence) Option (2) correctly eliminates a sentence that does not support the main idea. Option (1) incorrectly moves the topic sentence from the beginning of the paragraph. Option (3) removes an important supporting detail. Option (4) moves a detail out of logical order. Option (5) retains a sentence that does not support the main idea.

30. **(2) change rose to risen** (Usage/Verb forms) Option (2) uses the correct past participle form of the verb *rise*. Option (1) incorrectly uses a plural helping verb for the singular subject *cost*. Option (3) inserts an unnecessary comma. Option (4) is incorrect because *colonial* is not a proper adjective and should therefore not be capitalized. Option (5) uses an incorrect verb form.

31. **(5) postage, yet it costs** (Sentence structure/ Fragments) Option (5) corrects the fragment by giving it a subject and joining it to an independent clause to make a compound sentence. Options (1), (2), (3), and (4) do not show the relationship between the ideas in the sentence and fragment, nor do they fix the fragment with correct punctuation.

32. **(5) does** (Usage/Subject-verb agreement) Option (5) is correct because the third person singular verb *does* agrees with the third person singular subject *U.S. Postal Service*. Option (1) is not a third person verb form. Option (2) is a plural verb form. Option (3) is a plural verb form and shifts the tense. Option (4) also incorrectly shifts the tense.

33. **(1) you, our valued customers,** (Mechanics/ Commas around appositives) Option (1) is correct because commas are required before and after the nonessential appositive *our valued customers*. Options (2), (3), and (4) omit one or both of the necessary commas. Option (5) creates two sentence fragments.

34. **(5) change were to was** (Usage/Subject-verb agreement) Option (5) is correct because the singular verb *was* agrees with the singular subject *service*. Option (1) removes a comma needed after an introductory element. Option (2) replaces the correctly spelled adjective *high* with its homonym, *hi*. Option (3) is incorrect because a common noun such as *holiday* is not capitalized. Option (4) inserts an unnecessary comma between the subject and verb.

35. **(5) are** (Usage/Verb tenses) Option (5) correctly uses the present tense, which is indicated by the phrase *At this time*. Options (1), (2), (3), and (4) are incorrect verb tenses for the sentence.

36. **(4) features requested by our customers to make** (Sentence structure/ Run-ons) Option (4) correctly links the related thoughts in all the clauses of the run-on by subordinating some ideas and reducing repetition and wordiness. Options (1), (2), (3), and (5) do not lead to smooth, effective sentences that accurately restate the meaning of the original text.

37. **(4) with sentence 12** (Organization/Paragraph divisions) Option (4) correctly begins a new paragraph when the main idea shifts. Options (1), (2), and (3) involve sentences that are details related to the main idea of paragraph C. Option (5) creates a new paragraph with a detail that should be in the fourth paragraph.

38. **(1) insert is after goal** (Sentence structure/ Fragments) Option (1) corrects the fragment by inserting the missing verb. Option (2) supplies an incomplete verb form. Option (3) does not supply a main verb for the sentence. Option (4) inserts an unnecessary comma.

39. **(2) quarters, and** (Mechanics/Commas in compound sentences) Option (2) correctly puts a comma before the coordinating conjunction *and* that joins the independent clauses in this compound sentence. Option (1) lacks the comma before *and*. Option (3) incorrectly puts the comma after *and*. Option (4) creates a sentence fragment. Option (5) incorrectly places commas both before and after *and*.

40. **(1) change is to are** (Usage/Subject-verb agreement) Option (1) is correct because the plural verb *are* agrees with the plural subject *tips*. Option (2) inserts an unnecessary comma. Option (3) uses an incorrect verb form. Option (4) incorrectly changes a singular possessive to a plural possessive. Option (5) incorrectly changes the singular possessive to a plural.

41. **(3) If this label is missing,** (Sentence structure/ Modifiers) Option (3) correctly changes the dangling modifier at the beginning of the sentence into an introductory dependent clause. Options (1), (2), (4), and (5) do not lead to smooth, effective sentences that fix the problem of the dangling modifier and restate the meaning of the original sentence.

42. **(2) replace You with If that's the case, you**
(Organization/Transitions) Option (2) is correct because it supplies a transition that relates the meaning between sentences 7 and 8. Option (1) moves a supporting detail to an illogical place. Option (3) supplies an inappropriate transition. Option (4) moves a detail out of the paragraph in which it belongs. Option (5) removes an important detail.

43. **(2) remove the comma after frame**
(Mechanics/ Commas) Option (2) correctly removes the unnecessary comma separating the subject and verb. Option (1) inserts an unnecessary comma between two items. Option (3) incorrectly supplies a second subject, the pronoun *it,* which unnecessarily repeats the meaning of *space.* Option (4) replaces the correctly spelled *than* with its homonym.

44. **(1) replace it with the guardrail** (Usage/ Pronouns) Option (1) correctly replaces an unclear pronoun with its antecedent. Options (2) and (3) incorrectly remove necessary commas around the parenthetical term *moreover.* Option (4) uses an incorrect verb form. Option (5) replaces a noun with a pronoun, making the meaning of the sentence less clear.

45. **(5) change your's to yours**
(Mechanics/Spelling possessives) Option (5) corrects the sentence by removing the unnecessary apostrophe from the possessive pronoun. Option (1) is incorrect because the plural verb *are* agrees with the plural subject *programs.* Option (2) incorrectly changes a plural to a singular possessive. Option (3) inserts an unnecessary comma. Option (4) incorrectly changes a plural to a singular possessive.

46. **(2) change who's to whose** (Mechanics/ Spelling possessives) Option (2) is correct because the possessive pronoun is needed in the sentence, not the contraction of *who is.* Option (1) inserts an unnecessary comma. Option (3) is incorrect because the plural verb *are* agrees with the compound subject of the clause, *income* and *history.* Option (4) is incorrect because the plural verb *have* agrees with the subject of the clause *who,* which refers to *buyers.* Option (5) replaces the correctly spelled preposition *for* with its homonym, *four.*

47. **(1) payments, or they** (Sentence structure/ Compound sentences) Option (1) is correct because the original sentence is a compound sentence in which the clauses are correctly joined with a conjunction and comma. Option (2)

omits the necessary comma. Option (3) creates a run-on. By omitting *or,* option (4) does not show the reader the relationship between the two ideas. By omitting the second subject but keeping the comma, option (5) is incorrectly using a comma to separate the two verbs in a compound predicate (*offer* and *allow*).

48. **(2) limits. Buyers** (Sentence structure/Comma splices) Option (2) corrects the comma splice by making the second independent clause its own sentence. Option (1) is a comma splice. Option (3) is a run-on. Option (4) uses an inappropriate connecting word and is incorrectly punctuated. Option (5) omits the comma needed between independent clauses in a compound sentence.

49. **(4) has** (Usage/Verb tenses) Option (4) is correct because the simple present tense is required in the sentence—*the Veterans Administration has.* Options (1), (2), (3), and (5) use other present tenses or the past or future tense.

50. **(2) buy, including** (Sentence structure/ Subordination) Option (2) combines the sentences smoothly by making the detail in the second sentence subordinate to the first. Option (1) is the original, somewhat awkward wording. Option (3) leads to an incorrectly worded sentence. Options (4) and (5) are wordy and awkwardly constructed.

SIMULATED TEST (Pages 245–262)

1. **(5) change academy to Academy**
(Mechanics/ Capitalization) Option (5) is correct because all elements in the name of a specific organization are capitalized. For the same reason, option (4) is incorrect. Option (1) is incorrect because a common noun like *nominee* is not capitalized. Option (2) incorrectly removes the comma needed before a nonessential appositive. Option (3) incorrectly inserts an unnecessary comma between two items.

2. **(2) awards, yet it** (Sentence structure/ Fragments) Option (2) corrects the fragment by inserting a subject and making a compound sentence with an appropriate conjunction and comma. Option (1) is the original fragment. Option (3) creates a comma splice. Options (4) and (5) do not lead to a smooth, effectively structured sentence.

3. **(1) Oscars are awarded in many film categories.** (Organization /Topic sentences) Option (1) is the best choice of topic sentence because it is a general statement of the main idea

of the paragraph. Options (2), (3), and (4) do not relate to the main idea. Option (5) is too specific to be a topic sentence.

4. **(4) remove for the** (Sentence structure/Parallelism) Option (4) is correct because it removes the two words that make the last item in the series not parallel with the other phrases. Option (1) incorrectly inserts a subject pronoun when the sentence already has a subject (*Some*). Option (2) is incorrect because the plural verb *are* agrees with the plural subject *Some*. Option (3) removes a comma needed to separate items in the series. Option (5), the original, is not parallel in the series.

5. **(3) industry based** (Mechanics /Commas) Option (3) is correct because it eliminates an unnecessary comma. There is no reason for the comma in the original, option (1). Option (2) creates a sentence fragment. Options (4) and (5) use incorrect verb forms.

6. **(5) change they to the awards** (Usage/Pronouns) Option (5) corrects the vague antecedent of the pronoun *they* by replacing it with a noun. Option (1) is incorrect because the plural verb *are* agrees with the plural subject *Oscars*. Option (2) inserts an unnecessary comma. Option (3) incorrectly changes plural nouns to possessive singular nouns. Option (4) creates a run-on sentence.

7. **(2) remove the comma after Oscars** (Mechanics/ Commas) Option (2) is correct because it eliminates an unnecessary comma. Option (1) is incorrect because a comma is needed after the introductory element. Option (3) is incorrect because the singular verb *is* agrees with the singular subject *film*. Option (4) incorrectly replaces the singular pronoun *its*, which refers to *film*, with a plural pronoun. Option (5) is incorrect because the possessive pronoun is needed in the sentence, not the contraction for *it is*.

8. **(4) change you're to your** (Mechanics/ Spelling possessives and homonyms) Option (4) is correct because the possessive pronoun *your*, not the contraction for *you are* as in the original, is needed in the sentence. Options (1) and (2) incorrectly shift the verb tenses in the two clauses of the sentence. Option (3) inserts an unnecessary comma.

9. **(5) are committed** (Usage/Subject-verb agreement) Option (5) is correct because the plural verb *are* agrees with the plural subject *we*.

Options (1), (2), (3), and (4) are all singular verbs. Options (2), (3), and (4) also incorrectly shift the tense of the verb.

10. **(2) When you need a cracked or broken windshield replaced,** (Sentence structure/Modifiers) Option (2) correctly inserts a subordinating conjunction and a subject and verb into the dangling modifier, changing the phrase into a subordinating clause. Options (1), (3), (4), and (5) do not correct the error.

11. **(4) client. It** (Sentence structure/Run-ons) Option (4) correctly divides the two independent clauses into two complete sentences. Option (1) is a run-on. Option (2) uses an inappropriate connecting word and is missing the necessary comma. Option (3) uses an inappropriate connecting word. Option (5) creates a comma splice.

12. **(2) move it to follow sentence 8** (Organization/Unity and coherence) Option (2) correctly moves a supporting detail to its logical place in the paragraph. Options (1), (3), and (5) do not. Option (4) incorrectly removes the important piece of information.

13. **(5) no correction is necessary** (Usage/Subject-verb agreement) Option (1) incorrectly shifts the verb tense to the future. Option (2) is incorrect because the singular subject *looks* agrees with the singular subject *Everyone*. Option (3) supplies an incorrect verb form. Option (4) inserts an unnecessary comma.

14. **(2) will have** (Usage/Verb tenses) Option (2) is correct because the time phrase *the next morning* is a clue that the future tense is needed. Options (1), (3), (4), and (5) are incorrect verb tenses for the sentence.

15. **(1) is by following these steps to get a** (Sentence structure/Modifiers) Option (1) correctly places the modifier *from a friend's car* next to the noun it describes, *jump-start*. Options (2), (3), (4), and (5) move the modifier to unclear positions and change the meaning of the sentence.

16. **(4) replace breaks with brakes** (Mechanics/ Spelling homonyms) Option (4) corrects the homonym error because *brakes*, not *breaks* as in option (5), are stopping mechanisms in cars. Option (1) uses an incorrect verb form. Option (2) inserts an unnecessary comma. Option (3) removes the comma between the two independent clauses, both with *you* as the understood subject.

Answers and Explanations

17. **(4) change batteries to battery's** (Mechanics/ Spelling possessives) Option (4) correctly changes a plural noun to a singular possessive. Option (1) creates a sentence fragment. Option (2) uses a pronoun without a clear antecedent. Option (3) inserts an unnecessary comma.

18. **(5) with sentence 13** (Organization/Paragraph divisions) Option (5) correctly begins a new paragraph when the main idea shifts to disconnecting the cables. Options (1), (2), (3), and (4) are details that relate to the main idea of paragraph C.

19. **(2) have taken** (Usage/Verb forms) Option (2) uses the correct participle verb form to use with *have*. Option (1) is an incorrect verb form. Option (3) is an incomplete verb form because the helping verb *have* is needed. Options (4) and (5) incorrectly shift the verb tense.

20. **(3) battery. Now** (Sentence structure/Comma splices) Option (3) corrects the comma splice by making the two independent clauses into two complete sentences. Option (1) is the original comma splice. Option (2) creates a sentence fragment. Option (4) creates a run-on sentence. Option (5) uses an inappropriate connecting word.

21. **(4) replace affects with effects** (Mechanics/ Spelling) Option (4) is correct because the noun *effects,* meaning *results,* not *affects* meaning *to influence* as in the original, option (5), is needed in the sentence. Option (1) incorrectly capitalizes the common noun *medical profession.* Option (2) is incorrect because the singular verb *continues* agrees with the singular subject *profession.* Option (3) is incorrect because it is plural and shifts the verb tense.

22. **(2) replace Cholesterol with In turn, cholesterol** (Organization/Transitions) Option (2) inserts a transition to make the relationship between the ideas in sentences 2 and 3 clearer. Option (1) moves a detail to the position of the topic sentence in the paragraph. Options (3) and (5) move the detail to illogical positions within the paragraph. Option (4) incorrectly removes the important supporting detail.

23. **(2) percent by eating** (Sentence structure/ Fragments) Option (2) is correct because it joins the fragment to a complete thought and correctly shows the relationship of ideas. Option (1) is the original sentence fragment.

Option (3) uses an inappropriate coordinating conjunction. Option (4) is incorrectly punctuated and, along with option (5), uses an inappropriate connecting word.

24. **(3) is encouraged** (Usage/Subject-verb agreement) Option (3) is correct because *is* agrees with the singular, collective subject *public.* Option (1) is incorrect because it is plural. Option (2) is an incomplete verb form. Option (4) is incorrect because it is plural and shifts the tense to the past. Option (5) is an incomplete verb form for this sentence.

25. **(4) change helps to help** (Usage/Subject-verb agreement) Option (4) is correct because the plural verb *help* agrees with the plural compound subject *meat, beans, and oat bran.* Option (1) replaces a correctly spelled word with its homonym. Option (2) removes the comma needed between items in a series. Option (3) inserts an unnecessary comma between the subject and the verb. Option (5) inserts an unnecessary comma.

26. **(5) your eating and exercising habits can** (Sentence structure/Subordination) Option (5) moves the two important details from the second sentence—eating and exercising—into the first sentence. Options (1), (2), (3), and (4), do not lead to smooth, effective sentences.

27. **(3) magnates, May Foods and Brans United,** (Mechanics/Commas around appositives) Option (3) correctly places a comma before and after the nonessential appositive *May Foods and Brans United.* Options (1), (2), and (4) are missing one or both commas. Option (5) inserts an unnecessary comma between the two names.

28. **(1) UGO, whose cereal** (Sentence structure/ Subordination) Option (1) correctly combines the details of the two sentences by subordinating the information in the second sentence and eliminating repetition. Options (2), (3), (4), and (5) do not lead to smooth, effective sentences and change the meaning of the original text.

29. **(4) year, despite** (Sentence structure/ Subordination) Option (4) effectively subordinates the information in the second independent clause to the first and removes repetition. Option (1) is the original wordy and awkward sentence. Option (2) removes a necessary comma. Options (3) and (5) create fragments.

30. **(2) began** (Usage/Verb forms) Option (2) corrects the verb form by using the simple past, which is consistent with the first verb in the sentence, *listed*. Option (1) is the original incorrect verb form. Options (3) and (5) incorrectly shift the tense to the present and are both plural. Option (4) is an incorrect verb form and is plural.

31. **(5) replace their with its** (Usage/Pronouns) Option (5) is correct because the singular possessive pronoun *its* matches the antecedent *United Seed Company.* Option (1) removes the comma needed after an introductory element. Option (2) is incorrect because *Company* is part of the organization's name and should be capitalized. Option (3) is incorrect because the singular verb *continues* agrees with the singular subject *United Seed Company.* Option (4) replaces a correctly spelled word with its homonym.

32. **(1) with sentence 5** (Organization/Paragraph divisions) Option (1) correctly begins a new paragraph when the main idea shifts to other divisions in the corporation. Options (2), (3), (4), and (5) are details related to that main idea.

33. **(2) put** (Usage/Verb tenses) Option (2) is correct because the logical sequence of the sentence requires the simple present tense. Options (1), (3), (4), and (5) incorrectly shift the tense to the continuous present, the present perfect, the past perfect, or the future.

34. **(4) move sentence 11 to follow sentence 8** (Organization/ Unity and coherence) Option (4) is correct because it reorders the sentences more logically, putting the sentence with advice about which utensil to use after the sentence about moving the chicken. Option (1) moves the topic sentence out of the paragraph. Options (2) and (3) remove important supporting details. Option (5) does not correct the incoherence in the paragraph.

35. **(5) The meat will cook best with just that single move, so you** (Sentence structure/Modifiers) Option (5) correctly fixes a dangling modifier by inserting a subject and using the correct verb form. Options (1), (2), (3), and (4) do not lead to smooth, effective sentences.

36. **(2) don't see** (Usage/Verb tenses) Option (2) is correct because the present tense (*don't = do not see*) is needed in the second clause to be consistent with the present tense used in the first

clause (*It's = It is*). Option (1) is in the past. Options (3), (4), and (5) incorrectly shift the tense to the present perfect or the past or present continuous.

37. **(4) insert is after readiness** (Sentence structure/ Fragments) Option (4) corrects the fragment by adding a missing verb. Option (1) replaces a correctly spelled word with its homonym. Option (2) incorrectly changes a singular possessive to a plural. Option (3) inserts an unnecessary comma.

38. **(2) insert a comma after time** (Mechanics/ Commas after introductory elements) Option (2) is correct because an introductory clause needs a comma after it. Option (1) replaces a correctly spelled word with its homonym. Option (3) incorrectly shifts the verb tense from present to present perfect. Option (4) is incorrect because the contraction for *you are* is required in the sentence, not the possessive pronoun.

39. **(1) service at a reasonable price** (Sentence structure/Parallelism) Option (1) is correct because it changes a clause into a prepositional phrase that is parallel with the prepositional phrase that precedes it. Options (2), (3), (4), and (5) do not correct the error in parallel structure.

40. **(5) will see** (Usage/Verb forms) Option (5) corrects the verb form and uses the future tense, which is appropriate in the sentence because it is describing an action that will come. Option (1) is the original incorrect verb form. Options (2), (3), and (4) are correct verb forms but incorrect tenses for the sentence.

41. **(5) change have developed to developed** (Usage/ Verb tenses) Option (5) is correct because the logical sequence of the sentence requires the simple past tense in the second clause. Option (1) removes a subordinating conjunction and therefore creates a comma splice. Option (2) inserts an unnecessary comma. Option (3) removes the comma needed after the introductory clause. Option (4) is incorrect because *Test* is part of a proper noun and should be capitalized.

42. **(3) remove sentence 4** (Organization/Unity and coherence) Option (3) correctly eliminates a sentence that does not support the main idea. Option (1) moves the topic sentence from the beginning of the paragraph to an ineffective position at the end. Option (2) removes an important detail that leads into the main idea

expressed in the second paragraph. Option (4) incorrectly moves the topic sentence from the second paragraph into the first paragraph.

43. **(3) change hospital to Hospital** (Mechanics/ Capitalization) Option (3) is correct because *hospital* is part of a proper noun—the name of a specific hospital—and should be capitalized. Option (1) removes the comma needed after the introductory transitional element. Option (2) inserts an unnecessary comma. Option (4) is incorrect because the singular verb *requires* agrees with the singular subject *job*. Option (5) incorrectly replaces a plural with a singular possessive.

44. **(5) reviews, and I** (Sentence structure/Compound sentences) Option (5) is correct because it joins closely related independent clauses with a needed comma and a coordinating conjunction to make a compound sentence. Option (1) is the original that does not flow easily. Option (2) creates a run-on. Option (3) creates a comma splice. Option (4) omits the necessary comma in the compound sentence and changes the meaning (it makes the supervisor the one who receives the commendation).

45. **(3) change are to is** (Usage/Subject-verb agreement) Option (3) is correct because the singular verb *is* agrees with the singular subject *merchandise.* When a compound subject is joined by *or,* the verb should agree with the last subject. Option (1) incorrectly changes a plural to a possessive. Option (2) inserts an unnecessary comma. Option (4) replaces a correctly spelled word with its homonym. The preposition *for* is needed in the sentence, not the number word *four.*

46. **(2) Another questionable tactic, called a kickback,** (Sentence structure/Modifiers) Option (2) places the modifier next to the noun it is modifying. Options (1), (3), (4), and (5) do not reconstruct the sentence so that the modifier is clear and the sentence accurately restates the meaning of the original text.

47. **(3) change them to they** (Usage/Pronouns) Option (3) correctly replaces an object pronoun with a subject pronoun as the subject of the second independent clause in the sentence. Option (1) incorrectly changes a plural noun to a plural possessive. Option (2) incorrectly removes the comma needed between the two independent clauses. Option (4) incorrectly changes a plural noun to a singular possessive.

48. **(1) cash, and** (Mechanics/Commas in compound sentences) Option (1) is correct because the original sentence has two independent clauses joined with a comma and an appropriate coordinating conjunction. Option (2) creates a run-on. Option (3) creates two choppy sentences, with the second sentence beginning with a coordinating conjunction. Option (4) omits the comma needed in a compound sentence. Option (5) creates a comma splice.

49. **(3) insert a comma after start** (Mechanics/ Commas in series) Option (3) is correct because *one third at the start* is the first item in a series and requires a comma after it. Option (1) removes the comma needed after the introductory element. Option (2) incorrectly shifts the tense to the past. Option (4) inserts an unnecessary comma within the third element of the series. Option (5) incorrectly changes the parallel structure of the items in the series by making the last item a clause.

50. **(1) change Do'nt to Don't** (Mechanics/Spelling contractions) Option (1) correctly places the apostrophe so that it takes the place of the missing *o* in the contraction for *do not.* Option (2) incorrectly shifts the tense from present to present perfect. Options (3) and (4) replace correctly spelled words with their homonyms.

Sentence Structure (Unit 1)

When you edit your own writing or a passage on the GED Language Arts, Writing Test, ask yourself and check for the following:

❑ **Are all sentences complete?**
Each sentence has a subject and verb and expresses a complete thought.
Example: *Sarah had a good day.*

❑ **Are all sentences correctly punctuated?**
There are no run-on sentences and no comma splices. Each sentence has correct end punctuation.
Example: *Sarah had a good day at work.*

❑ **Are ideas combined smoothly and effectively in compound sentences?**
Equal ideas in independent clauses are connected with an appropriate coordinating conjunction and a comma.
Example: *She had written a memo, and her boss complimented her.*

❑ **Are ideas combined smoothly and effectively in complex sentences?**
A main idea is connected with additional information by an appropriate subordinating conjunction.
Example: *Because her meeting was running late, she had to skip lunch.*

❑ **Are details combined smoothly and effectively?**
Sentences vary in amount of detail and structure, without series of short, choppy sentences.
Example: *Sarah works in a downtown real estate office five days a week.*

❑ **Do items in series have parallel structure?**
Items in series are expressed in the same form and separated by commas.
Example: *Her duties are to handle incoming calls, place print ads, and write televised listings.*

❑ **Are modifiers clear and understandable?**
Modifying words and phrases are placed near the words they describe.
Example: *Going home, she felt good about her day's work.*

Organization (Unit 2)

When you edit your own writing or a passage on the GED Language Arts, Writing Test, ask yourself and check for the following:

❑ **Is the text divided into paragraphs where appropriate?**
Each paragraph has a main idea and supporting details that explain that idea.

❑ **Is each paragraph unified and coherent?**
The ideas in each sentence of a paragraph clearly support and relate to the main idea, and the ideas are presented in a logical order.

❑ **Does each paragraph have a topic sentence?**
The topic sentence states the main idea of the paragraph.

❑ **Do transitions show how ideas are related?**
Clue words and phrases connect one sentence to the next related sentence and one paragraph to the next related paragraph.

Example:

Many people want to own their homes, but owning can be expensive and stressful. **For one thing,** you need to come up with a down payment. **For another,** repairs can be costly, and repair companies can be unreliable. ~~Our teenaged babysitter is pretty unreliable, too.~~ **Finally,** property taxes are another hidden expense. **All told,** home ownership can be worrisome and costly.

The topic sentence is circled. Transitions are identified in bold text. A sentence that is irrelevant to the main idea is crossed out.

Usage (Unit 3)

When you edit your own writing or a passage on the GED Language Arts, Writing Test, ask yourself and check for the following:

❑ **Do all subjects and verbs agree?**

Singular subjects have singular verbs.
Example: *Baseball is a popular sport.*

Compound and plural subjects have plural verbs.
Example: *Football and basketball are popular too.*

Subjects and verbs agree, regardless of interrupting phrases or inverted order.
Example: *A very popular sport at the Olympics is figure skating.*

❑ **Are verb tenses consistent and correct?**

The past, present, and future tenses of verbs correctly show the timing of actions.
Example: *I go to Wood County Community College.*
Example: *Last fall I enrolled in a GED course.*
Example: *Next spring I will pass the GED Test.*

❑ **Are verb forms correct?**

The past and participle forms of verbs, especially of irregular verbs, are used correctly.
Example: *My 90-year-old grandmother has seen some strange things in her lifetime.*

❑ **Are pronouns used correctly?**

Pronouns agree with their antecedents in person, number, and gender.
Example: *Matt takes the bus to his job every day.*

Subject pronouns are used as subjects.
Example: *He likes the company that he works for.*

Object pronouns are used as objects of verbs or prepositions.
Example: *Matt's boss has promised him a raise.*

The antecedent of each pronoun is clear.
Example: *Matt and his boss are talking about Matt's idea for improving customer service.*

Mechanics (Unit 4)

When you edit your own writing or a passage on the GED Language Arts, Writing Test, ask yourself and check for the following:

❑ **Are words capitalized correctly?**
> Proper nouns and adjectives are capitalized. Common nouns are not.
> **Example:** *The Sands family is going to Mexico this fall.*

❑ **Are commas used correctly?**
> Commas separate independent clauses in a compound sentence. They set off an introductory clause or phrase. They separate items in a series. They appear before and after a nonessential appositive. They are not used where there is no clear need for them.
> **Example:** *They are leaving on September 10, and they won't return for two weeks.*

❑ **Are words spelled correctly?**
> The apostrophe is placed correctly in each contraction and possessive. Contractions and possessives that sound alike are not confused. Other homonyms are not confused.
> **Example:** *They can't wait to go there.*

Spelling Demons

Here are some homonyms and other commonly confused words. You may want to write each in a sentence and then compare the spelling you used with the meaning given here. Check the words that give you trouble. Then work on learning to spell them.

❑ accept (to receive)
❑ except (to exclude)

❑ advice (words that try to help or tell what to do)
❑ advise (to tell what to do)

❑ affect (to influence)
❑ effect (a result)

❑ be (to exist)
❑ bee (an insect)

❑ board (piece of wood)
❑ bored (uninterested)

- ❏ brake (to stop)
- ❏ break (rest period; to damage or destroy)

- ❏ capital (city that is seat of government; very important; money to invest)
- ❏ capitol (building where legislature meets)

- ❏ complement (to go with)
- ❏ compliment (flattering words)

- ❏ council (group or committee)
- ❏ counsel (to advise; advice)

- ❏ course (path, track)
- ❏ coarse (rough, textured)

- ❏ dear (sweet; priceless)
- ❏ deer (an animal)

- ❏ feet (plural of foot)
- ❏ feat (achievement)

- ❏ for (to be used as; in favor of; meant to belong to)
- ❏ four (the number 4)

- ❏ grate (shred)
- ❏ great (very good)

- ❏ hear (to listen)
- ❏ here (in this place)

- ❏ hour (60 minutes)
- ❏ our (belonging to us)

- ❏ knew (to be certain of)
- ❏ new (latest, additional)

- ❏ know (to have information)
- ❏ no (negative; not; opposite of *yes*)

- ❏ lessen (to decrease)
- ❏ lesson (something taught)

- ❏ let (to allow)
- ❏ leave (to go away)

- ❏ lose (to fail to win or to keep)
- ❏ loose (not tight)

Writer's Checklist

- ❏ made (created)
- ❏ maid (cleaning person)

- ❏ mane (hair of a lion)
- ❏ main (chief, most important)

- ❏ meat (flesh of an animal that is eaten)
- ❏ meet (to get together)

- ❏ one (the number 1)
- ❏ won (past tense of *win*)

- ❏ pane (window glass)
- ❏ pain (hurt)

- ❏ passed (went by)
- ❏ past (a time before)

- ❏ plane (flat surface; airplane)
- ❏ plain (simple, ordinary)

- ❏ poll (a vote)
- ❏ pole (a long piece of wood or other material)

- ❏ principal (main)
- ❏ principle (rule, belief)

- ❏ right (correct; opposite of *left*)
- ❏ write (to form words)

- ❏ roll (to turn over; a type of bread)
- ❏ role (a part played)

- ❏ scene (a view; part of a play or movie)
- ❏ seen (past participle of *see*)

- ❏ sight (the ability to see)
- ❏ site (place, location)

- ❏ sit (to rest one's body)
- ❏ set (to put something down)

- ❏ some (a few)
- ❏ sum (total amount)

- ❏ stationary (not moving)
- ❏ stationery (writing paper)

- ❑ too (also, very)
- ❑ two (the number 2)
- ❑ to (part of infinitive verb form; in the direction of)

- ❑ wait (to stay around for someone or something)
- ❑ weight (how heavy something is)

- ❑ way (path, direction)
- ❑ weigh (to measure the heaviness of something)

- ❑ where (what place)
- ❑ wear (to have clothing)

- ❑ whether (if)
- ❑ weather (climate)

- ❑ whole (entire)
- ❑ hole (opening)

- ❑ wood (what trees are made of)
- ❑ would (verb expressing a wish)

Spelling List

With some practice and concentration, you can improve your spelling ability. Here is a list of the most commonly misspelled words. Write the words as someone reads them to you. Make a list of the ones you spelled incorrectly. You may find it easier to master the ones you missed if you learn the correct spelling of ten to twelve words at a time.

a lot ☐	American ☐	auxiliary ☐	capital ☐
ability ☐	among ☐	available ☐	capitol ☐
absence ☐	amount ☐	avenue ☐	captain ☐
absent ☐	analysis ☐	awful ☐	career ☐
abundance ☐	analyze ☐	awkward ☐	careful ☐
accept ☐	angel ☐		careless ☐
acceptable ☐	angle ☐	bachelor ☐	carriage ☐
accident ☐	annual ☐	balance ☐	carrying ☐
accommodate ☐	another ☐	balloon ☐	category ☐
accompanied ☐	answer ☐	bargain ☐	ceiling ☐
accomplish ☐	antiseptic ☐	basic ☐	cemetery ☐
accumulation ☐	anxious ☐	beautiful ☐	cereal ☐
accuse ☐	apologize ☐	because ☐	certain ☐
accustomed ☐	apparatus ☐	become ☐	changeable ☐
ache ☐	apparent ☐	before ☐	characteristic ☐
achieve ☐	appear ☐	beginning ☐	charity ☐
achievement ☐	appearance ☐	being ☐	chief ☐
acknowledge ☐	appetite ☐	believe ☐	choose ☐
acquaintance ☐	apply ☐	benefit ☐	chose ☐
acquainted ☐	appreciate ☐	benefited ☐	cigarette ☐
acquire ☐	appreciation ☐	between ☐	circumstance ☐
address ☐	approach ☐	bicycle ☐	citizen ☐
addressed ☐	appropriate ☐	board ☐	clothes ☐
adequate ☐	approval ☐	bored ☐	clothing ☐
advantage ☐	approve ☐	borrow ☐	coarse ☐
advantageous ☐	approximate ☐	bottle ☐	coffee ☐
advertise ☐	argue ☐	bottom ☐	collect ☐
advertisement ☐	arguing ☐	boundary ☐	college ☐
advice ☐	argument ☐	brake ☐	column ☐
advisable ☐	arouse ☐	breadth ☐	comedy ☐
advise ☐	arrange ☐	break ☐	comfortable ☐
aerial ☐	arrangement ☐	breath ☐	commitment ☐
affect ☐	article ☐	breathe ☐	committed ☐
affectionate ☐	artificial ☐	brilliant ☐	committee ☐
again ☐	ascend ☐	building ☐	communicate ☐
against ☐	assistance ☐	bulletin ☐	company ☐
aggravate ☐	assistant ☐	bureau ☐	comparative ☐
aggressive ☐	associate ☐	burial ☐	compel ☐
agree ☐	association ☐	buried ☐	competent ☐
aisle ☐	attempt ☐	bury ☐	competition ☐
all right ☐	attendance ☐	bushes ☐	complement ☐
almost ☐	attention ☐	business ☐	compliment ☐
already ☐	audience ☐		conceal ☐
although ☐	August ☐	cafeteria ☐	conceit ☐
altogether ☐	author ☐	calculator ☐	conceivable ☐
always ☐	automobile ☐	calendar ☐	conceive ☐
amateur ☐	autumn ☐	campaign ☐	concentration ☐

conception ☐
condition ☐
conference ☐
confident ☐
congratulate ☐
conquer ☐
conscience ☐
conscientious ☐
conscious ☐
consequence ☐
consequently ☐
considerable ☐
consistency ☐
consistent ☐
continual ☐
continuous ☐
controlled ☐
controversy ☐
convenience ☐
convenient ☐
conversation ☐
corporal ☐
corroborate ☐
council ☐
counsel ☐
counselor ☐
courage ☐
courageous ☐
course ☐
courteous ☐
courtesy ☐
criticism ☐
criticize ☐
crystal ☐
curiosity ☐
cylinder ☐

daily ☐
daughter ☐
daybreak ☐
death ☐
deceive ☐
December ☐
deception ☐
decide ☐
decision ☐
decisive ☐
deed ☐
definite ☐
delicious ☐
dependent ☐
deposit ☐
derelict ☐
descend ☐
descent ☐
describe ☐
description ☐

desert ☐
desirable ☐
despair ☐
desperate ☐
dessert ☐
destruction ☐
determine ☐
develop ☐
development ☐
device ☐
devise ☐
dictator ☐
died ☐
difference ☐
different ☐
dilemma ☐
dinner ☐
direction ☐
disappear ☐
disappoint ☐
disappointment ☐
disapproval ☐
disapprove ☐
disastrous ☐
discipline ☐
discover ☐
discriminate ☐
disease ☐
dissatisfied ☐
dissection ☐
dissipate ☐
distance ☐
distinction ☐
division ☐
doctor ☐
dollar ☐
doubt ☐
dozen ☐
dyed ☐

earnest ☐
easy ☐
ecstasy ☐
ecstatic ☐
education ☐
effect ☐
efficiency ☐
efficient ☐
eight ☐
either ☐
eligibility ☐
eligible ☐
eliminate ☐
embarrass ☐
embarrassment ☐
emergency ☐
emphasis ☐

emphasize ☐
enclosure ☐
encouraging ☐
endeavor ☐
engineer ☐
English ☐
enormous ☐
enough ☐
entrance ☐
envelope ☐
environment ☐
equipment ☐
equipped ☐
especially ☐
essential ☐
evening ☐
evident ☐
exaggerate ☐
exaggeration ☐
examine ☐
exceed ☐
excellent ☐
except ☐
exceptional ☐
exercise ☐
exhausted ☐
exhaustion ☐
exhilaration ☐
existence ☐
exorbitant ☐
expense ☐
experience ☐
experiment ☐
explanation ☐
extreme ☐

facility ☐
factory ☐
familiar ☐
farther ☐
fascinate ☐
fascinating ☐
fatigue ☐
February ☐
financial ☐
financier ☐
flourish ☐
forcibly ☐
forehead ☐
foreign ☐
formal ☐
former ☐
fortunate ☐
fourteen ☐
fourth ☐
frequent ☐
friend ☐

frightening ☐
fundamental ☐
further ☐

gallon ☐
garden ☐
gardener ☐
general ☐
genius ☐
government ☐
governor ☐
grammar ☐
grateful ☐
great ☐
grievance ☐
grievous ☐
grocery ☐
guarantee ☐
guard ☐
guess ☐
guidance ☐

half ☐
hammer ☐
handkerchief ☐
happiness ☐
healthy ☐
heard ☐
heavy ☐
height ☐
herd ☐
heroes ☐
heroine ☐
hideous ☐
himself ☐
hoarse ☐
holiday ☐
hopeless ☐
horse ☐
hospital ☐
humorous ☐
hurried ☐
hurrying ☐

ignorance ☐
imaginary ☐
imbecile ☐
imitation ☐
immediately ☐
incidental ☐
increase ☐
independence ☐
independent ☐
indispensable ☐
inevitable ☐
influence ☐
influential ☐

initiate	☐	loneliness	☐	occurrence	☐	piece	☐
innocence	☐	loose	☐	ocean	☐	plain	☐
inoculate	☐	lose	☐	offer	☐	plane	☐
inquiry	☐	losing	☐	often	☐	playwright	☐
insistent	☐	loyal	☐	omission	☐	pleasant	☐
instead	☐	loyalty	☐	omit	☐	please	☐
instinct	☐			once	☐	pleasure	☐
integrity	☐	magazine	☐	operate	☐	pocket	☐
intellectual	☐	maintenance	☐	opinion	☐	poison	☐
intelligence	☐	maneuver	☐	opportune	☐	policeman	☐
intercede	☐	marriage	☐	opportunity	☐	political	☐
interest	☐	married	☐	optimist	☐	population	☐
interfere	☐	marry	☐	optimistic	☐	portrayal	☐
interference	☐	match	☐	origin	☐	positive	☐
interpreted	☐	mathematics	☐	original	☐	possess	☐
interrupt	☐	measure	☐	oscillate	☐	possession	☐
invitation	☐	medicine	☐	ought	☐	possessive	☐
irrelevant	☐	million	☐	ounce	☐	possible	☐
irresistible	☐	miniature	☐	overcoat	☐	post office	☐
irritable	☐	minimum	☐			potatoes	☐
island	☐	miracle	☐	paid	☐	practical	☐
its	☐	miscellaneous	☐	pamphlet	☐	prairie	☐
it's	☐	mischief	☐	panicky	☐	precede	☐
itself	☐	mischievous	☐	parallel	☐	preceding	☐
		misspelled	☐	parallelism	☐	precise	☐
January	☐	mistake	☐	pare	☐	predictable	☐
jealous	☐	momentous	☐	particular	☐	prefer	☐
journal	☐	monkey	☐	partner	☐	preference	☐
judgment	☐	monotonous	☐	pastime	☐	preferential	☐
		moral	☐	patience	☐	preferred	☐
kindergarten	☐	morale	☐	patients	☐	prejudice	☐
kitchen	☐	mortgage	☐	peace	☐	preparation	☐
knew	☐	mountain	☐	peaceable	☐	prepare	☐
knock	☐	mournful	☐	pear	☐	prescription	☐
know	☐	muscle	☐	peculiar	☐	presence	☐
knowledge	☐	mysterious	☐	pencil	☐	president	☐
		mystery	☐	people	☐	prevalent	☐
labor	☐			perceive	☐	primitive	☐
laboratory	☐	narrative	☐	perception	☐	principal	☐
laid	☐	natural	☐	perfect	☐	principle	☐
language	☐	necessary	☐	perform	☐	privilege	☐
later	☐	needle	☐	performance	☐	probably	☐
latter	☐	negligence	☐	perhaps	☐	procedure	☐
laugh	☐	neighbor	☐	period	☐	proceed	☐
leisure	☐	neither	☐	permanence	☐	produce	☐
length	☐	newspaper	☐	permanent	☐	professional	☐
lesson	☐	newsstand	☐	perpendicular	☐	professor	☐
library	☐	niece	☐	perseverance	☐	profit	☐
license	☐	noticeable	☐	persevere	☐	profitable	☐
light	☐			persistent	☐	prominent	☐
lightning	☐	o'clock	☐	personal	☐	promise	☐
likelihood	☐	obedient	☐	personality	☐	pronounce	☐
likely	☐	obstacle	☐	personnel	☐	pronunciation	☐
literal	☐	occasion	☐	persuade	☐	propeller	☐
literature	☐	occasional	☐	persuasion	☐	prophet	☐
livelihood	☐	occur	☐	pertain	☐	prospect	☐
loaf	☐	occurred	☐	picture	☐	psychology	☐

Column 1	Column 2	Column 3	Column 4
pursue ☐	scissors ☐	sweat ☐	visitor ☐
pursuit ☐	season ☐	sweet ☐	voice ☐
	secretary ☐	syllable ☐	volume ☐
quality ☐	seize ☐	symmetrical ☐	
quantity ☐	seminar ☐	sympathy ☐	waist ☐
quarreling ☐	sense ☐	synonym ☐	ware ☐
quart ☐	separate ☐		waste ☐
quarter ☐	service ☐	technical ☐	weak ☐
quiet ☐	several ☐	telegram ☐	wear ☐
quite ☐	severely ☐	telephone ☐	weather ☐
	shepherd ☐	temperament ☐	Wednesday ☐
raise ☐	sheriff ☐	temperature ☐	week ☐
realistic ☐	shining ☐	tenant ☐	weigh ☐
realize ☐	shoulder ☐	tendency ☐	weird ☐
reason ☐	shriek ☐	tenement ☐	whether ☐
rebellion ☐	siege ☐	therefore ☐	which ☐
recede ☐	sight ☐	thorough ☐	while ☐
receipt ☐	signal ☐	through ☐	whole ☐
receive ☐	significance ☐	title ☐	wholly ☐
recipe ☐	significant ☐	together ☐	whose ☐
recognize ☐	similar ☐	tomorrow ☐	witch ☐
recommend ☐	similarity ☐	tongue ☐	wretched ☐
recuperate ☐	since ☐	toward ☐	
referred ☐	sincerely ☐	tragedy ☐	
rehearsal ☐	site ☐	transferred ☐	
reign ☐	soldier ☐	treasury ☐	
relevant ☐	solemn ☐	tremendous ☐	
relieve ☐	sophomore ☐	tries ☐	
remedy ☐	soul ☐	truly ☐	
renovate ☐	source ☐	twelfth ☐	
repeat ☐	souvenir ☐	twelve ☐	
repetition ☐	special ☐	tyranny ☐	
representative ☐	specified ☐		
requirements ☐	specimen ☐	undoubtedly ☐	
resemblance ☐	speech ☐	United States ☐	
resistance ☐	stationary ☐	university ☐	
resource ☐	stationery ☐	unnecessary ☐	
respectability ☐	statue ☐	unusual ☐	
responsibility ☐	stockings ☐	useful ☐	
restaurant ☐	stomach ☐	usual ☐	
rhythm ☐	straight ☐		
rhythmical ☐	strength ☐	vacuum ☐	
ridiculous ☐	strenuous ☐	vain ☐	
right ☐	stretch ☐	valley ☐	
role ☐	striking ☐	valuable ☐	
roll ☐	studying ☐	variety ☐	
roommate ☐	substantial ☐	vegetable ☐	
	succeed ☐	vein ☐	
sandwich ☐	successful ☐	vengeance ☐	
Saturday ☐	sudden ☐	versatile ☐	
scarcely ☐	superintendent ☐	vicinity ☐	
scene ☐	suppress ☐	vicious ☐	
schedule ☐	surely ☐	view ☐	
science ☐	surprise ☐	village ☐	
scientific ☐	suspense ☐	villain ☐	

Writing Checklist

The Writing Links activities that you worked on throughout this book helped you to develop some basic writing skills. These skills will be necessary for writing an effective essay on Part II of the Writing Test. When you write—either personal writing or more general writing—ask yourself and check for the following:

❑ Does the writing have a clear introduction, middle, and conclusion?

❑ Does each new main idea have its own paragraph?

❑ Are all sentences complete and clear?

❑ Are there interesting and specific details and examples?

❑ Are there vivid, specific modifiers that will help a reader see what I am describing?

❑ Are there specific action verbs?

❑ Is the point of view throughout the writing consistent?

❑ Does the writing stay on topic? Are all ideas related to the topic?

❑ Is the use of sentence structure correct and appropriate? (See checklist on page 314.)

❑ Is the organization effective and clear? (See checklist on page 315.)

❑ Is the usage of English correct? (See checklist on page 316.)

❑ Are the mechanics of writing—capitalization, punctuation, and spelling—correct? (See checklist on page 317.)

antecedent the particular noun or phrase that a pronoun is substituting for or refers to. Example: The people and their pets sat in the waiting room. (*People* is the antecedent of *their*.)

appositive a word or phrase that explains or gives additional information about a noun or pronoun. Example: Sara, the right fielder, has the highest batting average.

clause a group of words with a subject and verb. An independent clause expresses a complete thought; a dependent, or subordinate, clause does not.

collective noun a word that stands for a group of people or things. When the group is acting as one, the collective noun is considered a singular subject and takes a singular verb. Example: The committee meets every Friday.

comma splice two independent clauses incorrectly separated only by a comma. Example: Pack your bags, leave town.

complex sentence an independent clause and a subordinate clause, connected by a subordinating conjunction. Example: If the restaurant is closed, we will have to eat at home.

compound sentence two independent clauses connected by a comma and a coordinating conjunction (*and, but, or, for, nor, yet, so*). Example: We traveled by boat, and we had a wonderful time.

conclusion the end of a piece of writing that restates the main idea

conjunctive adverb a word that shows the relationship between two ideas. In a compound sentence, a semicolon precedes the adverb and a comma follows it. Example: He had to leave; however, his report is on the desk.

contraction a word formed from two words that are combined and shortened by leaving out letters. An apostrophe takes the place of the missing letters. Example: *he's (he is)*. One exception: *won't (will not)*.

coordinating conjunction a word that connects equal elements, such as the independent clauses in a compound sentence (*and, but, or, for,*

nor, yet, so). Example: She works hard, but her performance could improve.

dangling modifier a phrase placed at the beginning of a sentence that lacks the subject the modifier is describing. Example: Reaching under the bed for the ball, the cat scratched his hand.

essay a piece of writing of several paragraphs or longer that explains the writer's view on a topic

future perfect tense a verb tense that expresses a future action that will begin and end before another action begins. Use *will have* with the past participle. Example: He will have completed the paint job by the end of the week.

future tense a verb tense that expresses a future action or condition. Use the helping verb *will* or *shall* with the future. Example: You will see your brother next week.

gender relates to whether a pronoun is masculine, feminine, or neuter.

helping verb (also called *auxiliary verb*) a verb used with the main verb to make participle forms. The helping verbs are forms of the verbs *be, do,* and *have*. Example: We will buy the new computers.

homonyms words that sound alike but have different spellings and meanings

indefinite pronoun a noun substitute that makes a general reference to a person, place, or thing. Example: Anyone can answer the phone.

independent clause a group of words that has a subject and verb and expresses a complete thought. Example: With hard work, they all passed the test.

introduction the beginning of a piece of writing that tells the reader what will be written about

irregular verb a verb whose past forms are not made by adding *-d* or *-ed* to the simple present. Example: *begin* (present), *began* (past), *begun* (past participle)

journal a notebook in which you can write anything that you like

main idea the central organizing idea of a paragraph, often expressed in the topic sentence

misplaced modifier a descriptive word or phrase placed too far from the word or phrase it describes. Example: Joey bought the car from the neighbor with the broken headlight.

number singular or plural

paragraph a group of related sentences that develops a single main idea

parallel structure a series of words, phrases, or clauses in a sentence that are written in the same grammatical form. Example: We spent the money because we earned it, wanted it, and needed it.

parenthetical expression a word or phrase that adds nothing essential to the meaning of a sentence

past participle the principal part of a verb that uses a helping verb to form the present perfect, future perfect, and past perfect tenses. Example: They have loaded the truck.

past perfect tense a verb tense that expresses an action that began and ended before another past action began; it is formed by using the helping verb *had* with the past participle. Example: We had chosen to stay home before we realized the party was for us.

past tense a verb tense that expresses an action that took place or a condition that was true in the past. Example: We talked for hours yesterday.

perfect tense a verb tense that expresses a complex time relationship. The perfect tense consists of a helping verb that is a form of *have* plus the past participle. Example: I have walked that way many times.

person a pronoun form that depends on who is being referred to. First person: *I, we, me, us, my, mine, our, ours.* Second person: *you, your, yours.* Third person: *he, she, it, they, him, her, hers, them, his, its, their, theirs*

personal narrative a piece of writing in which the writer tells a story about himself or herself

personal pronoun a word that can be used in place of the name of a person, place, or thing. Example: Give the keys to her.

point of view the perspective from which something is written. It may be written from the writer's first-person point of view, from the reader's second-person point of view, or from someone else's third-person point of view.

possessive a word that shows ownership. Example: (singular) Harriet's project; (plural) the girls' hats.

preposition a word that shows direction (*to, from*), location (*next to, behind*), or time (*before, since*). Example: We found the wallet on the sidewalk.

present perfect tense a verb tense that expresses an action that was completed or a condition that was true at some indefinite time in the past. It also refers to an action that began in the past and has continued into the present. It is formed using either *have* or *has* with the past participle. Example: She has worked long and hard on that report.

present tense a verb tense that expresses an action that is happening now or that happens regularly, or one that describes present conditions. Example: He runs every morning.

pronoun a word used in place of a noun, which names a person, place, or thing. Example: Lisa is eighteen, so she is old enough to vote.

pronoun shift an error that occurs when the person or number of a pronoun changes within a sentence or paragraph. Example: When one is riding in an elevator, you never know who will get on.

proper adjective an adjective that is formed from a proper noun. It is always capitalized. Example: American landscape, Italian bread.

proper noun a noun that names a specific person, place, or thing. Proper nouns are always capitalized. Example: Henry, the Alamo, the Declaration of Independence.

regular verb a verb that forms its principal parts by adding *-d, -ed,* or *-ing* to the present form

run-on sentence two or more independent clauses that are joined as one sentence without proper punctuation and/or connecting words. Example: In time I hope to get my GED I will look for a better job.

sentence fragment an incomplete sentence. A fragment does not express a complete thought. It may lack a subject or complete verb, or it may begin with a subordinating conjunction. Example: We need to stop for gas. <u>Running on empty</u>.

simple sentence a group of words that has a subject, a verb, and one idea. Example: Today is Sunday.

subject a word or phrase that names who or what a sentence is about. Example: Jim found a great job.

subject-verb agreement the subject and the verb in a sentence must both be singular (referring to one) or plural (referring to more than one). Example: <u>We know</u> the scheduled time for the concert. (plural subject, plural verb)

subordinate clause (also called a dependent clause) a group of words that has a subject and verb but is *not* a sentence because it does not express a complete thought. Example: As we finished cleaning up.

subordinating conjunction a connecting word that sets up a relationship of unequal rank between the ideas in two clauses. Example: I will go to the party <u>even though</u> I may have to leave early.

supporting detail a statement that explains the main idea of a paragraph by giving a specific detail, an example, or a reason

topic sentence a sentence that states the main idea of a paragraph

transition a word or phrase that signals the relationship from one idea to the next. Example: Apply the brake. <u>Then</u> shift into reverse.

unclear antecedent an error that occurs in writing when the reader cannot be sure of the antecedent of a pronoun. Example: Mike and Fernando took off in <u>his</u> car.

unity and coherence a quality of a paragraph in which all the sentences are about one main idea and are in logical order

verb a word that tells what the subject is or does. Example: Lanny <u>is</u> a great friend. He <u>gives</u> me a ride each day to work.

verb tense the form of a verb that communicates when an action takes place or when a condition is true

Index

Language Arts, Writing, Part I

Name: _____ Class: _____ Date: _____

○ Pretest   ○ Posttest   ○ Simulated Test

1 ① ② ③ ④ ⑤	11 ① ② ③ ④ ⑤	21 ① ② ③ ④ ⑤	31 ① ② ③ ④ ⑤	41 ① ② ③ ④ ⑤
2 ① ② ③ ④ ⑤	12 ① ② ③ ④ ⑤	22 ① ② ③ ④ ⑤	32 ① ② ③ ④ ⑤	42 ① ② ③ ④ ⑤
3 ① ② ③ ④ ⑤	13 ① ② ③ ④ ⑤	23 ① ② ③ ④ ⑤	33 ① ② ③ ④ ⑤	43 ① ② ③ ④ ⑤
4 ① ② ③ ④ ⑤	14 ① ② ③ ④ ⑤	24 ① ② ③ ④ ⑤	34 ① ② ③ ④ ⑤	44 ① ② ③ ④ ⑤
5 ① ② ③ ④ ⑤	15 ① ② ③ ④ ⑤	25 ① ② ③ ④ ⑤	35 ① ② ③ ④ ⑤	45 ① ② ③ ④ ⑤
6 ① ② ③ ④ ⑤	16 ① ② ③ ④ ⑤	26 ① ② ③ ④ ⑤	36 ① ② ③ ④ ⑤	46 ① ② ③ ④ ⑤
7 ① ② ③ ④ ⑤	17 ① ② ③ ④ ⑤	27 ① ② ③ ④ ⑤	37 ① ② ③ ④ ⑤	47 ① ② ③ ④ ⑤
8 ① ② ③ ④ ⑤	18 ① ② ③ ④ ⑤	28 ① ② ③ ④ ⑤	38 ① ② ③ ④ ⑤	48 ① ② ③ ④ ⑤
9 ① ② ③ ④ ⑤	19 ① ② ③ ④ ⑤	29 ① ② ③ ④ ⑤	39 ① ② ③ ④ ⑤	49 ① ② ③ ④ ⑤
10 ① ② ③ ④ ⑤	20 ① ② ③ ④ ⑤	30 ① ② ③ ④ ⑤	40 ① ② ③ ④ ⑤	50 ① ② ③ ④ ⑤